Doing Ethics In Journalism

CREDITS

Page **Source**

1 "Diana's Hunters: How Quarry Was Stalked," September 10, 1997; Copyright © 1997 by The New York Times Company. Reprinted by permission.

Reuters (file photo of Princess Diana appeared in *St. Petersburg Times* September 11, 1997). Reprinted with permission.

15 "Who'll run for Adams' seat?" March 22, 1992, *Seattle Times*, by Mark Matassa, photo by Mark Harrison. Reprinted with permission.

" 8 more women accuse Adams," special reprint, originally published March 1 and 2, 1992, Page 1, *Seattle Times*. Reprinted with permission.

52, 55 "Aids in the heartland," special reprint, June 21, 1989, *St. Paul Pioneer Press*, story by Jacqui Banaszynski, photos by Jean Pieri. Reprinted with permission.

67 "Streets of Despair $20 sex for a $20 bag," January 19-23, 1992, *The Hartford Courant*. Copyright © The Hartford Courant. Reprinted with permission.

71 "Dark Alliance," front of special reprint section, first printed August 18-20, 1996, Page 1, *San Jose Mercury News*, by Gary Webb. Reprinted with permission.

76 " 2 Cowboys Accused of Sexual Assault," January 1, 1997; Copyright 1997 by *The Austin American Statesman*. Reprinted with permission

79 *The Raleigh News and Observer*. Reprinted with permission.

82 "McVeigh took responsibility for bombing, reports say," February 28, 1997, *Dallas Morning News Web Page* as it appeared on the cover of Quill magazine. Reprinted with permission.

"McVeigh admitted bombing, memos say," March 1, 1977, Page A1, *Dallas Morning News*, by Pete Slover. Reprinted with permission.

87 "An apology is long overdue," May 5, 1996, Page E 9, *Northwest Arkansas Times*, by Mike Masterson. Reprinted with permission.

91 "4 Weeks: The Campaign the World Watched," October 20-November 17, 1991, special reprint, Page 1, *Times–Picayune*. Reprinted with permission.

126 "Lost in media frenzy: ethics, compassion," February 9, 1996, Page 10A, the *St. Petersburg Times*, photo by Robert Rogers. Reprinted with permission.

"Cheryl comes home," February 9, 1996, Page 1B, *the St. Petersburg Times*, staff writers. Reprinted with permission.

129 "Family and media shaped outcome of Cheryl's story," February 11, 1996, Page 1B, the *St. Petersburg Times*, by Andrew Z. Galarneau. Reprinted with permission.

165 "When do the ends justify the means?" March 1997, *Quill* magazine. Reprinted with permission.

174 "TV mimics Okla. Bombing in security test," April 13, 1997, *The Tampa Tribune*. Reprinted with permission.

186 Nameplate of the *Daily Southtown*, August 15, 1993. Reprinted with permission.

193 "Violence, fires erupt after police kill driver," October 25, 1996, Page 1A, the *St. Petersburg Times*, staff writers. Reprinted with permission.

Doing Ethics In Journalism

A Handbook with Case Studies

THIRD EDITION

Jay Black
University of South Florida, St. Petersburg

Bob Steele
The Poynter Institute for Media Studies

Ralph Barney
Brigham Young University

Allyn and Bacon
Boston · London · Toronto · Sydney · Tokyo · Singapore

A Viacom Company
160 Gould Street
Needham Heights, Massachusetts 02494

Internet: www.abacon.com

ISBN 0-205-28535-X

Printed in the United States of America

10 9 8 7 6 5 4 3 2 1 02 01 00 99 98

Acknowledgments

This handbook on journalism ethics was first proposed in 1987 by Carolyn Carlson, past president of the Society of Professional Journalists and chairman of the SPJ Ethics Committee. SPJ Ethics Committee Vice Chairman Dan Bolton coordinated fund-raising and publishing efforts of the project, which first appeared in 1993 as a Society of Professional Journalists publication. After a series of SPJ national and regional workshops and seminars at numerous news organizations around the country, the book was revised for publication as a textbook by Allyn and Bacon in 1995. The third edition was released in limited numbers for the 1997 SPJ national convention.

Donors

Financial support has included gifts from the Ethics and Excellence in Journalism Foundation, Oklahoma City, Okla.; The Sigma Delta Chi Foundation, Greencastle, Ind.; The Knight-Ridder, Inc. Fund; the Freedom Forum, Arlington, Va.; James S. Copley Foundation, La Jolla, Calif.; and the generous donation of staff time, facilities and related services by the Poynter Institute for Media Studies, St. Petersburg, Fla. and the Universities of Alabama and South Florida St. Petersburg.

Contributors

This project would not have been possible without major contributions of time and effort by graduate students and journalists Rick Kenney and Eric Eyre, who did much of the case study interviews and reporting, plus bibliographic research, and Susan Keith, copy editor. The book drew substantially on members of the SPJ national ethics committee. Those who contributed both as writers and editors for this and earlier editions included: Douglas E. Beeman, Riverside (Calif.) *Press-Enterprise;* Dan Bolton, Riverside (Calif.) *Press-Enterprise;* Fred Brown, *Denver Post;* Joann Byrd, *Seattle Post-Intelligencer;* Carolyn S. Carlson, The Associated Press, Atlanta; Casey Bukro, *Chicago Tribune;* Eric Deggans, *St. Petersburg Times;* Caroline Dow, Evansville University, Evansville, Ind.; Jerry Dunklee, Southern Connecticut State University, New Haven; Ted Frederickson, University of Kansas, Lawrence, Kan.; Don Fry, Scott Libin, Keith Woods and Aly Colon, Poynter Institute for Media Studies, St. Petersburg, Fla.; Paul Husselbee, Ohio University; Kleyton Jones, San Francisco State University, San Francisco; Sherrie Mazingo, University of Southern California, Los Angeles; Anne Nunamaker, Howard University, Washington, D.C.; Mike Nickel, Marin (Calif.) *Independent Journal;* Sandy Rivera, KHOU-TV, Houston; Cliff Rowe, Pacific Lutheran University, Tacoma, Wash.; Kevin Smith, Miami University; Paul Steinle, University of Miami, Coral Gables, Fla.; Peter Sussman, Berkeley, Calif.; Rebecca Tallent, Oklahoma City, Okla.; Georgiana Vines, The Knoxville (Tenn.) *News-Sentinel;* and the staff of the *Sacramento Bee.*

Principal authors Jay Black, Bob Steele, and Ralph Barney thank all of the above, and the thousands of journalists , journalism instructors and journalism students who have responded so positively to earlier versions of the book. Special thanks go to Christopher Roberts of the *Birmingham* (Ala.) *News,* who designed the first two editions of the book, and Molli Gamelin, designer of the third edition. Cover art for the present edition was based on the first edition's design, by Kevan Barney and Jon Miles.

196 "Media criticized for disturbance coverage, February 20, 1997, Page 11B, the *St. Petersburg Times*, by Kelly Ryan. Reprinted with permission.

199 "Readers deserve explanation for offensive sports column," May 5, 1997, *The Miami Herald*, by Doug Clifton. Reprinted with permission of The Miami Herald.

209 "Three killed in wreck," April 12, 1996, Page 1, *The Post* by Wendy Zang. Reprinted with permission.

211 Front of the opinion page, April 15, 1996, Page 2, *The Post*. Reprinted with permission.

215 Front Page, February 7, 1997, *The Arizona Republic*. Reprinted with permission of The Arizona Republic and Phoenix Newspapers Inc.

219 "Now life or death," June 19, 1996, Page 1A, *San Jose Mercury News*, by Sandra Gonzalez, photo by John Burgess. Reprinted with permission.

223 "Another tragedy of youth," *Daily Press*, July 31, 1993, Page 1A, by Matt Murray, photos by Kenneth D. Lyons. Reprinted with permission.

227 "Thompson sees no need for aid, so far," June 18, 1992, Page 10A, *The Milwaukee Journal*, by Steve Schulltze, photo by Carl D. Hoyt. © Journal Sentinel Inc., reproduced with permission.

230 Front Page, A1, metro edition, September 23, 1996, *The Courier–Journal*. Reprinted with permission.

Front Page, A1, Indiana edition, September 23, 1996, *The Courier–Journal*. Reprinted with permission.

242 Page 1A, April 9, 1992, *USA TODAY*. Copyright 1992, USA TODAY. Reprinted with permission.

246 Front Page, 1A, May 20, 1997, *Grand Forks Herald*. Reprinted with permission.

248 "Angel Appears in GF, EGF," May 19, 1997, 1A, *Grand Forks Herald*. Reprinted with permission.

251 "A life ruined," October 28, 1996, Page 3A, *St. Petersburg Times*. Reprinted with permission.

"Media certainly share the blame," October 31, 1996, Page 14A, *St. Petersburg Times*. Reprinted with permission.

"Stick to Facts: Richard Jewell Case Not News Media Shining Moment," November 4, 1996, Page 15A, *The Ledger*. Reprinted with permission.

"The Accused: How Richard Jewell and His Lawyers Seek Revenge on the Media," January 3, 1997, The Wall Street Journal. Reprinted by permission of *The Wall Street Journal*, © 1997 Dow Jones & Company, Inc. All Rights Reserved Worldwide.

"Nauman: Media Ethics Code Little Help to Richard Jewell," November 3, 1997, *The Sacramento Bee*. Reprinted with permission

268 "Life, Death, Crack: Night and Day with the High Horror," October 15, 1989, *Detroit Free Press*. Reprinted with permission.

272 "Undocumented Journey to the Promised Land," August 1996, Page 1, special section, Copley Newspapers Inc., story by Lynne Walker, photo by Jeffrey Brown. Reprinted with permission.

Table of Contents

Chapter Eight: Photojournalism

Chapter Nine: Privacy

Chapter Ten: Source/Reporter Relationships

DIANA KILLED IN CAR CRASH

Diana, Fayed spent final hours in Paris dodging photographers

Lawyer: Photo shows driver blinded by flash

The blood on journalists' hands

Reuters files (1996)

Diana makes clear her disdain for the paparazzi as their mutually beneficial relationship soured.

In pursuit of Diana, little else mattered

■ Two members of the hard-core paparazzi offer an unapologetic look at the relentless targeting of Diana.

© New York Times

LONDON — The paparazzi who made their living from the endless pursuit of Diana, Princess of Wales, called it "being looned" — the moment when Diana would lose her cool and flail wildly at the photographers she often accused of making her life a misery.

DRUGS DETECTED: Prosecutors say car's driver had Prozac, another medicine in his blood. 8A

To Mark Saunders and Glenn Harvey, among the hardest of the hard-core Diana paparazzi, such incidents, which took place with increasing regularity and vehemence in the last years of her life, were sure signs that "The Loon," as they not-so-affectionately called Diana, was at best fragile and at worst unstable.

But Harvey and Saunders, who published a book last year called *Dicing With Di*, are so stubbornly unapologetic in their description of life among the Diana-following paparazzi that it is hard to imagine any target who would not have cracked under the pressure.

In an interview Tuesday, Harvey recounted how he and his colleague followed Diana relentlessly for years, taking pictures of her at the gym, on the street, on vacation, with boyfriends, with her sons, with her ex-husband and leaving restaurants, department stores and her therapists.

Please see **DIANA** 8A

Doing Ethics in Journalism

Introduction

These paragraphs are being written in the aftermath of yet another flurry of media self-analysis, this time over the coverage of the death of Diana, Princess of Wales. What role did paparazzi and the tabloids have in the tragic accident and its aftermath? Does the public distinguish between the tabloids and mainstream media, or have the lines become blurred? How are responsible media to handle an inherently sensational event without pandering to base instincts? Are talk shows and other forums that encourage public criticism of news media significant agencies of accountability, or mere window dressing? Has journalism ethics bottomed out, or are the intense self-examinations a sign of progress?

The questions continue; the answers rarely satisfy.

Sometimes journalism students, in their academic programs and as they watch professional journalists, feel some discomfort at what journalists do on the job. Students attracted to journalism by a desire to report and write or photograph often are not prepared to deal with angry readers, viewers and sources. Those students hoping to reform journalism and bring it into a kinder and gentler era experience inner turmoil when their ideals meet up with reality—when, for instance, they learn firsthand that journalism sometimes involves intruding upon people's solitude, or pulling news from reluctant sources, or sharing distressing news with a community that would rather not learn of it.

A woman who phoned one of this book's authors said she had experienced such feelings a decade earlier when she had been a journalism student. All she had wanted to do was to write for a living, she said. But she shunned journalism because of what to her were its repulsive practices, and after graduation went to work in government and foundation organizations.

After ten years of observing government and other social institutions at work, she concluded that if the world is to be saved from selfish self-destruction it would be the journalists, in all their objectionable practices, who would do it. She said she wanted to study journalism ethics.

We wish her well. Her idealism is admirable; her journey will not be without some obstacles.

When challenged about their professional behavior, journalists and journalism faculty members often become defensive, offering unconvincing excuses or poorly expressed reasons for what they believe are solid decisions. Students, in these circumstances, can be forgiven for their own difficulties in reconciling the conflicts they feel as they contemplate a professional life in the field.

It is not surprising that both journalists and journalism students become frustrated—students because it is the rest of their professional lives they are contemplating, and journalists because they realize their gut reactions are not adequate either to make or explain tough ethical decisions.

If used properly, this text can go a long way in helping journalists make better ethical decisions and explain them when challenged. It can also help students recognize the critically important role they can play if they choose to continue in the field and become vigorous and courageous journalists. The book should not be viewed as a directory of correct answers and quick fixes for ethics problems. Such a book does not exist.

Doing Ethics: A Craft and a Skill

This book describes the connection between excellent journalism and ethical journalism. It includes case studies that are examples of thoughtful, powerful and principled reporting. It also includes cases where regrettable decisions teach important lessons. Commentary and analysis help put the cases in context.

This book's approach should lead to excellent journalism. It can also help stem the tide of mounting resentment from a highly critical public.

This approach is **doing** ethics, a belief that good ethical decision making in journalism is a craft and a skill comparable to good writing, good photography and good editing.

- **Doing ethics in journalism** must be both learned and developed.
- **Doing ethics in journalism** is reasoned, principled and consistent thinking about how journalists can maximize their truthtelling obligation while minimizing harm to vulnerable news sources and consumers.
- **Doing ethics in journalism** is about individual responsibility.
- **Doing ethics in journalism** is about being accountable.
- **Doing ethics in journalism** is about the critically important contribution excellent journalism makes to society.

"Doing ethics" with this handbook will not resolve all your dilemmas. It suggests an approach to making better ethical decisions. We hope this book helps you reason to a solution on your own and gives you a stronger rationale and vocabulary to defend and justify the tough calls.

To the practitioners: This book tries to systematically cover the ethical dilemmas reporters, photographers, producers and editors encounter most frequently. It challenges you to work through a variety of cases, some of which are well known, some of which have not received the time of day. You'll hear from others who have had to make tough calls, often on deadline. You'll read some observations about what seemed to have gone right and where things may have gone awry. In your spare time, or during a newsroom retreat, a few minutes with this book might help you and your colleagues "front end load" a decision making process that you can later apply on deadline. If you do as thousands of your colleagues have done with the first two editions of *Doing Ethics in Journalism*, you'll keep the book handy, next to your stylebook and dictionary, where you can pull it out on occasion.

To students and instructors: The beauty of "doing ethics" in the classroom rather than the newsroom should be self-evident. In the quiet of the academic setting students and instructors can systematically explore many nuances of decision making—without penalty. Working through hypotheticals or even revisiting real case studies with impunity is a luxury that comes with college. Students and instructors can raise more questions than they can answer, and can leave some of the tough questions hanging, without ever having to really invade privacy, break a promise to a source, run afoul of officials, or offend audiences.

Once they have learned what sorts of questions to ask and what effects their decisions are likely to have, students will be far better prepared to apply these skills while under fire. Indeed, deadlines are not the time to start thinking about journalism ethics. The time to decide whether it is appropriate to intrude upon a private moment of grief occurs long before the photographer adjusts the F-stop. Deadlines are a good time to "plug in" the decision making skills that have developed from the academic give-and-take. When students occasionally suggest that classroom ethics cases aren't real, we reply that this is all for the better, that they'll be far better able to handle the tough calls once they've slogged through the easier ones in class.

This does not mean that studying ethics in the classroom will lead to self-censorship and timidity. On the contrary. As we stress throughout this book, the primary role of the journalist is to get and report truthful news, to remain independent of forces that would pollute the channels of communication, to minimize harm, and to be accountable. Therefore, we explore questions of power and independence with a constant eye toward excellence: How can journalists do the best job possible, without compromising their fundamental role? In the pages that follow we raise questions about acting out of principle, understanding professional and social values, and recognizing conflicting loyalties. All the while, we do so with an eye toward encouraging positive, proactive and ethical journalism.

This is not a primer for wimps.

One other point: This book is not an introduction to journalism, but an intermediate or advanced text on applied ethics. It assumes that working journalists and instructors and students will bring to bear their own experiences on reporting, editing, dealing with sources and audiences, etc. Therefore, the language of the profession can be brought into the classroom to enhance deliberations about ethics.

The first part of the book introduces the important role of courageous and constitutionally-protected journalism. It explores rights versus obligations, and notes the importance of individual and collective decision making. The second chapter introduces professional codes of ethics; they are helpful, but not the be-all and end-all for making ethical decisions. The 1996 revision of the Society of Professional Journalists' code of ethics helps frame the discussion. Chapter 3 shows how a checklist of journalistic duties and provocative questions is applied to a Pulitzer Prize-winning series. Three separate voices may be heard in this part of the book: Ralph Barney was primary author of chapter 1, Jay Black of chapter 2, and Bob Steele of chapter 3. (All three authors contributed to the four sub-sections of chapter 2, in which the SPJ code's guiding principles are explored.)

The major section of the book defines specific types of problems, categorizing them and providing examples of common ethical dilemmas. It focuses on concerns such as accuracy and fairness, conflicts of interest, deception, diversity, photojournalism issues, invasion of privacy and source-reporter relationships. In our interviews with hundreds of journalists and in our search through codes of ethics and the growing literature of journalism ethics, these types of issues surfaced most frequently. Those who have used earlier editions of this book will note that 14 of the older edition's 31 case studies have been preserved, and 31 new cases have been added. Nearly all the new cases are drawn from 1996 and 1997 incidents.

In some of the case studies, we propose solutions, but we often merely offer the sorts of probing questions that discerning reporters and editors should ask and answer for themselves en route to more justifiable journalism.

At the beginning of each section is a succinct introduction to the general topic, followed by a checklist of important questions to ask when facing an ethical dilemma. After each chapter's case studies you will find excerpts from print and broadcast codes of ethics and relevant thoughts from other journalists. A careful reading of these sections will show some intriguing differences in handling ethical challenges, and may be useful to news organizations producing or refining their own codes or policy statements.

In the back of the handbook is a comprehensive annotated bibliography of the field, for those who want to pursue these issues more extensively. It is organized to follow the book's structure; a general introductory set of readings is followed by references to each of our case-study categories.

The book is dedicated to excellence and ethics in journalism. Enjoy.

Jay Black, University of South Florida St. Petersburg
Bob Steele, The Poynter Institute for Media Studies
Ralph Barney, Brigham Young University

September, 1997

Defining Ethics and Morality

Ask a layperson what he or she means by ethics or morality, and you're likely to hear that these subjects deal with the nature of human values and moral conscience, of choosing and following the "right" rather than the "wrong," and of understanding and applying standards that have been set down by a group, association or community. These definitions are useful for openers, but our fuller understanding of the issues ... might be better based on some of the insights and definitions posed by philosophers over the ages.

Ethics is based on the Greek word *ethos*, meaning character, or what a good person is or does in order to have a good character. In general, ethics deals with the philosophical foundations of decision making, of choosing among the good and bad options that one faces. *Morality*, on the other hand, comes from the Latin *mores*, and refers to the way or manner in which people behave. Thus *morality* has come to mean socially approved customs, or the *practice* or application of ethics. (One easy way to remember the distinction, according to a philosopher with a sense of humor, is to think of ethics as behavior that occurs above the neck, and morality as behavior that occurs below the neck!)

Ethics, in short, may be seen as being concerned with that which holds society together or provides the stability and security essential to the living of human life. Ethics as a branch of philosophy involves thinking about morality, moral problems, and moral judgments. It deals with "owes" and "oughts," what obligations we owe or to responsibilities we have toward our fellow humans, what we "should do" to make the world a better place. It is unlike law, which is a bottom-line, minimalistic enterprise that tells us what we *can* do or what we *can* get away with. When we describe the practicing of ethics, of putting these ideas to work, we are talking about "doing ethics."

—Source: Jay Black and Jennings Bryant, *Introduction to Media Communication, 4th Ed.* (Dubuque, Iowa: Brown and Benchmark, 1995), pp. 540-541.

Professional Journalism Organizations' Codes of Ethics

Society of Professional Journalists

Preamble

Members of the Society of Professional Journalists believe that public enlightenment is the forerunner of justice and the foundation of democracy. The duty of the journalist is to further those ends by seeking truth and providing a fair and comprehensive account of events and issues. Conscientious journalists from all media and specialties strive to serve the public with thoroughness and honesty. Professional integrity is the cornerstone of a journalist's credibility.

Members of the Society share a dedication to ethical behavior and adopt this code to declare the Society's principles and standards of practice.

Seek Truth and Report It

Journalists should be honest, fair and courageous in gathering, reporting and interpreting information. Journalists should:

- Test the accuracy of information from all sources and exercise care to avoid inadvertent error. Deliberate distortion is never permissible.
- Diligently seek out subjects of news stories to give them the opportunity to respond to allegations of wrongdoing.
- Identify sources whenever feasible. The public is entitled to as much information as possible on sources' reliability.
- Always question sources' motives before promising anonymity. Clarify conditions attached to any promise made in exchange for information. Keep promises.
- Make certain that headlines, news teases and promotional material, photos, video, audio, graphics, sound bites and quotations do not misrepresent. They should not oversimplify or highlight incidents out of context.
- Never distort the content of news photos or video. Image enhancement for technical clarity is always permissible. Label montages and photo illustrations.
- Avoid misleading re-enactments or staged news events. If re-enactment is necessary to tell a story, label it.
- Avoid undercover or other surreptitious methods of gathering information except when traditional open methods will not yield information vital to the public. Use of such methods should be explained as part of the story.

• Never plagiarize.

• Tell the story of the diversity and magnitude of the human experience boldly, even when it is unpopular to do so.

• Examine their own cultural values and avoid imposing those values on others.

• Avoid stereotyping by race, gender, age, religion, ethnicity, geography, sexual orientation, disability, physical appearance or social status.

• Support the open exchange of views, even views they find repugnant.

• Give voice to the voiceless; official and unofficial sources of information can be equally valid.

• Distinguish between advocacy and news reporting. Analysis and commentary should be labeled and not misrepresent fact or context.

• Distinguish news from advertising and shun hybrids that blur the lines between the two.

• Recognize a special obligation to ensure that the public's business is conducted in the open and that government records are open to inspection.

Minimize Harm

Ethical journalists treat sources, subjects and colleagues as human beings deserving of respect. Journalists should:

• Show compassion for those who may be affected adversely by news coverage. Use special sensitivity when dealing with children and inexperienced sources or subjects.

• Be sensitive when seeking or using interviews or photographs of those affected by tragedy or grief.

• Recognize that gathering and reporting information may cause harm or discomfort. Pursuit of the news is not a license for arrogance.

• Recognize that private people have a greater right to control information about themselves than do public officials and others who seek power, influence or attention. Only an overriding public need can justify intrusion into anyone's privacy.

• Show good taste. Avoid pandering to lurid curiosity.

• Be cautious about identifying juvenile suspects or victims of sex crimes.

• Be judicious about naming criminal suspects before the formal filing of charges.

• Balance a criminal suspect's fair trial rights with the public's right to be informed.

Act Independently

Journalists should be free of obligation to any interest other than the public's right to know. Journalists should:

• Avoid conflicts of interest, real or perceived.

• Remain free of associations and activities that may compromise integrity or damage credibility.

• Refuse gifts, favors, fees, free travel and special treatment, and shun secondary employment, political involvement, public office and service in community organizations if they compromise journalistic integrity.

- Disclose unavoidable conflicts.
- Be vigilant and courageous about holding those with power accountable.
- Deny favored treatment to advertisers and special interests and resist their pressure to influence news coverage.
- Be wary of sources offering information for favors or money; avoid bidding for news.

Be Accountable

Journalists are accountable to their readers, listeners, viewers and each other. Journalists should:

- Clarify and explain news coverage and invite dialogue with the public over journalistic conduct.
- Encourage the public to voice grievances against the news media.
- Admit mistakes and correct them promptly.
- Expose unethical practices of journalists and the news media.
- Abide by the same high standards to which they hold others.

(Sigma Delta Chi's first Code of Ethics was borrowed from the American Society of Newspaper Editors in 1926. In 1973, Sigma Delta Chi wrote its own code, which was revised in 1984 and 1987. The present version of the Society of Professional Journalists' Code of Ethics was adopted in September 1996.)

Radio-Television News Directors Association

The responsibility of radio and television journalists is to gather and report information of importance and interest to the public accurately, honestly, and impartially.

The members of the Radio-Television News Directors Association will accept these standards and will:

1. Strive to present the source or nature of broadcast news material in a way that is balanced, accurate and fair.

   A. They will evaluate information solely on its merits as news, rejecting sensationalism or misleading emphasis in any form.

   B. They will guard against using audio or video material in a way that deceives the audience.

   C. They will not mislead the public by presenting as spontaneous news any material which is staged or rehearsed.

   D. They will identify people by race, creed, nationality, or prior status only when relevant.

   E. They will clearly label opinion and commentary.

   F. They will promptly acknowledge and correct errors.

2. Strive to conduct themselves in a manner that protects them from conflicts of interest, real or perceived. They will decline gifts or favors which

would influence or appear to influence their judgments.

3. Respect the dignity, privacy and well-being of people with whom they deal.

4. Recognize the need to protect confidential sources. They will promise confidentiality only with the intention of keeping that promise.

5. Respect everyone's right to a fair trial.

6. Broadcast the private transmissions of other broadcasters only with permission.

7. Actively encourage observance of the Code by all journalists, whether members of the Radio-Television News Directors Association or not.

(This version of the RTNDA Code of Ethics was adopted in 1987.)

National Press Photographers Association

The National Press Photographers Association, a professional society dedicated to the advancement of photojournalism, acknowledges concern and respect for the public's natural-law right to freedom in searching for the truth and the right to be informed truthfully and completely about public events and the world in which we live.

We believe that no report can be complete if it is not possible to enhance and clarify the meaning of words. We believe that pictures, whether used to depict news events as they actually happen, illustrate news that has happened or to help explain anything of public interest, are an indispensable means of keeping people accurately informed; that they help all people, young and old, to better understand any subject in the public domain.

Believing the foregoing we recognize and acknowledge that photojournalists should at all times maintain the highest standards of ethical conduct in serving the public interest. To that end the National Press Photographers Association sets forth the following Code of Ethics, which is subscribed to by all of its members:

1. The practice of photojournalism, both as a science and art, is worthy of the very best thought and effort of those who enter into it as a profession.

2. Photojournalism affords an opportunity to serve the public that is equaled by few other vocations and all members of the profession should strive by example and influence to maintain high standards of ethical conduct free of mercenary considerations of any kind.

3. It is the individual responsibility of every photojournalist at all times to strive for pictures that report truthfully, honestly and objectively.

4. Business promotion in its many forms is essential, but untrue statements of any nature are not worthy of a professional photojournalist and we severely condemn any such practice.

5. It is our duty to encourage and assist all members of our profession, individually and collectively, so that the quality of photojournalism may constant-

ly be raised to higher standards.

6. It is the duty of every photojournalist to work to preserve all freedom-of-the-press rights recognized by law and to work to protect and expand freedom-of-access to all sources of news and visual information.

7. Our standards of business dealings, ambitions and relations shall have in them a note of sympathy for our common humanity and shall always require us to take into consideration our highest duties as members of society. In every situation in our business life, in every responsibility that comes before us, our chief thought shall be to fulfill that responsibility and discharge that duty so that when each of us is finished we shall have endeavored to lift the level of human ideals and achievement higher than we found it.

8. No Code of Ethics can prejudge every situation, thus common sense and good judgment are required in applying ethical principles.

Public Radio News Directors Incorporated

Whereas Public Radio News Directors Incorporated (PRNDI) was formed in December 1984 to enhance news and information programming, and

Whereas PRNDI was formed to encourage professional development, and

Whereas PRNDI is to foster events to pursue developmental goals of journalists, producers, editors, independent contractors, students, and volunteer news and public information aides, and

Whereas PRNDI members serve many communities and interests that deserve news programs of the highest standards of honesty, fairness, integrity, balance, compassion, and technical quality;

Now, therefore Public Radio News Directors Incorporated does advance and call upon members to follow this code of ethical conduct ...

1) Prepare and deliver news programs accurately to maintain public trust. All errors of fact, bias, or omission must be corrected immediately.

2) Strive to eliminate personal, station, or community bias and balance matters of race, creed, religion, ethnic origin, gender, and sexual preference.

3) Recognize, understand, and vigorously pursue our public's right-to-know laws. Members must evaluate the merit and news value of materials provided by anonymous sources. After deliberation, members must insure the sanctity of those sources based upon right to privacy and guard against its violation.

4) Make efforts to name those who provide newsworthy information and avoid all sound presentations not generated at the news site.

5) Responsibly evaluate the newsworthiness of all broadcast items and guard against undue pressure from non-news personnel.

6) Honor legitimate requests to hold or embargo newsworthy material provided in advance.

7) Avoid making false representations to obtain materials from those who might otherwise object to discussing matters with reporters, editors, producers, independent contractors, student aides, or volunteers under your direction.

8) Inform news sources when conversations are being taped.

9) Make no promises or guarantees to report, promote, or advance materials without true news value.

10) Avoid the reality or perception of all conflicts of professional and personal interests. These include rejection of gifts, favors, commissions, privileges, or special access which cloud perception.

11) In every case possible, maintain a separation of duty during station pledge drives and other fund-raising efforts. If possible, this separation should include all news-related personnel.

12) Reconsider the associations with community events, service projects, boards, councils, or commissions when conflicts of interest arise and to work to assign stories on those organizations to reporters.

13) Avoid employment that involves work for politicians, corporations, companies, sponsors, underwriters, or station donors which strain professional obligation and public trust.

14) Avoid participation in any event (marches, demonstrations, picketing, rallies) that compromise professional integrity and future news or public information assignments.

15) Maintain and upgrade these standards as circumstances require.

16) Require all news employees, independent contractors, producers, editors, talent, aids, and volunteers under member direction to adhere to these standards.

And,

Upon acceptance of these standards, members should advance them by personal action. By doing so, members maintain a standard of excellence which enhances the value of the news delivered. Members doing so provide worth to their stations, their communities, and the employees under their direction. This provides the public with a trustworthy product that is beyond reproach.

(The PRNDI Code of Ethics was adopted on July 27, 1991.)

Chapter One

The Role of the Journalist

With startling regularity, journalists and newsrooms find themselves vigorously discussing whether to run stories they know will cause a storm of discussion on talk shows and in the streets.

Debates rage over publishing unproven accusations of sexual harassment against powerful figures (U.S. Sens. Brock Adams of Washington and Robert Packwood of Oregon are two fairly recent ones), or naming alleged rape victims (NBC News and the *New York Times* in the case of William Kennedy Smith), or juvenile offenders.

More recently, questions revolve around whether public accusations of improprieties or other behavior that invade the privacy of a celebrity (Frank Gifford or Diana, Princess of Wales) or a public figure (the Gennifer Flowers "affair" with Bill Clinton) should be plucked from tabloid newspapers and given wider distribution in the "mainstream" press.

The questions may not be whether such stories should be published, but how well journalists reason and explain decisions that cause obvious and grievous harm to an individual, even a public official. Sen. Adams denied the accusations, for example, calling them unfounded. He soon announced he would not seek re-election in 1992, charging irreparable harm to his political and personal reputation. Media did not publish similar accusations against Sen. Packwood, on the other hand, and Mr. Packwood was re-elected, only to spend the first two years of his new term defending himself unsuccessfully after the accusations did finally appear.

Television talk shows inevitably pit defenders of publication against critics of the press. Unfortunately, the critics most often carry the day, correctly pointing to the harm. This happens largely because journalists and their defenders find it difficult to spell out clearly and convincingly why the media often have a moral obligation to publish such stories.

Rights versus Obligations

Defenders tend to speak of the *right* rather than the moral *obligation* to publish such material. It is as if insistent assertions of the right to publish would somehow turn away attacks and public outrage. The *right* to publish, granted by the First Amendment to the U.S. Constitution and confirmed by judicial decisions, is widely documented and discussed in civics classes and history lectures. But the *obligation* to distribute information, which resides in the soul of a journalistic ethic, is rarely discussed. It is the *why* of this process that demands articulation, so that the public can understand and appreciate the journalist's motives for telling so much.

Journalists are often denounced and ridiculed for invoking First Amendment rights in their demands for access to sensitive information. They are bitterly criticized as they invade privacy in pursuit of information. The citizens' sense of justice often demands that journalists act differently. Journalists are accused of selfishly claiming special privileges for themselves while victimizing others, particularly in privacy invasions. Later in this book we explore cases in which journalists published the name of the benefactor of a city destroyed by floods who did not want to be identified publicly, published gory photographs of shooting and accident victims, and carried racist and homophobic language. Often, the strongest critics in such cases are those who feel threatened by media disclosures or practices, those who have a vested interest in passive media. These public people often try to convince the rest of the public, often successfully, that journalists are jackals. The grieving families of the victims and a brief FBI suspect in the Atlanta Olympics bombing, as well as many others, would agree.

The right to publish is widely documented and discussed in civics classes and history lectures. But the obligation to distribute information, which resides in the soul of a journalistic ethic, is rarely discussed.

The force and durability of the accusations cause the industry to smart. Journalists are jostled into introspection, asking whether traditional rules still apply and what, in a complex world, they *should* do to serve a critical society.

- What moral obligation did the news industry have to cover the Persian Gulf War, challenging official information and revealing public policy issues?
- Does ethics require publication or temporary withholding of names of suspects or other public figures named in police reports?
- Is it obligatory or optional to expose extramarital escapades and drug experimentation of political candidates, or are other issues more important and useful in the election process?
- What moral obligation requires a reporter to keep sources confidential, and when may those sources ethically be "burned"?
- Is it a moral obligation of journalists to detect and warn about impending

disasters, such as resulted in the $150 billion bailout of the collapsed savings and loans industry?

• How can journalists balance their obligations to tell truth, remain independent and minimize harm during such volatile crises as the 51-day standoff between federal agents and Branch Davidians in Waco, Texas?

News people increasingly are perplexed about how to handle problems that until recently seemed black and white.

Until the gulf war, combat had never been viewed live by both sides on a single commercial television outlet. Cable News Network kept the world informed, blow by blow. In other wars, the military has generally controlled the communications systems. Direct portable satellite transmission and cellular telephones allowed many journalists to bypass that control in the gulf.

When rape and sexual attacks never got to court without evidence of a brutal assault, torn clothing, bruises, and evidence of resistance, the procedures for news coverage were clearly prescribed. Today, in a more sensitive society, ambiguities between accused and accuser make old coverage policies seem inadequate.

What moral burden rested on the *Seattle Times*, for example, to find provable truths before it published allegations of sexual harassment against a sitting U.S. senator, particularly when a similar accusation had been investigated and dismissed by a government agency? By the same token, what allowed Oregon media, when confronted with repeated complaints about Sen. Packwood's proclivities, to keep silent as he ran for re-election and largely deprived the state of his representation for two years while he tried to defend himself?

Can journalists argue that they ought not be expected to be so expert in finance that they could detect approaching financial disaster, such as the fragility of junk bonds or the collapse of savings and loans, months or years before disaster struck?

When thousands of Los Angeles buildings were torched when rioting erupted after the controversial Rodney King verdict in 1992, what moral rules directed helicopter-borne camera operators to broadcast live pictures showing where dangers lay or where there were no police? Such coverage provided sensitive information to two disparate groups—frightened citizens and marauders.

Complicating the journalist's mission are the public relations experts who make favorable information abundantly available while obscuring the trail to unfavorable information.

As these dilemmas arise, often requiring decisions on deadline, journalists must search beyond the dogma of news values and tradition for help. A critical tool in the search is a greater understanding of the ethical role a journalist plays in making the wheels of society turn, and in keeping those wheels on. Later in this chapter, we will see how an appreciation of that role can help us better understand journalistic behavior during the 1993 Waco, Texas tragedy, and how it might help journalists cope with the next "Waco."

SUNDAY

WASHINGTON'S LARGEST NEWSPAPER • COPYRIGHT © 1992, SEATTLE TIMES COMPANY

8 more women accuse Adams

Allegations of two decades of sexual harassment, abuse – and a rape

Sen. Brock Adams has sexually harassed and physically molested female employees and associates over the past two decades, according to eight who say they are victims.

U.S. Sen. Brock Adams

INSIDE: The women's stories, and what psychologists say about why it is difficult for women in such circumstances to come forward. Pages 3-4.

Please see ADAMS on Page 2

A story that had to be told

Please see EDITOR on Page 2

Stock market closes at 3,275.27
Closing NYSE prices F6

The Seattle Times Page 5

UW great Heinrich dead at 61 B 1

Finding time for Derrick

As the Sonics beat Cleveland, Karl weighs lineup change. B 1

35¢

The Seattle Times

MONDAY
March 2, 1992
44 pages

WASHINGTON'S LARGEST NEWSPAPER ■ COPYRIGHT 1992, SEATTLE TIMES COMPANY

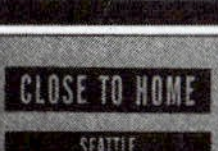

Pregnant pause

Mothers-to-be wait for buses to get to prenatal care. C 3

Gai's Bakery merges with S.F. bread baker

Combining of companies is part of expansion strategy. F 8

Resentment brews over state berths

Private schools are targets in battle of Class B teams. B 4

INSIDE STORIES

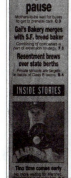

Tino time comes early

No more waiting for Martinez, Mariners have spot for him. B 1

Basketball star dies

BROCK ADAMS: Out of the race

Who'll run for Adams' seat?

Mark Harrison / Seattle Times

Sen. Brock Adams hugs daughter Kokie and wife Betty at a news conference yesterday after announcing that he will not seek re-election.

Scramble on after senator withdraws

by Mark Matassa
Times staff reporter

Sen. Brock Adams' decision to end his re-election campaign throws the Senate race wide open, with several candidates claiming a new advantage and some Democratic strategists scrambling to flesh out what they say is a weakened, inadequate field.

Adams withdrew from the race yesterday – but vowed not to resign from the Senate – after The Times reported allegations by eight women that he had sexually harassed or abused them over the past two decades.

At a news conference in his campaign headquarters in downtown Seattle, the senator denied the allegations in the strongest terms, decrying The Times' copyright newspaper stories as poor journalism and suggesting the report was part of a politically motivated conspiracy.

"I've never harmed anybody in my life," he said with his wife, Betty, and daughter Kokie at his side. "I just don't know why or who or what these people are doing."

Nevertheless, he said, the charges were so damaging to his campaign, to his family, to his staff and to himself that he chose not to continue his candidacy.

"This is the saddest day of my

Journalism is Different

The journalist's social role is critical, but it is little understood by the public and poorly explained by the profession. While most journalists talk about protections the Constitution and the courts offer the journalist, few explain to critics and the public **why** society protects journalists. What are the foundations of the First Amendment and favorable court interpretations? *Seattle Times* executive editor Michael Fancher described the painstaking procedures *Times* staffers followed in assuring fairness in the Brock Adams case, yet he still cited "traditional standards" to be met for publication. (Recall for a moment the traditional standards for deciding what is news, standards you first learned in journalism school or on the job: conflict, novelty, prominence, proximity, impact, recency, etc. These traditional standards may be suitable for defining routine news coverage, but they have no ethical or philosophical foundation. In short, these definitions of newsworthiness are amoral. Relying upon them to defend yourself against an accusation of questionable ethics can't satisfy an intelligent critic. In fairness to the *Seattle Times*, we must add that its editorial staff did go beyond these minimalistic standards; many other journalists, however, never get that far.)

Unlike other professionals who have institutionally defined social roles and ethics, journalists have been left to their own devices in working out their social roles and in determining their ethics, and then in justifying those roles and ethics to the public.

Surgeons, in contrast, enjoy a clear mandate. It is unthinkable that most of us would pick up a knife and cut on a friend. Yet the surgeon has that specific moral charge: Inflict some pain and shed some blood, but be sure to bring more benefit than trauma to the patient. Thus the surgeon has a role bestowed and protected by society: Shed blood for a greater good. Likewise, a military commander has a role that morally justifies sending people to their deaths and inflicting death on an enemy, presumably for a greater good.

While it is generally accepted that surgeons have a moral right to shed blood, and generals in certain circumstances may morally end the lives of human beings they do not know, it is more difficult to define the journalist's role.

Journalists are not licensed, as are surgeons, nor are they hired, legitimized, and controlled by government, as are generals. Thus individual journalists and the profession as a whole must work out their own role definitions according to (1) their perceptions of what society needs, and (2) an ethical recognition that Constitutional protection must not knowingly be socially destructive. Because it would be silly for a society to protect a class of people who are hastening its destruction, it must be assumed that journalists bear a strong moral obligation to avoid conscious social damage.

A substantial amount of unjustifiable social damage can be avoided if journalists satisfy themselves that what they publish, however controversial it may be, has a high probability of being the truth. While truth is sometimes difficult to identify, the journalist, nevertheless, should generally err in favor of disclosure, rather than withhold information in cases in which probability of truth is high.

In a society that protects people who speak or write, any person (literate or illiterate, learned or ignorant, socialized or rebellious, passive or outraged) may become a journalist without standards imposed either by government or professional groups. Even regulation by society at large in the form of intimidating public opinion, while often formidable, is difficult to enforce because of the Bill of Rights. First Amendment protection slows suppression, even by the compelling power of public opinion, until society considers and discusses restrictions.

A big problem for journalists as they compare their duties to those of the surgeon and the general is that their discussions all too often begin by citing law rather than explaining the moral obligations that journalists are attempting to fulfill. Defenders talk of the *right* to publish, rather than the *reason* they

A Letter from the Editor

These pages are a reprint of the first two days of a story about U.S. Senator Brock Adams as it was reported by the *Seattle Times*. The *Times* story itself has become the subject of wide journalistic discussion because of its reliance on unnamed sources and because the senator subsequently ended his bid for re-election.

As I say in a front-page explanation to our readers, we believe this story had to be told ....

Having worked on the story for more than three years, the reporters and editors were convinced the allegations were true. Our dilemma was that none of the victims would allow us to use her name, despite our ongoing attempts to persuade them to go on the record.

Our choice was to publish nothing of these allegations or to publish a story without naming the women. We decided that a responsible approach was to publish the claims of women who were willing to sign statements affirming the truth of their allegations and acknowledging they might have to face him in court should he sue us. Eight of the women agreed.

We would have preferred to publish a story with all parties named. Because that wasn't possible, we believe what we did was the only responsible course we could follow.

We make this reprint available to help you better examine our discussion and to contribute to an open discussion of the issues concerning confidential sources in investigative journalism

— Michael R. Fancher, Executive Editor

publish. There is a tendency by journalists to wrongly assume the public understands the rationale behind First Amendment protections. Just as the public now questions basic assumptions about the environment and natural resources, so journalists are being pressed to answer basic questions about their function.

Journalists distribute information, a traditional role that often puts the journalist at odds with individuals and power brokers who want to keep power by controlling information.

The democratic principle supporting quality journalism has been expressed by philosopher Carl Friedrich. He wrote that since everyone is fallible in making decisions, society needs the collective judgments of many fallible people to produce valid social decisions and solve social problems. The journalist is the central figure in improving the odds that good decisions will be made. He or she provides key information that will assist the populace in giving informed consent to public proposals. Constantly opposing the journalists, for good reasons of their own, are those with competing strong ideas about how the world should turn out, and a corresponding commitment to promote their own agendas. Discouraging journalists from distributing contrary information is a common way true believers attempt to advance causes.

Journalists must decide for themselves, rather than having others decide for them, what information they will distribute, and what form that information will take.

Because information helps ensure informed consent, the principle of open communication has a unique standing in American society. In that context, ethical reasoning requires a considerably different approach than is common in professional ethics. The First Amendment and subsequent court rulings give journalists unparalleled freedom to inform the fallible without government interference.

The conscientious journalist needs to deal with the moral question of social contract. In this case, it is a question of journalists' contracts with their audience: What contract is created between me and my reader or viewer when that person buys my newspaper or spends time watching my newscast?

In a democratic society, the audience is expected to process a much broader range of information than in other cultures.

When we speak of journalism ethics, then, we speak not of regulated behavior, the phenomenon most familiar to us as we look at the activities of doctors, lawyers, plumbers, and others who follow professional codes. In journalism, we speak of the far more important concepts of "reasoned" and "principled" behavior. Journalists must decide for themselves, rather than having others decide for them, what information they will distribute, and what form that information will take. Even professional groups, without authority to keep journalists from practicing their craft, may not tell the journalist how to perform.

Most discussions of professional ethics imply the existence of documented restrictions on ethical behavior as a means to protect society. Such restrictions are expected to be universally accepted and mandatory. A free society, however, specifically rejects most speech and press restrictions. Therefore, mandatory standards for journalism are rightly unenforceable and unworkable. Judicial interpretations of the First Amendment consistently resist pressure to insist that journalists be licensed. Thus, anybody can be a journalist without fear of being prohibited from practicing the craft (or being de-pressed or ex-communicated, if you would).

This absence of professional discipline makes journalistic codes, including the new SPJ Code of Ethics, more advisory than mandatory. That is in sharp contrast to the enforceable codes of the legal and medical professions, and a source of concern to those who see a need to "control" anyone who possesses the kind of power the media are perceived to have. But it also means that journalists, individually and collectively, have a greater need for an articulated sense of ethics than do the more regulated professionals.

Into the Arena of Principle and Reason

There are several propositions journalists should be aware of as they participate in principled and reasoned decision making. These propositions, abbreviated here, are expanded in other ethics publications, but they provide a starting place for someone working to understand and defend the journalistic role.

First, society is committed to the possibility of the free flow of information as a means of a) informing the population so its members may b) make informed decisions which c) combine with thousands or millions of other decisions d) to contribute to the strength of society or determine how society will treat its individual members.

Second, the journalistic mission is often obscured because information control is related to power. Distribution of information is a redistribution of power. Thus, because the traditional function of the journalist is the distribution of information, the journalist is often at odds with individuals and entities wishing to retain power by controlling or withholding information.

Distribution of information is a redistribution of power.

Distribution of information can be a mixed bag. All information may help someone while at the same time harming others. Disclosure about nursing home abuses may benefit patients by improving care. However, it also reduces the power of nursing home operators, placed in a public spotlight, to control their own operations. Nursing home disclosures may also cause anxiety, and even guilt feelings in families who comfortably assume family members in *all* nursing homes are receiving competent, caring treatment.

Surgeons cut people open, generals commit lives to combat. Both life-and-death or pain-inflicting functions have strong public support. Journalists do their job by taking power from groups bent on retaining or accumulating it. They then redistribute power to the public by disseminating information. Brock Adams had the power to run again for the Senate, but the *Seattle Times* story gave the public information which diminished his power. The citizens of Washington, with more information, gained the power to decide if Brock Adams should continue to hold public office. The citizens of Oregon, on the other hand, with silent media, made their electoral decisions in a significant information vacuum, not having critical information that may have affected their votes significantly.

The journalist is likely to be immersed in a variety of differing loyalties and ties that affect the pure gathering and distribution of information: the desire to win fame and fortune; biases for or against social institutions or individuals; conceptions about what a journalist or investigative reporter is, or does, etc. Such pressures may blunt the journalist's moral judgment, producing faulty journalistic decisions. The public then suffers from distorted information.

Despite the journalist's service to audiences, those largely defenseless and unorganized groups seldom express themselves. They contrast with special interest groups which, because they tend to be extremely vocal, create an impression of a public opinion outpouring. This book is concerned with giving voice to the voiceless, those who have minimal leverage or position in society. The voiceless can then air their views, along with the views of more vocal special interests, to produce legitimate public opinion which, in turn, can be understood and enhanced by the news media. Communications media thus fulfill their basic functions of communicating—making experiences common or sharing information—and mediating—coming between and pulling together various interest groups.

A society that trusts the media to keep it informed has mixed feelings about those media. Minimizing harm while trying to keep audiences fully informed requires that journalists formulate justification mechanisms to defend publishing decisions. Those defenses must go beyond mere restatements of traditional journalistic rights or unquestioned institutional norms. They need to be articulated journalistic obligations.

Beyond Waco

Press performance before and during a 51-day armed standoff between the followers of David Koresh and federal agents near Waco, Texas, offers a classic example of the conflicting obligations described in this chapter. It tests the principles of disclosure we have discussed. It is a case worthy of study and discussion for what it tells us about journalists' roles and their relationship to power. The concern was such that the Society of Professional Journalists put together a special task force to examine media behavior in the face of accusations that the media were responsible for much of what went wrong in Waco.

The conflict is between several rights: the public's rights to know about weapons stockpiles and child abuse accusations and law enforcement agencies' rights to investigate in comparative anonymity instead of being pressured by public opinion to justify themselves during the process.

The eyes of the world were on Waco from the morning of Feb. 28, 1993 when four federal agents and several Branch Davidians were killed in a massive effort to arrest David Koresh at his fortress-like compound. Warrants had been issued charging him with firearms violations.

For our purposes the story had begun months earlier, however, with an investigation project by the Waco *Tribune-Herald* into stories of child abuse and arms stockpiles coming out of the compound which housed Koresh and his religious followers.

After more than eight months of research and writing, the *Tribune-Herald* produced a series of stories which deplored local law enforcement's apparent lack of interest in the matter. Federal agents asked that the newspaper delay publishing the stories, citing its own reasons. The newspaper complied, for nearly a month, but not just because of the government's request. Editor Bob Lott said the month was used to polish the stories and arrange security for reporters and editors who had worked on the series. The newspaper published the first story on Saturday, February 27, the day before the federal raid.

The newspaper decided that sharing the information was more important than whatever benefits might have accrued from following authorities' request to delay publication. This was an important judgment call.

The request for delay by law enforcement investigators represents the first of several ethical dilemmas centered on power redistribution. The Bureau of Alcohol, Tobacco, and Firearms would, so long as the story was not published, retain the power to investigate and act at its own speed, or to ignore the issue if it were so inclined. It could follow its own strategic plan in the matter.

Upon publication of such unsettling stories, however, public agencies feel a pressure to act. They have little choice once the community becomes aware of a potential problem in its midst (in this case, an accelerating stockpiling of armaments, and reports of children being sexually abused—right next door). The disclosures expose a consensus that must thereafter be taken into consideration by all the citizens in the area.

The newspaper decided that sharing the information was more important than whatever benefits might have accrued from following authorities' request to delay publication. It was an important judgment call.

A federal agent later said the timing of the raid against the Branch Davidians was not connected to the newspaper's publishing plans. However, questions have been raised about whether the story alerted the compound to expect some law enforcement action, or whether the media somehow intensified the conflict and bore some responsibility for the deaths resulting from the assault, and perhaps even for the length of the standoff by denying raiding officers the benefit of surprise. Nevertheless, the siege began.

Prominent among other accusations of media transgression were instances in which broadcasters, without consultation with authorities, allowed David Koresh airtime to deliver his messages live. In another case, a radio station carried a taped message from Koresh after authorities asked the station to do so. Koresh's promises to release children in return for airtime were not kept.

The dilemmas posed by the Waco siege involve media obligations in conflict with government rights to resolve conflicts and maintain an orderly society. A secondary question asks about conditions under which the media should become "agents of government" in delaying publication, or in agreeing to help government strategies by relinquishing—or at least sharing—control of their media. First thoughts tend to compel cooperation with government, but separation of government and media, an important element in a successful watchdog system, suggests such cooperation should come only after careful consideration.

Law enforcement agents undoubtedly feel most comfortable conducting raids and sieges in a spotlight substantially dimmer than that provided by media scrutiny.

The two main conflicts, however, are whether the newspaper should have printed the story in spite of government requests for continued delay and whether the media are justified in bypassing government agents in a siege/hostage situation in which lives are at stake in order to provide alternative views of government enforcement-in-process.

A justification for the media is that the community has a right to know of potential dangers within its borders. As in so many other situations, the question of how serious a danger may be is a matter of human judgment, both by journalists and by the government. These judgments may be affected by the self-interest of both parties, but it would be the moral obligation of both parties to make the decision with more than their own selfish interests in mind.

Different journalists will arrive at different decisions, acceptable under the First Amendment. The concern, however, is that editors deliberate carefully and consider audience and community well-being, both requiring principle and reason, as paramount in their concerns.

Conclusion

In using this handbook, then, one must recognize the paramount importance of distributing information to a democratic society. Once that role is understood as a primary obligation, journalists can use moral reasoning and can follow principles, rather than routine and tradition, in making ethical decisions. Those decisions should support journalists' obligation to distribute necessary information fully, while avoiding unnecessary harm and holding themselves accountable.

The remainder of this book is devoted to guiding journalists through a decision making process that will protect society by supporting the full disclosure of information and giving voice to the voiceless, while protecting innocent individuals from needless harm.

Chapter Two

Codes of Ethics and Beyond

Ever since the first journalist began assembling the first information for the first news story, people have been concerned about journalism ethics. Millions of words have been spoken, and thousands of pages written, about identifying and resolving the tough calls journalists face while gathering and reporting the news.

However, for all the work that has been put into ethics over the years, the job is nowhere near finished. In the words of Philip Meyer, author of *Ethical Journalism*, journalists are still ethically confused. As a profession, journalists have come a long way in their ability to identify ethical issues and dilemmas. However, they have a long way to go before knowing how to resolve those problems carefully and systematically. Journalists have heightened their sensitivity far more than they have expanded their decision making skills.

Much of the credit and a fair share of the blame for this confusing state of affairs can be laid at the feet of those who invoke codes of ethics as the panacea. At best, the codes have helped define many of the problems and have kept the profession alert to its responsibilities to gather and report news thoroughly and accurately and to remain vigilant toward governmental and other forces that would usurp the media's independence. At worst, codes have short-circuited journalists' ability to act as independent decision makers.

Pros and Cons of Codes

One of the prerequisites of a profession is to have its own code of ethics. Codes of ethics are supposed to act as the conscience of the professional, of the organization, of the enterprise. A code of ethics falls somewhere between societal and personal values on the one hand and law on the other. A code is not as subjective as personal beliefs and opinions, nor as rigid and enforceable as the law.

The strength of an ethics code is a function not only of its various principles and mandates, but of its legitimacy and power in the eyes of those for whom it is written. The code will be obeyed because individuals willingly subject themselves to ethical standards above and beyond their own personal beliefs or because the code has specific provisions for enforcement which they fear should they violate it.

Even the best codes have built-in limitations. Codes of ethics identify useful lists of sins, and to some extent outline truly noble behavior. They are of some use to newcomers who need a road map that points out troublesome ethical intersections, sharp corners, and the biggest potholes. They also have some public relations value to an industry that tries to convince the public of its seriousness about ethics. But codes cannot delineate all the territory likely to be encountered, and they aren't much help when negotiating the vast foggy terrain through which journalists travel daily. As a result of these natural limitations to codes, many journalists erroneously conclude that there are no useful guidelines, that each ethical decision is made *ad hoc* or independently of all other decisions.

The goal of this book is like the goals of moral philosophers throughout history: to help individuals and groups make ethical decisions that are morally defensible, and to base those decisions on justification processes that hold true from situation to situation, person to person, time to time. The authors of *Doing Ethics in Journalism* hope to help journalism students and practitioners systematically work through ethical dilemmas because of an articulated ethical mission, a dedication to *doing the right thing for the right reasons*. To accomplish such a complex goal requires more than a code.

Law ≠ Ethics

Ethics is not the same as law, and ethical constraints are not the same as legal rules. Ethics articulates what we ought to do in order to be moral individuals and professionals, while law concentrates on the bottom line below which we should not fall. Ethics deals with ideal behaviors, while law deals with minimal standards. There is a common tendency today to equate ethical standards with legal standards, and for victims of unethical behavior to seek legal remedies for perceived ethical lapses. This is a false equation and a fundamental misconception of the relationship between law and ethics. For instance, invasion-of-privacy laws widely permit the publication of information that, for reasons of ethics, taste, compassion or professionalism, some news media would not publish or broadcast. Identifying a rape victim is an example. This handbook does not purport to address the legal boundaries of the gathering and publication of news. Rather, it analyzes the ethical questions of journalists' behavior and decisions.

Bruce W. Sanford, counsel to the nation's oldest and largest journalism organization, the Society of Professional Journalists (SPJ), writes, "History teaches that the most effective way to promote ethical behavior is through discussion and information, not enforcement."

In an article in the Associated Press Managing Editors publication *Ethics Codes: Sunrise or Sunset?*, Sanford quotes Geoffrey Hazard, who makes a good case for relying on a deliberative process rather than a list of dos and don'ts:

> Ethical principles can be established only as a result of deliberation and argumentation. These principles are not the kind of thing that can be settled by fiat, agreement or by authority. To assume that they can is to confuse ethics with lawmaking, rule-making, policy-making and other kinds of decision making.

For the past decade or so, SPJ members have been debating the pros and cons of enforcement procedures for their code. Some maintain that a professional organization without the means and willingness to censure code violators is undeserving of the public trust. Others insist that the constitutionally protected enterprise of journalism had fought too hard and long for freedom from outside control, and should not impose any more control over itself than absolutely necessary. Still others argue that to enforce the code would invite litigation financially devastating to the Society and establish precedents that would serve the purposes of those seeking a universal standard of conduct enforceable in court. Still others claim that the wording of the Society's code combines lofty idealistic statements and minimal standards of performance in such a way as to render the code unenforceable in the first place.

In 1987, SPJ deleted from its code of ethics a clause requiring journalists to "actively censure" code violators. In its place, the Society promised a strong education program that stressed ethics and encouraged journalists to adhere to the code's honorable ideals. Preeminent among these ideals was the desire "to preserve and strengthen the bond of mutual trust and respect among American journalists and the American people." That bond is based on both credibility and ethics, the former being the profession's image, the latter its substance.

The code as revised in 1987 also called on journalists in print and broadcasting to frame individual and institutional codes of ethics. However, in their fear that having clearly articulated standards would play into the hands of lawyers, many journalists appeared to back away from the hard but necessary work of spelling out precisely what they believe is ethically proper. Nevertheless, many other journalists have been cautiously attempting to draft or revise their newsrooms' codes or policy manuals.

The 1996 SPJ Code

Codes of ethics, like muscles, brains and old house pets, wither and atrophy unless they are exercised occasionally. The SPJ code is no exception.

SPJ has had a written code since 1926, very early in the organization's history. (At the time the group was known as Sigma Delta Chi, or SDX.) It borrowed the American Society of Newspaper Editors' canons of journalism, which served SDX until it drafted its own code in 1973, in the aftermath of Watergate. The 1973 code, unanimously approved by delegates to the national convention, was amended several times in the ensuing years. The 1987 amendment, as noted earlier, dropped the "censure" clause and replaced it with an "education" clause.

A decade of changing technologies, changing managements, changing marketplaces, changing roles, changing reputations and changing dilemmas suggested to the nation's largest organization of journalists that it was time once again to change its code of ethics. A two-year effort that involved thousands of SPJ members from hundreds of chapters and the work of several committees resulted in adoption of a totally new code in 1996. It was framed around a set of three guiding principle proposed in earlier editions of *Doing Ethics in Journalism*: to seek truth, to minimize harm, and to remain independent. However, a fourth principle was added, in light of myriad discussions concerning the need for journalists to hold themselves publicly accountable. The fourth principle is not an enforcement clause *per se*, but it is as close to one as SPJ has had since 1987. The debate over enforcement continues.

The Preamble

The five sentences constituting the preamble to the SPJ code of ethics claim, in lofty language, what it is that professional journalists stand for:

> Members of the Society of Professional Journalists believe that public enlightenment is the forerunner of justice and the foundation of democracy. The duty of the journalist is to further those ends by seeking truth and providing a fair and comprehensive account of events and issues. Conscientious journalists from all media and specialties strive to serve the public with thoroughness and honesty. Professional integrity is the cornerstone of a journalist's credibility.
>
> Members of the Society share a dedication to ethical behavior and adopt this code to declare the Society's principles and standards of practice.

This preamble sets the stage for the set of four fundamental guiding principles (truth, harm, independence and accountability), and more specific lists of the profession's generally accepted standards of practice. It is significant to notice that the guiding principles are abstract and idealistic, whereas the standards of practice are much more specific. Unlike many codes, however, both components tend to be framed in the affirmative ("Thou shalt") rather than the negative ("Thou shalt not"). This was a conscientious choice on the part of the code writers, believing as they did that more professional, ethical behavior will result from conscientious application of principles than from blind obedience to minimalistic rules.

Principles and Questions

Members of the SPJ Ethics Committee, bolstered by thoughtful observers of journalism and by work across the spectrum of ethical decision making, believe it is possible to help journalists weigh the ingredients of a good ethical decision without compromising deadlines. The following four principles (and subsequent checklists of 10 questions) are intended to help journalists work their way through an ethical dilemma.

These are not "fault" standards that can be trotted out by libel lawyers seeking to discover some bottom line of propriety below which journalists may have fallen.

These are not "fault" standards that can be trotted out by libel lawyers seeking to discover some bottom line of propriety below which journalists may have fallen. Rather, they are provocative models for clear thinking, drawn from interviews with several hundred working journalists, the contents of more than 100 news media codes of ethics and policy statements, and the insights of many philosophers and news media critics. The object is to help journalists recognize ethical dilemmas when they arise, to explore the complexities of decision making, to resist moralizing, and to recognize the limits of blind obedience to customs and codes. Throughout this book, we will see how these principles and questions play out in the decision making process.

Guiding Principles for the Journalist

Seek Truth and Report It. Journalists should be honest, fair and courageous in gathering, reporting, and interpreting information.

Minimize Harm. Ethical journalists treat sources, subjects and colleagues as human beings deserving of respect.

Act Independently. Journalists should be free of obligation to any interest other than the public's right to know.

Be Accountable. Journalists are accountable to their readers, listeners, viewers and each other.

The next section of this book—four "mini-chapters"—explores how each of the four principles plays out in the world of journalism. It is important to note, at this early juncture in the discussion, that the four guiding principles are intended to work in tandem, and not alone. That is, a given ethical dilemma entails a balancing act between or among two or more of the principles.

How, for instance, can one seek and report truth without disrupting the status quo and causing a certain amount of harm? And how can journalists act independently while being held accountable? The tendency to polarize these two sets of principles is very tempting, indeed. But there is a better way.

Journalists frequently maintain that they are justified in causing harm during the gathering and reporting of information the general public needs to know about. Be that as it may, the choice should not be either-or. A good choice probably rests somewhere along a continuum: How much harm is necessary in order to tell how much important truth? (Do you name a rape victim or identify a sexual predator, citing community interest? Is it necessary to photograph a badly disfigured youth who happens to be in the midst of an unpleasant lawsuit?)

All else being equal, journalism's first objective is to seek out and report truth. Ethical journalists do not revert to minimizing harm as the first step when doing journalism, but as a second step. The harm principle is not invoked as a means of blunting criticism, or currying favor, or avoiding having to do substantial truthtelling. All too often journalists "wimp out" when better journalism—and more civic good—would have resulted from putting truthtelling and minimizing harm in their proper contexts.

Likewise, a balance between independence and accountability must be sought. Journalists, bolstered by the First Amendment and a history of favorable court rulings, are cantankerously independent. Traditionalists in the craft worry about "face licking" journalism. They don't think the recent public journalism movement is healthy, because they see it as a lessening of journalism's hard-fought independence. Sharing trade secrets and airing dirty laundry (the ombudsman movement, news councils, etc.) could chip away at the nascent profession's mystique, because such exercises in public accountability allow the barbarians to cross the moat.

Upon closer examination, it is perfectly reasonable for journalists to maintain enough independence to remain free from external and internal pressures that dilute the truthtelling enterprise, while simultaneously recognizing that as professionals we are accountable to our readers, listeners, viewers and each other.

It's time to reframe the thought process. We can accomplish this by avoiding the either-or polarization of ethical decision making. Instead, picture journalism's guiding principles on a set of horizontal and vertical axes.

"Bad" journalism occurs when we do a lousy job of truthtelling and when sources or subjects are harmed for no good reason. ("Low/Low" on the horizontal and vertical axes.) "Better" journalism might occur when we cause a lot of harm (disrupting people's comfort zones) during the process of telling highly significant truths ("High/Low") or when we cause only a small amount of

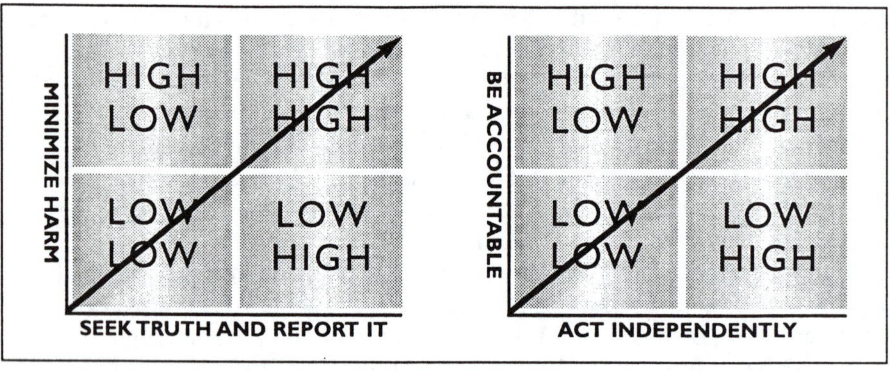

harm while telling an insignificant story ("Low/High"). Ethical and excellent journalism, of course, maximizes the amount of truth and the minimization of harm.

The same goes for the principles of independence and accountability.

The bulk of this book shows how journalists in 45 case studies attempted to deal with these four principles, consciously or not, when making decisions on deadline.

Ask Good Questions to Make Good Ethical Decisions

Drawing on the work of the Poynter Institute for Media Studies, SPJ also recommends the following checklist of 10 questions intended to help journalists work their way through ethical dilemmas. The questions are phrased in user-friendly, common-sense language, but reflect much deeper philosophical concerns over moral rule and duties, consequences, loyalties and knowledge.

Not all of the questions can be asked and answered on deadline, nor should they be. But to the extent the questions are dealt with ahead of time—"front-end loading," as it were—the questions can help journalists avoid a great many stumbling blocks. The questions are also particularly useful during a *post mortem*, when staff members have the luxury of a few moments to try to learn from one experience in order to better cope with the next one.

The ten questions:

1. What do I know? What do I need to know?
2. What is my journalistic purpose?
3. What are my ethical concerns?
4. What organizational policies and professional guidelines should I consider?
5. How can I include other people, with different perspectives and diverse ideas, in the decision making process?
6. Who are the stakeholders—those affected by my decision? What are their motivations? Which are legitimate?

7. What if the roles were reversed? How would I feel if I were in the shoes of one of the stakeholders?

8. What are the possible consequences of my actions? Short term? Long term?

9. What are my alternatives to maximize my truthtelling responsibility and minimize harm?

10. Can I clearly and fully justify my thinking and my decision? To my colleagues? To the stakeholders? To the public?

Neither of the lists above—the four guiding principles and the 10 questions—is etched in granite. Both are culled from a variety of sources, and subject to considerable debate. Indeed, one of the blessings and one of the curses of journalism in a democracy is the lack of agreement over its fundamental values or guiding principles. Some say there are none; others admit to one or some combination of the above. The authors of this book and the Society of Professional Journalists choose to propose rather than impose these principles and questions, believing that they adequately reflect the values and struggles of an industry in search of its professional ethic.

Indeed, one of the blessings and one of the curses of journalism in a democracy is the lack of agreement over its fundamental values or guiding principles.

If journalists are reminded that the fundamental obligations to report truthfully and fully are intertwined with concerns over independence and minimizing harm, while holding themselves accountable, the press and its publics will both benefit. Likewise, if awareness of those principles leads journalists to ask systematically and then answer key questions about journalistic purposes, rules, stakeholders, and consequences, there is a much greater likelihood that the decision will be ethically justifiable.

To say a decision has been "ethically justified" does not necessarily mean the decision will be popular. It merely means that ethical principles have been applied in such a way that a disinterested but fully informed public would agree that the decision maker was careful and did not act capriciously. Indeed, some of the toughest dilemmas have been resolved in ways bound to displease many stakeholders, particularly sources, audiences, and advertisers. Journalists are used to not being loved. At the same time, a commercially based information industry cannot risk permanently alienating the public and cutting access to sources. So there is some ambivalence built into the journalism ethics enterprise. The key is not to overreact, neither rigidly and blindly following codes or trade practices on the one hand nor amorally pandering on the other.

Codes of Ethics

General Introductory Material

The Society of Professional Journalists

Members of the Society of Professional Journalists believe that public enlightenment is the forerunner of justice and the foundation of democracy. The duty of the journalist is to further those ends by seeking truth and providing a fair and comprehensive account of events and issues. Conscientious journalists from all media and specialties strive to serve the public with thoroughness and honesty. Professional integrity is the cornerstone of a journalist's credibility.

Members of the Society share a dedication to ethical behavior and adopt this code to declare the Society's principles and standards of practice.

Beaumont* (Texas) *Enterprise

Newspapers succeed as businesses and as public institutions only to the extent the readers believe in the integrity and honesty of the people who work for them.

People who enter the newspaper business take on a position of great power and influence. Because of the power and the public visibility that goes with it, people in journalism, like people entering the public eye in politics, entertainment or the arts, also take on unusual responsibilities and surrender some of the rights enjoyed by ordinary people.

Montreal* (Quebec, Canada) *Gazette

A newspaper's greatest asset is its integrity. Respect for that integrity is painfully won and easily lost. It is maintained by constant attention to a host of minor details on a day-to-day basis.

Charlotte* (N.C.) *Observer

When a newspaper talks about ethics, ordinarily it has in mind the sinners and saints of the world at large. A major function of the U.S. daily press is a ceaseless calling-to-account of public officials. That chore is vital in a quite literal sense: Without the press's continuing attention, the muscular but delicate division of American political power would collapse.

But who calls the press to account? Ultimately, the readers do, but a casual glance through U.S. newspapers will confirm that their stewardship is not rigid. Bad newspapers can prosper. In the short-term economic sense, then, the *Observer*'s ethics policy is unnecessary. A fair number of people will buy the paper whether or not it is written and edited by people who think about the ethical implications of their actions. So when a newspaper like the *Observer* adopts an ethics policy, it does so as a matter of self-discipline. The newspaper is powerful; the *Observer*'s ethics policy is a way, perhaps awkward, of trying to see that the power is used fairly. Awkward, because that amount of self-consciousness may seem prissy. Awkward, because no policy can cover every situation.

And no policy can supplant the editors' obligation to hire men and women of character. But in the gray areas, where private lives and public responsibilities may meet, a policy can offer some guidelines.

Gannett (Washington, D.C.) News Service

Correct ethical conduct is particularly at the heart of the operation of a company engaged in communications with and on behalf of the public. In all matters and in all divisions, the highest professional standards must be practiced in every Gannett activity to guarantee the independence and the integrity of all our news, editorial, information, advertising, and marketing services. In every case, necessary safeguards must be maintained to prevent any action or any association that might reflect adversely, directly or indirectly, upon Gannett.

Grand Forks* (N.D.) *Herald

Because this newspaper cannot properly function without the trust and respect of its readers, we recognize an obligation to maintain the highest professional and ethical standards in the collection and presentation of the news.

We also recognize a duty to defend vigorously the principle of freedom of the press, not on our own behalf but in the general public interest. Freedom of the press belongs to the people. It must be defended against encroachment or assault from any quarter, public or private. The individual journalist has a responsibility to defend that principle at all times by resisting efforts to distort, suppress, or censor the news.

The pledge made more than 100 years ago by our founder, George B. Winship, remains this newspaper's guiding principle: "It will be the people's paper, run strictly in their interests, guarding jealously their rights, and maintaining boldly their cause."

New York *Daily News*

Journalism carries heavy responsibilities in a democracy. It is called upon to discover and report the truths which a free people … must have to make informed decisions regarding their destiny.

To meet its obligations, the profession must be free to pursue truth without fear or interference. This is why the press is singled out for special protection under the First Amendment to the Constitution.

But to be free of outside coercion is not enough. Reporters, editors and publishers must also be free of internal coercion, the subtle personal or economic influences which can corrode impartiality. More than that, they must avoid even the appearance of bias, for this can destroy public trust just as quickly as genuine corruption.

Like most other institutions, the press is under attack. We are being harassed by government officials and judges. Our motives and methods are challenged. Our fairness is questioned. Our credibility with the public is undermined.

In this climate, it is more important than ever that we act fairly and responsibly in reporting the news, that we reject any conduct—any conflict of interest or special favor—which might lessen public confidence in our integrity.

Professional tradition and lively individual consciences are the best defenders of journalistic ethics. But many issues, equivocal or morally ambivalent, are difficult to decide in concrete terms. Because this is so, it seems advisable to have specific guidelines for the *News*.

Philadelphia Inquirer

A vigorous and courageous press is one of the guarantors of a democratic community. Therefore, the *Inquirer* has both the right and the obligation to pursue the truth, without bias or favor, in all matters of public interest and importance, believing that a fully informed populace is the best guarantee of freedom and justice.

The *Inquirer* is responsible to its readers for the accuracy and fairness of its work. We should, therefore, be as accessible to those readers as humanly possible. In all our contacts with members of the public, we should strive to let them know that we are seeking the truth, that we are open-minded, and that we want to listen to what they have to say.

San Jose* (Calif.) *Mercury News

A profession that subjects people and institutions to intense and constant scrutiny must itself maintain the highest of principles.

The integrity we earn by maintaining our principles is our most valuable asset. Without it, we lose the public trust essential to a vigorous and effective press. That integrity is seriously eroded by conflicts of interest, as well as the appearance of conflict.

This code is intended to offer ethical guidelines to help avoid such conflicts. It cannot envision all circumstances in which ethics must be considered. It is intended to be an aid to common sense and individual conscience, not a substitute for them. Ultimately, individuals are accountable for their actions in areas not covered specifically in this code.

Seek Truth and Report It

Journalists should be honest, fair and courageous in gathering, reporting and interpreting information.

The average citizen cannot directly see, smell, hear or feel enough to make sense of all the conflicting "truths" vying for shelf space in the global marketplace of ideas. Sorting and filtering information and presenting it to audiences is a task that falls to those who choose to become journalists. Journalists must do their best to find and report information that will come as close as humanly possible to preparing the audience for what is ahead, or for explaining why a significant event occurred.

It is the vigor with which the journalist approaches the gathering of significant information and the fidelity with which it is reported that determine whether the images in audience member's minds are equal to the reality they will encounter. That challenge is reflected in nearly all of the 45 case studies in Part Two of this book. They show how journalists grapple with their mission to gather and report truth in the public's interest. The cases also show how that mission often clashes with other journalistic principles of minimizing harm, remaining independent and being accountable.

Journalists do not operate in a vacuum. A huge cottage industry thrives on creating misleading or heedless images for selfish purposes. Since journalists stand in the gateway to the media, they bear the brunt of pressures to mislead. One way to help ensure that truth is in the marketplace for audiences is for journalists to strive for pluralistic views in each story. That is, multiple sources in stories provide alternative views that allow individuals to make good decisions. The five case studies in chapter 10 emphasize the complexity of the source/reporter relationship.

Under the principle, "Seek Truth and Report It," the SPJ code says journalists should:

• **Test the accuracy of information from all sources and exercise care to avoid inadvertent error. Deliberate distortion is never permissible.**

• **Diligently seek out subjects of news stories to give them the opportunity to respond to allegations of wrongdoing.**

• **Identify sources whenever feasible. The public is entitled to as much information as possible on sources' reliability.**

• **Always question sources' motives before promising anonymity. Clarify conditions attached to any promise made in exchange for information. Keep promises.**

• Recognize a special obligation to ensure that the public's business is conducted in the open and that government records are open to inspection.

By quickly naming Richard Jewell as the prime FBI suspect in the Atlanta Olympic Park bombing, journalists created an immediately accurate image of the man the FBI suspected, but also formed false expectations about who ultimately would be charged with the act (see "Public and Private Jewell," case #38). In quickly naming Timothy McVeigh in the Oklahoma City federal building bombing, and later—a month before his trial—saying he had confessed to the crime, journalists not only created the immediate image of the suspect, but reliably named the person who ultimately would be convicted of the bombing (see "McVeigh's Confession Goes Online," case #5).

The good journalist develops techniques for assembling a body of information that has high probability of being true. The journalist then works with society in an ongoing sifting process to produce what will turn out to be Truth—truth with a capital T.

These two examples illustrate the complexity of the journalist's task in finding and reporting the truth. Journalists should not become the dupes of manipulators—FBI agents who immediately improved their images and reputations for acting quickly in the face of a public danger in fingering Jewell; unnamed members of McVeigh's defense team who had still undetermined motives for claiming McVeigh had confessed; etc. Journalists should carefully evaluate information for its credibility and likely durability under scrutiny.

The good journalist develops techniques for assembling a body of information that has high probability of being true. The journalist then works with society in an ongoing sifting process to produce what will turn out to be Truth—truth with a capital T. Whatever truth is produced by the process will shape social decisions and help determine how well society and its institutions will function. To generate this information requires journalists to wear different hats, but mostly it requires a pluralistic mind set that will tend to assure that truth is discoverable.

At some point the journalist, audience, and time should cooperate to sift and sort until some sort of Truth comes clear, or until audience members have the tools they need to decide what is *their* truth. This recognizes, of course, that a Truth for a pro-choice individual may legitimately be different from Truth for a pro-lifer. And, just as audience members have different truths, so do sources and journalists. Numerous case studies address the elusive nature of truth (for examples, see "The CIA Crack Contra-versy," case #2; "David Duke and the *Times-Picayune*," case #7; "We Don't Do Rumors. Or Do We?" case #9; and all six cases in chapter 7, "Diversity"). The SPJ code acknowledges this when it says journalists should:

• Tell the story of the diversity and magnitude of the human experience

boldly, even when it is unpopular to do so.

- **Examine their own cultural values and avoid imposing those values on others.**
- **Avoid stereotyping by race, gender, age, religion, ethnicity, geography, sexual orientation, disability, physical appearance or social status.**
- **Support the open exchange of views, even views they find repugnant.**
- **Give voice to the voiceless; official and unofficial sources of information can be equally valid.**

If the information bundle the journalists present to their audiences is seriously flawed, distorted images in the public mind will produce decisions that will not be consistent with realities. When those images are misleading, media credibility drops and people turn to other sources. Those sources may be other, better journalists, but they may also be self-seeking persuaders whose power relies on misleading.

The goal, of course, is a society whose citizens collectively make better informed decisions about their public institutions and the way the system works. Such a society minimizes accumulations of power in the hands of those who seek to gain and manipulate power for their own selfish ends. As we move toward such a society, a great many pressures are brought to bear on the journalism enterprise.

Some pressures are external, as journalists recognize that virtually all their sources are determined only to provide the information *they* want to provide, and to protect the information that does not serve them well. The good journalist is in constant battle to unearth that information. Others pressures are internal, from within the journalist's own organizations as favored sources and causes are protected, or as management monitors stories for their effects on various bottom lines (ratings, circulation, advertising revenues, public opinion, friends, etc.). These pressures are discussed more fully in the upcoming discussion of journalistic independence, another of the profession's four guiding principles, and they are reflected in many of the case studies in chapters 4 ("Accuracy and Fairness") and 5 ("Conflicts of Interest").

Given the pitfalls, encouraging journalists to seek truth and report it to audiences is a simple task compared to the problems of truly achieving the goal. Our opening chapter's discussion of the role of journalism emphasized the challenge. While similar rumors surfaced in Washington and Oregon in the early 1990s about sexual harassment and abuse by U.S. senators from those states, journalists responded differently. The *Seattle Times* wrote a story, based on separate accusations by nine women about the abuses of Sen. Brock Adams. In the aftermath, Sen. Adams withdrew from his campaign for re-election. In Oregon, on the other hand, newspapers declined to disclose similar information about Sen. Robert Packwood. His power remained in place through a re-election campaign and it was only after the *Washington Post* disclosed the accusations that Sen. Packwood had to begin defending himself. As it turned out, journalistic protection of the senator's power effectively denied Oregon the services of a senator for nearly two years during Sen. Packwood's defense and ultimate resignation from the Senate. Oregon journalists let power remain untouched, to the ultimate detriment of their state's citizens.

The democratic experience counsels caution in allowing power to concentrate, as it did for Adams and Packwood. This explains why journalists need to gather and distribute truthful, complete information as a reliable way of ensuring some power balances. This is not an easy task in any case, but it is complicated when a society seems to not want to know, when individuals seem to not want power to control their own lives, and when many of us seem to not want to have our myths shattered. Perplexing examples of this tendency are seen in three of the case studies found in chapter 6, "Deception": ABC's hidden camera coverage of poor food handling practices in Food Lion stores (case #20); a reporter who went undercover to discern the truth about casualties of the Persian Gulf War (case #21); and reporters who secretly taped sources to confirm allegations of wrongdoing in the University of Kentucky basketball program (case #22). All three cases revealed problems many audience members would have preferred not to know about. Power was redistributed as a result of journalists' effort in each case.

As seen throughout this book, but especially in the discussions of accuracy and fairness, deception, privacy and photojournalism, journalists face a variety of temptations to take short-cuts—and end runs—when seeking and reporting truth. That is why the SPJ code says journalists should:

- **Never plagiarize.**
- **Make certain that headlines, news teases and promotional material, photos, video, audio, graphics, sound bites and quotations do not misrepresent. They should not oversimplify or highlight incidents out of context.**
- **Never distort the content of news photos or video. Image enhancement for technical clarity is always permissible. Label montages and photo illustrations.**
- **Avoid misleading re-enactments or staged news events. If re-enactment is necessary to tell a story, label it.**
- **Avoid undercover or other surreptitious methods of gathering information except when traditional open methods will not yield information vital to the public. Use of such methods should be explained as part of the story.**
- **Distinguish between advocacy and news reporting. Analysis and commentary should be labeled and not misrepresent fact or context.**
- **Distinguish news from advertising and shun hybrids that blur the lines between the two.**

Couple the external pressures with the internal workings of journalists and it sometimes seems a miracle that truth is found at all in critical instances. This is a reason the Society of Professional Journalists Code of Ethics seems to belabor the obvious about Truth. The fact is, journalists have substantial obstacles, both from outside and inside themselves, to overcome in order to act ethically in gathering and distributing Truth.

Examples abound testifying to the elusiveness of Truth, suggesting we often must be forced to a relatively low standard in accepting something as Truth, with the hope that public scrutiny will either confirm it or lay the matter to rest. Did O.J. Simpson kill his ex-wife and her friend? Were paparazzi responsible for the deaths of Princess Diana and her companions? Our feelings about those incidents, as with so many things, may not be so informed by what we know as by our biases, our prior experiences, or our preconceptions about social institutions and about how the world ought to be. These often have an impact on what journalists choose to call Truth and therefore become part of what journalists need to guard against in order to produce a version of Truth that will stand the test of time. Truth is the version that subsequent information cannot discredit.

The code admonition to journalists to Seek Truth and Report It encourages journalists to conscientiously work their way through minefields of daily confusion.

The code admonition to journalists to Seek Truth and Report It encourages journalists to conscientiously work their way through minefields of daily confusion. The highest compliment a journalist can be paid is to have members of the audience repeatedly be able to say "I knew that was going to happen," or "I was ready for that one."

Minimize Harm

Ethical journalists treat sources, subjects and colleagues as human beings deserving of respect.

That admonition is no small challenge in a profession that often demands assertive behavior and split-second decision making in the pursuit of truth and the disseminating of information. Minimizing harm is difficult to accomplish when reporting on a tragedy; when accusing public officials of wrongdoing; when publishing or broadcasting unpleasant news about our society.

Yet, the principle of minimizing harm is both logical and essential. Its roots are deep within ethical theory, as espoused by Mill, Kant, Aristotle, Rawls and others.

Minimizing harm is reflected in the time-honored appeal to "treat others as you yourself wish to be treated." It is embedded within the "walk a mile in the shoes of another" maxim.

Minimizing harm is connected to the values of humaneness: fairness, compassion, empathy, kindness, respect. It is based on our responsibility to treat others with decency and to allow them their dignity even in the worst of circumstances. It is connected to a concern for the consequences of our actions.

The principle of minimizing harm prescribes that ethical individuals treat others as deserving of respect, not merely as a means to one's own ends, no matter how important we see those ends to be. In journalism, that means we must show concern for those we cover, those who give us information and those we work with, even as deadlines, competition, ratings and circulation pressures, great stories and our own career goals are weighing heavily upon us.

This principle of minimizing harm all too often clashes head-on with the principle of truthtelling. These principles, however, are seldom mutually exclusive. Our challenge as ethical journalists is to gauge the significance and importance of the truth we are pursuing, and to anticipate, estimate and understand levels of harm we may cause through our actions in gathering and disseminating information.

Then we must be adept at developing, considering and implementing alternative courses of action that honor, to the greatest degree possible, both the truthtelling and the minimizing harm principles.

A number of the cases in this *Doing Ethics in Journalism* book demonstrate this process of searching for alternatives that maximize truthtelling while minimizing harm.

Editors at the *Daily Press* in Newport News-Hampton, Virginia, included the family members of a murdered teenager in their decision making on the use of a particularly powerful photo of the victim's body. Editors also expanded the story to give context to the this murder in relation to the national issue of teen murders (see "Covering Victims," case #33).

Print and television photojournalists in Florida made a decision, in consultation with supervisors, not to photograph a terribly disfigured young man as he came to court to testify in a civil trial. They wanted to spare him what was sure to be additional pain. Instead, those news organizations used file photos of him from before the accident (see "A 'Cool' Decision," case #39).

Journalists at WCCO-TV in Minneapolis chose several reporting and storytelling alternatives in producing a report on a woman undergoing an abortion. The anchor's lead-in prepared the viewers for what many might find an offensive story by telling them what was coming up; the photojournalist on the story shot and edited the tape to both meaningfully reveal the procedure and to recognize viewers' sensibilities; the reporter used only the woman's first name to honor her request for confidentiality (see "Abortion Coverage on Deadline," case #10).

In reporting on race and racism in high schools in South Chicago high schools, the *Daily Southtown* decided to quote teenagers by name and to use racial slurs in the stories since "language and sensitivity were what this story was about," according to one editor. But, editors chose an alternative in one case, leaving out the name of a Hispanic female student who was dating a black student without her parents' knowledge, in order to protect her from her stepfather's potential ire (see "Covering Racism," case #25).

Editors of several papers in New Jersey grappled with whether to name a convicted child molester who was the central figure in a federal appeals court case related to the Megan's Law debate. While some papers named the man, other editors chose not to use his name until the court case was settled, recognizing the profound impact identifying him might have on the man's life (see "Megan's Law," case #40).

Two Seattle newspapers applied great scrutiny to rumors about improper behavior by that city's mayor, delaying coverage until information could be verified and put in context (see "We Don't Do Rumors," case #9).

In each of these cases the journalists involved faced the challenge of honoring their duty to disseminate meaningful information about significant stories while recognizing their actions might greatly harm someone. They searched for and applied alternatives to minimize the harm while still reporting the essence of the story.

You will also find cases in the book where the minimizing harm principle was ignored, avoided or dishonored. Some of those news organizations reporting the Richard Jewell case lost sight of Jewell the person in their zealous chase for a story (see case #38). Much the same happened with some of the reporting on the Dallas Cowboys' players implicated in a reported rape case (see case #3). Some television stations in Phoenix covering a man's plunge from a 400-

foot tower were less than sensitive in their treatment of onlookers or viewers (see case #31). And controversy continues over how *USA Today* handled its reporting on Arthur Ashe when the newspaper learned he had AIDS (see case #36).

The minimizing harm principle included in the SPJ Code of Ethics calls on journalists to uphold both professional and personal ethical principles in their work. Thoughtful journalists and committed news organizations find ways to make that happen. The code expands the minimizing harm principle by asking journalists to:

• **Show compassion for those who may be affected adversely by news coverage. Use special sensitivity when dealing with children and inexperienced sources or subjects.**

We can learn from the approach used by WCCO-TV (Minneapolis, Minn.) reporter Trish Van Pilsum, who says she approaches every story knowing of the potential for revictimizing vulnerable people. "I'll always approach the family without cameras and very low key. I'll say, 'It's very important I don't make this situation worse for you.'"

• **Be sensitive when seeking or using interviews or photographs of those affected by tragedy or grief.**

Suzanne McCarroll, a reporter for KCNC-TV in Denver, says she often writes short notes to people she hopes to interview regarding a tragedy, believing the note is less intrusive and invasive than a phone call or a knock on the door. McCarroll says she allows herself to feel the emotion of those who are grieving so she can better understand their vulnerability. And, when someone does not want to do an interview, she respects that. "It's not their obligation to talk to the media," she says. "I always think they're doing us a favor by talking with us. They have every right to say 'No.'"

• **Recognize that gathering and reporting information may cause harm or discomfort. Pursuit of the news is not a license for arrogance.**

When the *San Jose Mercury News* ran a front-page photo of convicted child killer Richard Allen Davis holding up both of his middle fingers, the paper's editor added a column to readers both explaining his decision and seeking their opinion. More than 1,200 readers responded. The editor said that response indicates people want to "feel a part of the paper and are desperate to understand why we do what we do." (See case #32.)

• **Recognize that private people have a greater right to control information about themselves than do public officials and others who seek power, influence or attention. Only an overriding public need can justify intrusion into anyone's privacy.**

Chip Scanlan, now director of the writing program at the Poynter Institute, was a reporter for Knight-Ridder's Washington Bureau writing about product liability lawsuits against tobacco companies. He was interviewing the widow of a smoker who died of lung cancer. She showed him her photo albums and then took him on a tour of her house. Standing in her bedroom, she looked over at the bed she had shared with her husband, saying "Would you believe it? I take his aftershave lotion and spray it on his pillow just so I can smell him. Just the smell of it makes me feel like he's with me."

Scanlan said there "was no doubt in my mind that this was a powerful way to convey her loss. At the same time, the detail seemed so intimate. I made a point of telling her I wanted to use it in the story and asked if she'd have any objection. She didn't, but I asked her again before the story ran. I really sympathized with her loss. At times like this, I know that my low-key approach helps me get the material I need to tell the story, but I want to make sure I am not abusing the privilege."

• **Show good taste. Avoid pandering to lurid curiosity.**

Reporting on the JonBenet Ramsey murder provided significant ethical challenges to Colorado news organizations. The publication by the *Globe* tabloid of graphic crime scene photos posed a particular ethical challenge. "We reported the story about the stolen pictures. We reported the story about the guys in the photo lab arrested for it, but we never showed the pictures," said Patti Dennis, news director for KUSA-TV in Denver, in an interview with the *Rundown* newsletter. "If we showed the pictures, we would have been doing exactly what the *Globe* was doing. We could tell the story without showing the pictures."

• **Be cautious about identifying juvenile suspects or victims of sex crimes.**

WSOC-TV in Charlotte, North Carolina, had the only video of a reunion between a mother and her 2-year-old daughter who had been missing for four days. The station had interviewed the mother and identified the little girl in previous reports to increase the chances of her being found. However, when it learned the child had been raped by her abductor the station stopped using her and her mother's name in order to afford the same protection they would give to other victims of sex crimes. And it explained its decision to viewers, indicating why it was no longer using the name.

• **Be judicious about naming criminal suspects before the formal filing of charges.**

The Richard Jewell case is the high-profile reminder here (see case #38).

• **Balance a criminal suspect's fair trial rights with the public's right to be informed.**

The *Dallas Morning News* dealt with that challenge in covering the Timothy McVeigh trial. Its decision demonstrates the dilemma of reconciling tension between the First and Sixth Amendments. (See case #5.)

The principle of minimizing harm is very important in journalism given the significant freedom journalists have to do their work and the potential harm that they can cause. However, minimizing harm is secondary to the primary principle of journalism: to seek the truth and report it as fully as possible.

In those rare instances where the level and extent of harm is so profound that it outweighs the importance of the truth to be told, journalists should consider actions that give priority to minimizing the harm.

In most situations, however, both principles can be honored by choosing alternative courses of action that maximize the goal of truthtelling and show respect, fairness and compassion to all affected.

Act Independently

Journalists should be free of obligation to any interest other than the public's right to know.

If $50,000 from a documentary subject to help with production costs does not rob a public broadcasting station producer of the independence to present an honest view, how large a check would it take?

When journalists moonlight for political candidates and causes, or capitalize on their celebrity, can we accept the argument that what they do in their private time is nobody's business but their own?

If a reporter marries a high profile politician, is her history of fairness and thoroughness enough to justify keeping her on a public affairs beat, or should she serve in another capacity?

Does chartering a jet to reunite family members who have been subjects of an ongoing news story change the nature of that story and affect public credibility?

Are small news operations allowed to accept freebies and junkets, whereas those big enough to pay their own way are somehow taking the higher road? That is, is there a price tag on ethics?

What is the ethical value of a brick wall between editorial and business-advertising departments of news media? Is it realistic in today's climate?

When attempting to answer the above perplexing questions, journalists would do well to consider the standards of practice SPJ has built into the "Act Independently" section of its code of ethics. The code says journalists should:

- **Avoid conflicts of interest, real or perceived.**
- **Remain free of associations and activities that may compromise integrity or damage credibility.**
- **Refuse gifts, favors, fees, free travel and special treatment, and shun secondary employment, political involvement, public office and service in community organizations if they compromise journalistic integrity.**
- **Disclose unavoidable conflicts.**
- **Be vigilant and courageous about holding those with power accountable.**
- **Deny favored treatment to advertisers and special interests and resist their pressure to influence news coverage.**
- **Be wary of sources offering information for favors or money; avoid bidding for news.**

Independence when making professional and personal decisions is critical if ethical journalists are to help audiences create accurate and useful pictures of reality. Because of their position in society, journalists often decide whether the public ever hears opinions that are at odds with those at the centers of power. However, pressure and ignorance tend to limit journalistic independence.

Pressure is often difficult to resist because of implicit or explicit promises of rewards or punishment by sources and others who have a vested interest in having stories told in their favor. In addition, ignorance can rob journalists of the ability to act independently.

It seems that the profession has not resolved these issues, if one can draw conclusions from journalism's numerous codes of ethics and from much of the shop talk and trade literature on journalism ethics. More than half of all the contents of the 100-plus codes of ethics analyzed for this book were devoted to exploring the nature of conflicts of interest and journalistic independence. The largest single chapter in this book is chapter 5, "Conflicts of Interest," with its eight case studies and page after page of excerpts from ethics codes. Regardless of what the codes say, the industry is still confused about the separation of professional duty and personal or political ties (see "Journalists Supporting Politicians," case #12, and "To Love and Work in Denver," case #13). Meanwhile, competition and corporate bottom lines give rise to other concerns (see "Checkbook Journalism," case #14; "A National Guard Trip," case #15; "KQED and the Vintner," case #16; and "Editorial Independence and Car Dealers," case #17). And we haven't fully resolved one of the oldest ethical problems in the business—the balancing of professional independence and financial self-interest (see "CNN Conflicted," case #18, and "Freebies and Junkets," case #19).

One of the moral problems here is that the social system that protects journalists also assures that journalists are constantly wooed or bullied by sources and others bent on serving their own self-interest.

One of the moral problems here is that the social system that protects journalists also assures that journalists are constantly wooed or bullied by sources and others bent on serving their own self-interest. Pressures come from those who try to divert a journalist's loyalty away from audiences and steer it toward narrower vested interests. These vested interests seldom serve the best interest of audience members.

Because those who pressure journalists generally do not have the resources to reach audiences directly, they must seek their goals through the existing mass media. Even billionaire Ross Perot conducted his presidential campaigns through the mass media. He used his money to reduce the number of intermediaries between him and the audiences by talking directly to television audiences using his visual aids. Still, the media owned the audiences.

Those without Perot's resources must pass through an increasing number of intermediaries (typically gaining favor first with beat reporters). Their goal, of course, is to have their message reach audiences with as much of its original intent intact as possible, and with as little contradictory addition as possible. Most sources are very happy if reporters fail to seek the contradictory views that ensure broader discussion for audiences.

Audiences are most often unseen and unfelt (they tend not to exert direct, effective pressures in specific instances), yet they are those to whom journalistic loyalty is most socially important.

To act independently implies acceptance of a heavy responsibility—recognition that independence in ignorance, or misguided zeal, can be destructive and is morally indefensible.

Independent action requires periodic questioning of professional rules, and of the newsroom orthodoxy. Thoughtful acceptance of rules is important; thoughtless acceptance of newsroom rules is difficult to defend morally for an independent person. A dynamic, changing, pluralistic society has a vested interest in continuing analysis and refinement of rules—journalism's rules included.

To be usefully independent one needs several interrelated character and professional traits:

1. Be knowledgeable—Strive to know enough to make independent decisions. Generate your own knowledge from numerous sources. Never believe you know enough; always assume there are other facets to any information you have. Develop a continuing self-education program by reading widely to immunize yourself from being manipulated on complex issues. Above all, avoid the false security of believing you know as much as you need to know about a topic.

2. Be tough-minded—Be able to resist seductive persuasions of those who would use your distaste for conflict to manipulate you. Develop tough negotiation skills as a way of successfully defending your principles and positions, and of seeking information your sources are reluctant to provide.

3. Have a secure personality—Develop confidence in your own thought processes and abilities, through experience and knowledge, so you trust your own judgments. This toughens you for the principled battles you will fight. Journalists uncertain about their role are far more likely to be manipulated than journalists with a sense of mission, a sense of stewardship.

4. Know the audience—Know your audience well enough to be confident of its subdivisions and their needs. Be aware that audience pressures on journalists pale beside the pressures exerted by sources and other vested interests. Journalistic news values were developed with audience needs in mind, but may not be valid in all cases today, since audience needs change in a changing society.

5. Listen critically—Always be aware of the specific self-interest of sources and seek other inputs into stories. Routinely develop multi-source, unusual-source stories. Develop a wide range of economists as sources, for example. Views of economists of color and of both genders may be as important to audiences as high profile economists of various theoretical schools.

6. Be analytical—Develop critical skills in recognizing and appropriately evaluating the conflicting values present in most stories. Be able to weigh values of your own survival versus loss of credibility (assuming a source/subject's $50,000 donation truly would *not* create a conflict) and the damage that would do to your ability to serve audiences to make the decision that history will show was, on balance, the most morally defensible.

7. Be disclosive—Recognize the cleansing power of disclosure and be secure enough to defend your actions before your audiences and sources, trusting in their ultimate judgments.

8. Be persuasive—Effectively use skills in moral suasion in maintaining your independence in the face of determined power. Be able to argue effectively with colleagues and supervisors for the moral course. Recognize that there will be wins and losses, but seek to build wins over the long haul.

9. Be willing to sacrifice—Most pressures are brought on journalists with an assumption their sacrifice threshold is low. To act ethically often requires some sacrifice; therefore, willingness to sacrifice for principle must be developed early.

Be Accountable

Journalists are accountable to their readers, listeners, viewers and each other.

The statement from the SPJ code of ethics seems innocuous enough. On its face it is perfectly logical. After all, why shouldn't journalists be accountable to their audiences and to each other?

The principle is reasonable, but its execution is problematic.

The code of the nation's largest organization of news professionals says journalists should:

- **Clarify and explain news coverage and invite dialogue with the public over journalistic conduct.**
- **Encourage the public to voice grievances against the news media.**
- **Admit mistakes and correct them promptly.**
- **Expose unethical practices of journalists and the news media.**
- **Abide by the same high standards to which they hold others.**

These are the "standards and practices" that fall under the code's accountability principle. They define the construct. They make clear that journalism does not exist in a self-interested vacuum, but in an environment of reciprocity. They list the stakeholders, those who have the right to call journalists into account for meeting or falling short of their own and their audiences' expectations. They follow—but do not contradict—the code's principle of independence, suggesting that while seeking independence from the forces of corruption journalists remain inexorably connected to others.

American journalism has a long history of cantankerous independence, a resistance to criticism from others and even from within its own ranks.

There's a problem, however. Based in part on the existence of a Constitutional amendment which says "Congress shall make no law ...," American journalism has a long history of cantankerous independence, a resistance to criticism from others and even from within its own ranks. The battles to sustain First Amendment freedoms are instructive. In general, they have resulted in the sense that government can hold journalists accountable for their behaviors—in matters of libel, privacy, copyright, obscenity and the like—only after the fact. Prior restraint is another matter altogether. Some journalists have taken this relationship with government to another, more problematic level, arguing that calls for accountability by members of the public and even by other journalists somehow violate the news media's First Amendment privileges.

For nearly three-quarters of a century, journalism organizations have struggled with ways to build accountability and/or enforcement into their codes of ethics. The Society of Professional Journalists is no exception. For a variety of reasons, it has never had an effective enforcement mechanism. Its present code, framed primarily by "ideal expectation" guiding principles and positive rather than minimalistic standards and practices, does not lend itself to rigid enforcement. It does, however, address the core issue of accountability by reminding journalists that they can and should be called to judgment by the public and by other professional journalists. (The code wisely avoids issues of accountability to government; after all, it is a code of ethics, not a body of law.)

If journalists decide to hold themselves accountable to the public and peers, what forms does that accountability take? The most obvious might be the several journalism reviews (*American Journalism Review, Columbia Journalism Review, St. Louis Journalism Review*); journals put out by professional organizations (*Quill, IRE Journal, Nieman Reports, The American Editor, Masthead*, etc.); trade and academic publications (*Editor & Publisher, Broadcasting and Cablecasting, News Photographer, Newspaper Research Journal, Media Studies Journal, Journal of Mass Media Ethics*, etc.). The struggling ombudsman movement (fewer than 40 for the nation's 1,500 daily newspapers) and the stagger-step press council "movement" also come to mind. So do the op-ed pages, the talk shows, and the media review sections of the daily press. And, of course, the nation's hundreds of journalism schools, in which press criticism is flourishing.

All in all, however, the "calling journalists to judgment" business is of questionable impact on an industry more committed to independence than to accountability.

All in all, however, the "calling journalists to judgment" business is of questionable impact on an industry more committed to independence than to accountability.

Many of the case studies in this book demonstrate the difficulty of significant, sustained accountability within daily journalism. Some cases are included because they exemplify unusually courageous and open-minded journalism; they show how the bonds with readers, viewers and listeners can be strengthened at a time of diminished credibility. Others seem to be more like after-the-fact rationalizations, excuses drafted to ward off external criticism.

Interesting examples include:

• The intramural and public debate over whether a reporter had gone too far in drawing conclusions about the U.S. government's connection to Latin American drug lords and domestic crack ("The CIA Crack Contra-versy," case #2), and whether a columnist had made racially insensitive comments in a tongue-in-cheek sports piece ("A Columnist's Edge Cuts Skin Deep," case #28).

• An apology by a new editor for a reckless hatchet job perpetrated by his predecessor ("An Overdue Apology in Arkansas," case #6).

• A school paper's commitment of a full page of editorial soul searching over how to cover a tragic automobile accident ("On Campus: Tragedy at Ohio University," case #30).

• A call for public response to an offensive photograph—a *post mortem* that drew some 1,200 responses ("Dear Reader: 'An Indelible Photo,'" case #32).

• An explanation of why a newspaper felt compelled to seek out and publish the identity of a community benefactor who had hoped to remain anonymous ("Unmasking the Grand Forks Angel," case #37).

In these and other cases we can see that going public with our decision making processes is not always a panacea. Sometimes when audiences better understand why we did what we did, they empathize with our dilemma and lower their lances. On other occasions, our attempts at accountability merely confirm audiences' worst suspicions about how news is made.

It has been said that journalism is not thin-skinned, but that it has no skin at all. If the industry has a serious claim on professionalism, and if it seeks to build and sustain bonds with audiences, and if it hopes to retain independence from government control, it will do well to carefully address the notion of accountability. The fourth leg of the SPJ code of ethics acknowledges the importance of balancing accountability with the other three principles: seeking and reporting truth, minimizing harm, and acting independently.

Chapter Three

Making Ethical Decisions

Doing ethics in journalism is not just deciding between two choices, right and wrong, when facing an ethical dilemma. True ethical decision making is much more difficult and complex. It's about developing a range of acceptable actions and choosing from among them. It's about considering the consequences of those actions. And it's about basing decisions on obligation, on the principles of the journalist's duty to the public. True ethical decision making is also about public justification, the ability to explain clearly and fully the process of how and why decisions are made.

Ethical decision making entails competition among values such as truthtelling and compassion, courage and sensitivity, serving the public and protecting individual rights. Indeed, ethical decision making is a fundamental element of everyday journalism. Just as we think of writing, editing and photography as essential skills that are part of our craft, the ability to make good ethical decisions in the face of difficult challenges is also a great skill, which can be taught and learned.

And, just as we develop techniques to improve our skills as reporters, photojournalists and editors, we should continually develop our technique for doing ethics. This chapter is all about how journalists make ethical decisions.

Excellence and Ethics

To appreciate the decision making process, let's focus on the powerful connection between excellent journalism and ethical journalism. We will look at a success story, one in which good decisions were made for right reasons. One basis for using such an example is that all too often we think of ethics as highly restrictive, admonishing ourselves or others to avoid certain behaviors, or to feel ashamed for having overstepped certain boundaries. We would do better to think of ethics as more proactive, a thought process that helps us

ST. PAUL PIONEER PRESS DISPATCH

AIDS IN THE HEARTLAND

A special reprint of the Pulitzer Prize-winning series

Story by
Jacqui Banaszynski
Photographs by
Jean Pieri

Chapter I

Reprinted from
Sunday, June 21, 1987

Bert Henningson and Dick Hanson stand outside their 100-year-old Glenwood, Minn., farm, their emotional retreat from the physical ravages of AIDS.

Life's simple pleasures, like harmonizing at the old farm house piano, continue despite Hanson's illness.

Continued on next page

do the right things.

When Jacqui Banaszynski wrote her series of reports on "AIDS in the Heartland" for the *St. Paul* (Minn.) *Pioneer Press* in 1987, she had some tough ethical decisions to make at virtually every step in the reporting process. The series was about AIDS, about two gay men, about life and eventually death on a Minnesota farm. The ethical issues were many: a responsibility to inform the public, invasion of privacy, harm to family members, questions of taste about language and photos, potential manipulation of sources, confidentiality, promisekeeping and the two-way exploitative relationships between the journalists and the people they were reporting on.

The ethical and the journalistic challenges were great. The stakes were high. The public needed to know much more about AIDS in our society. At the same time, the potential harm to the subjects of the story was great. And there were significant questions about journalistic independence. Banaszynski and photographer Jean Pieri carried out their truthtelling responsibility with dedication and great skill. They also exhibited significant compassion and sensitivity in their reporting. Their paper was committed to publishing a powerful story about a painful issue. Excellence and ethics were tied together. "AIDS in the Heartland" received considerable public acclaim and earned both the Pulitzer Prize and The Society of Professional Journalists Distinguished Service Award.

Decision Making Processes

This case provides an appropriate blueprint to apply a decision making model for doing ethics. Banaszynski and her colleagues at the *St. Paul Pioneer Press* had to make important and difficult ethical decisions that had a significant impact on the public, the subjects of the story and the newspaper itself. The journalists' careful and systematic process of making those decisions serves as a model for other journalists. While this case of long-form journalism provides the grist for such an analysis, there are other cases of deadline reporting outlined later in the handbook where the decision making process is analyzed.

There are two basic ways to make ethical decisions. One is to decide what to do by weighing the consequences of your actions. The second is to decide according to the principles of duty. It is tempting to think of these alternatives as mutually exclusive, but in the real world, the lines between them get somewhat blurred.

Consequences

Let's address the consequences approach first. Working as they do for commercially based media whose products are distributed to mass audiences, journalists quite naturally think in terms of the consequences of their behaviors. This approach allows journalists to weigh the good and bad impact of their actions in each situation, believing each story is in some ways unique. Unfortunately, because of all the variables in daily journalism (deadlines, competition, pressure from peers, sources, audiences, advertisers, and the like), many journalists think the only guideline is to do whatever it takes to make a particular assignment turn out well. Indeed, journalists often say they covered a certain story because the good that resulted outweighed whatever bad happened.

While weighing consequences is one way to make ethical decisions, the approach has its shortcomings. For one thing, this approach can place a disproportionate weight on justifying actions that serve the greatest good for the greatest number of people. Those individuals or issues that represent a minority perspective can easily lose out in a good-versus-bad equation. Furthermore, merely achieving the greatest good for the greatest number may not be the best ethical decision, because of its unfairness to vulnerable people.

This balancing of good-versus-bad impact also relies heavily on the ability of the decision maker to anticipate the outcome of the action, which is generally difficult. It's one thing to speculate about short-term consequences, but altogether a different thing to determine all the long-term effects of an action.

Ultimately, consequence-based decision making leads to an ends-justifying-the-means thought process. It's all too easy in the face of competition and deadlines to rationalize a particular action by saying, "Well, the result turned out O.K." Such thinking allows us to take advantage of people in trying to reach a particular goal. Applying this greatest-good-for-the-greatest-number thinking to the AIDS series raises the likelihood that the subjects of the story could be exploited by using them as means to an end. In this case, where journalists are working with individuals who are vulnerable to a variety of harms, the ends-justifying-the-means approach is highly problematic.

Ultimately, consequence-based decision making leads to an ends-justifying-the-means thought process.

Jacqui Banaszynski could have limited herself to consequentialist decision making in her work on "AIDS in the Heartland." She could have said that the amount of good coming to the public from reading the story would outweigh the bad, either in terms of harm to the subjects of the stories or the bad that comes from offending readers, which leads to harm to the newspaper for having run such a controversial series. However, as we shall see, the *St. Paul Pioneer Press* relied on a different set of standards to justify its reporting.

The Principles of Duty

If making ethical decisions by looking at consequences has so many shortcomings, is there a better way? This is where the second approach, making

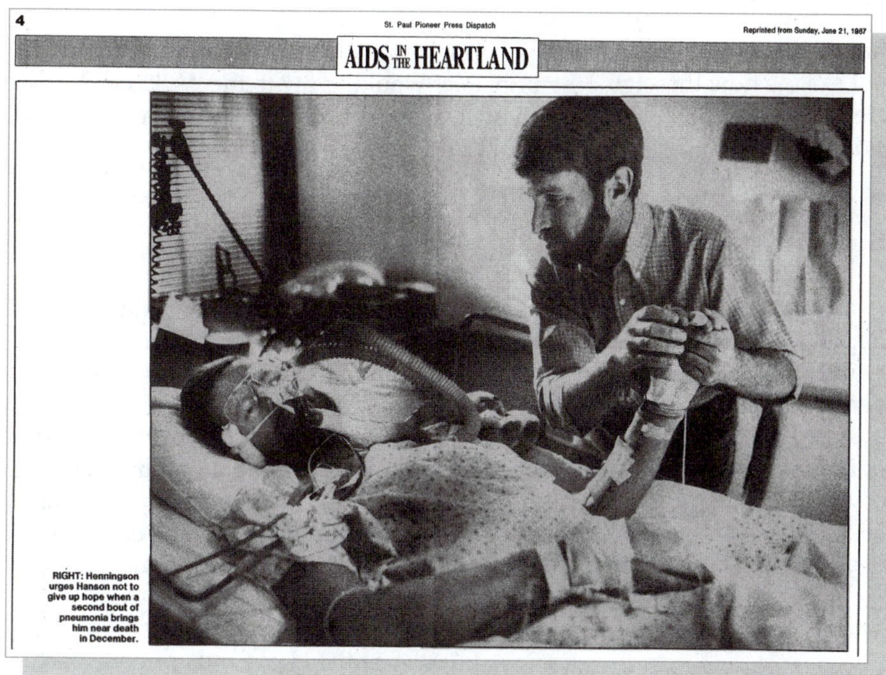

4 St. Paul Pioneer Press Dispatch Reprinted from Sunday, June 21, 1987

AIDS IN THE HEARTLAND

RIGHT: Henningson urges Hanson not to give up hope when a second bout of pneumonia brings him near death in December.

decisions according to the principles of duty, provides a strong alternative. One does not act according to an ends-justifying-the-means logic. Rather, one raises and then responds to questions of obligation: What should a good person do to behave well? What basic duties or responsibilities ought one to obey or pursue, regardless of the consequences?

The principles of duty are the guideposts. As we have already argued in this book, the duty of distributing truthful information is the foundation of journalism. Truthtelling is a justifiable principle even when it may cause some harm. Likewise, gathering and reporting information as fully, accurately and courageously as possible are ethical duties. The fact that some sources, news subjects, or advertisers seek to control information to maintain the status quo or protect their power base does not override the duty to maintain journalistic independence, which is essential to fulfill the truthtelling mandate.

There are other duties inherent in doing ethical journalism. Many of these duties were described in Chapter 1 of this handbook. The fundamental "Guiding Principles for the Journalist" (truthtelling, independence, minimizing harm and remaining accountable) incorporate such duties as keeping oneself informed; engaging and educating the public; giving voice to the voiceless; holding the powerful accountable; guarding the media's stewardship role; seeking out and disseminating competing perspectives without being unduly influenced; remaining free of conflicts of interest; being compassionate to sources, subjects, and colleagues. Journalists have a range of personal and professional obligations to keep promises and to "do good" and to "minimize harm" in their actions, both in gathering and reporting the news.

Let's see how these guiding principles would apply to the "AIDS in the Heartland" series by looking at how it was reported and written, and by considering some of Jacqui Banaszynski's decision making processes.

Seek Truth and Report It

Banaszynski clearly fulfilled the primary principle: "To Seek Truth and Report it as Fully as Possible." She did a great deal of research and preparatory interviewing to make sure she was well grounded on the issues. She demonstrated the courage to develop the story in the face of resistance from sources and even skeptical colleagues. She said it took her team "almost a year of false starts" to gain access to the people who would open their lives to news coverage. And once Banaszynski and photographer Pieri began reporting on Dick Hansen and Bert Henningson, they spent hundreds of hours on the story over the course of a year, including full-time reporting for about three months. It was a commitment that reflected sincere and serious journalism.

Truthtelling speaks to the responsibility of journalism to cover those people who normally may not have access to the media and to cover those issues that need light shined upon them.

"AIDS in the Heartland" not only factually informed readers, it also educated the public about a significant public policy issue and about its human side. "It was above all a love story," Banaszynski would later write. "It was a rare glimpse into a homosexual relationship—the kind of relationship that mystifies most and disgusts many. But that has become an undeniable part of our culture." And her writing and Pieri's photography were certainly compelling, fine examples of excellent journalism that would engage readers.

Furthermore, Banaszynski honored her responsibility to be honest and fair in her gathering and reporting. She was forthright with Dick Hansen and Bert Henningson, the subjects of her story, about what she planned to do. "I asked Hansen if we ... could try to tell the whole story of AIDS—life and death, love and hate, family support and family strife. Finally, I said, 'Dick, understand I'm asking you to do the whole story, beginning to end .... We both know you're going to die. I'm asking if I can watch you die.' "

Banaszynski was honest with her subjects about what she wanted to do and why. "I had an obligation to report intensely personal and painful events honestly—and yet to do so with respect for the subjects." And she was clear with them about what the impact might be of such a probing story. "We talked about the potential invasion of his privacy, about the inevitable anger of his relatives, about the scorn the story would generate, about the logistics of a reporter and photographer having access to the most personal aspects of his life, about negotiating the rough water of mutual trust."

One element of this principle of truthtelling is to give voice to the voiceless. Truthtelling speaks to the responsibility of journalism to cover those people who normally may not have access to the media and to cover those issues that need light shined upon them. According to Banaszynski, "We were struggling to find a focus, searching for a story that would go a step beyond the informational coverage of AIDS, a story that would not only humanize the AIDS crisis but enlighten and, perhaps, nudge society toward a more compassionate understanding of this stigmatized killer."

Minimize Harm

The second guiding principle for journalists is to "Minimize Harm," an obligation that encompasses both personal and professional responsibility. Banaszynski and Pieri were faced with telling what was bound to be an intrusive story about a controversial issue while being compassionate and showing respect for all those involved.

Here the balance between the principles of maximizing truthtelling and of minimizing harm becomes challenging.

It was not an academic question for Banaszynski, but a practical one. "What kind of deals do I cut that are ethical to them (the sources)? To me? To the readers? Can I selectively lie to my readers? We start making compromises. We start looking for alternatives."

For Banaszynski, choosing among alternatives to promote truthtelling while minimizing harm was an essential step in the decision making process. "I agreed I wouldn't talk with Bert's ex-wife because Bert convinced me she was too vulnerable."

Banaszynski also talks about leaving a certain quote out of her story because of the pain the words would have caused to Dick Hansen's family. "I realized I had achieved my effect without putting in that line (from Dick's brother) about 'putting a bullet in (Dick's) head.'" Banaszynski also agreed not to write about Bert Henningson's medical status until he gained a farm loan. "I told him I'd give him as much time as possible to get the loan, then we cut a deal that he'd have to trust me." That decision was another example of choosing an alternative to help maximize the truthtelling principle while minimizing harm to the story's subjects.

Act Independently

The third guiding principle for journalists is to "Act Independently." Jacqui Banaszynski realized that she could not entirely separate her professional and personal selves, yet the integrity of the story reflected her ability to remain independent. "The greatest challenge was to recognize my emotional involvement in the story—to use that emotion to breathe passion into my writing but to detach myself enough to remain focused on the truth." She was both introspective in her journalistic approach and methodical in her reporting techniques, particularly interviewing and observation.

"We discussed the ground rules," said Banaszynski, in describing the agreement she reached with her sources. "Everything I see goes in my notebook. I don't know how to not be a reporter .... I told them I would tell them about what I would write but I wouldn't show them my copy." Yet she did not act rigidly. She told Dick and Bert that "when we talk and I don't use my notebook, it's not on the record, but I'll come back to you later to ask about it."

Although Banaszynski would not show Dick and Bert her copy, she was willing to negotiate with other family members both to gain access for interviews and to protect their vulnerability. She described how she listened to family members talk for four hours, "telling their pain ... what a psychotherapist would pay big money to see." Because of the willingness of the family to talk, she reached an agreement with them. She offered to call each of them back independently and tell them how she quoted them and how she described them. If they could convince her that she had erred, she would change it. "Nobody asked me to change anything," she said. "They hated the story but they all think it was fair."

As a journalist, Banaszynski actually enhanced her independence by her willingness to have her work challenged by sources.

As a journalist, Banaszynski actually enhanced her independence by her willingness to have her work challenged by sources. This approach gave her access to important information and perspectives that heightened accuracy, and deepened and broadened the context of her stories.

Banaszynski also recognized that she had to have a clear understanding with her subjects about the importance to her of both getting close to her sources and remaining at a distance. "When we came (to the farm) we'd get big hugs and pumpkin pie. I'd say, 'Beep-Beep, Reporter-Alert,' and remind them what I was doing."

She knew how important it was to engage in collaborative ethical decision making with photographer Jean Pieri and with the editors all during the reporting and writing process. She described how she and Pieri would debrief at key points, saying to each other, "Do you know what we've done here? We both know we've crossed a line we've never crossed before."

Because she knew she was "crossing lines," Banaszynski says she also worked closely with the editors on the ethical implications of her reporting. "I'd also be very, very honest with my editors, to the point of beating it in the ground .... I told them they needed to read my copy and watch me more carefully than any story I've ever done to make sure I'm not whitewashing this and making heroes out of these guys." Banaszynski credits editors with giving her the "compassionate guidance ... the unerring faith ... and the disciplined editing" to deal with the "delicate balance" of reporting such a story. Certainly the collaborative role of the editors in questioning, supporting and inspiring the reporter strengthened both the independence and the truthtelling principles.

Be Accountable

Finally, journalists are asked to be accountable to their audiences and to one another—and, by extension, to other stakeholders, including sources and story subjects. As discussed in the previous chapter, this principle has numerous components, some of which applied to the "AIDS in the Heartland" story.

During the development of the series, the paper was nudged into accountability by the reporter and photographer, after editors at the *Pioneer Press* made a decision designed to "minimize harm" by not running a particular photo. The decision was based on the photo's potential impact not on the subjects of the story, but on the readers, and by extension, on the paper and its ability to meet its goals.

The photo showed Dick and Bert kissing. Pieri and Banaszynski both argued strongly for using the photo. According to Banaszynski, "The editors said 'no way ... you are going to lose people for that one picture.' I said to my editors, 'I think you're making the wrong decision.' It was honest journalism to use that picture. To not run it was dishonest." The editors prevailed, believing that too many readers would be offended by that picture, with diminished impact for the overall story. The photo did not run. As an alternative, Banaszynski convinced her editors of the importance of including explicit details about Dick's and Bert's sex lives in the story.

On a broader level, the paper held itself accountable by going public with its decision making. Executive editor Deborah Howell recounted the process in a column following the awarding of the Pulitzer Prize; the column was reproduced in a special reprint. Howell explained why the paper tackled the difficult and sensitive story, noting that the assignment "required a particular combination of sensitivity, toughness, tenacity and dedication to journalistic excellence."

Howell observed that not all *Pioneer Press* readers shared the staff's happiness in winning a Pulitzer:

> After the first article in the series appeared, many let us know they did not want to read about gay people or AIDS. Some felt we were glorifying homosexuality.
>
> But by the time the final installment ran, the tide turned. We received many letters of praise. One, from a federal judge, said: "Your series humanized and focused a terror that is swiftly becoming pervasive. Your work was sympathetic but objective and in a most skillful fashion helped teach the community to care."

Another, from a 56-year-old state Capitol security guard, said "Each chapter both tore me apart and also gave me a great sense of serenity in how the two dealt with the disease. In all honesty, all three chapters produced tears ...."

Getting letters like that from readers is, in the long run, more important than winning prizes. Prizes are nice, but they don't touch people's hearts.

Beyond Gut Reactions to Reflection and Reasoning

One of the challenges we face in the process of ethical decision making is to heighten our level of moral reasoning, to expand our skills at doing ethics. Many journalists say they make ethical judgments based on their "gut reactions." While it is natural to respond initially in such a way, these gut reactions only provide an entry point for confronting an ethical dilemma.

At this gut-reaction level, we tend to see ethics in stark black and white, suggesting that the distinction between right and wrong is quite clear and that the answer is intuitively obvious. We stake out our position, argue strongly, and don't really listen to contrasting views or consider alternative solutions. Sometimes we say our course of action is obvious because we have a rule we must follow, such as "never use deception to get a story," or "we don't cover suicides," or "don't offend the readers or viewers with graphic pictures." Such rules may have been laid down by editors or staffers for good pragmatic reasons, but blind obedience to them is not the same as making an ethical decision. Ethical decision making is very seldom that simple.

It is important for journalists to be willing to struggle with the gray area of ethical dilemmas, to develop the capacity to recognize competing principles within a case, to hear opposing positions.

It is important for journalists to be willing to struggle with the gray area of ethical dilemmas, to develop the capacity to recognize competing principles within a case, to hear opposing positions. We must move beyond our gut reactions and standard operating procedures, and get to reflection and reasoning. We must question whether the situation presents an exception to the rule. We search for alternative actions that can maximize our responsibility to inform the public while minimizing the harm to those involved in the story.

Ask Good Questions to Make Good Ethical Decisions

One way to accomplish this higher level of ethical decision making is to ask good questions of ourselves and of others, questions that force us to see shades of gray, questions that challenge us both to consider the consequences of our actions and to honor our fundamental journalistic duties. By asking good questions at key points in the decision making process, we prompt conversation and collaboration, and we force a higher level of justification beyond mere rationalizing.

In Chapter 2, we suggested a list of ten questions that expand ethical decision making to a stronger level of reasoning. These questions can be used in any ethical dilemma, from coverage of tragedy to investigative stories, from conflict of interest to manipulation of photos.

Let's now apply these ten ethical questions to the "AIDS in the Heartland" case.

1) What do I know? What do I need to know? This question about knowledge demands that journalistic excellence be a standard for measuring responsible actions. Jacqui Banaszynski was aware that AIDS was a major issue deserving significant scrutiny. She recognized that she needed to know more about AIDS, from medical, political and sociological perspectives. She needed specific details about Dick's and Bert's health and their relationship to decide how to pursue the story and what deals to make with her subjects and sources. The newspaper made a major commitment to this story in terms of time invested by the reporter and photographer to give depth and breadth to the gathering of information.

2) What is my journalistic purpose? It was essential for Banaszynski and Pieri to be clear on why they were doing what they were doing. They had a duty to provide meaningful information to their readers about a significant issue. They had to uphold the guiding principles of truthtelling and independence, despite resistance from those who would prefer not to read such stories. As *St. Paul Pioneer Press* managing editor Mark Nadler put it, this series "was an attempt to debunk some of the stereotypes of AIDS and to lift the shroud of ignorance from the disease."

3) What are my ethical concerns? The journalists also had an obligation to recognize potential harm to various stakeholders, those affected by decisions. There were issues of invasion of privacy and possible public scorn for Dick and Bert and their families. There was also potential harm to the readers who might be offended by graphic language or photos. And there was potential harm to the credibility of the paper if readers blamed the journalists. Some readers accused the paper of "glorifying homosexuality, trading on death, exploiting a family's private pain." The journalists had to decide whether the harm they might cause would be compensated by the good of creating public understanding.

4) What organizational policies and professional guidelines should I consider? Banaszynski and the editors at the *St. Paul Pioneer Press* needed to weigh the paper's past positions on reporting about AIDS and sexual issues as well as the paper's policies on the relationships between reporters and sources. What policies existed for use of graphic language and photos? They also had to consider professional standards of fairness and accuracy.

5) How can I include other people, with different perspectives and diverse ideas, in the decision making process? Banaszynski made a point of talking with editors at key points to make sure they were checking her approach to reporting the story. She did the same in collaborating with Pieri, who brought a different perspective to the information-gathering process. The fact that one of the editors at the paper had a brother who was gay helped broaden the perspective of those involved in the decisions. Finally, the year-long intense interaction with the two main subjects and their families provided a broad range of insights and viewpoints.

6) Who are the stakeholders—those affected by my decision? What are their motivations? Which are legitimate? The stakeholders are all those individuals and groups affected by the decisions and actions of the journalists. In the case of "AIDS in the Heartland," stakeholders included Dick and Bert, their families, neighbors, readers, makers of policy, the newspaper and the journalists themselves. The reporters and editors periodically had to challenge their own motivations to assure themselves the story was motivated primarily by truthtelling rather than just the forces of competition, professional recognition, or economic gain. Banaszynski recognized that Dick and Bert had their own reasons for participating in the story, as did their families when they agreed to be interviewed. The reporters had to weigh all these competing interests against one another.

7) What if the roles were reversed? How would I feel if I were in the shoes of one of the other stakeholders? It's one thing to recognize who the stakeholders are, but quite another to have compassion and empathy for them. Recognition can be a detached intellectual process. Compassion and empathy are emotional processes, calling for journalists to imagine themselves subjected to similar intense reporting. Thus the *Pioneer Press* team had to empathize with the situations, feelings and motivations of the stakeholders.

8) What are the possible consequences of my actions? Short term? Long term? Banaszynski described how she told her sources what impact the stories could have on them. She recognized the value of telling this story to her readers, of educating and engaging them about a gripping drama and a highly significant public policy issue. The editors also weighed the potential impact of various information and photos on the readers, and how that impact could have consequences for the paper, both in terms of the success of the AIDS story and the paper's credibility in the community.

9) What are my alternatives to maximize my truthtelling responsibility and minimize harm? At virtually every step in the reporting and writing process, Banaszynski, Pieri, and the editors considered choices for gathering and then presenting information. Banaszynski made what she called "deals" with certain sources to gain greater access to information, while providing some protection to those sources. Additionally, by immersing themselves in the daily lives of their subjects over a long period, the reporter and photographer enhanced their ability to tell a compelling story while never losing sight of the harm and benefit the stories would produce. Thus Banaszynski and her colleagues demonstrated the virtues of duty-based and consequence-based reporting.

10) Can I clearly and fully justify my thinking and decision? To my colleagues? To the stakeholders? To the public? "AIDS in the Heartland" is a splendid example of proactive, principle-based journalism. Within the series itself, in letters to the editor, and in editors' columns, the paper carried on a public dialogue so that readers could respond as a "fully informed jury." The *St. Paul Pioneer Press* journalists also had to make their case to the Pulitzer Prize committee, the Society of Professional Journalists and professional forums. At every stage, tough questions were asked, and in the process of answering them, Banaszynski and her colleagues proved themselves to be both excellent and principled journalists.

Conclusion

In this chapter, we have done a *post mortem* ethical analysis. Tough as it is to do this type of ethical decision making under daily deadline pressures, it can be done. We urge journalists to develop their skills at "doing ethics" by referring to these guiding principles and questions at every step in the newsgathering and reporting process. The development of expertise in the craft of ethical decision making is an essential step in achieving excellence in journalism.

"AIDS in the Heartland" has provided us with a good example of how journalists can do collaborative and reflective ethical decision making based on strong principles to produce courageous and excellent journalism. This series not only earned great professional recognition, but also provides a blueprint for how to "do ethics."

The next section of this handbook consists of a series of case studies taken from contemporary American journalism. There are cases involving long-form journalism, much like Banaszynski's and Pieri's coverage of AIDS, and there are cases dealing with breaking news in which ethical decisions were made within minutes of deadlines. In some cases, we fully apply the principles and questions to provide a complete ethical analysis. In others, we outline the cases and ask the readers to conduct the analysis for themselves.

Chapter Four

Accuracy and Fairness

The principles of accuracy and fairness stand at the very heart of journalism. Indeed, accuracy and fairness speak to the obligation of providing meaningful information to citizens who depend on its quality, authenticity and lack of bias to understand issues and to make important decisions.

Accuracy means "getting it right." It is an essential responsibility of individual journalists and news organizations. To provide wrong information is a disservice to the public and a sure way to erode the credibility of journalism.

Audiences deserve, and pay for, a reasonably accurate and unbiased picture of the world they live in. Every effort should be made to ensure that facts are correct and that information is presented in context. It is not appropriate to use deadlines, or competition, or personal excuses, or equipment problems, or staffing shortages, or any other reason to justify inaccuracies or bias.

Fairness means pursuing the truth with both vigor and compassion and reporting information without favoritism, self-interest or prejudice.

Accuracy and fairness mean challenging traditional definitions of news, ensuring coverage of societal issues and groups of people under-reported in the past.

Accuracy and fairness also mean portraying individuals and issues with a basic sense of open-mindedness, avoiding biased reporting, stereotypical portrayals, and unsubstantiated allegations.

To be sure, journalism can never tell the full truth in every story, because facts compete against each other, and additional facts and more information emerge over time. Many stories must be reported piecemeal, as they develop. But the fuller picture will come only from journalists committed to the fundamental principles of accuracy and fairness.

Accuracy Checklist

- Do you have a high level of confidence about the facts in your story and the sources that are providing them? If not, can you tell your story in a more accurate manner? If you have any doubts about your sources, can you delete them or replace them and achieve a higher likelihood of reliability?
- Have you attributed or documented all facts?
- Have you double-checked the key facts?
- Can you provide the properly spelled name and accurate telephone number of every source cited?
- Are you highly confident that all the factual statements in your story reflect the truth?
- Are you prepared to defend publicly your fact checking and whatever other measures were taken to verify your story?
- Are the quotes in your story presented fairly, in context?
- Are you quoting anonymous sources? Why are you using those sources? Are you prepared to defend publicly the use of those sources?
- Are you using any material, documents or pictures provided by anonymous sources? Why? What is your level of confidence about the validity of this material? Are you prepared to defend publicly the use of that material?
- Have you described persons, minority groups, races, cultures, nations, or segments of society—e.g. business-people, Vietnam veterans, cheerleaders—using stereotypical adjectives? Are such descriptions accurate and meaningful in the context presented?
- Have you used potentially objectionable language or pictures in your story? Is there a compelling reason for using such information? Would the story be **less** accurate if that language or picture were eliminated?
- Do your headlines (or broadcast promos or teases) accurately present the facts and context of the story to which they are referring?

Case Study #1

Streets of Despair

Summary

In January 1992, the *Hartford* (Conn.) *Courant* published a five-part series on drug addiction, prostitution and AIDS. Photojournalist Bradley Clift spent six months and reporter Mary Otto spent three months preparing "The Streets of Despair." Clift and Otto documented the lives of the people who live in the shadow of the state Capitol building in downtown Hartford.

Their project prompted a terrific response from the readers of the *Courant*. Hundreds of people called or wrote the paper to voice anger or praise for what the paper had done and to express horror about the reality it revealed.

Clift's photographs took readers to the back alleys and the shooting dens, where heroin and cocaine are rampant and women sell their bodies to feed their addictions. Clift's pictures showed women injecting needles into their arms, their legs, their feet and showed women propositioning men in a downtown restaurant.

Perhaps the most powerful and painful of the photographs showed young children, living with their mothers, who were trapped inside this bleak and deadly neighborhood.

Otto described life and death on the streets of Hartford. She wrote vividly about the drugs and the filth, about the disease and the pain. And she wrote about transsexuals and about oral sex.

She, like Clift, also painted a clear and tragic picture of the children who lived within "The Streets of Despair."

Many readers were outraged by the series, accusing the *Courant* of sensationalism and exploitation. Some said they hid the newspaper from their children. Others said the series was damaging to the neighborhoods, a local McDonald's restaurant and Trinity College, all of which were mentioned in the reports.

Perhaps the strongest reaction was to the *Courant's* decision to use real names and to show real faces. The editors at the paper had given their approval to the project only on condition that no confidentiality be granted, that every person be identified and speak on the record.

Assistant managing editor Terri Burke said the decision to use names was a matter of credibility, as well as one of impact. "If you wanted to tell the story in a way it had never been told before, it had to be done with names and faces."

Day 1

The Hartford Courant.

Established 1764

Streets of despair • Addiction, prostitution and the specter of AIDS

THIRD OF FIVE PARTS

$20 sex for a $20 bag

Photos by BRAD CLIFT
Stories by MARY OTTO
Of The Hartford Courant

[illegible]

▶ Continued next page

Clift also felt this policy was essential to the project. "We wanted to show the real in-depth side of what the addicts were thinking from their point of view .... This is a real person with a real life .... Some people we lost [because of the no-confidentiality policy], but by the end of the project some people came around [and permitted us to quote them] because they knew others were doing it."

Clift said there was another issue involved in the full-disclosure approach. "Some people want to write off drugs as a black or Hispanic problem. We wanted to make sure we reflected that this problem was with all sorts of people .... I found that most of the people out there were white women from the suburbs."

Otto said, "I think that people realize that a story is told in its particularity. A lot of people understood the need to name themselves in the story in the same way that they feel a bit passed over and disenfranchised in their lives. This was a chance to make a kind of contribution and have their voices heard. It's noble. It took a lot of courage."

Analysis

Accuracy in journalism demands that reporters and photographers provide the public with authentic information, both in terms of facts and context. Accuracy also requires strong attribution of information by identifying sources.

The *Courant*'s decision to use only real names and show real faces reflects a commitment to that obligation of accuracy. It was also a decision that was likely to cause some harm to the individuals involved in the story as well as to their families.

The paper did obtain written permission from all adults whose names were used and whose photographs were published and from the parents or legal guardians of all children.

That, of course, is primarily a legal issue. Ethically, the use of the names is more difficult to justify. As one reader wrote to the paper: "This publicity is bound to cause embarrassment and heartache to the families of the addicts. Children can be unduly harsh with innocent playmates who live under the cloud of such illegal activities."

Other readers argued the opposite, saying the probing revelations into the lives of these people were justified. "I hope these articles help people see that the addict could be any one of us or our children," wrote one reader. "If this graphic display of real-life addicts makes some child pass up 'the life' for another day at school, something momentous will have been accomplished."

The *Courant*'s reader representative, Henry McNulty, also saw the conflict between the value of the strong, direct reporting and the pain it caused. "Looking directly at a bleeding sore is never easy, but sometimes it must be done."

McNulty ended his thoughts on "The Streets of Despair" project by asking these questions:

• Were we fair to the subjects, to their families, to the neighborhood, to the city, to the readers?

• Did we cross the line from responsible reporting to sensationalism?

• Did we irreparably harm the families?

• Most of all, did we do what's right for the addicts' children shown in the series?

As McNulty said, "I doubt anyone has a perfect answer."

To his questions we might add several more, questions other journalists could ask when facing similar ethical dilemmas:

• Are we fulfilling our primary responsibility of **seeking the truth and reporting it as fully as possible?**

• Can we choose alternatives that will fulfill that obligation and minimize the harm to the most vulnerable individuals?

• Is our reporting also focusing on the "system failure" aspect of this story so that larger truths are being told?

• What can we do to prevent exploiting individuals as a means to our journalistic end, no matter how good our cause might be?

It took courage for Clift to embark on this story and to convince the editors at the *Courant* of its worth. It took Clift and Otto considerable courage to go into the streets to document this story. It took the editors courage to give the story the green light, to support it with resources and to publish it, knowing the paper would receive considerable criticism.

It was a story that needed to be told.

Case Study #2

The CIA Crack Contra-versy

Summary

The reprint of the *San Jose Mercury News* series "Dark Alliance" hit the desks of newspapers across America in the summer of 1996 with an unusual greeting from executive editor Jerry Ceppos. His letter began, "Dear Editor: At first I found the story too preposterous to take seriously."

Ceppos, it turned out, wasn't alone.

Several of the nation's largest newspapers criticized the *Mercury News*'s three-part series, challenging its findings and questioning the motives and skills of its author, investigative reporter Gary Webb.

The series alleged that two Nicaraguan drug dealers with connections to the CIA-backed Contra army—along with a Los Angeles drug dealer—had "opened the first pipeline between Colombia's cocaine cartels and the black neighborhoods of Los Angeles, a city now known as the crack capital of the world." (The series called one of the Nicaraguans "the Johnny Appleseed of crack cocaine.") The drug dealers funneled "millions in drug profits" to the Contras, the newspaper reported, adding that the ring "helped spark a crack explosion in urban America." All this took place at the same time the guerrilla army was being funded and advised by the CIA, the series reported. The *Mercury News* never flatly asserted that the CIA was behind any drug dealing or was even aware of it.

In his letter to editors Ceppos wrote, "A drug ring virtually introduced crack cocaine in the United States and sent the profits of the drug sales to the U.S.-government supported Contras in Nicaragua. All the while, our government failed to stop the drug sales .... In quiet, reasoned articles, Webb proved the case."

The *Los Angeles Times* didn't think so. Nor did the *Washington Post* and the *New York Times*, among other newspapers, which debunked the series. In October 1996, the *Mercury News* responded by publishing its own analysis of the series and its criticism. The lengthy piece was written by a reporter not connected to the original series.

Numerous issues surfaced regarding the series: the conduct of the reporter and editors, the role of the Internet and reaction from other media outlets.

Consider:

• The series did not establish a firm link between the CIA and drugs. Yet a logo that ran on the *Mercury News's* Web site—and in the reprints—depicted a

A SPECIAL REPRINT AUGUST 18-20, 1996

San Jose Mercury News

dayone:

How a cocaine-for-weapons trade supported U.S. policy and undermined black America

A MERCURY NEWS SPECIAL REPORT

'Crack' plague's roots are in Nicaraguan war

■ Colombia-Bay Area drug pipeline helped finance CIA-backed Contras ■ '80s effort to assist guerrillas left legacy of drugs, gangs in black L.A.

First of three parts

THE KEY PLAYERS

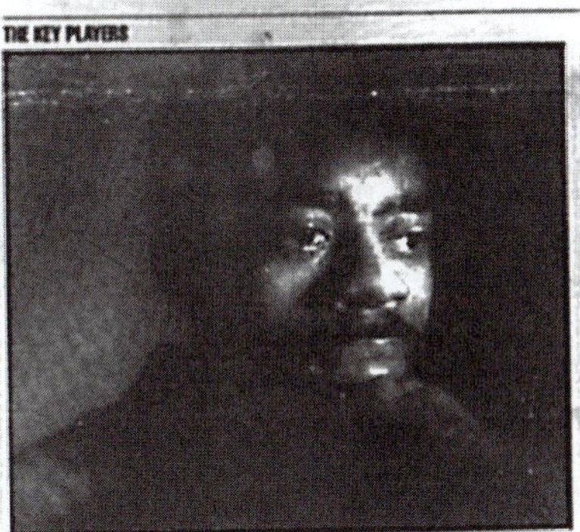

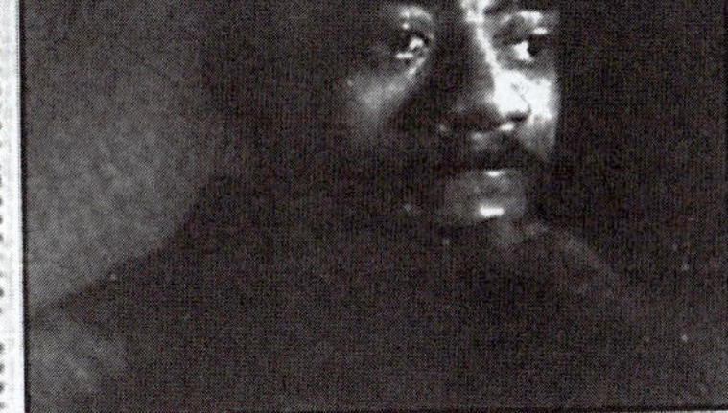

RICK ROSS: The street connection in the partnership that started a flood of cocaine into the United States.

more in Mercury Center

BY GARY WEBB — MERCURY NEWS STAFF WRITER

inside

On the Web: A guide to the Mercury Center presentation of "Dark Alliance" on its World Wide Web site. **PAGE 4**

How it began: Reporter Gary Webb tells about the tip that led him to the "Dark Alliance" story. **PAGE 7**

Reaction: Readers used the open forum in Mercury Center to comment on the series. **PAGE 8**

Follow-up: "Dark Alliance" outraged leaders in Los Angeles and in the nation's black community. **PAGE 8**

man smoking a crack pipe superimposed over the CIA seal. The logo did not appear in the newspaper. The logo was removed from the Web site only after a critical story appeared in the *Washington Post*. Ceppos told *American Journalism Review* that the logo was the newspaper's "main regret."

• The stories ignited anger and outrage, particularly in the African-American community. At first, when the series received a muted response, many black leaders suggested that if these sorts of suspicions had been raised concerning any other community, there would be widespread calls for congressional investigations and demands for government action. "People in high places were winking and blinking, and our children were dying," said U.S. Rep. Maxine Waters, a Los Angeles Democrat.

• According to *American Journalism Review*, Ceppos didn't read the entire series before it ran.

Critics of the series argued that the *Mercury News* had irresponsibly fanned suspicions about a government conspiracy to destroy black neighborhoods. Supporters, meanwhile, said that although some aspects of the newspaper series may have been hyped, the general thesis—that drug dealers associated with the Contras sold cocaine in South-Central Los Angeles at about the time the crack explosion began—should not have been brushed aside.

• The *Washington Post, L.A. Times* and *New York Times* led the charge in dismantling the series. (Not all media reaction was unfavorable.)

The *L.A. Times's* three-part condemnation of the series covered six and a half pages—more than the *Mercury News's* original pieces. In its 5,000-word attack, the *Washington Post* called the series "weak on evidence." *Post* ombudsman Geneva Overholser wrote that the *Mercury News* series was "seriously flawed ... reported by a seemingly hotheaded fellow willing to have people leap to conclusions his reporting couldn't back up." However, Overholser also called the *Post*'s attack a "case of misdirected zeal" and concluded that "the *Post* (and others) showed more passion for sniffing out the flaws in San Jose's answer than for sniffing out a better answer themselves."

After re-examining "Dark Alliance" with seven *Mercury News* reporters and editors, Ceppos acknowledged in a May 1997 column that the series had "shortcomings," was "oversimplified" and fell short of his journalistic standards.

"... We fell short at every step of our process, in the writing, editing and production of our work," Ceppos wrote in the column, which appeared on the front page of the *Mercury News's* Sunday opinion section. "Several people here share that burden .... But ultimately, the responsibility was, and is, mine."

Ceppos wrote that the *Mercury News* presented only one interpretation of complicated, sometimes conflicting evidence; oversimplified the complex issue of how the crack epidemic in America grew; created impressions, through imprecise graphics and language, that were open to misinterpretation; and failed to label the amount of money involved in the drug ring as an estimate.

The reporter, Gary Webb, who has been reassigned to a *Mercury News* bureau in Cipertino, California, and instructed not to report further on the case, has stood by his story. In an interview with the *Washington Post*, Webb called Ceppos' column "very bizarre" and in some cases "misleading." He added: "I'm not happy about it at all. It's rather nauseating."

Analysis

Two keys to judging this story lie in the motives and competency of both the reporter and the *Mercury News* editors. If Gary Webb's purpose was to attract readers and draw attention to himself with only sketchily supported declarations, the story would be difficult to defend, because a reporter's conviction that the truth is being told is a bedrock necessity of journalism. Similarly, then, the conviction must be supported by solid reporting.

Assuming his sincerity and some substantive competence, the arena in which Webb was operating is a particularly secretive one, meaning that an intense search for story information is only the first step in the truthtelling process. Others must come forward with their information once the first step is taken.

If, after conducting serious, professional fact-gathering, Webb had a high level of confidence in his thesis about the drug explosion and its victims, his only course was to start the public discussion. If the story as far as he could take it had merit, it could attain a life of its own as more information was disclosed.

Webb certainly started the discussion, but its direction might be questioned. It would appear that the media critics cited above looked more at his methods and information than at either confirming or discrediting the story *per se*. This could certainly raise the question of whether journalists are not sometimes more conditioned to protect icons—often their sources—than to provide information the public needs.

While it is important to ask publicly whether the story was solid, the emphases of the critics suggest they were more intent on disciplining a rogue colleague than on seeking truth themselves.

While it is important to ask publicly whether the story was solid, the emphases of the critics suggest they were more intent on disciplining a rogue colleague than on seeking truth themselves. Nevertheless, journalists calling colleagues to account is a healthy practice.

Because of the secretive nature of both drug dealers and the Central Intelligence Agency, and because the minority community portrayed as victims of the drug explosion sees itself as neglected by the media, the agenda raised by Webb has inherent value. However, partial repudiation of its own story and reporter suggests the *Mercury News* was not as persuaded as Webb that his information and conclusions were sound. It is interesting to note that the newspaper waited until external criticism reached a crescendo before conducting its own self-examination; a bit more front-end editing and soul searching probably would have been more productive than the *post hoc* scrambling Ceppos and others engaged in. That said, public accountability remains a valuable component of the entire journalistic enterprise.

As is often the case, perhaps the whole truth of the "Dark Alliance" will never be told. Yet the story ran, seeking to illuminate dark corners, and the reporter's own newspaper and other media called the account into question.

Some questions that could be asked in the production of this and related news stories:

- What standards of fairness should apply to public discussion about government agencies? Does their power to control information about themselves (particularly the more secretive agencies, such as the CIA) require a different standard of fairness as we engage the public in an open discussion?
- Is there any justification, such as marketing, for including elements in your promotional material that were not fully supported by the story itself (the CIA logo on the Web page and in reprints)? Should newsrooms and marketing departments be held to the same standards of truthtelling, fairness and accuracy?
- How morally defensible is it to present a united front (the newspaper defending its reporter) against outside criticism when members of your own staff may agree with some of the critics?
- What level of proof should a reporter have before drawing conclusions about such matters as a vague connection between the CIA and a drug explosion in a minority neighborhood?
- What level of proof would justify inciting an African-American (or any other) neighborhood's anger against a government agency, as was done in this case? Can discussion born of public anger be considered healthy?

Case Study #3

Cowboys in Trouble

Summary

For several years, media coverage of the off-field behavior of the NFL Dallas Cowboys has required extensive help from cops and courts reporters. The news has been so extreme it has been difficult to distinguish among real events, pseudo-events, and events made up out of whole cloth.

In late 1996, a Dallas woman claimed she had been raped at gunpoint by All-Pro tackle Erik Williams and another man at Williams' home while All-Pro receiver Michael Irvin videotaped the goings-on.

The incident was first reported publicly by Marty Griffin, an investigative reporter at KXAS-TV, Ch. 5, an NBC affiliate in Fort Worth. Griffin, heavily promoted in the competitive Dallas-Fort Worth market as one of the station's "public defenders," had achieved success and notoriety for his access to sources with less than sterling reputations. As the *Wall Street Journal* later reported: "Mr. Griffin had the scoop because the woman called to tell him first; he says he sent her to police." The article described Griffin as "probably best-known for a hidden-camera expose last May of Mr. Irvin, during an alleged cocaine buy, in which his source who videotaped the incident was paid $6,000 for the tape by Mr. Griffin's station."

Local media quoted KXAS news director Dave Overton as admitting the station had used the woman as a source in some of its reporting on the Cowboys. But he said the station never paid her for information and she was by no means considered an employee. In fact, the woman was often identified in media reports as a topless dancer—the occupation through which she had made the acquaintance of Irvin, Williams and other Cowboys.

Once Griffin went public with news that police were investigating Irvin and Williams, law-enforcement officials held a news conference to confirm it. Media were quick to pick up on the story, reporting the woman's accusation and the players' denials before police had had a chance to consider whether to file charges. Many media outlets followed the story by recounting sundry other recent run-ins Cowboys players, including Irvin and Williams, had had with the law.

Regarding the rape allegation, Irvin was quoted as saying, "I don't know anything about it. I have not done anything in any way, shape or form to violate my probation .... I've done enough bad things to my family and teammates. But in this case I've done nothing." Later he angrily said that he was

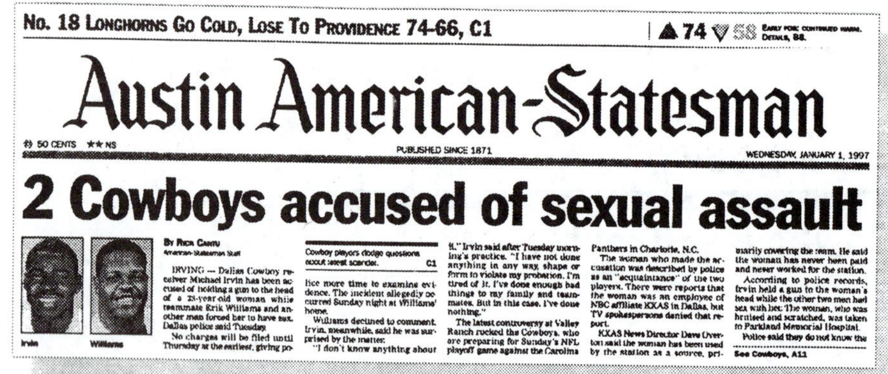

No. 18 Longhorns Go Cold, Lose To Providence 74-66, C1 | ▲74 ▽58 Early fog; continued warm. Details, B8.

Austin American-Statesman

50 CENTS ★★NS PUBLISHED SINCE 1871 WEDNESDAY, JANUARY 1, 1997

2 Cowboys accused of sexual assault

Irvin Williams

By Rich Cantu
American-Statesman Staff

IRVING — Dallas Cowboy receiver Michael Irvin has been accused of holding a gun to the head of a 23-year-old woman while teammate Erik Williams and another man forced her to have sex, Dallas police said Tuesday.

No charges will be filed until Thursday at the earliest, giving police more time to examine evidence. The incident allegedly occurred Sunday night at Williams' home.

Cowboy players dodge questions about latest scandal. C1

Williams declined to comment. Irvin, meanwhile, said he was surprised by the matter.

"I don't know anything about it," Irvin said after Tuesday morning's practice. "I have not done anything in any way, shape or form to violate my probation. I'm tired of it. I've done enough bad things to my family and teammates. But in this case, I've done nothing."

The latest controversy at Valley Ranch rocked the Cowboys, who are preparing for Sunday's NFL playoff game against the Carolina Panthers in Charlotte, N.C.

The woman who made the accusation was described by police as an "acquaintance" of the two players. There were reports that the woman was an employee of NBC affiliate KXAS in Dallas, but TV spokespersons denied that report.

KXAS News Director Dave Overton said the woman has been used by the station as a source, primarily covering the team. He said the woman has never been paid and never worked for the station.

According to police records, Irvin held a gun to the woman's head while the other two men had sex with her. The woman, who was bruised and scratched, was taken to Parkland Memorial Hospital.

Police said they do not know the

See Cowboys, A11

anxious to see whether reporters "rewrite, reprint, rerun all these things about what happened Sunday night when you find out I wasn't even at Erik's house."

The initial story, after all, was front-page news in Texas newspapers and received front-page play in many sports sections elsewhere.

A police investigation verified Irvin's claim, and neither he nor Williams was charged. The woman recanted her story and was charged with perjury. Griffin, the TV news reporter who first reported her allegations, was suspended by his station from appearing on air. In July 1997, Irvin and Williams settled a defamation suit against Griffin and KXAS for a reported $2 million.

Irvin also was adamant that news media give equal play to the fact that the police investigation and the woman's confession had cleared him of any wrongdoing. The *Dallas Morning News* gave the recantation and the conclusion of the investigation against the players front-page play. So did many other newspapers, including the *New York Times*, which carried a George Vecsey column headlined simply, "Headline For Irvin: Innocent."

Said Nels Jensen, a deputy sports editor in charge of Cowboys coverage at the *Morning News*: "We take into account where ongoing stories were played originally. At news meetings we often ask, 'Did this ever make 1A?' We did the same treatment after she recanted as when police announced the investigation."

Analysis

Paragraph after paragraph of high-minded pronouncements extolling the virtues of accuracy and fairness in journalism notwithstanding, sometimes it's almost impossible to ignore our gut instincts about a potential news story. This is especially true when we've "been there, done that"—when we've already heard the same unsavory news about the usual suspects, and the news has proven to be true. Times like these call for some very careful decision making.

Who among us wouldn't lend credence to yet another set of charges against the likes of Michael Irvin, described by *Times* columnist Vecsey as "already on probation for possession of cocaine, a rich and arrogant football player with a sordid reputation"? How do we overcome our natural instincts, how do we ignore those voices whispering in our journalistic ears that "Here we go again"?

At the outset of this chapter on accuracy and fairness, we reminded ourselves that accuracy and fairness speak to the obligation of providing meaningful information to citizens who depend on its quality, authenticity, and lack of bias to understand issues and to make important decisions. We said that accuracy means "getting it right," and that fairness means "pursuing the truth with both vigor and compassion, and reporting information without favoritism, self-interest, or prejudice."

The Society of Professional Journalists' new code of ethics tells us to be judicious about naming criminal suspects before the formal filing of charges. Under normal circumstances, the code's advice rings true. However, this was not a normal news story.

The story broke on television, because the woman making the accusation initially sought out KXAS-TV's Marty Griffin—for attention?—rather than police. This fact alone should have caused journalists to have a gut check, but apparently the competitive nature of the market and the possibility that the woman's case had merit precluded cautious and systematic decision making. It was a news story, one that cried out to be told.

The *Dallas Morning News* story about the Cowboys led with the "news" that the players had been accused of the sexual assault; only later in the story did we find the statement that no charges would been filed until police had more time to examine evidence.

The players' denials must have seemed as predictable, self-serving and problematic to the reporters as they did to many readers and viewers. Given the history of Irvin and Williams, wasn't it reasonable to suspect that the accuser was more likely than the Cowboys to be speaking truthfully? It might have been reasonable, but it wasn't prudent, as time proved.

As the case against the Cowboys collapsed, media accountability increased. It is gratifying to note that the *Dallas Morning News* gave the woman's recantation and police conclusions the front page play they deserved. Too often, accusations of wrongdoing receive front-page play, while resolutions—particularly resolutions favorable to the accused—get buried somewhere inside the paper.

And the punishment handed out to television reporter Marty Griffin may serve to alert other journalists not to confuse news-breaking with news-making.

As Vecsey concluded:

> The rest of us can learn a few lessons, too. Don't idolize athletes first, and then vilify them later, until we know the details. Even America's Team deserves America's legal premise: Innocent until proven guilty.

Case Study #4

Using the "N" Word in North Carolina

Summary

In April 1996, Don Follmer, spokesman for the speaker of the House in North Carolina, called a group of protesting University of North Carolina housekeepers and students "niggers and wormy kids" in what he thought was a private conversation with Associated Press reporter Dennis Patterson.

Follmer uttered the racial slur in the doorway of Patterson's office in the North Carolina General Assembly building's press room. Another reporter overheard the remark and told others. No journalists, including Patterson, reported the remark until two weeks later when Raleigh *News & Observer* reporter Joseph Neff heard about it. Neff pursued the story. He discussed it with the newspaper's state editor and assistant managing editor, both of whom agreed that Follmer's racist comments were newsworthy.

Neff confronted Follmer about the remark, and Follmer admitted he had used the racial slur. Neff wrote a front-page story about the comment, and three days later, North Carolina House Speaker Harold Brubaker fired Follmer.

Neff said he never had any doubts that he should report Follmer's conversation with Patterson.

"The speaker of the House is the second most powerful person in state politics," Neff said. "And you have his spokesman standing in a public place, very loudly making racist jokes about state employees. To me, this was a no-brainer."

Neff said Follmer had used "nigger" during an interview with another *News & Observer* reporter a year earlier, but the reporter chose not to use the racial slur in a story.

"Anyone in the '90s should know better," Neff said. "It isn't a word you toss around like that."

Follmer said the "niggers and wormy kids" comment was made in jest while "letting off steam." He said he was "under a lot of stress" that day and protesters who had entered the General Assembly building were disruptive.

"It just got away from me," Follmer said. "I used an unfortunate word in a private setting. I just popped off in a private conversation."

Follmer's admission, however, was not enough to eliminate the controversy that his comments had stirred on the university campus and in state government.

Neff questioned Follmer's boss, Brubaker, who said his staff was "color-

Brubaker spokesman admits using racial slur

Press secretary says conversation was private

Brubaker's spokesman says he's still on the job after racial slur

Group seeks Brubaker meeting

UNC housekeepers who were the object of a racial slur by House Speaker Harold Brubaker's spokesman want an explanation.

This act just won't play, Don

Brubaker fires aide over slur

Democrats say action overdue

Follmer's lesson: The media have tolerated divisive racial slurs for too long

blind" and never used racist language. Follmer said he advised Brubaker to fire him, and the House speaker did.

Patterson declined to comment on why he didn't report Follmer's remarks.

In an interview with Neff, he said he sometimes engaged in "politically incorrect" banter with Follmer, but that he never used racial slurs. In a story distributed by the AP, Patterson said he had told Follmer to "be careful" with his remarks but didn't consider writing about them.

"It was a casual conversation, not an interview, and I was working on something else," Patterson said in the AP story.

Follmer, a 20-year journalist before switching to state politics, said he had overheard numerous conversations that included racist and foul language but chose not to report them.

"If I had been in that boy's shoes, I never would have reported the story," said Follmer, who has retired and lives in the mountains of east North Carolina.

Follmer blamed the controversy on the popularity of "gotcha" journalism and "political correctness."

"These days people will take an inflammatory statement like that and try to smear somebody," he said. "They need to lighten up. Just report the news. And have a sense of humor."

Analysis

Holding the powerful accountable is at the heart of journalism's truthtelling responsibility.

The primary role of reporters is to inform and educate the public in a clear and compelling way on significant issues. By just about any definition, Don Follmer's comments are newsworthy. Racial slurs are significant, especially when coming from the lips of a powerful state employee.

Reporter Neff took an appropriate course of action in reporting and writing this story, including giving Follmer an opportunity to respond. It was important that Neff learned that this significant indiscretion on Follmer's part was not an aberration, but a repeat offense. In fact, one wonders why the *News & Observer* ignored Follmer's racial insensitivity the first time around.

It is also appropriate to challenge the AP reporter's decision to ignore Follmer's racial slur "because I was working on something else." That attitude is a warning to all journalists, telling us that we may be too chummy with those we cover, too unwilling to hold them accountable for improper behavior.

When facing a story of a similar nature journalists should consider their responsibility for both factual and contextual accuracy. While it is important to report a particular instance of racial insensitivity, it is at least as important to report about that moment within the scope of race relations in our society.

Case Study #5

McVeigh's Confession Goes Online

Summary

Seven hours before its newspaper hit print, the *Dallas Morning News* posted a story on its World Wide Web site reporting that Timothy McVeigh, then a suspect in the Oklahoma City bombing, had confessed to the crime to a defense team investigator.

The Web article stated that McVeigh had told his lawyers that he had driven the truck used in the bombing and decided on a daytime attack to ensure a "body count." The bombing at the Alfred P. Murrah federal building killed 168 people and injured 500. The story on the *Morning News* Web site appeared on the day prospective jurors were required to turn in court questionnaires.

The *Morning News* found itself at the center of attention almost immediately, not only because of the story's content, but because of its method of distribution. It was the first time that a newspaper had broken a major story online before its printed edition was published.

McVeigh's lead attorney, Stephen Jones, accused the *Morning News* of jeopardizing his client's right to a fair trial. At a news conference, Jones called the report "irresponsible" and "sensational." He also suggested that the newspaper had stolen the information, "hacking" into his computer files. At one point, Jones claimed that the defense team had fabricated the documents that the *Morning News* had used in its story.

After several days of reporting different responses from Jones, the *Morning News* published a graphic showing how the attorney's positions had changed.

Calling Jones's accusations "totally untrue," *Morning News* editor Ralph Langer said the newspaper obtained the information legally—though he did not explain how the *Morning News* accessed the defense files.

"Clearly, we would not publish a story if we weren't confident of the quality of information we have," Langer said in the *Morning News* article published the morning after the initial Web story appeared.

Langer said *Morning News* editors decided to first publish the confession on the newspaper's Web site because the newspaper wanted to deliver a "blockbuster" story to readers as soon as possible. The story had been written and edited by mid-afternoon, then quickly posted to the Web.

In addition, a *Morning News* reporter had interviewed government officials, prosecutors and Jones—all of whom knew a story was going to be published about McVeigh's confession—and the newspaper feared being scooped by its

Netscape: The Dallas Morning News: The Front Page

Location: http://www.dallasnews.com/index.html

The Dallas Morning News

dallasnews.com

February 28, 1997 3:15 p.m.

MCVEIGH TOOK RESPONSIBILITY FOR BOMBING, REPORTS SAY

McVeigh saw 'body count' as best way to make statement in Oklahoma City bombing, defense reports state

Suspect's attorney disputes reliability of documents

© 1997 The Dallas Morning News

Texas & Southwest: Oklahoma City bombing suspect Timothy McVeigh says a "body count" in the April 1995 explosion was necessary to get a point across to the government, according to confidential defense reports.

Timothy McVeigh Photo by Associated Press.

"We needed a body count to make our point."

LINCOLN BEATS HIGHLAND PARK, 64-46, FOR STATE TOURNAMENT BERTH. PAGE 1B.

The Dallas Morning News

Texas' Leading Newspaper | Dallas, Texas, Saturday, March 1, 1997 | 9 Sections | 50 Cents

McVeigh admitted bombing, memos say; his attorney disputes documents' credibility

By Pete Slover
Staff Writer of The Dallas Morning News

Timothy McVeigh has described for his defense team how he bombed the Oklahoma City federal building, saying the daytime attack left a "body count" intended to get a point across to the government, according to confidential defense reports.

In the documents, examined by *The Dallas Morning News*, Mr. McVeigh implicated his former Army buddy and codefendant Terry Nichols in the plot but insisted he alone drove the explosives-filled truck that destroyed the Alfred P. Murrah Federal Building on April 19, 1995.

Mr. McVeigh's lead attorney, Stephen Jones, called *The News* report "irresponsible" and "sensational" at a news conference Friday evening in Denver.

■ Lawyer certain client can get impartial jury. 23A

He suggested that either the newspaper had obtained stolen documents or the documents were fake. At one point he said the reports may have been furnished by someone with ill will toward the paper.

The reports quoted by *The News* "do not resemble anything that's in our office," Mr. Jones said after a hastily convened meeting with the judge in the case, U.S. District Judge Richard Matsch.

Mr. Jones initially declined to answer when asked whether Mr. McVeigh had ever admitted the crime to him, citing a gag order by the judge and attorney-client privilege.

"I can't tell you what he said in my interviews," he said.

Later in the news conference, Mr. Jones denied that Mr. McVeigh had ever made comments reflected in the reports.

Ralph Langer, executive vice president and editor of *The News*, said the newspaper obtained the documents legally.

"Clearly, we would not publish a story if we weren't confident of the quality of the information we have," Mr. Langer said.

Prosecutors and lawyers for Mr. Nichols had no comment, but Mr. Nichols has pleaded not guilty and denied any part in any illegal activity related to the bombing.

Both defendants face possible death sentences if

Please see McVEIGH on Page 23A.

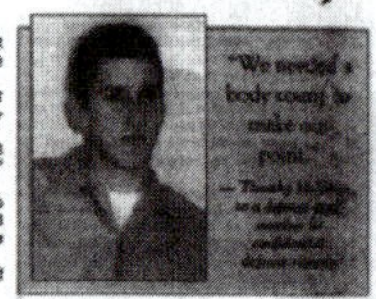

competitors, Langer said.

Some critics charged that the newspaper wanted to avoid any prior restraint attempts by Jones, but Langer said Jones never threatened to ask a judge to block the story.

In *Quill,* Langer wrote that he, other editors and the newspaper's attorney had discussed whether to publish McVeigh's confession over parts of several days before the story appeared on the Web. The decision process, he said, covered basic questions concerning the use of material from defense files and the possible impact on the trial.

"We had concern about the trial but, ultimately, came to believe that the information in that part of the material was of national importance and that we were obligated to publish it," Langer said.

Prosecutors, the judge and McVeigh's defense team later agreed that the *Morning News* report would have no effect on the trial. McVeigh ultimately was convicted and sentenced to death.

Analysis

The publication in the *Dallas Morning News* of the purported confession of Timothy McVeigh offers a classic case in journalism ethics. Just as important, it offers a significant case study in the process of ethical decision making.

At its core, this case is about competing principles and conflicting values. It is about the tension between the First and Sixth amendments. It is about duty and responsibility, about consequences and alternatives. It is about fairness to the accused, concern for the families of victims, and respect for the judicial process. It is also a case about public service, journalistic independence, and competitive instincts.

Clearly there are legal issues, but why, when, what and how to publish are essential ethical decisions. While ethics is about right and wrong, it is prudent to resist the temptation to cast a thumbs up or thumbs down on the *Morning News'* actions. Ethical decision making is more complex than that.

Additionally, we are missing pieces of the puzzle necessary to evaluate the newspaper's decisions. We have not seen the documents the *Morning News* used as the basis for its story. Nor were we in the newsroom to observe and hear the deliberations on the decision to publish.

Morning News editor Ralph Langer said the paper had an obligation to publish the story about McVeigh's alleged confession because "the information in that part of the material was of national importance and ... we were obligated to publish it."

Since the public did not have the same access to the documents as the *Morning News,* Langer is asking us to make a considerable leap of faith in accepting its reasons. It is appropriate, therefore, to be more detailed in explaining how it reached its decision. We want to know why the paper decided to publish the story on that weekend. And it's very important to understand to what degree journalists considered the interest of the victims and victims' families.

Until we know more, it is best to hold the *Morning News* accountable by challenging rather than cheering or condemning.

The case has high stakes on many levels for all of the affected parties. The editors of the *Dallas Morning News* still need to tell us more about their decision making process. That public accountability will help all of us judge whether the newspaper responsibly fulfilled its journalistic obligation.

—In *Quill,* Bob Steele suggests a series of questions that would have informed the *Morning News*'s decision to publish McVeigh's purported confession. The questions deal with issues of news-gathering techniques, sources, authenticity, fairness, consequences, independence, publishing, process and accountability. See "Until we know, let us challenge," *Quill,* April 1997, pp. 28-29.

Fairness

Checklist

- Is the meaning distorted by over- or under-emphasis?
- Are facts, quotations, photos and graphics in proper context?
- Have you given this story the length and display appropriate to its importance, and have you presented it with dignity and professionalism?
- Are the headlines and teases warranted by the text of the stories? Is their tone consistent with the story?
- Have you done your best to report all sides of the story, not just one side or, just as problematic, two artificially polarized points of view?
- Have you been compassionate in your reporting?
- Have all relevant people, particularly those who may be affected or harmed by the story, been given an opportunity to reply? If they have not been reached or have no comment, have you explained why in the story?
- If sources are not fully identified, is there a justifiable reason?
- When substantive errors or distortions appear in your paper or on the air, do you admit and correct them voluntarily, promptly and with a prominence comparable to that given the inaccurate statement or statements?
- Are you fostering an open dialogue with your readers, viewers and listeners? Do others, both in the newsroom and outside it, feel the story is fair to those involved?

Case Study #6

An Overdue Apology in Arkansas

Summary

As a journalism professor at Ohio State University for five years, Mike Masterson preached to his students about truth and responsibility. When he left the university to become editor of the *Northwest Arkansas Times,* he felt an obligation to live up to those words.

Less than a year after taking over the news side of the paper, Masterson, a former award-winning reporter, conducted his own investigation of controversial news coverage of a 1992 Fayetteville, Arkansas, mayoral candidate, Dan Coody.

Masterson concluded that the newspaper, under a different editor and owner, had fostered a vicious smear campaign against Coody, "wildly galloping over an innocent man's reputation with false rumors, leaving deep and lingering scars in the process."

The week before the election in 1992, the *Times* repeated innuendoes about Coody raised by other mayoral candidates. An editorial questioned Coody's mental stability. The newspaper warned of a mysterious and unexplained past in Texas. The rumors later were proved false.

The *Times* also hired a private investigator to look into Coody's past.

After the election, which Coody lost by 550 votes, he filed a libel suit against the *Times,* claiming the newspaper had maliciously published false reports that cost him the election and ruined his good name. Coody won the libel suit at the local level, but the decision was overturned by the Arkansas Supreme Court. The U.S. Supreme Court refused to hear Coody's appeal in 1995.

As the new editor in town, Masterson had heard much talk about the case.

"The impact of it was so substantial, it created an 8.5 on the emotional Richter Scale in this community," Masterson said.

Four years after the mayoral race, Fayetteville residents were writing letters to the editor about how the newspaper had unfairly treated Coody. Reporters were still getting phone calls about the race.

Masterson decided to look into the matter on his own. For two months, he pored over stacks of court depositions, internal memos and newspaper clippings.

In the court documents, Masterson discovered a letter from former *Times* publisher David Stokes to the newspaper's corporate owner in Chicago. In the letter, Stokes called Coody a "left-winger that has a large following of the '60s crowd."

Sunday, May 5, 1996 — Opinion — Northwest Arkansas Times

An apology is long overdue

The *Times'* actions in 1992 left an unwarranted stain on one man

A LONG STORY

BEGAN ON 'OCT. 29'

PAPER HIRED PRIVATE EYE

UNDERSTAND 'ARMED ROBBERY'

SECRETIVE CANDIDATE

MAXIMUM IMPACT

ELECTION DAY STORIES

LINGERING IMPACTS

NEW PUBLISHER AGREES

It's time for Coody's facade to come off

Coody provides details of early life

Rumors flying after mayoral election

Tales of the tape

Times publisher defends probe into past of mayoral candidate

In correspondence and conversations Stokes also accused Coody of being arrested in Texas on charges of armed robbery and writing bad checks, as well as serving time in prison, according to court documents. Coody, however, did not have a criminal record.

In a 1992 editorial, "It's Time for Coody's Facade to Come Off," which was published three days before the election, the newspaper accused Coody of misleading people about "who he is."

Two weeks after the election, Stokes was fired by the newspaper's corporate owner, Thomson Publishing. He could not be reached for comment.

After reviewing the documents and articles in 1996, Masterson decided an apology to Coody was long overdue. The newspaper, he said, had an obligation to tell the truth and help "erase the stain" it had placed on Coody's reputation.

Masterson met with the newspaper's new publisher and proposed writing an investigative news story or editorial column. The publisher opted for the column.

"Dan Coody and his family felt the brunt force of the power with which newspapers are entrusted," Masterson wrote in the column. "His story is a good example of why so many people distrust the press today. And it is one more reason why we all are mandated to do our job responsibly without arrogance, assumptions or malice toward anyone.

"When we knowingly fall short of that, even three years later, we should be willing to step forward and apologize for the damage we inflict. Otherwise how can we be trusted?"

Coody remains bitter over the treatment he received from the *Times*, but he hopes that Masterson's conduct might serve as a model for other newspapers.

Coody noted that his libel case did not receive national media attention until after Masterson issued the apology.

"The media should have been outraged at what the newspaper did from the start," Coody said. "The media wonder why they have a credibility problem. This is why. The media never want to expose a bad apple among themselves."

Analysis

This case study is all about minimizing harm and about accountability, two concepts that mesh neatly with questions of journalistic fairness. It also reminds us of the important distinctions between law and ethics.

The *Northwest Arkansas Times* caused unnecessary harm to Dan Coody and to community civic life in 1992. Several years later—appellate court decisions notwithstanding—the consequences of bad journalism remained as a festering boil on the newspaper's conscience. The lesson taught by former professor and new editor Masterson is that it's never too late to apologize, to set the record straight, to minimize harm.

If we were to take the convenient (some might say the "corporate") approach to the issue of liability, we would conclude that the Supreme Court's refusal to hear Coody's libel appeal settled the matter in the newspaper's favor. However, the fact that lawyers won the case on legal grounds does not mean the paper was morally justified in its treatment of Coody. Libel law makes it increasingly difficult for a public figure to collect damages. In their belief that a free press is better than a controlled press, the courts have made plaintiffs such as Coody prove quite clearly that journalists have acted with reckless disregard of the truth, that they have an "attitude" that a reasonable society should not tolerate. Apparently Coody wasn't able to prove his case to the court's satisfaction.

> ***(T)he fact that lawyers won the case on legal grounds does not mean the paper was morally justified in its treatment of Coody.***

However, his case was compelling to Masterson, as it should have been.

Masterson, using an ethical rather than a legal frame of mind, recognized full well that more than Coody's reputation was at stake. The reputation of the newspaper whose editorial control he inherited was also at stake.

In an all-too-rare display of accountability, Masterson went public with his apology to Coody, an apology that reminded readers why press credibility is at a precariously low point but reiterated the journalistic mandate for responsibility and fairness.

In its discussion of accountability, the Society of Professional Journalists' code of ethics says journalists should clarify and explain news coverage and invite dialogue with the public over journalistic conduct, admit mistakes and correct them promptly, expose unethical practices of journalists and the news media, and abide by the same high standards to which they hold others. Three years may not be "prompt" for a correction, but on all other criteria Masterson's investigative column met the SPJ standards for accountability.

If the *Northwest Arkansas Times* had referred to this book's "Fairness Checklist," there is little likelihood Masterson would ever have had to conduct the investigation or issue the apology. Were the concepts of fairness frontloaded into the gate-keeping process of the newspaper staff back in 1992, there is little likelihood the smear campaign would ever have been conducted.

This is not to discourage news media from conducting hard-hitting investigations of political candidates. Far from it. To function well, a community's civic life demands a vigorous and courageous press, one not afraid to turn over rocks, dig up dirt, and pass judgment. But such digging and judging should be done with constant reliance upon the tools of fairness.

Case Study #7

David Duke and the *Times-Picayune*

Summary

"Our state was shaken to its core. And the newsroom of the New Orleans *Times-Picayune* quaked with it, knowing that our future was at stake. It was a battle for the soul of the electorate, and we found ourselves in the thick of it."

That's how Jim Amoss, editor of the *Times-Picayune*, described the 1991 Louisiana governor's race that featured David Duke running against former Gov. Edwin Edwards.

Amoss and his colleagues faced a quandary at what he called "the intersection of personal belief and journalistic ethics." It was, he said, "a far trickier ethical morass covering a former Klan leader whose newfound rhetoric disguised his longstanding beliefs, whose following among one's readers is sincere and massive, whose election would mean social and economic disaster, but whose opponent is a scoundrel."

The *Times-Picayune* decided to publish a series of hard-hitting editorials to head off a Duke election. That series, "The Choice Of Our Lives," ran for five consecutive days, taking up the full editorial column of the paper.

There was clearly a point of view. "We decided that the election of David Duke was to be avoided at all costs. We felt it was our obligation to show why that was so .... Once the editorials were out there, there could be no doubt where we stood," said Amoss.

There was also no doubt about the stance of Keith Woods, an African-American and city editor of the *Times-Picayune*. "[Duke's] election would leave those of us who care with two choices," wrote Woods in his biweekly op-ed column. "[We could] work to heal the racial alienation and hatred that [Duke] has so totally laid bare and so deftly exploited, or leave." Woods said he would have to leave Louisiana if Duke were elected. "Someone else will have to fight that battle, though, because I cannot live in a state governed by a bigot."

Beyond the series of editorials, the *Times-Picayune* mounted a strong effort in its news coverage on the campaign. Woods said, "The passion behind our editorial writing was also behind sending 40 people out to produce a volume of reporting on this election and on Duke." He said they "did not have people trying to uncover new truths about Edwards .... And for a lot of people there was no distinction between the editorials and the news coverage .... It wasn't a blurring of lines. It was an erasing of the lines."

The Times-Picayune

4 WEEKS

The campaign the world watched

DAVID DUKE lost the election, but was the center of attention.

STAFF PHOTO BY TED JACKSON

EDWIN EDWARDS receives a blessing from Elder Paul Morton at the Greater St. Stephen Church. Edwards built a unique coalition to beat Duke. STAFF PHOTO BY JIM SIGMON

A few days after Louisiana voters catapulted former Ku Klux Klansman David Duke into the gubernatorial runoff, one of the state's leading pollsters called The Times-Picayune with a startling prediction: Duke would win his battle against Edwin Edwards.

The reason was simple. Voters hated Edwards. Many had decided Duke would be the lesser evil. Others thought he would be ineffective, and, therefore, harmless.

For Duke to lose, the pollster said, someone had to do something.

The following 27 pages tell the story of how a newspaper and its state rallied to preserve the tolerance and respect for human dignity that bind us as a community.

For its part, The Times-Picayune published a series of five editorials examining how Duke and Edwards might compare as governor. It ran extensive profiles of both candidates, including excerpts from Duke's chilling 1985 interview in which he said he did not believe the Holocaust had occurred. It inaugurated a feature called "To Tell the Truth," examining the candidates' assertions and comparing those claims with the facts. It focused the talents of more than 40 reporters, photographers and columnists on the governor's race.

When the returns were in, Edwards had gotten more votes than any gubernatorial candidate in Louisiana history.

REPRINTED FROM THE OCTOBER 20 TO NOVEMBER 17, 1991 ISSUES OF THE TIMES-PICAYUNE

Yet, Amoss points out that the paper did not print mindless allegations, sought comment from both sides, did not avoid negatives on the other candidate, and fully acknowledged flaws on both sides. Amoss says the *Times-Picayune* has been "the premier news organization investigating Edwards" over 15 years, and its special pre-election coverage included a half page of excerpts of Edwards's most damaging testimony from his racketeering trial.

Amoss feels the paper was truly responsible in its overall coverage. "Each story is fully journalistically defensible," he says. Woods echoes that belief, saying the paper sought balance and fairness on each story. "The editorials had a strong voice and strong point of view, unquestionable in their slant. The news stories read like good news stories."

Woods said the paper "had to decide whether we could view [Duke] as a hurricane or as a 'How's the weather?' candidate." As Woods put it, "If we treated him as normal, we would have been advocating David Duke. We could not be neutral no matter what we did."

Amoss also viewed the paper's dilemma as a Hobson's choice. "We were accused by many, including many on our own staff, of abandoning all principles of journalism .... Yet, if Duke were elected, I knew the paper would be held culpable to a large extent, just as we were when he was defeated."

Woods said he "felt particularly uncomfortable" during the weeks leading up to the election, and that in the newsroom "we talked about this election non-stop. There was a poison in the air .... Reporters crying, depression, constant bickering."

Amoss said, "The emotional pitch of those weeks could be gauged by the edgy mood of our news meetings, or by the number of staffers offering to write op-ed pieces about some aspect of the election." He said the paper received hundreds of letters and phone calls about its election coverage, most from angry Duke supporters. On four occasions, the *Times-Picayune* devoted the full op-ed page to letters from readers.

After the election, Woods asked some of his colleagues for their views. "Journalistically, ethically, I wanted him defeated," said one *Times-Picayune* journalist. Said another, "My goal was to provide information to fair-minded persons so we could vote against him."

Yet it was clear to at least some at the paper that there were both short-term and long-term consequences of their actions. As one journalist put it, "It was for the major good, but I'm not sure we didn't damage the instrument."

For Woods, the *Times-Picayune's* approach to the election was justified. "I'm absolutely, unequivocally supportive of what we did, despite how uncomfortable I felt and what anxiety it caused." Still, Woods said it "would be egotistical" to give the paper credit or blame for any power it had over the results of the election. "If we affected the voters," he said, "I think it was marginal."

For Amoss, this story was "all-consuming," whereby the paper was "caught between our own convictions and the imperative that we be trustworthy chroniclers." In the end, he felt that "to a certain extent, the ethical dilemmas were solved by the momentum of the story itself. Duke **was** the story, for the media, the readers, the voters. You either voted for Duke or you didn't vote for Duke. To a great degree, that exonerates news organizations. They are tracking what the story has become. The focus already was on Duke. It was incumbent upon the newspaper to explore that phenomenon."

Analysis

The journalists at the *Times-Picayune* faced considerable and complex ethical dilemmas in their coverage of David Duke and the Edwards-Duke gubernatorial election. This case highlights why news organizations must have strong journalistic and ethical principles as guideposts, as well as the capacity for good decision making under intense pressure.

Journalists at the *Times-Picayune* deserve credit for their process of decision making, even if one disagrees with the positions the paper took, the logic of its editors or some of their actions. There was considerable newsroom deliberation and collaboration to explore ramifications and alternatives. The extensive use of letters to the editor provided both contrary views and a forum for public debate.

Furthermore, one must recognize the great courage the editors displayed when facing that "intersection of personal belief and journalistic ethics." They made a very difficult decision knowing full well they would face disagreement and condemnation from both the public and from journalism.

Only extraordinary circumstances justify a newspaper's using so much energy and so many of its resources on a single focus, much less mounting a strong and specific effort to defeat a particular candidate. The burden is on the news organization to clearly and fully explain to the public why it is diverging from traditional approaches to reporting on an election. That same public disclosure is necessary for the paper to justify why it would allow its reporters and editors to become involved in the editorial campaign.

Although the circumstances of this case are unique, other news organizations can certainly benefit from the experiences of this case, as the *Times-Picayune* and its readers faced "The Choice of Our Lives."

A further analysis of this case might be based on a series of questions:

- Did the *Times-Picayune* honor the journalistic principles of truthtelling and informing the public?
- Was the paper fair in its journalistic mission and its reporting? How do you define "fairness" in a story like this?
- What elements of the decision making process suggest that reason, rather than emotion, prevailed?
- What are the consequences when the public or staff members feel a paper blurs or erases the difference between editorials and news coverage?
- Should the unusual circumstances of this case have been a factor in how the *Times-Picayune* resolved its ethical dilemmas, as editor Jim Amoss suggests?
- Should a news organization ever mount what some would call "a cru-

sade" against a political candidate? Was this a case where the stakes were so great that the paper had "an obligation" to take a strong position?

• Should reporters and editors write editorials or opinion columns while also writing on or editing campaign coverage? What are the consequences of such actions?

• Did the "all-consuming" nature of this story prevent or exonerate the paper from fulfilling other aspects of its journalistic mission?

• Did the *Times-Picayune* uphold or compromise its independence and ability as a "trustworthy chronicler?" Was that a risk worth taking in this case?

• Given the clear intention of the paper to prevent a Duke election, was there "a greater good" to be achieved by the strong editorials and intensive reporting?

• What alternatives might the *Times-Picayune* have considered to fulfill its varied and competing responsibilities to the public?

• What impact might the *Times-Picayune* coverage of this election have on the paper's credibility and its ability to cover other important issues in the future?

Case Study #8

Admiral Boorda Suicide

Summary

When he committed suicide May 16, 1996, Admiral Jeremy Boorda was the Navy's top officer, a highly decorated veteran of the Vietnam era who had risen from the enlisted ranks to command NATO as it engaged in its first offensive action.

Boorda killed himself roughly an hour before was to be interviewed by *Newsweek* correspondents about whether he had worn a medal for valor that he hadn't earned. In the aftermath of the tragedy, *Newsweek* and other news organizations were accused of hounding Boorda to his death, which provoked the magazine and other media members to do a little soul-searching over the question: Is any story worth a life?

Although the Pentagon did not blame *Newsweek*, it was clear that Boorda changed his lunch plans and went home to kill himself upon learning that reporters were on their way to ask him unsettling questions. Boorda's suicide note, the *Washington Post* reported, "indicated he was not taking his life in the belief he had been caught in a lie, but out of fears that the media would accuse him of one and blow it out of proportion." Navy spokesman Admiral Kendall Pease said, however, "*Newsweek* did nothing wrong."

Some media critics, however, did blame *Newsweek* and other news organizations that had begun to investigate Boorda for what syndicated columnist Nat Hentoff called a story that "had no legs." *Newsweek* acknowledged that letter-writers complained vociferously about the magazine's role, and some canceled subscriptions.

In a "full accounting" by its media critic, Jonathan Alter, the magazine looked inward to examine whether it had violated some unwritten but understood ethical tenet. After chronicling how the story idea had been generated—a Washington-based outfit called National Security News Service provided documents and photos showing Boorda began wearing the valor pin in the 1980s, then stopped—and how the reporting process had taken shape—part-time contributing editor David Hackworth was working on the story with Washington bureau chief Evan Thomas and national security correspondent John Barry—Alter concluded that *Newsweek*'s position was "defensible."

Acknowledging the sometimes grave consequences that journalism can produce, Alter also raised the issue of "whether the story was worthy or not. Was it too trivial to pursue?" Although Hentoff and others believed so, some current and former military officers disagreed. Among them was Hackworth, a retired Army colonel often referred to as the nation's most highly decorated officer. Accompanying Alter's article was an essay by Hackworth, titled "Why Medals Matter." Referring to an officer's wearing of decorations he is not entitled to, Hackworth wrote: "There is no greater disgrace."

Hackworth's involvement in the story included this ironic footnote: Almost a year to the date after Boorda's suicide, CNN and CBS reported that Hackworth also had military decorations he hadn't earned. Hackworth told CNN he had learned he was not entitled to a Ranger tag and a second Distinguished Flying Cross. Hackworth said he had listed the medals on the resume posted on his personal page on the Internet but removed them.

CNN reported that Hackworth may have made an honest mistake—just as Boorda claimed he had.

Analysis

This is a troubling case study about journalistic fairness. Whenever the public jumps to the conclusion that the media have caused egregious harm, it is time to take stock—regardless of the merits of the public's opinion.

It may be a mark of lingering Vietnam-born media paranoia among the military over what most civilians would consider a trivial story: A man at the top of the military ladder takes his own life rather than face a reporter's questions.

Whenever the public jumps to the conclusion that the media have caused egregious harm, it is time to take stock—regardless of the merits of the public's opinion.

Reporters often must weigh the effect of reporting a story when determining whether audiences need any particular information. Each time a reporter inquires into an individual's personal behavior, there is risk that the source will react in an extreme way. However, it's unlikely *Newsweek* reporters could have anticipated Admiral Boorda's suicide.

Still, reporters must have been aware that their story would be more than an embarrassment to Boorda. It was bound to damage an otherwise honorable officer's professional reputation.

A former officer, who himself was later found to have worn undeserved medals, took a strict stance in calling such behavior "no greater disgrace"—a difficult statement for most civilians to comprehend.

Truth is important, and comprehensive media reports relating to public figures are doubly important.

But, the suicide aside, harm to Boorda's reputation may have been difficult to justify when considering the usefulness of the information to *Newsweek* readers. On the other hand, scrutiny of public figures and such mundane behavior as wearing unearned medals is critically important if citizens are to make informed judgments about their leaders.

If Boorda had told the reporter he would commit suicide if the story ran, would the reporter have been justified in killing the story? Such threats do occur. In this case, the *Newsweek* reporters would probably have been puzzled at the extremity of the response. Their puzzlement, however, might have led to more thorough understanding of and better reporting on the military, a complex institution whose value system is not well understood by all journalists.

In the aftermath of Boorda's suicide, public discussion of the matter was effective in holding *Newsweek* accountable, whatever the magazine's justification. The soul searching conducted by *Newsweek's* Alter was commendable—not just as a PR effort on behalf of the magazine, but as an ethical post mortem. It's likely reporters familiar with the Boorda case will make greater efforts to determine the impact of their stories on their sources as they decide whether the story is worth the potential harm.

Case Study #9

We Don't Do Rumors. Or Do We?

Summary

"When someone is spreading a false rumor in order to get attention, it creates a dilemma: Should you confront the rumor head-on, even if it means giving the perpetrator the attention he wants? Or should you ignore the rumor, even if it means that some people may wonder if it's true?"

The speaker was Seattle Mayor Norm Rice, who was at the time a candidate for governor of Washington. Rice described the conflict at a press conference in May 1996, more than two years after a former city employee began what the *Seattle Post-Intelligencer* called a "scattershot campaign of accusation and vitriol against Rice."

Seattle-area media had heard the accusations and checked them out. *P-I* managing editor Kenneth F. Bunting recalled that "there was little that was credible about the scenario" maintained by Kurt Hettiger, who was fired from the water department in late 1993. Said Bunting: "To believe the incident as Hettiger had detailed it, one had to also believe that the police department, the fire department, emergency transport drivers, the hospital and the media had all engaged in an elaborate conspiracy to cover it up."

Seattle Times executive editor Michael R. Fancher wrote in his first column after the Rice press conference, "Our conclusion was that the rumors were false."

The rumor was that Rice had been shot by his wife when she discovered him a in a sex act with his deputy mayor. The story was told in dozens of letters and faxes to Rice and other officials, and in fliers Hettiger distributed in downtown Seattle, asking, "Who Shot Mayor Norm B. Rice?"

The day Rice announced his candidacy for governor, a caller brought up the rumor on Mike Siegel's "Hot Talk" radio show. Siegel, an afternoon host on KVI-AM, said he had heard the rumor and would look into it further. (He hired a private investigator and said the detective could not substantiate the story.)

Over the next several weeks, conservative talk shows across the state discussed the rumor.

Rice said he decided to fight back after Siegel's April 11 show, which was simulcast in Spokane. During the show, called "The Truth About Norman B. Rice," a former Seattle police officer repeated Hettiger's claim. Siegel labeled it a "rumor" and said he had heard it from "a variety of sources who are very credible." He called on Rice to publicly deny the allegation.

About that time, Bunting, the *P-I*'s managing editor, wrote a memo directing that the paper should not report the allegations in the absence of "credible, on-the-record sources with first-hand knowledge of the purported incident itself AND, not or, the supposed cover-up."

A few weeks later, Rice invited the media and others to a press conference. There, Rice's announcement, Bunting said, "changed the story .... We had never been close to running a story about the accusations in the fliers .... On the other hand, there was never much consideration of NOT doing a story once we learned that the mayor was planning to dramatically confront them."

"We had never been close to running a story about the accusations in the fliers .... On the other hand, there was never much consideration of NOT doing a story once we learned that the mayor was planning to dramatically confront them." —Kenneth F. Bunting

The *P-I* advanced the press conference at the top left corner of the front page May 11, describing the rumor in the eighth paragraph: "Initially, Hettiger contended Constance Rice shot her husband in the wrist after she found him having sexual relations with then Deputy Mayor .... A later version says another member of the mayor's family shot Rice in the shoulder."

The report recounted Hettiger's history with the city and Rice, identified the former deputy mayor and quoted him saying: "It's so preposterous .... But it does hurt people, because people do believe it."

In contrast, the next day's *Seattle Times* previewed the press conference with eight paragraphs leading a "Political Notebook" on page B4. The column characterized the tales as "bizarre rumors about the mayor's personal life."

At the press conference, Rice denounced the allegations as "ludicrous, outrageous and untrue," without mentioning the specific allegations. His wife, Constance, surprised the gathering by saying she never could have been involved in a shooting, because she hated guns: Her father had been murdered.

Siegel's listeners heard the press conference live. That afternoon, Siegel apologized to Rice and his family on the air.

The next day, Rice took off on a campaign tour called "Taking the High Road With Rice."

Siegel was fired two weeks later for damaging the reputation of Fisher Broadcasting Inc. by airing the rumors. But his talk show career continues: He is on 22 stations in Washington, via the Michael Siegel Network.

Rice lost in the Democratic primary September 17 but garnered more votes than the top Republican vote-getter. Reporting on a poll conducted in the two days before the primary, the *Times* interviewed a resident of southwest Washington who said when she considered Rice, "I heard something about a scandal; I don't know what it was about or how it was resolved, but that made me not want to vote for him."

Times editor Fancher said after the primary, "There is no way to know whether the rumors hurt him or whether he helped himself by standing up to Siegel .... Most of the post-election analysis has focused on other things." He added that "Rice said he got off to a slow start, and attributed part of that to the distraction of the rumors, but didn't cite them as a significant factor in his loss."

Despite his apology to the mayor, Siegel continued to defend his actions on a panel at the convention of the Association for Education in Journalism and Mass Communication in California in August. He said of the rumor: "For three years it had been brought to my attention, and I had rejected it because it was a rumor. When something happens spontaneously on the air as this did, it was handled in the proper manner."

Siegel's primary point in Anaheim was, "Talk radio is not journalism, and I don't think the standards that we should be judged by should be from those traditional standards .... We are in effect the town meeting ... what we do is to try to get people involved. I like to talk about enlightenment and empowerment and entertainment—entertainment being the key."

Analysis

Like most ethical dilemmas, the choice between publishing no details and publishing more details creates a conflict among principles we are loathe to violate. Consider three of the Guiding Principles for Journalists: seek truth and report it as fully as possible, act independently and minimize harm.

The Seattle papers had sought truth in the rumor itself and found none. The new truth was that the rumor was spreading and Rice had called a press conference to denounce it. Reporting those truths as fully as possible would seem to argue for more details about the rumor's content.

Reporting the truth is intended to keep the public informed. Telling people more allows them to evaluate specifics rather than speculate what the specifics might be.

Yet the public may not want journalists to report rumors. In his "Inside the Times" column May 19 executive editor Fancher wrote that David Boardman, the paper's regional-enterprise editor, was influenced by *Front Porch Forum*, the paper's dialogue with readers. Boardman told him that readers "want us to put these things in the proper perspective in the political process."

Another of the guiding principles would have us minimize harm. Reporting all we know likely would hurt Rice, the former deputy and their families. Or so it seemed: If a reliable medium reports a rumor, it lends the tale legitimacy. A rumor that might be true is more damaging to the subject than a tale with no recognition from trustworthy quarters. (The media's apparent blessing also rewards those who invent or spread rumors and, so, encourages harm.)

But what became different in May is that Rice consented to this harm. When he called a press conference, he agreed to have the information made public and understood that the media could (make that "would") report more than he was reporting. If people give informed consent to some treatment, they don't get to complain when it happens. We usually think that holding or seeking public office implies consenting to diminished privacy and greater public scrutiny. (Though probably not to the point of tawdry rumors. If rumor is the issue, then consent would require a specific agreement.)

Minimizing harm is always good. But when we weigh that goal against informing the public in a case in which the subject has agreed to the harm, the obvious course seems to be telling the public.

A third principle tells us to act independently. From a distance, that appears to be what is happening. But political observers told Michael Paulson of the *P-I* Capitol Bureau that "the mayor's action appeared to be intended not only to limit the damage from the rumors but also to be a calculated gamble to garner attention and sympathy for a gubernatorial campaign that could use a boost in the opinion polls."

Obviously, the more we go along with a political initiative, the less independence we show. If the Rice campaign went public for the sake of sympathy, then the more coverage the rumor got, the more the paper would be helping that cause.

We don't recommend falling for manipulation or appearing to. Still, even sophisticated, skeptical, independent journalists may find themselves manipulated by professionals.

If we believed the Rice camp was trying solely to kill the rumor, then we should print more, not less. If this seemed to be a self-serving grab for sympathy, the best way to resist the influence and exhibit independence would be to publish not one more syllable than necessary.

When the information we have seems to point in all directions, the answer often is more reporting.

—This is an edited version of an article written by Joann Byrd for the Poynter Institute Web site.

Case Study #10

Abortion Coverage on Deadline

Summary

Journalists covering the abortion issue often find themselves facing ethical dilemmas. That was the case on July 3, 1989, the day the U.S. Supreme Court upheld a Missouri law restricting abortion.

It was clearly **the** news story of the day, and news producers at WCCO-TV in Minneapolis wanted to give the abortion issue a strong play on their 10 p.m. newscast. The decision was made to focus on a woman having an abortion that day.

The station contacted Minneapolis abortion clinics. Some agreed to ask their patients if they would be willing to be interviewed. At about six o'clock, one woman agreed. Her appointment was for 6:30, so the news crew rushed to the clinic.

According to WCCO-TV news producer Julie Kramer, the "woman had no restrictions as far as questions. She asked only that her last name not be used and her face not be shown." The station agreed.

Kramer described how the events of the evening unfolded:

"The crew came back with the tape between 8 p.m. and 8:30 p.m. A debate began then over whether the story should air. Some thought it was too inflammatory. Others thought it tasteless. Others thought it was blatantly pro-choice. The crew was baffled. When they'd left, the newsroom seemed enthusiastic about the story.

"The 10 p.m. producer didn't want to air it that night, suggesting that it could run the next evening, or maybe never. An anchor insisted that the other side be given comparable time in the same section. The news director was called at home. He was concerned about the controversial nature of the piece.

"The field producer and the photographer couldn't spend as much time arguing in favor of the story as they'd like, because they needed to spend their time producing and editing the story. The producer felt that since the news of the day, the Supreme Court decision, was written with both views in section one, it was not necessary to balance every abortion view in the newscast with the opposing side.

"The news director decided that to be fair, we should broadcast a string of sound bites from an interview earlier in the day with the local archbishop. After the piece was edited, the producer had the photographer change some suction scenes she felt were too graphic."

The story aired on WCCO's 10 p.m. newscast that night, followed by the interview comments from the archbishop.

Analysis

This case is an example of ethical decision making under deadline pressure, and it's important to note that the story did make it on the newscast that night. The journalists at WCCO-TV were faced with making some tough calls, weighing consequences and considering alternatives on an important story. They did not succumb to paralysis of analysis.

There were several issues at play. Fairness was a factor, as some in the newsroom felt the story was biased toward the pro-choice position on abortion. Interestingly, one could argue the opposite, suggesting that the graphic scenes of the abortion and the revelation by the woman that this was her second abortion reinforced the pro-life position.

It is an issue not easily resolved. Perhaps the best a journalist can do in such a situation is recognize one's personal biases, do collaborative decision making to gain diverse input, and present factual information from competing sources. Sometimes an imperfect alternative is chosen to resolve a fairness struggle, as in this case with the use of the archbishop's interview to provide a competing perspective on abortion in the same newscast.

Yet, to believe that every story can be perfectly balanced can restrict good journalism. Instead it is productive to recognize that each story can be fair, although balance might better be achieved over time and through continuing coverage of an issue.

Balance is a noble goal, elusive though it is. Yet, to believe that every story can be perfectly balanced can restrict good journalism. Instead it is productive to recognize that each story can be fair, although **balance** might better be achieved over time and through continuing coverage of an issue.

Another issue in this case deals with "taste," which is truly an ethical issue because it deals with the potential for harm to individuals as well as the obligation to tell the truth. To show video of an abortion procedure certainly raises the possibility of offending some viewers, by harming their sensibilities or even emotionally traumatizing them. At the same time, it's important to present as clear and compelling pictures of the procedure as possible in order to bring the viewers an accurate account of what took place.

Abortion is a highly controversial and important public policy issue in our society. Journalism best serves the citizens when it provides meaningful information on such important issues, even when some might be offended. It is possible to minimize that harm to viewers, however, by choosing alternatives that allow for a clear understanding of what happened, yet protect to some degree the sensibilities of the public.

In the end, the principle of truthtelling must take precedence over the principle of minimizing harm, except in those exceptional situations where the harm is truly extreme and clearly outweighs the value of the information that is to be left out of a story.

In most cases, journalists can resolve these competing obligations, honoring both. In the case of the WCCO coverage of the abortion, the photographer shot the video with alternative editing possibilities in mind. He recognized that he must be sensitive in how he took pictures, both out of respect for the woman undergoing the abortion and eventually for the viewers who would see the videotape. Yet he knew that he must provide enough video to give the story context as well as accuracy.

Another alternative for minimizing harm while providing potentially offending information is to provide a warning. Introductory comments by the anchor might alert viewers to the nature of the upcoming material, preparing them for its impact and giving them the choice not to watch.

Another issue in this case was how the reporter and photographer dealt with the woman having the abortion. What are the pros and cons of agreeing to the woman's request that her last name not be used and her face not be shown?

The authenticity of all news reports is enhanced by fully revealing the identities of those involved in stories, be they sources of information or subjects of coverage. Yet it's clear that in order to avoid using individuals as mere means to a journalistic end, reporters must sometimes grant confidentiality and anonymity in order to protect those who are quite vulnerable.

Making such ethical decisions on fairness and balance, taste and confidentiality places great demands on individual journalists and news organizations. These decisions can be made best by individuals who think about ethics on a regular basis, not just when a crisis occurs.

Ethical decision making is a craft and a skill, much like writing or editing or taking pictures. If journalists develop and practice this skill, then they can make good decisions on tough issues, even when those calls must be made on deadline.

Case Study #11

Naming Victims of Sexual Abuse

Summary

Orange County (Calif.) *Register* reporter Susan Kelleher faced difficult ethical decisions when she learned the state medical board was investigating a local gynecologist over complaints that he molested four of his patients.

Kelleher used the information to write a short story that appeared in the back of the Metro section on New Year's Eve—a day, she said, "when not many people read the paper." Then she started getting calls. Some women wanted the medical board's telephone number. Some women said they, too, had been molested by the doctor. While the most recent incident was just four years earlier in 1987, two of the incidents on which the complaints were based occurred in the 1960s.

Kelleher began taking the women's names and phone numbers. Some were hesitant, and others agreed to give only a false name. "They were very, very fearful," according to Kelleher.

And the stories they told were chilling. Many of the women said Dr. Ivan Clifford Namihas masturbated them when they had their feet in the stirrups. Others accused the doctor of performing laser surgery without adequate anesthesia and of performing unnecessary surgery. The physician allegedly told several patients they had genital warts. He also allegedly told one woman she had AIDS, although a later check with another doctor revealed she did not.

After the first five women called, Kelleher thought the paper should do another story on the doctor and the allegations against him. By the time 14 women had called in the three to four weeks after the initial story, Kelleher said, "I was absolutely convinced we should do a story."

But how?

The paper's policy was normally not to name victims of sexual abuse. The paper's policy normally did not allow unnamed sources either, particularly sources making accusations. Kelleher, who opposed using the names, argued that the paper should follow its policy on sexual abuse victims and quote the women anonymously. There were many allegations being made against the doctor. Kelleher said the sources would have been unwilling to be quoted by name.

There were other problems as well: Kelleher feared that requiring her to use the names might kill the story until the state medical board acted; furthermore, she and the editors feared that they might get beaten by the *Los Angeles Times's*

Orange County Edition.

Assistant managing editor Ken Brusic decided that the names were necessary. He felt, and managing editor Tonnie Katz and editor Chris Anderson agreed, the situation was different from other cases of sexual abuse because medical board complaints, unlike police reports, are confidential. Without the protection of that legal privilege, the paper could be in jeopardy if it ran the allegations without the names of the accusers.

The editor's decision forced Kelleher to try different strategies to get her story. She promised each of the women to whom she talked that she wouldn't do a story unless she had three of them recounting similar stories on the record. That way, Kelleher reasoned, no one woman would become the focus of allegations or retribution. "That put a lot of women at ease," Kelleher said. She also told the women "to think about it" for 24 hours before making a decision on allowing their names to be used. And finally, she told each woman she could change her mind at any time before publication.

Kelleher said she let the women retain control as much as possible. "They couldn't control what was in the story, but they could control whether **they** were in the story." By the time the story ran, 25 women had come forward to Kelleher; only four agreed to allow their names to be used.

When the story ran, the *Register* included a warning to readers about graphic language in the story. In an accompanying letter to readers, Anderson explained why the *Register* published what it did: "Normally we edit out such language or paraphrase strong quotes. We have not [done so] here because we felt they were essential to the stories ... to understand the difference between a gynecological exam and the charges of sexual abuse."

Anderson also explained that the newspaper deviated from its normal policy on using the names of sexual abuse victims because "the charges against Namihas were so strong" that the allegations must be on the record. The editor also told readers how the reporter dealt with the women making the allegations.

Kelleher said she believes publishing the names gave the story far more credibility and impact than if the newspaper's policy had been followed and the names had not been published.

In July 1992, the state medical board revoked Namihas's medical license.

Analysis

This case is a good one on which to apply the Guiding Principles for Journalists presented earlier in this book. It is also a good case in which to raise questions about motivations that drive journalists' decisions:

• Did the *Orange County Register* fulfill its responsibility to inform the public about a significant issue?

• Did it give voice to the voiceless and hold the powerful accountable? Did the reporter and the paper protect their independence while seeking out important sources of information?

- Did the journalists show compassion for those affected by their actions?
- Has the newspaper been accountable for its decisions?

Some important questions of fairness must be asked in this case.

- Did the paper give the accused physician a reasonable opportunity to respond to the allegations against him?
- Did the paper put the allegations and facts into context by seeking information from other sources beyond the patients and the doctor?
- Were the motivations of the paper driven by a responsibility to reveal a significant story about the abuse of power?
- How great were the motivations to beat the competition to the story?
- In deciding the paper must name the victims who were making the allegations, was the paper truly recognizing the importance of solid and direct attribution?
- Did the warning to readers about the explicit language in the story help minimize harm?

This case also provides good examples of applying some of the questions suggested in the "Making Ethical Decisions" chapter.

Editors at the paper were willing to consider and reconsider their organizational policy on the naming of victims of sexual abuse. They asked whether the facts in this case warranted a valid exception to the policy.

Clearly reporter Susan Kelleher was willing to "walk in the shoes of the stakeholders" in this story, particularly the women who were making the allegations of sexual abuse.

She also maximized her truthtelling responsibility and minimized harm by negotiating with her sources to encourage them to come forward while giving them a meaningful level of protection.

This case had consequences related to fairness, revelation of important information, protection of the vulnerable, accountability of the powerful, and credibility of the story and of the paper. The reporter and the editors had to consider both short- and long-term implications of their actions.

Importantly, the *Orange County Register* fulfilled its responsibility to justify publicly the paper's decision making process by explaining to readers **why** it used explicit language in the story and **how** the reporter dealt with her sources.

Accuracy and Fairness

What the Codes Say

Spokane (Wash.) ***Spokesman-Review***

Credibility of the news reports is the cornerstone of the newspaper. Our readers expect the news reports to be accurate, honest fair, balanced and free of distortions or influence which business, advertising and political interests might try to impose on news content.

Business, advertising and political interest of management personnel must not be allowed to influence news content. While recognizing that the newspaper is a for-profit business, the editorial department must retain its special status as watchdog for the readers, inherent in which is the responsibility to report stories regardless of the economic or political ramifications.

The newspaper should report matters regarding itself or its personnel with the same vigor and candor as it would other comparable institutions or individuals.

Wilmington (Del.) ***News Journal***

News Journal recognizes that the power it has as the dominant source of information for residents of Delaware and adjacent areas carries with it special responsibilities to face the public with politeness and candor, to avoid the appearance of arrogance and to listen to the voiceless.

Accuracy and impartial reporting and editing should be the hallmarks of the *News Journal.*

Reporters should not comment editorially on stories they are covering and should not write about events in which they're personally involved. Each of us should avoid public involvement in, and expression of opinion about, controversial issues. The editorial page and opinion columns are the places for such expressions. Each of us should be wary of expressing opinions in casual conversation or elsewhere that may then be cited by others as a basis for charging news-slanting.

San Jose **(Calif.)** ***Mercury News***

The *Mercury News* strives to operate with fairness, accuracy and independence.

It strives to be diligent in its pursuit of the truth without regard to special interest and with fairness toward all. Although the law does not require it, the *Mercury News* whenever possible seeks opposing views and solicits responses from those whose conduct is questioned in news stories.

The *Mercury News* strives to guard against inaccuracies, carelessness, bias or distortion through either emphasis or omission.

Errors, whether made by the reporter, editor or source, shall be acknowledged. When an error has been made, it shall be acknowledged in a straightforward correction, not disguised or glossed over in a follow-up story. Corrections and clarifications shall appear in a consistent location.

Associated Press Managing Editors

The newspaper should guard against inaccuracies, carelessness, bias or distortion through either emphasis or omission.

It should admit all substantive errors and correct them promptly and prominently.

Beaumont* (Texas) *Enterprise

The readers must be able to assume that what we give them in the news columns is the clear, unembellished truth as best we can determine it. Although we should strive always to present the news to the readers in terms that show them the impact of the news on their lives, we should not attempt to do their thinking for them or reach conclusions for them unless we label it as opinion or analysis.

Every *Enterprise* reporter and photographer should be able to answer yes to the six-question checklist for accuracy and fairness:

1. Are my facts straight? Have I checked them and double-checked them?
2. Do I have it all? Are my facts thorough, and am I presenting them in context?
3. Are the facts in balance? Have I given everyone who could be affected by this story a chance to comment or explained to the readers why I was unable to do so?
4. Do the readers have a legitimate right, need or desire to know this information? Is this even worth a story? Are the readers' tax dollars involved? Are their health and safety at issue?
5. Have I told this story in sufficient depth to relate it in understandable terms to the reader's interests in that information? Do the readers realize what it means to them and why I'm bringing it to them?
6. Have I given this story length and display in keeping with its importance, and have I presented it with dignity and professionalism?

Columbus* (Ga.) *Ledger-Enquirer

Accuracy

These newspapers make every reasonable effort to guard against inaccuracies, carelessness, bias or distortion, by commission or omission.

When substantive errors or distortions do appear in our papers, we admit and correct them voluntarily, promptly and with a prominence comparable to that given the inaccurate statement or statements.

Integrity

Our newspapers strive for impartial treatment of issues and dispassionate handling of controversial subjects. We provide forums for exchange of comment and criticism, especially when such comment is opposed to our editorial positions. Editorials and other expressions of the writer's opinion and judgment are clearly labeled or identified as such for the reader.

When reporters write personal columns or news analyses, they refrain from expressing opinions about persons and issues they cover in news stories.

Our newspapers report the news without regard for our own interest. We do not give favored news treatment to advertisers or special-interest groups. We report matters regarding ourselves and our staff and families with the same standards we apply to other institutions and individuals.

We do not use the paper to push our personal agendas or solve personal problems. Nor do we use our special access to the newspaper to benefit friends, relatives or associates. We identify ourselves and our organization to those from whom we are gathering information for publication. We do not plagiarize.

Honolulu Advertiser

Accuracy in reporting the news is the mark of a professional. It is a standard of excellence toward which we must always strive.

1. Every effort will be made to avoid errors or inaccuracies. There is no excuse for failure to check a fact or allegation.

2. Our headlines and pictures should accurately reflect the stories they accompany or represent.

3. Mistakes should be corrected promptly and candidly. It is impossible to avoid all errors; it is easy to correct errors. In making the correction, we must not be reluctant to admit we erred.

Orange County* (Calif.) *Register

Accuracy, fairness, integrity, impartiality—these are of paramount importance in reporting the news. These are the marks of any credible news story, the cement of any lasting trust between journalist and reader. Hence, the following guidelines:

1. Every story should be free of errors or inaccuracies. Every reasonable attempt should be made to check a fact or allegation before publication of a story.

2. Headlines and graphics should accurately reflect the stories they accompany or represent.

3. Mistakes of substance will be corrected speedily and sincerely. When they appear in the *Register*'s pages we will unhesitatingly admit our inexactness or wrongness and respond in an appropriate manner.

4. Any person or group whose reputation is attacked should expect a reasonable attempt at simultaneous or prompt rebuttal.

5. In news stories of controversy, all pertinent viewpoints should be presented.

6. Sources of quotations should be attributed except in cases when the reason for concealing the identity of sources is clear in the story or when concealment is otherwise innocuous.

7. If during the reporting of a news story it becomes necessary for the newspaper to promise confidentiality to a source, that promise will be kept.

8. Articles of opinion and analysis shall be clearly identified as such. The publisher's opinions shall be confined to the editorial page except under extraordinary circumstances. Advertisements shall be clearly discernible from editorial copy.

9. The *Register's* management and staff shall be committed to the truth uncorrupted by special interest.

Scripps Howard Newspapers Inc.

It is essential that each of us maintains the highest standards of conduct as we go about the business of informing the public with accuracy, truth and fairness, and without suspicion that any of us does what he or she does for personal gain.

Washington* (D.C.) *Post

This newspaper is pledged to minimize the number of errors we make and to correct those that occur. Accuracy is our goal; candor is our defense. Persons who call errors to our attention must be accorded a respectful hearing.

All China Journalists' Association

Journalists are not allowed to cover and issue news from the considerations of the interests of the individuals or small groups, not allowed to take advantage of the public opinion tool held in their hands to vent personal spites, or make biased reports.

Journalists should implement the guiding principle of "letting a hundred flowers blossom and a hundred schools of thought contend," respect science and stress practice, and never pass willful judgments or take arbitrary side.

Norfolk (Va.) *Virginian-Pilot*

A number of techniques commonly used in fiction writing must be avoided. Among them:

- The telescoping of time so that, for example, events that actually happened during several days are reported as happening in an single day.
- Vivid description of scenes that the writer could have not seen or had specific knowledge of.
- Passages conveying that the reporter knew what an individual was thinking or feeling without having been told.

Obscenity

What the Codes Say

Philadelphia Inquirer

Our policy on the use of profanity, obscenity and blasphemy is based on the premise that the *Inquirer* should appeal to the widest possible audience. Unlike movies, whose rating system warns potential viewers of the kind of language they will be exposed to, newspapers should offer a G-rated product every day. It is true, of course, that society's attitudes are changing and that we now freely use some language that a few years ago was thought to be too frank. Still, there is a danger of being more tolerant than our audience as a whole; we should carefully monitor the use of profanity, obscenity and blasphemy and restrict it to extraordinary circumstances.

Central to any decision is this question: Is an important journalistic purpose served by the use of the questionable language? The harsher the language, the more important and serious our purpose must be. This means that we have to refrain from publishing some quotations that we ourselves would find funny; in the interest of simply entertaining our readers, we should not resort to language that might offend many of them.

This is an area in which only the broadest sort of guidelines can apply. A word or phrase that may be used in one context may be entirely objectionable in another. When in doubt about whether any language is appropriate, ask for guidance. The practice of referring those decisions helps maintain uniform standards throughout the paper. The following guidelines are intended to help editors make decisions in this area.

The use of any questionable language is almost exclusively limited to quoted material. It should be rare indeed that our own writers employ it.

Generally, if a news subject utters profanity, obscenity or blasphemy when no one is present but one or two reporters, we will not use it. The decision becomes more difficult when the number of listeners is larger and the personage of the speaker more important. When President Carter said in public of a potential campaign opponent, "I'll whip his ass," that was deemed to be a situation in which the verbatim quotation was justified.

Sometimes language that is not in itself profane, obscene or blasphemous might be objectionable on the ground of taste. On the other hand, we should not hesitate to write in clinical terms on matters pertaining to human anatomy, sex and excretory functions when relevant to the news.

In most cases, when language is deleted from a quotation, an ellipsis will be inserted to indicate that something is missing. Occasionally—and on approval of a ranking editor—it is permissible to suggest the word or phrase by using the first letter of the word followed by an em dash. The use of "bleep" and "bleeping" as substitutes for profanity is restricted to the sports pages. Most decisions concerning the use of questionable language should be resolved by departmental editors and copy-chiefs. These line editors may determine when circumstances warrant the use of expletives such as "hell" and "damn." Line editors may also authorize the use of such terms as "goddamn," "son of a bitch" and "bastard" when the speaker is a reasonably important person, the audience is a fairly substantial one, or the quotation is in a long, serious piece in a section of the paper such as "Review and Opinion" or "Inquirer Magazine." When the circumstances are not clear-cut, or if stronger language or a question of taste is involved, the executive editor or managing editor must be consulted. In the absence of these editors, the editor in charge must be consulted. Hard-core obscenities such as "shit," "fuck," "piss," "cocksucker," "motherfucker" and their variations may be used only by express approval of the executive editor or the managing editor.

Detroit Free Press

Our guiding standard is whether an important journalistic purpose is served by using objectionable language. The harsher the language, the more

Move Something: Testing the *Inquirer* Policy

The *Philadelphia Inquirer's* stand on publishing obscenity was tested in 1985. A group of radical black activists who referred to themselves as "MOVE" was engaged in a continuing confrontation with Philadelphia city officials. In the heat of the rhetoric, Ramona Africa, minister of communications for MOVE, sent the following letter to Mayor Wilson Goode. The letter was reprinted, in a photocopied form rather than being typeset, in the *Philadelphia Inquirer* on May 20, 1985, p. 11.

> *Any body who think they gone jump on MOVE, wipe us out and leave an example of a well organized plan is out they god damn mind. When you come here it aint gone be swift and clean it's gone be a mess. MOVE gone see to that .... If MOVE go down, no only will everybody in this block go down, the knee joints of America will soon fall and we mean it .... Before we let you muthafuckas make an example of us we will burn this muthafuckin house down and burn you up with us.*

The war of words escalated. Police dropped an incendiary device on MOVE headquarters. The MOVE house and five dozen surrounding houses were consumed by fire. Eleven MOVE members died, including five children under the age of 12, and 250 residents were left homeless.

important our purpose should be. Only the broadest sort of guidelines can apply; a word or phrase that is newsworthy in one context may be entirely objectionable in another. The use of any obscene or tasteless language is limited to quoted material. The speaker and the audience are of primary importance in determining whether any obscenity will be reported. Generally, when an obscenity is deleted in a quotation, hyphens will stand for all but the first letter. Harsh obscenities may be used only with approval of a managing editor. See the *Free Press* style guide for more details.

Grand Forks* (N.D.) *Herald

We won't publish potentially offensive language merely for its shock value. We will publish profanities and obscenities, almost always in direct quotation, when their use is essential to the point, tone or mood of a significant story.

Washington* (D.C.) *Post

The *Washington Post* as a newspaper respects taste and decency, understanding that society's concepts of taste and decency are constantly changing. A word offensive to the last generation can be part of the next generation's common vocabulary. But we shall avoid prurience. We shall avoid profanities and obscenities unless their use is so essential to a story of significance that its meaning is lost without them. In no case shall obscenities be used without the approval of the executive editor or the managing editor or his deputy.

St. Paul* (Minn.) *Pioneer Press

We are a family newspaper and will not use four-letter words, profanity or obscenities if they can be avoided. Ask yourself, is it in good taste to use the word? If the answer is no, then ask yourself, is it essential to the story to use it? Often we can "tell it like it is" without hitting our readers with every four-letter word uttered or written by those in the news. If the word is essential—its elimination would make the story meaningless or distort its significance—use the first letter of the word and dashes to indicate the rest. Exceptions: goddamn, crap, ass, bastard can be used in full if the above criteria are met. Make it s.o.b. Final decision on whether to use such terms and, if so, in what form, will be made by the city editor in local copy and the news editor in wire copy, both in consultation with the managing editor. Business editors will consult the executive business editor; sports editors will consult the executive sports editor.

Chapter Five

Conflicts of Interest

The success of a free press is reflected in the ability of journalism to honor a primary loyalty to the public. Journalistic principles of truthtelling and independence work together to honor that loyalty. In order to seek truth and report it as fully as possible, journalists must be independent.

Journalists must remain free of associations and activities that may compromise their integrity or damage their own or their organizations' credibility. (Don't forget: Credibility is what others think of us; ethics is what kind of people we actually are. One is image, the other substance.) Journalists must seek out competing perspectives without being unduly influenced by those who would use their power or position counter to the public interest.

Conflicts of interest occur when individuals face competing loyalties to a source or to their own self-interest, or to their organization's economic needs as opposed to the information needs of the public.

Journalism carries a terrific responsibility in our society, for no other profession does what journalism does. No other individuals have the primary and constitutionally protected role of regularly informing and educating the public in a meaningful way on significant issues. To abdicate that responsibility, to put awards or friendships or self-interest or economic gain ahead of public benefit is unacceptable and unethical.

Editors and reporters in small towns face particularly difficult challenges because of the unique nature of their personal and professional loyalties. They are far more likely than their metropolitan colleagues to be tugged by ties of friendship with sources, commitments to local institutions, and the simple fact that they come face to face with their readers on a daily basis. In rural communities, there tends to be a vacuum in leadership, which often impels communities to draft all competent and willing citizens—including journalists. And the readers have a proprietary interest in the newspaper (not legal, but social). In this setting the journalist may have a responsibility to be a part of the community and may behave in ways that would be a conflict of interest in a larger community.

The cases in this section, while not reflecting the full range of potential conflicts-of-interest issues, raise essential questions about obligations and competing loyalties. The accompanying excerpts from codes of ethics provide specific guidelines various news organizations use to guard against conflicts and to ensure journalistic independence. More than half of all the sections in all the news media codes reviewed for this project were devoted to conflicts of interest, and we offer a generous sampling of that soul-searching.

Conflicts of Interest

Checklist

- Because of the enormous responsibility journalists have to the public, they must be aware of any situations that create a real or perceived conflict of interest. Individual journalists must weigh their obligations against the impact of:
    - involvement in particular activities
    - affiliation with causes or organizations
    - acceptance of favors or preferential treatment
    - financial investments
    - outside employment
    - friendships

- Newspapers and broadcasters play a dual role in a community, as journalists and as corporate citizens. While these roles are not mutually exclusive, media leaders must guard with vigilance their organizations' stewardship role in society. They must also insure that their primary obligation to the public is not eroded by other legitimate goals, such as:
    - a quest for economic gain
    - the interest of being a good corporate citizen
    - the concern for their own employees
    - the desire to be competitive in the marketplace

- In the end, individual journalists might do well to ask themselves:
    - Am I being independent?
    - Could my action harm my integrity or my organization's integrity?
    - Is the mere appearance of a conflict enough to diminish my credibility?
    - Am I willing to publicly disclose any potential conflicts?

Case Study #12

Journalists Supporting Politicians

Summary

A Detroit television anchor contributes $2,600 to Republicans. A New York TV anchor gives $1,000 to Steve Forbes during the 1996 presidential campaign. And a Texas television anchor acts as master of ceremonies for a gubernatorial candidate during a campaign swing through the state.

Journalists who contribute to political candidates have come under fire in recent years. Critics charge that journalists who support politicians are jeopardizing their credibility by taking a public position. Voters and opposing political candidates question whether such journalists can remain fair in their reporting.

Journalists who contribute to politicians say what they do in their private time is nobody's business but their own. They insist they can contribute to one side in a political race and remain fair to both candidates.

During the 1994 Texas governor's race between Ann Richards and George W. Bush, news anchor Mike Snyder of KXAS in Dallas acted as master of ceremonies during rallies for Bush at several campaign stops. Snyder often introduced Bush as "the next governor of Texas."

Two weeks before the election, which Bush eventually won, the Richards campaign questioned the use of Snyder as master of ceremonies at Bush functions. A competing Dallas TV station reported the story, which was picked up by the Associated Press and several Texas newspapers. KXAS executives yanked Snyder off the air (with pay) while conducting an investigation. In interviews, Snyder said since he's an anchor who doesn't actively report on campaign issues, he should be allowed to do as he pleases during his time off. Snyder also said the Bush campaign never paid him for his work. He was a volunteer.

The same year, a Detroit television news anchor gave more than his time to Michigan politicians; he gave his money: $2,600 in campaign contributions. WJBK news anchor Rich Fisher, who moderated a gubernatorial debate for the station and reported on politics, paid $1,100 to the National Republican Senatorial Committee and $1,000 to the Michigan Republican Party. He also contributed a $500 gift to the campaign of U.S. Senate candidate Spencer Agraham.

Fisher told the *Detroit Free Press* that his political beliefs never affected his reporting. "I go out of my way to be fair," Fisher said. "What I choose to do in my private life should remain private. The fact that I anchor television news does not mean I shouldn't have a private life. I'm a taxpayer. I'm a citizen. I vote."

WJBK's news director, Mort Meisner, defended his anchor. "Rich reports the news fairly," Meisner told the *Free Press.* "His reputation is 100 percent beyond reproach. He has a lot of integrity."

In a similar case, Chuck Scarborough, news anchor for WNBC in New York, wrote a $1,000 check to the Steve Forbes campaign in 1995. Forbes, who was seeking the Republican nomination for president, made Scarborough's contribution public when he filed his contribution list with the Federal Election Commission. The Associated Press reported it.

Embarrassed by the revelation, WNBC announced that as long as Forbes remained a candidate, Scarborough would not be allowed to report on the presidential race. Newspapers later reported that Scarborough also had given money to the Bob Dole campaign. WNBC released a statement saying Scarborough had acknowledged an "error in judgment." The station extended his presidential-race-reporting ban for the rest of the campaign. He remained news anchor.

Analysis

This case demonstrates both the importance of the principle of independence and the thorny nature of conflicts of interest. The television news anchors in Detroit, New York and Dallas were forced to choose between competing loyalties: to the politicians they supported, or to the public they serve in their role as journalists.

The principle of independence calls on journalists to remain free of associations or activities that may compromise their integrity or damage their credibility. It is essential for individual journalists and news organizations to honor that principle if they are to be effective in fulfilling the primary obligation of journalism: seeking truth and reporting it as fully as possible.

The involvement of the news anchors seems especially problematic in this case, given their high visibility in their communities and their prominent role in presenting the news.

While the respective controversies focused on the actions of the journalists, the management of the television news stations must also accept responsibility for how this situation developed. Did the stations have reasonable policies addressing this issue? Did the management of the stations remain vigilant to the potential conflict of interest? Were station managements really willing to take action to resolve the conflicts, or were their actions merely "brushfire" responses forced by the revelation of the conflicts in newspaper stories? Finally, were the stations open and honest in disclosing to the public the nature of the problem and the stations' resolutions to the problem; that is, how ethically did they meet the test of accountability?

These cases speak to the importance of news organizations' having a clear standard regarding political involvement or activism on community issues. Such a standard could be extended to involvement in controversial public policy issues, such as abortion, nuclear power or civil rights.

News managers should not expect that every member of their staff naturally understands the news organization's position on conflicts, nor should there be an assumption that all journalists share the same personal position on such ethical matters.

News managers should not expect that every member of their staff naturally understands the news organization's position on conflicts, nor should there be an assumption that all journalists share the same personal position on such ethical matters. Some journalists may feel so passionately about a particular issue that they feel they **must** become involved.

The reality is that journalism would not function well in our society if journalists were to easily cast aside their role as independent observers and recorders of events.

Independence is an essential principle for journalists, part of the foundation upon which fairness rests. The obligation of journalists to remain free of associations and activities that may compromise their integrity or damage credibility is not to be taken lightly.

Any decision by a journalist to become involved in an activity that could lead to such compromise should weigh potential consequences, including the individual's being reassigned or eventually even leaving the news organization. Ideally, reporters and editors should discuss such potential conflicts as early as possible in the decision making process. **Front end** thinking allows for more collaboration, provides the time for more alternatives to be considered, and minimizes the likelihood of crisis management and serious impact on individuals and the organization.

Cases like these serve as good examples of how important it is for journalists to consider both the short- and long-term implications of their actions.

Case Study #13

To Love and Work in Denver

Summary

When reporter Lesley Dahlkemper and Mike Feeley, a state senator from a Denver suburb, started dating in the early 1990s, she gave up covering politics for Colorado Public Radio in favor of covering education, hoping to pre-empt potential conflicts of interest. But when Feeley decided in 1997 to run for governor and the couple decided to marry, Dahlkemper—a widely respected eight-year veteran at KCFR—soon found herself out of a job.

That unpleasant resolution resulted after months of debate and hand wringing at KCFR. Initially, Dahlkemper and station news director Kelley Griffin said, the talk had been tentative and hypothetical. "For a year and a half, the subject was broached, batted around, but never seriously discussed," Dahlkemper said. Although discussions preceded Griffin's appointment as news director, "I would say the station didn't walk it all the way through," Griffin said. "We've never said, 'If you were this, then this.' I did find in an old file folder, on yellowed paper, our ethics policy. It was actually pretty sound, but it had not been distributed for some time."

The situation escalated in May 1997 when Feeley officially announced he would explore a run at the governorship. The press release announcing that decision also mentioned he would marry Dahlkemper, whom the release identified as a Colorado Public Radio reporter, May 25.

The dividing line in the issue, first blurry, became clearer: The station believed Dahlkemper could not continue to cover the news without creating at least the appearance of conflict of interest; she did not believe her credibility could be compromised. "I had stated clearly that I would have no role in his campaign—which made his political consultants nuts," Dahlkemper said.

While seeking expert advice from media ethicists and researching examples of similar situations at other media outlets, Griffin sought to balance the station's desire to retain Dahlkemper while not appearing to compromise the news staff, which comprised three full-time reporters, two hosts, a news researcher and a news director.

"I started talking to people about what this would mean to the newsroom," Griffin said. "Nobody said it wouldn't matter at all. Some people would say she could cover some things—but would (her reporting) work covering some things and not others? And with our staff size, could we afford that?

"The political reporter already was ... talking to all the prospective candidates, and we felt we could easily be charged with favoring one candidate, or ignoring something to overcompensate, or saying something negative about another candidate."

While Dahlkemper was preparing to return to work after her wedding, the station considered alternative roles for her and granted her time off to consider reassignment. One idea was to establish an arts beat and put Dahlkemper on it. "We thought about adding it," Griffin said, "but again, one of the issues here is a tax for funding the arts."

The perception of a conflict of interest was a nagging issue that wouldn't go away. "There was this whole question of, 'What if the *Denver Post* ran a big story about (Feeley's) campaign? Why didn't Colorado Public Radio do that?'" Griffin said.

"And there is much more to behaving ethically than merely avoiding conflicts of interest. There's hard work, respect, objectivity, fairness, compassion, thoroughness, a healthy skepticism."
—Fred Brown

And so, "we determined we would create a position outside the newsroom for the duration of the campaign," Griffin said. The job might have entailed fund-raising, a music research project, producing prototype programs, "even doing some outside reporting for National Public Radio," Griffin said.

Dahlkemper held fast to her conviction that "there was no direct conflict, no immediate impact," and resigned rather than accept reassignment, which, she felt, would have meant admitting that her professional credibility could be compromised by her marriage to a possible gubernatorial candidate.

"What became lost in the mix was the station's reputation and my track record for integrity," Dahlkemper said. She wanted the opportunity, at least, to prove her impartiality through her performance.

Two local newspaper columnists at least partly agreed with her after her resignation.

The *Denver Post*'s Fred Brown, incoming national president of the Society of Professional Journalists and former chair of its ethics committee, wrote: "... performance is more important than perception. And there is much more to behaving ethically than merely avoiding conflicts of interest. There's hard work, respect, objectivity, fairness, compassion, thoroughness, a healthy skepticism. Dahlkemper didn't lose those qualities when she became Mrs. Candidate."

Sue O'Brien of the *Post* wrote: "Why not see if common-sense guidelines could work? Share the problem with KCFR listeners—probably one of the most thoughtful and articulate groups of media consumers anywhere—and let them make their own judgments about spin."

The news director and her reporter still disagree over two key points: a possible distinction between a conflict of interest and the appearance of such conflict, and whether KCFR ultimately chose the best option when it lost a solid journalist.

"Appearance can undermine your credibility," Griffin said. "We rely on public perception that we don't have anything more to do than to report the truth."

Said Dahlkemper: "I think the perception of conflict of interest became all-consuming."

Griffin: "Part of what we were trying to do, in doing things ethically, was to be sure we've built the proper walls the proper height. And if we removed her from the newsroom, that would show we had done what we could."

Dahlkemper: "The question remains, can a reporter continue as a reporter if her spouse is elected to political office? I had hoped Colorado Public Radio would've broken new ground on this."

Today, Colorado Public Radio has a new written ethics code that is being distributed to staffers. Griffin said she also was considering having staffers sign a form consenting to the code.

"In creating the policy and talking about it, we created a climate where people understand that you have to tread lightly and you have to disclose," Griffin said. "It's the framework that reporters need to bring to everything. To have people think of it whenever the potential arises.

"In Lesley's case, the conflict issue was there even before the marriage, during her relationship with Mike Feeley. I don't think we looked hard enough at that."

Analysis

It is true, as the *Denver Post's* Fred Brown argued, that KCFR reporter Lesley Dahlkemper did not lose her journalistic skills or her ethical principles by getting married to a politician. Yet that action clearly raised complications for her public radio station. The equation was changed and the status quo was not acceptable.

To be sure, Dahlkemper had a personal right to begin a relationship with and eventually marry Feeley. However, KCFR had a clear responsibility to protect the credibility of the station's news operation. Management believed that credibility might be eroded if listeners, politicians or citizens questioned the station's ability to fairly and meaningfully cover Feeley's political activities or other political issues.

To her credit, news director Kelley Griffin searched hard for alternative resolutions to this ethical challenge. She sought outside expertise. She weighed how other news organizations dealt with similar cases. Griffin considered a range of resolutions, while recognizing the potential conflicts with each possibility.

While a news manager certainly owes some loyalty to employees, the primary loyalty goes to the public. That should be reversed only in exceptional cases.

A thoughtful and principled news manager searches for win-win solutions, and that is what Griffin was attempting in keeping Dahlkemper employed at KCFR while removing her from journalistic situations where she and the station faced clear conflict. Dahlkemper was sincere in her belief that her journalistic standards would not be compromised because of marriage to Feeley. However, that position is basically indefensible. It is impossible to prove a negative. Dahlkemper cannot prove that her personal life would not improperly influence her journalistic work. No matter her intentions, she could not *prove* that she might not bend too far one way or another in her reporting on issues that might involve her politician husband. She could not *prove* that her choice of sources, her angle on stories, her tone of delivery was fair. And she could not prove that her reporting was fair when some people might believe her conflict was irreconcilable.

In some cases where a journalist clearly has a conflict of the nature of Dahlkemper's, the news organization has a large enough news staff to shuffle people around to eliminate conflict, protect the individual's job and still meaningfully cover the news. At a small station like KCFR that did not seem possible.

The station offered Dahlkemper a reasonable, short-term solution to the conflict by moving her away from news coverage. That approach was imperfect, but it kept Dahlkemper at the station, allowed for another reporter to cover political issues, and kept open the process of creating a different solution after the campaign, including returning Dahlkemper to the news staff.

In these cases the news organization must show respect for employees and do everything possible to resolve ethical dilemmas fairly. Sometimes that involves a parting of the ways. In a profession where journalists necessarily point the finger of conflict of interest at powerful people, a news organization must set a very high standard for itself to avoid its own conflicts, real or perceived.

Case Study #14

Checkbook Journalism

Summary

Each year there are 50,000 or so runaways in Florida. Few are newsworthy. Cheryl Ann Barnes may have been the exception.

Barnes, 17, lived with her grandparents in Bushnell, Fla. She was a senior at South Sumter High School, worked as a clerk at Evans Hardware and sang alto in the choir in the Pentecostal Potters House International Church in Wildwood, Fla. By all accounts, she was religiously devout.

Barnes' father and mother were separated in 1989 and later divorced. In December 1995, her father married an 18-year-old who was his daughter's classmate and, by some accounts, her best friend.

One morning the following month, Cheryl Barnes left home in her 1988 Mazda but didn't show up for school. After her grandparents alerted officials that the girl was missing, and the event received local print and broadcast attention, a spokesman for Sumter Sheriff's Office said, "It's 99.9 percent an abduction."

Four days later, given the lack of evidence (no car, no personal belongings, no reported sightings, no witnesses), Sheriff James L. "Jamie" Adams Jr. began to back away from his department's earlier assertion that Cheryl had been abducted. On TV, he pleaded with Cheryl to come home if she had run away.

The disappearance received intense regional and national attention, prompted largely by Cheryl's grandmother, who had "befriended" reporters at the Bushnell home and shared with them home videos of Cheryl singing in the church choir.

On January 18, 1996, Cheryl was found sitting in a snow drift in New York, disoriented and somewhat incoherent, wearing a bulletproof vest. She left police with the impression that she had been molested. She was taken to the psychiatric ward of a Manhattan hospital with amnesia, where she was labeled a 21-year-old Jane Doe.

Three weeks later, with Barnes still unidentified, WABC-TV in New York ran footage of Cheryl supplied by Tampa's ABC affiliate, WFTS-TV. A hospital nurse recognized Cheryl as the Jane Doe amnesia victim and notified authorities. The Barnes family was contacted in Bushnell, and Cheryl talked to the family by phone that evening. Tampa's WFTS broke the story on Wednesday night's news, after getting the scoop from New York ABC affiliate WABC.

Minutes after the news broke, news director Bob Jordan of Tampa's WFTS offered to charter a jet to fly the family to New York City, in exchange for 24

Cheryl comes home

Missing teen is regaining memory, but the mystery of her odyssey persists

Pieces of the puzzle are still missing

By JUSTIN BLUM, KELLY RYAN and DAVID BALLINGRUD
Times Staff Writers

She left, it is now thought, quietly and with forethought.

She returned five weeks later, bewildered and confused, embraced by a tearful family and a relieved town, besieged by a media horde of O. J. Simpson-like proportions.

"I wasn't sure at all that I had any friends left, but I was amazed when I got here to see you all," she said, standing on a porch table under the floodlights of television trucks at her grandparents' home near Bushnell. "For so long, I thought there was nobody," she said, her hands shaking.

Cheryl Ann Barnes is home. But there are as many questions as answers about the journey of a 17-year-old girl who turned up in a New York snowbank, wearing a bulletproof vest and saying she knew neither her name nor her past.

■ Her grandmother, Shirley Barnes, said she still thinks Cheryl was abducted. Investigators say she ran away. She says she does not remember.

If she did run, why?

■ Sumter County sheriff's officials said Thursday they are investigating statements Cheryl made suggesting sexual abuse in the family by her father, William Barnes Jr.

Barnes vigorously denied Cheryl was abused.

"I love my daughter, but not that way," he said. "It's not true."

■ Sumter County Sheriff Jamie Adams and Bushnell police Chief Eddie Lovett described Cheryl's journal entries as proof that the deeply religious girl ran away from home.

"They said all along they thought the key was in those journal entries," sheriff's spokesman Gary Brannen said.

Please see **CHERYL** 11A

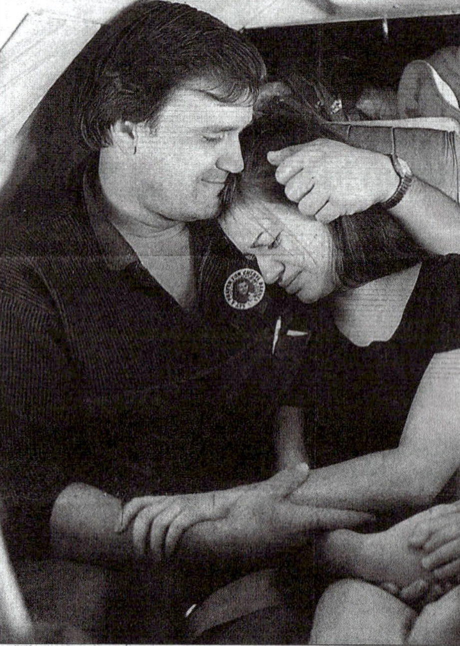

Times photo — BILL SERNE

Cheryl Barnes sits with her dad, William Barnes Jr., during the plane ride Thursday from New York to Tampa. Parts of her memory are returning. She recognized her dad when she saw him in the hospital.

■ Officials look to entries in Cheryl Ann Barnes' journal for clues to her disappearance. **Excerpts, 10A**

■ The media play a big part in the family's reunion. Did they sidestep ethics? **10A**

Friends, family prepare welcome

By KELLY RYAN and ANDREW GALARNEAU
Times Staff Writers

Across Sumter County, residents rejoiced Thursday that five weeks of terror had ended happily with Cheryl Ann Barnes' return home.

Her classmates at South Sumter High led the charge, quickly assembling a blue banner bearing seniors' signatures to hang outside her house to welcome her. They packaged heart-shaped cookies, delivered flowers and constructed a wreath of angels for 17-year-old Cheryl.

"They are just glad to have her back," said senior class adviser Karen Cloud, who teaches Cheryl. "They don't really care what happened. You can't describe the happiness — I feel like my prayers have been answered."

Cheryl returned to her grandparents' house, where she lived, after 6 p.m. Thursday to a crowd that cheered and clapped to see her in person. Some held signs saying, "Sumter County loves you."

The bittersweet reunion begins to bring closure to a case that has gripped this close-knit community since Cheryl disappeared outside a bank Jan. 3.

Sumter authorities are saying Cheryl ran away in a case that ended in New York when a nurse saw her picture on the news and recognized her as an amnesia patient. Cheryl began to remember her friends and family Thursday night as she saw them at her house, but her family said she still has a long way to go.

Throughout Sumter County, few were concerned with getting answers to their questions right away.

"It really doesn't matter to me," said senior Beth McLauchlan, who has known

Please see **FRIENDS** 11A

Times photo — ROBERT ROGERS

Cheryl Barnes is surrounded as she returns home Thursday night. The teenager was smiling and happy until the cameras went on.

Lost in the media frenzy: ethics, compassion

hours of exclusive rights to the story. Cheryl's grandmother reportedly turned down the offer, saying it wouldn't be fair to the other television stations.

Tampa Bay media organized a Lear Jet to fly the Barnes family to New York City late Wednesday after it appeared there would be no commercial jet with available seats from Tampa to New York until Thursday evening. The Lear Jet was chartered, at a cost of $8,314, by Daniel Webster, news director of the Tampa Fox affiliate, WTVT-TV. The local TV stations arranged to pool coverage and money for the event, including the family's New York hotel (Grand Hyatt) and limousine transportation. The *St. Petersburg Times* and *Tampa Tribune*, having learned the Barnes family would be on the chartered jet, arranged to pay for one seat apiece but were not to join in the reporting pool. Departure of the family from the Tampa airport was delayed for up to a half hour to provide dramatic video for the 10 p.m. Wednesday newscast on WTVT. (Other local newscasts are at 11 p.m.)

At the hospital, Barnes appeared to be partially recovering from her amnesia and recognized her father and grandmother.

The reunited family and the Florida journalists returned to the Tampa airport in the chartered jet the next day, strategically just in time for the opening of the local evening news. The Fox station (WTVT) flew the family from the Tampa airport to an immense community homecoming in Bushnell on its own helicopter, an event covered live on WTVT by another helicopter.

Allegations of sexual abuse by Cheryl's father surfaced from comments made by some of her friends and reportedly from her older sister and from statements Cheryl had made to a minister she had met while on the road in January. The abuses reportedly had occurred eight or nine years earlier, but were denied by Cheryl's father, William Barnes Jr., at several points during the media feeding frenzy in New York, Tampa and Bushnell.

William Barnes, saying he and his current wife were unemployed and in need of money to pay for his daughter's hospital stay and ongoing medical care, said he was negotiating with national television talk shows for the Cheryl Barnes story. "If there is some money or some benefit to come out of this, we'll take it," Barnes told reporters, adding that he would allow his daughter to be interviewed only if the program could be sensitive to her needs and offer her psychological help. (At about this same time the sheriff's department released pages from Cheryl's diary to the media, which duly printed and broadcast some of the sections that revealed her emotional struggles.)

Several days later, William Barnes appeared on the *Montel Williams Show*. Cheryl Barnes did not. The show was titled, "They're Saying My Daughter Ran Away Because I Abused Her."

Analysis

This case is titled "Checkbook Journalism," but it is much more complex and compelling than that. The case could have come under any number of journalism ethics labels, and in any number of places in this book:

- Feeding frenzy and the loss of journalism independence.
- Costs and rewards of beating up a story for sweeps weeks.
- The perils of getting too close to your sources (symbiotic journalism?).
- What happens when a little-girl-lost family morality tale turns sour.

The following analysis considers all of the above issues.

The story, which took up a disproportionate amount of time and space in the Tampa Bay news media, enjoyed a short shelf life. Media critics noted that the story was made to order for the February sweeps, but that once Cheryl returned home and rejoined her church choir, and her father's questionable behaviors had been duly noted, the story died a natural death. The mere fact that the story dropped off the radar screen after having dominated local media for more than a month may indicate that there appeared to be little intrinsic value to the events and the people in question—at least in the minds of the journalists.

The mere fact that the story dropped off the radar screen after having dominated local media for more than a month may indicate that there appeared to be little intrinsic value to the events and the people in question—at least in the minds of the journalists.

The police and sheriff's departments in Cheryl's hometown initially told the media her disappearance was almost certainly an abduction. Among the reasons they offered for reaching this conclusion was that Cheryl "didn't fit the profile" of the typical runaway: She was a "deeply religious girl" who "wouldn't put her family through such pain." Yet there were indications to the contrary—indications that, the media learned later, convinced some officers from the start that she had left home voluntarily. These indications included some information available only to official investigators—her journal entries, for example—but some that was available and even known to the media.

Did the media ask enough questions? Should reporters have pressed for further insight from police and deputies as to why they believed someone had abducted Cheryl? Would more research, by computer or old-fashioned library work, have produced more informed skepticism on the part of those covering the story? Were they too accepting of the official account because it made for a more compelling story?

What if police had said there was a good chance Cheryl was a runaway? Most news organizations don't routinely cover such cases. (The most common reasons are that there are too many and that coverage sometimes encourages other kids looking for attention to mimic the behavior of runaways whose stories they see in the news.) Is that a good practice? Teenagers run away far more often than they are kidnapped. The issue of runaways affects far more families than abduction does. Did the media take the opportunity to examine

Family and media shaped outcome of Cheryl's story

■ It was a story made for headlines and broadcasts, and the missing girl's family and authorities helped feed reporters' interest.

By ANDREW Z. GALARNEAU
Times Staff Writer

Thousands of times each year, a distraught parent calls the police.

Another troubled Florida teenager is missing.

The police dutifully log in the statistic, but can do little more. Another runaway. More than 50,000 last year alone.

So when Cheryl Ann Barnes' loved ones called her discovery last week in a Manhattan psychiatric ward "a miracle", in a way, they may be right.

We now know that when the 17-year-old senior didn't make it to South Sumter High School on Jan. 3, all the images the first news reports conjured up — the simple, safe small town besieged by an abduction and evil — were apparently not accurate.

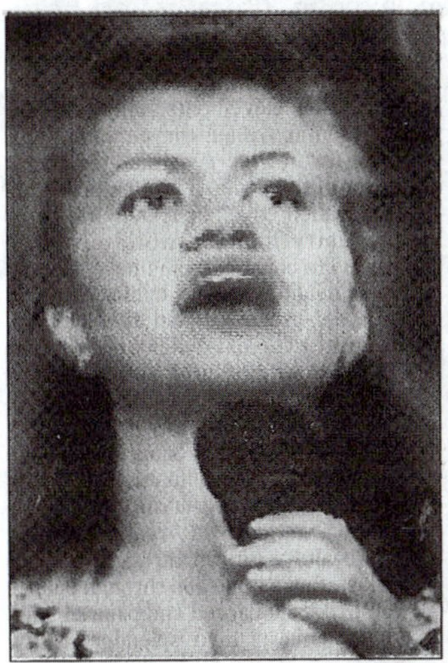

Times files

The Barneses showed reporters a video of Cheryl performing in church.

the problem, its causes, warning signs and ways to prevent or deal with such situations?

Several suggestions have surfaced as possible explanations for Cheryl's leaving home. Clearly, her family situation was neither typical nor ideal. One particularly titillating detail was her father's marriage, just a month before Cheryl's disappearance, to an 18-year-old from Cheryl's school. Did the media treat that element of the story appropriately? Was it a legitimate part of the story at all?

How about the reports that Cheryl's father might have molested her? Did or could anyone properly attribute the allegations? When did that become appropriate to report—if at all? How about her father's criminal record: his 1995 drunk-driving conviction and subsequent parole violation, and his 1980 conviction in Chicago for contributing to the sexual delinquency of a minor?

Should police have released Cheryl's journal entries? Does their releasing the material make it okay to publish or broadcast?

How important are the actions of the competition? Using the journal and the molestation allegations as examples: If one station or paper uses the material, does that make it okay for their competitors to do the same? After all, "it's out there ...."

How close should journalists get to their subjects? In the two or three days surrounding Cheryl's homecoming, TV reporters seemed to be positioning themselves as dear personal friends with whom the Barnes family had bonded in the weeks since Cheryl's disappearance. Was it posturing, or had the journalists been taken in, literally and figuratively, by the Barnes family since early January? Had the weeks of cozying up to the grandparents (using the Barnes home as a press headquarters, eating Grandmother Barnes's homemade treats, gaining access to home videos of Cheryl, falling prey to a small town's compassion for one of its missing children) cost journalists their independence and thus their capacity to critically analyze the story? Did compassion get the better of them? Was any of the on-air emotion artificial? Does it matter?

The plane! The plane!

Coverage pools are not uncommon on stories of such huge interest among the media. But this one came about in an unusual way: The night of her discovery in a New York hospital, WFTS offered to fly Cheryl's family to New York and back in a chartered jet at the station's expense in exchange for 24 hours of exclusive access to the family. The cost was more than $8,000. Is that an attempt to buy a story? Is it different from offering a news source actual money for a story? Or is it more like flying a guest in to appear on a talk show?

The Barnes family (growing more media savvy with each passing day) rejected WFTS's offer but accepted a proposal to make the trip by chartered jet once all five local TV stations got involved. WTVT provided a reporter and photojournalist to fly with the family and to provide tape to all five stations. Was it then a legitimate pool arrangement?

At least once on the round trip (and twice, by some accounts) WTVT delayed departure of the plane in order to cover its takeoff live on the station's newscast. New director Daniel Webster says it was a matter of only 10 minutes—though others claim it was more like half an hour—and he says it's not a decision he would necessarily make that way again. Should he have made it that way in the first place? Jets can make up that much time in the air, and the reunion happened sooner, because of the charter arrangement, than it would have had the family taken a commercial flight. What harm, if any, did the delay do?

Cheryl's return to Florida the next day dominated local newscasts. Some TV news managers even decided to interrupt regular programming to carry her airport arrival. How much coverage is too much? One local station, WFLA, an NBC affiliate, decided to move on to other stories significantly sooner than its competition, and WFLA had the day's highest ratings for the day's newscasts. But WFLA regularly wins the local news ratings race. WFTS, which seemed to have more coverage (at least in sheer volume of time) than anybody else, had the highest early-evening newscast ratings in its brief history. How much is too much?

The reunion and hours immediately following it were understandably tearful, but Cheryl seemed to compose herself each time she had a few private moments with her family. By several accounts, she lost her composure and nearly collapsed on a couple of occasions when the bright lights went on and the crush of media surrounded her. Did the crews covering her homecoming treat Cheryl with the consideration she deserved?

That homecoming also reunited some of Cheryl's feuding family members. Several media outlets carried accounts of a physical fight between Cheryl's mother, who had flown in from Arizona, and her grandmother, with whom Cheryl lives. That fight resulted in a 911 call. Was that legitimate news?

In the week following Cheryl's return home, the TV stations that had cooperated on coverage of her homecoming began to bicker—publicly, once the newspaper picked up on it. WTVT began running promotional spots claiming to have been "a step ahead of the competition" on the story with "exclusive" video its crew shot in New York. The other stations say that violated their agreement that anything the pool crew got would be available to all participants, and that there would be no claims of exclusivity. At least one of those other stations, WFLA, said on that basis that it would not pay its roughly $2,000 share of the trip's cost.

And at about the time the TV stations were turning on each other, Cheryl's father was entertaining offers for national publicity and—in some cases—money from TV talk shows. There was a rumor of a book deal, and Barnes said he frankly hoped the family could make some money off the story, because he had lost his job due to all the time he took off work while Cheryl was missing.

Is it possible the Barneses were manipulating the media? The police? Did they know more than they admitted?

Broadcast news pros told a class of journalism ethics students that, under deadline pressure and amidst heavy competition, they were forced to make crucial decisions in less than a minute. Some chided the students (who were critical of the choices made) for not having a sense of the "real world." In fact, aren't all such decisions made on the experiences of a lifetime, and not within a vacuum in a minute? Shouldn't journalists recognize that considerations of professional values/pressures/loyalties/principles/etc. provide the framework for decisions that only appear to be made in a minute? And shouldn't those journalists be able and willing to articulate such variables to satisfy the legitimate inquiries from students, viewers, news sources and other stakeholders?

—Other versions of this case were written by Scott Libin of The Poynter Institute and Jay Black for The Poynter Institute Web site and the *Journal of Mass Media Ethics* (Vol. 11, No. 2, pp. 119-128).

Case Study #15

A National Guard Trip

Summary

When, if ever, should a reporter accept a free trip in order to cover a story? Is that "junket journalism," or can it be a legitimate way to cover important events?

The Bangor *Daily News* bureau chief in Presque Isle, Maine, received an invitation to join employers and public officials who were flying to a National Guard training site in Gagetown, New Brunswick, nearly 200 miles away. Military issues are important in that region. There are 1,000 Guard members in Aroostook County in northernmost Maine, an area that has also been home to a bomber base targeted for closing.

The helicopter trip was sponsored annually by an organization whose sole purpose is to educate employers, public officials and the public about the National Guard. A Guard spokesman felt the trip would help foster understanding between employers and Guard members.

The bureau chief was interested in joining the group to talk to employers about the problems and benefits of having employees who are members of the Guard. She also was interested in seeing the training site in Gagetown, one of the largest training facilities in Canada.

There are no commercial flights between Presque Isle and Gagetown and no bus service. A chartered flight would cost about $1,000. Driving to and from the training site would take the better part of a day.

The newspaper contacted the representative of the group sponsoring the trip and asked if the paper could pay the reporter's way for the helicopter trip. The newspaper was told it couldn't pay.

The bureau chief consulted with her editors, and the decision was made to send her on the helicopter trip anyway, after determining what stories she would develop as a result of the trip.

Analysis

This is a case in which a news organization must weigh its actions according to the principles of truthtelling and independence. The journalists involved also must consider the consequences of their decisions, both short-term and long-term.

Some questions to raise when mulling over this type of dilemma:

• Can the newspaper fulfill its news-gathering and reporting responsibilities to the public if the paper is accepting a free trip from the people being covered? On the other hand, can the newspaper properly inform its readers about potentially important stories if their coverage is limited by economic or logistical reasons?

• How valuable is it for the community to understand, through the newspaper, the program that involves many of its citizens every summer? Is the story valuable enough that the paper should risk compromising its integrity or damaging its credibility by accepting the free trip?

• Where does the "free" stop? If the sponsoring group was also offering free meals to those who made the helicopter trip to the training site, should the newspaper accept those free meals?

• How would reasonable people respond to this dilemma? Would they agree that the benefit of coverage of the National Guardsmen outweighs the risk that a free trip might cause the reporter to unduly favor the National Guard in that or subsequent stories? Or that she might be overly critical in her reporting in an effort to prove her independence?

• What other alternatives might the newspaper have considered to cover the story while also recognizing economic concerns? Could the newspaper have used a freelance reporter? Could the story have been reported from Presque Isle without going on the free helicopter trip? Could the reporter have driven to the training camp, possibly reporting several stories on the trip to help justify the travel time involved?

Finally, when a decision has been reached, the news organization would do well to hold itself accountable, by sharing its decision making with its readers:

• What level of disclosure should the newspaper make when reporting the story? Should the story include specific mention that the reporter traveled at the expense of the sponsoring organization? Should an editor write a column explaining the decision making process the paper followed?

News organizations benefit from having clear guidelines on such issues as conflicts of interests, junkets and freebies. Such guidelines provide guideposts for making good decisions. Guidelines also provide standards for consistency, combating the tendency "to slide down the slippery slope" by taking every case as something new.

When it comes to junkets and freebies, is it harder for a small news organization to take the high road on ethics than it is for a larger organization?

Case Study #16

KQED and the Vintner

Summary

When executives and San Francisco public television station KQED announced to their board of directors that the station was planning a documentary on Napa Valley vintner Robert Mondavi, they never anticipated the uproar that would be ignited by the proposed program.

In a report, the board was told that the station hoped the documentary would air on PBS's "American Master's Series" and that a $50,000 research grant had been secured from the nonprofit American Center for Wine, Food and the Arts, a potential underwriter for the program as well.

The funding sounded fishy to KQED board member Sasha Futran, a part-time journalist who researched the American Center for Wine, Food and the Arts and discovered the center was primarily financed with a $6 million donation from Robert Mondavi and had close personnel ties to his winery. Mondavi was chairman of the center's board. The American Center's marketing director called Mondavi its "visionary." The center's executive director had previously been vice president of Robert Mondavi Winery.

Futran called the documentary "paid programming," adding, "Someone is paying for a documentary about themselves. This raises some very serious journalistic questions of ethical integrity."

Station executives defended the project. They said the documentary would focus on the growth of the wine industry, using "Mr. Mondavi as a frame of reference." They also said:

- the $50,000 was research money, not production money;
- the show itself would be cultural programming ("lifestyle and growth of the Napa Valley") and therefore didn't have to adhere to the stricter PBS standards for funding public affairs shows;
- the American Center had more than 100 benefactors in addition to Mondavi and was not a stand-in for the Mondavis;
- "neutral" contributors would be solicited for the remainder of the documentary's $600,000 cost.

Both the station and American Center told news reporters that KQED would retain total editorial control.

Faced with a barrage of unwelcome publicity, station executives eventually canceled the program and returned $50,000 to the American Center. The station president, however, defended the funding of the proposed document, saying, "Questions about the American Center's funding, raised publicly by a member of KQED's board of directors, created an inaccurate perception of conflict and have resulted in negative news coverage, damaging the project's viability."

A week later, the *San Francisco Chronicle*, citing numerous KQED internal documents, disclosed that the station's agreement with the American Center was the result of negotiations with marketing officials at Mondavi and that all preliminary correspondence to the station was on the letterhead of the Robert Mondavi Winery, not the American Center. The *Chronicle* also reported that KQED had pitched the documentary to the winery as a highly flattering portrayal of the vintner, titled "Robert Mondavi—A Profile."

PBS funding guidelines caution against problematic "connections between the funder's interest and the subject of the program." KQED sought the opinion of lawyers who echoed the station's assertion that "the Center was not given any of the indicia of editorial control or supervision which concerns PBS under its guidelines."

KQED's board later voted to adopt a short ethics policy described as a distillation of PBS guidelines. Critics said the new guidelines were vague and left the door open for the same kind of misjudgments that they said characterized the proposed Mondavi documentary.

Analysis

Conflict of interest, which involves seducing journalists from the object of their primary loyalties—their audience—has two flash points: the actual subverting of the message by the source and the appearance of luring the producer from that loyalty by the source.

In this case, it would appear a strong case could be made for the appearance of conflict, station protestations notwithstanding, because the money came from an entity that was an offspring of the industry from which the show's subject comes.

As more information became available, it appeared the conflict of interest was actual. It is difficult to foresee how the station, given terms of funding, could remain independent in the production. The cards, as so often happens, were stacked in favor of the funder, to the harm of a vulnerable audience relying on the producer's integrity.

The cards, as so often happens, were stacked in favor of the funder, to the harm of a vulnerable audience relying on the producer's integrity.

On the other hand, economic realities being what they are for public television stations, the lure of being able to shine the light on a seldom-seen industry, biased though it may be, or may be perceived to be, has some validity.

Yet, it appears clear the wine industry would have borrowed the integrity of the television station through funding if ties had not been disclosed. This, as so often occurs when media are manipulated, leads to a deliberate deception, by omission of information, of a vulnerable audience expecting to take at face value the station's declaration about the documentary's pedigree.

New economic realities can be expected to seduce producers into convincing themselves, and trying to convince others, that hard-won funding is pure and divorced from the content of the program.

Indeed, more funders are insisting on guiding the programming they pay for, increasing the probability of conflict of interest.

One solution when a station finds itself trapped into such a coalition is to disclose the conflict, clearly telling audiences the favorable programming was paid for by the subject of the story or his friends.

Perhaps the major transgression here is that KQED was unwilling to recognize and, therefore, unwilling to disclose the extent of the program's funding route in the topical industry. Whistleblowing notwithstanding, KQED did not demonstrate the level of accountability called for by the SPJ Code of Ethics.

In an ideal world, a disinterested automobile maker's association would provide funding for a vintner's documentary, clearly demonstrating low possibility of either the appearance or fact of conflict. However, in the world of new realities, perhaps the disclosure of ties may be the best that can be hoped for in an increasing number of circumstances.

Case Study #17

Editorial Independence and Car Dealers

Summary

A front-page story in the *Hartford* (Conn.) *Courant* cautioned readers about high-powered sales tactics that could be used by local auto dealers during an upcoming "car-sales blitz." The article appeared the same day as ads began running promoting car sales during "President's Week."

One dealer called the article "grossly untrue and slanderous." Some irate dealers began pulling their ads from the paper.

In response to the pullout and bitter dealer complaints, then-publisher and editor Michael Davies sent a letter of apology to the auto dealers and their advertising agencies. Davies told the dealers he was angry the story appeared without his knowledge or the review of a top editor—and on page one, at that.

He labeled as "unfair" a line in the story that begins, "Experts agree that not all dealers are out to rip off consumers ...." This statement angered dealers who said this line implied that only a few dealers are honest. The "experts agree" reference had been inserted by an editor on the originating desk.

Davies pointed out that the topic itself is newsworthy and that other stories in the *Courant* have been favorable to auto dealers. A reporter was assigned to do a story on the auto-dealer protest. The *Courant* also invited several of the dealers to the paper to discuss how news is produced under deadline. This invitation was not unique, as the paper had often invited business people and other members of the public to the paper to voice concerns or complaints. Four or five dealers accepted that invitation and gained a better understanding of how the paper operated. Some dealers, however, kept their advertising out of the paper, and some took their ads to competing media.

Davies' actions reportedly strained existing tensions between the business and editorial sides of the paper and had a chilling effect on some coverage. Reporters said they found themselves being more cautious on certain stories. Line editors said they now check with top editors on stories involving big advertisers.

Analysis

The virtues of editorial independence and the financial health of the newspaper come into conflict in this case. Media organizations are profit-making endeavors and must support themselves financially in a free-enterprise economy. Journalists and the public, however, worry about business "buying" the news functions of the media with advertising, thereby damaging the credibility of the news side.

Most advertisers do not realize they are buying the media's credibility when they buy space or time. They merely feel they are buying the audience, and they feel they have paid for the right not to have their advertising dollars neutralized by criticism.

Reporters and editors, on the other hand, have a moral obligation to empower audiences with everyday decision making skills, whether political or economic, such as buying an auto.

Perhaps the story would have caused less conflict if it had been more palatable to the auto dealers. More interviews with the dealers and more research might have provided the necessary cautionary information while softening what was viewed as a condemnation of the entire industry in Hartford.

As it is, the community may have reason to believe the newspaper is not credible when it comes to the auto industry. All elements have to live in some harmony in a community, making it necessary for journalists to understand and respect the economic role that auto dealers play.

Publishers and ad sales people, on the other hand, have an obligation to regularly explain to advertisers the information and persuasion functions of the newspaper.

Several questions might be raised when considering the conflicts raised in this type of journalism:

- What is the ethical value of separation between editorial and business-advertising departments of a newspaper?
- Would routine discussion among editors and reporters about the story have raised cautionary questions before the story ran and created the furor?
- How could an editor ethically arrive at a decision to delay running the story until after the special automobile promotion?
- Would such a discussion have resolved the problem so an important story could be run and the publisher-editor would not have felt the need to write an apologetic letter to auto dealers and ad agencies?
- What are the alternatives to appeasing the advertisers?
- Should the publisher appease the advertisers, back his staff, seek another solution or back off altogether?
- Both ethically and practically, would it be wise for editorial and advertising departments to confer more often to head off such problems?
- What role should senior editors play in reviewing stories of this sensitive nature, and how should they discuss this issue with the publisher and with the business side of the paper?
- What compromises are ethically acceptable when the financial and editorial functions of the newspaper conflict, as they did in this case? What should be the major considerations for each side?

Case Study #18

CNN Conflicted

Summary

Many media observers and television news consumers agree that CNN earned its stripes while reporting developments from the Persian Gulf War in 1990. The news organization's stature grew as, around the clock, correspondents dutifully filed stories no other media outlet could or would. CNN's journalistic reputation also blossomed during coverage of natural disasters and major trials in the mid-'90s.

By 1997, celebrity appeared to have gone to CNN's head.

Hollywood and Madison Avenue came courting, and CNN was seduced. Reporters and anchors began appearing as themselves in otherwise fictionalized films such as "The Lost World: Jurassic Park" and in an advertisement for Visa credit cards.

In a Visa print ad targeted at Generation X, 29-year-old CNN correspondent Jonathan Karl's wallet is featured. Scribbled notations detail his recent Visa purchases, at least one of which reveals his profession (expenses incurred while covering the presidential inauguration), and his press credentials are prominently displayed. Overall, the ad is plainly an endorsement of Visa and of some of the merchants listed in his purchases.

A spokesman for the agency that created the ad told the *Wall Street Journal* that Karl was not paid for the ad but that CNN executives who approved of his action thought it might bring him valuable exposure. It was stressed that Karl had done no wrong, since he sought the approval of his bosses.

In summer 1997, CNN correspondents and anchors appeared in the "Jurassic Park" sequel and in "Contact," a movie about scientists preparing to make contact with life from another planet. CNN explained that the idea was similar to "product placement" of name-brand soft drinks and cars, for example. Some CNN journalists, such as White House correspondent Wolf Blitzer, refused to appear in the movies.

The blurring of the line between reporting the news and selling a product raised the specter of an incident in 1992 in which Lou Dobbs, then the managing editor of business news for CNN, was strongly reprimanded by Tom Johnson, the news organization's president, for appearing in promotional videos for Wall Street firms—a gig that earned him $5,000-$10,000 per assignment. At the time, Johnson called for a "full review of all outside projects" by CNN journalists to examine whether there was any compromise in journalistic integrity.

When the issue resurfaced in 1997, provoking criticism from media observers and colleagues, Johnson decided to enact a policy that restricts its journalists from appearing in movies. (A July 15, 1997, *Washington Post* article said that ABC, CBS and NBC already had such policies.)

Johnson's swift actions earned praise in a press release from the Society of Professional Journalists, quoting a letter from its president, Steve Geimann. "It's about time that CNN pulled the plug on turning its responsible, professional journalists into Hollywood stars," Geimann wrote to Johnson. "Your action sends an important signal to other professional journalists that the separation between fact and fiction is what makes journalism an important and honored profession, and what makes movies fun and amusing."

"Your action sends an important signal to other professional journalists that the separation between fact and fiction is what makes journalism an important and honored profession, and what makes movies fun and amusing."

—Steve Geimann

In the case of correspondent Karl, who had been given approval by senior executives, Johnson, who claimed no prior knowledge of the advertisement, later disapproved, according to a *Journal* article. Johnson also determined that the ad violated CNN policy, and he made it clear to senior executives that it should not happen again, the *Journal* reported.

Analysis

CNN deserves credit for eventually responding with clarity and conviction in each of these instances, albeit after it hit some land mines along the way. Each of these cases involve the journalistic principle of independence. As presented in this handbook, **journalists should act independently, remaining free of associations and activities that may compromise their integrity or damage their credibility**.

Journalists face enough skepticism from the public without adding to it by muddying the waters between news and entertainment, between fact and fiction. It might seem good fun (and perhaps good marketing) for a news organization or its journalists to be featured in a movie or an advertisement. To do so, however, raises significant possibilities of conflict of interest or erosion of credibility.

How can a journalist or his news organization be perceived as fair in covering any stories about a major credit card company if that journalist was a pitchman for the company? What happens to a journalist's reputation and his news organization's credibility for covering Wall Street issues when he moonlights for one of the financial firms on his beat? How can a news organization legitimately cover the film industry if that news organization is a player rather than an observer?

Yes, journalists and their organizations can keep saying, "We remain objective. We have not been compromised by our involvement." But it is impossible to prove that point. You cannot prove that you haven't bent too far one way or the other. You cannot defend your decisions for what you did cover and what you didn't cover.

And, while you are fending off challenge and criticism, you are distracted from what you are supposed to be doing—reporting the news.

CNN's experience in each of these cases points out the importance of news organizations having clear policies and protocols for matters of journalistic independence and conflicts of interest. Guidelines and decision making processes protect both the organization and the individual.

The best time to handle an ethical issue is before it becomes an issue.

Case Study #19

Freebies and Junkets

Summary

Even Yogi Berra might have been at a loss for words.

When journalists accepted freebies during promotion of Disney World's 20th anniversary celebration in 1991, it was, *Editor & Publisher* noted, a la Berra, "like deja vu all over again."

So what was it when, five years later, the Yankees gave away or sold post-season tickets to selected New York City area reporters and editors?

Perhaps it was much the same thing when, say, Disney offered junkets to 10,000 journalists for its 1986 birthday bash. Or when it previewed EPCOT for journalists before it opened in 1981. Or when ....

Or when the issue arose again at Disney in 1996.

As the *Arizona Daily Star* reported, for example, three Tucson television stations "accepted gifts from or [were] pressured into providing coverage of Disneyland." The newspaper noted that at Disney's expense, two of the stations sent meteorologists to Anaheim to report on weather back in Tucson and a third sent a reporter and camera operator to Disneyland at the station's—not the newsroom's—expense, after running a contest coordinated by Disney and the station sales staff.

Disney (said) the company does not expect favorable coverage in exchange for complimentary trips and services ....

"Disneyland wanted us to do a new series, a couple of news stories to play along with this (contest) thing," KVOA-TV Ch. 4 news director Mick Jensen told the *Daily Star*. "I didn't want to do that .... What it finally boiled down to was (we reported) a story of our choosing. Our travel was picked up by the station .... I guess you could say our sales department paid for it, which was fine by me, since they got me into it anyway."

Disney spokeswoman Susan Roth told the paper that the company does not expect favorable coverage in exchange for complimentary trips and services, but that the freebies are to help reporters who cover the theme park experience it fully. "It's not a contract or anything," she was quoted as saying. "They never guarantee a story .... When a critic reviews a movie, they need to see it."

In the case of the Yankees, journalists who did not cover the post-season games—the non-working press—were given free tickets or at least access to tickets while many fans who waited in line for hours were shut out.

As Allan Wolper reported in *Editor & Publisher* in October 1996, team owner George Steinbrenner had faxed journalists an offer to watch the games with him in his luxury box. Some accepted the free tickets, Wolper noted, but others paid for them—as did politicians whom the papers criticized for doing so.

The ticket offer came at a time when Steinbrenner was trying to muster media support for a proposed new stadium.

Staffers at the *New York Times*, *Daily News* and Associated Press bought tickets to playoff games but denied receiving special treatment, Wolper reported. The managing editor of the *New York Post*, Marc Kalech, however, told *E&P*: "We didn't pay for our tickets .... Believe me, I won't be swayed by free tickets .... I still expect to get calls from Steinbrenner complaining about our coverage."

Joseph Lelyveld, *Times* executive editor, told *E&P*: "I don't understand the conflict. I do not see it as a good, ethical issue of the day. We paid for our tickets."

Bruce Weber, a *Times* reporter, bought a playoff ticket. Then, after being assigned to write about the situation and after reading a *Village Voice* article about it, decided not to buy a World Series ticket. He told *E&P*: "It seemed unseemly to me."

Weber's words echoed those from a decade earlier, when *E&P* quoted a *Times* editorial that said journalists who accepted freebies "debased" the profession and left the image that the press was "on the take."

Analysis

The issue here is not just freebies. It's also about privilege and power. Simply put, journalists and their news organizations should not accept gifts, favors, free travel and special treatment from news sources or subjects of coverage or from anyone else engaging in a power play.

Any individual or organization who used journalistic stature to obtain free tickets to those Yankees games was violating the principle of independence. The conflict of interest is clear. And while some argued that they paid for their tickets, there is still a strong conflict of interest if the opportunity and access to buying those tickets was a special one offered to journalists but not available to the general public whose interests journalists are supposedly serving.

> ***The issue here is not just freebies. It's also about privilege and power.***

Members of the public have every right to be skeptical and angry when they see journalists getting special treatment. Sure, those news organizations could say we "still reported the story fair and square." That defense carries little, if any, weight with those who raise the questions.

In the case of the Arizona television stations walking arm-and-arm with Disney, the ethics issues take on additional levels. There is definitely a real conflict of interest when a station allows Disney (or any other company, organization or individual) to pay for any part of coverage costs. Why should viewers believe anything about their coverage knowing those stations were, in essence, on the Disney payroll? (The fact that Disney is the parent company to one network is already problematic; that Disney seems to avail all journalists of its junkets doesn't lessen the ethical concerns.)

Just as important, a news organization sells its soul to the highest bidder when it determines its news coverage based on sales department priorities or the financial incentives offered by well-heeled corporations seeking publicity. News managers can argue all they want about how their coverage in those cases is fair and objective. Tell that to other businesses or organizations who don't get any coverage because they aren't willing to pay what amounts to a bribe.

Conflicts of Interest

What the Codes Say

Cable News Network

No outside employment by CNN employees or services rendered by CNN employees shall appear to be an endorsement by CNN or the employee of the product, service, or company in question; no employee shall act as a spokesperson for any outside interest or entity permit the use of his/her name, voice, likeness, biography and/or statements to promote or advertise any product, service or organization without the prior written consent of an executive vice president, or the president, of CNN.

PBS

Editorial integrity in public broadcasting programming means the responsible application by professional practitioners of a free and independent decision-making process which is ultimately accountable to the needs and interests of all citizens. Programming based on the principles of editorial integrity will guarantee journalistic objectivity, as well as fair and balanced presentation of issues ....

As surely as programming is our purpose, and the product by which our audiences judge our value, that judgment will depend upon their confidence that our programming is free from undue or improper influence. Our role as trustees includes educating both citizens and public policy makers to the importance of this fact and to assuring that our stations meet this challenge in a responsible and efficient way.

Norfolk (Va.) *Virginian-Pilot*

Editors, reporters and photographers should be sensitive to the use of bumper stickers, pins, badges or other signs that connect them to a particular candidate or social cause. Taking a public stand on openly controversial social issues will be strongly discouraged. For example, we expect any professional involved in news gathering for or against abortion or other similarly controversial social issues to refrain from allowing his or her name to be used in any way supporting or condemning abortion.

New York *Daily News*

The *Daily News* does not permit or condone bribes, kickbacks or any other illegal or improper payments, transfers or receipts. This prohibition is across-the-board; it applies to both giving and receiving. No employee shall offer, give, solicit or receive any money or anything else of value for the purpose of 1) obtaining, retaining or directing business, or 2) bestowing or receiving any kind of favored treatment ....

No company funds or assets may be contributed to any political candidate or political party, unless such contribution is expressly permitted by law. This prohibition relates only to the use of company funds or assets. It is not intended to discourage employees from making personal contributions to political candidates or parties of their choice through lawful company channels or otherwise. Employees must not, however, be reimbursed by the company in any way for such personal contributions.

Rochester* (N.Y.) *Democrat and Chronicle

Token gifts of less than $20 value may be accepted if it would be awkward to send them back. Such gifts include a pen, key chain, calendar or similar item.

All other gifts will be returned to the donor with the explanation that it is in violation of our policy to accept gifts. Bottles of wine or liquor shall be considered gifts of more than token value and may not be kept.

Albany (N.Y.) Capital Newspapers

We are mindful of the need to maintain our integrity and credibility. We do this by avoiding conflicts of interest and the appearance of conflicts of interest ....

General Conduct. As staffers, we must take care not to use newspaper property (for example, its name, its stationery, etc.) or our positions on our newspaper, for personal gain or advantage.

Outside Activity. Outside activity is so integral a focus of our concept of ethics that a subsection of the Guild contract discusses it. These standards reflect that spirit.

Staffers should avoid involvement in any activity which could compromise, or appear to compromise, the staffer's or the newspaper's capacity, ability or disposition to gather, report, write or edit, faithfully, factually, impartially and fairly. Connection with government is often the most unacceptable.

A staffer may engage in other employment or in contract work or volunteer work provided it does not interfere with the staffer's duties here and there is no conflict of interest involved.

So we may know of it and advise whether we perceive any such interference or conflict, such activity must be cleared in advance with the managing editor whenever any possibility of interference or conflict exists.

Associated Press Managing Editors

The newspaper and its staff should be free of obligations to news sources and special interests. Even the appearance of obligation or conflict of interest should be avoided.

Newspapers should accept nothing of value from news sources or others outside the profession. Gifts and free or reduced-rate travel, entertainment, products and lodging should not be accepted. Expenses in connection with news reporting should be paid by the newspaper. Special favors and special treatment for members of the press should be avoided.

Journalists are encouraged to be involved in their communities, to the extent that such activities do not create conflicts of interest. Involvement in politics, demonstrations and social causes that could cause a conflict of interest, or the appearance of such conflict, should be avoided.

Work by staff members for the people of institutions they cover also should be avoided.

Financial investments by staff members or other outside business interests that could create the impression of a conflict of interest should be avoided.

Stories should not be written or edited primarily for the purpose of winning awards and prizes. Self-serving journalism contests and awards that reflect unfavorably on the newspaper or the profession should be avoided.

Charlotte* (N.C.) *Observer

The News Columns

It goes without saying that no *Observer* staffer would ever show favoritism in the news columns in exchange for gifts or favors. So in most circumstances our concern is the appearance of conflict of interest, not actual conflict.

The best general guide to conduct is that we accept nothing of value for which we do not pay. To be specific: You go to lunch with a news source who picks up the tab. That's fine, and next time you pick up the tab and put it on your expense account. Someone courts you as a pipeline into the paper and wants to give you a bottle of whisky. Decline, with thanks, as gracefully as you can. We don't want to be sanctimonious about this, but we want our people to carry their weight.

In addition, there's an obvious reason not to write stories concerning outside interests in which you are involved unless your editors know of your involvement and your story discloses that involvement.

Outside Conduct

You have the right to determine what you do in your private life, and so does your spouse, but that private life might affect what newsroom duties you could take on.

Whenever a potential for conflict between personal and professional activities arises, prudence dictates open discussion with supervisors.

In general, be wary of political commitment, although this need not mean civic isolation. Part of our obligation as citizens is to make decisions about candidates and issues and act on them.

But it is also clearly part of our obligation as journalists to insure that our reputations as objective fact-finders are not blemished by a display of our political views.

Generally that means the public ought not be able to tell by our behavior how we feel about an issue or candidate.

Partly because the newsroom is a semi-public place, partly because readers don't make the same distinctions we do about who covers what, that guideline includes all of us—whether active in the coverage of political campaigns or not.

Moonlighting

Free-lance work on your own time is your own business, but practically there is potential for difficulty in several areas. Open discussion with supervisors is a clear necessity to avoid conflict.

Things That Come In The Mail

Gifts or promotion items of substantial value sent to staffers will be returned or given away to an appropriate public or charitable institution in the name of the donor. You should write the donor a polite but firm letter that explains our ethics policy and asks that you be excluded from future mailings.

Review Books

Reviewers may keep books and records given them to review or consider for review. You may keep books that are related to your work—books on grammar for the copy desk, on business for the business desk, reference works for the library, on golf for the golf writer, etc. The book editor may give books to reviewers if they are likely to further the reviewer's knowledge in a specialty area, whether or not the books are to be reviewed. Books and records that are not reviewed or that are not related to work will be given to public and quasi-public institutions, such as schools, prisons or hospitals.

Trade Shows, Press Conferences

Each department receives invitations to many events, often given by a business or a political figure, for which there is no charge or opportunity to pay. It is difficult to generalize because the occasions are so varied, but in general if you feel attending would be part of your work, you should not hesitate to accept.

Free Admissions

Also, the common journalistic practice of accepting free admission to news events, including those involving meals, does not create an ethical problem.

The Best Course

If a situation bothers you, tell someone about it, preferably your immediate supervisor. If that makes you uncomfortable, discuss it with the managing editor or editor. Clear the air.

Columbus* (Ga.) *Ledger-Enquirer

Our newspapers and each staff member must be free of obligations to news sources and special interests. Equally important, we must be free of any appearance of obligation or conflict of interest.

As a general guide, we accept nothing of substantial value for which we do not pay. We do accept admission to sports and entertainment events, etc., for the person covering or reviewing the event. But we do not accept complimentary tickets from sponsors of such events. That includes season passes, movie passes, circus and fair tickets, free memberships, press cut-rates and the like.

We do not accept gifts of any substantial value from news sources or special interests. What constitutes "substantial value" depends upon the situation, but a general guideline is anything worth more than $5.

Meals bought by news sources are permissible, so long as they are infrequent and the invitation is easily repayable by the staff member. Meals at civic clubs and other meetings being covered by staffers fall into the same category as tickets to sports and entertainment events; if they are offered free to on-duty reporters, we may accept.

We accept for review books, records and movie and theater tickets offered voluntarily by the publisher or theater (for reviewer and one guest only). Where they are not offered, the newspaper pays for those considered appropriate for review. Reviewers keep books and records. Books and records received but not reviewed become the property of the newspapers, for distribution as the editors decide. Staffers and editors who receive those materials should make them available to other departments.

We do not accept free out-of-town travel, except where other transportation is not available or appropriate, as in the case of a military trip; we then pay our pro-rata share of expenses where feasible.

In declining tickets, gifts and other favors, *Ledger-Enquirer* staff members should avoid rudeness and self-righteousness. We should express our appreciation and politely decline, explaining that the policy is as much in the would-be giver's interests as our own.

Staffers should never profit in any way, beyond salaries, from what they cause to be published in our newspapers.

Outside employment

Ledger-Enquirer staff members avoid any business arrangement, outside commitment or honorary position that may result in a conflict of interest.

Full or part-time employment by any other news organization is discouraged and must be approved in advance in writing by management. Similarly, staff members' employment by news sources or potential news sources is avoided, and staffers refrain from lending their names to commercial enterprises with no promotional value to our papers. Business interests that could conflict with a staff member's ability to report the news, or that would create the impression of such conflict, are avoided.

Professional work as stringers or free-lancers for newspapers, magazines, book publishers, news services, photo agencies and similar organizations headquartered and circulated principally outside our circulation area is usually acceptable. So is part-time teaching in local colleges and other professional or para-professional areas, so long as it does not interfere with newspaper duties. All arrangements of this kind, however, are discussed in advance with management.

Written material, art work, photos and negatives produced on company time and/or with company materials are company property. Any material or information developed by staff members for publication must be offered first to the *Ledger-Enquirer* before it is offered for sale or publication elsewhere.

As members of AP and Knight-Ridder, we make available to AP and the

KRN wire stories and photos we have published.

Causes and organizations

We exercise discretion in all relationships with causes and organizations. We encourage staff members to join and to perform voluntary services for local religious, cultural, social and civic organizations. We also believe that newspapers have the same community responsibility as other businesses in donating editors' and employees' time to civic undertakings. Staffers should let their supervisors know what groups they're involved with.

However, we recognize that our involvement as citizens may sometimes compromise or inhibit our professional responsibilities, and we judge each situation with that in mind. We are particularly conscious of the necessity to avoid personal involvement on either side of an issue about which we would be writing or editing stories for the newspapers. In that connection, we avoid paid or unpaid work for a politician or political organization, and we do not hold public office or accept political appointment to any position for which there is remuneration other than expenses.

We also are aware of the possibility that our personal involvement with organizations might create an appearance of newspaper bias or favoritism for the organizations. So we do not prepare publicity or serve on publicity committees for any groups, and we request that all businesses and organizations go through normal newspaper channels in seeking news coverage.

Staffers must discuss any doubts on ethical questions with a supervising editor. The burden to do so rests affirmatively on the journalist.

Detroit Free Press

Gifts, books, records: We accept nothing of value from news sources or from sources whose activities are, or are likely to be, the subject of news coverage by the *Free Press*. This includes free travel, merchandise, lodging, reduced rates or discounts available only to members of the media, free memberships in clubs or organizations, and loans of cash or merchandise. Unsolicited gifts should, where possible, be returned to the donor with a note explaining our policy. If this is not possible, the gift may be donated to charity with a note to the donor explaining the circumstances. Gifts of token or insignificant value may be accepted if returning them would be awkward or inappropriate. Meals and/or drinks shared with news sources should be paid for, wherever possible, by the staff member. When the cost of a meal includes an additional sum (for example, a $500-a-plate political fund-raiser), the staff member will pay the price of the meal and be reimbursed by the *Free Press*.

Books and records received for review purposes belong to the *Free Press*. Some books are distributed to staff members for background uses. Books and records assigned for review belong to the reviewer, but are not to be sold or exchanged. No one should derive any profit—either by resale or tax write-offs—from these books or records. Books not reviewed or otherwise distributed are donated to local libraries. Unreviewed records are given to charities.

Tickets: Free tickets to events for which the public must pay should not be accepted by staff members or members of their households in behalf of the staff member. Staff members required to attend events where press box facilities are not provided should purchase tickets and be reimbursed by the *Free Press.* Photographers and reporters assigned to cover sports or political events may use such facilities as review seats, press boxes, press galleries or press rooms which are necessary to cover the event. Access to press boxes or press galleries may be granted to other staff members when the access is necessary to developing information or skills.

Outside activities: Staff members should avoid outside activities that might conflict with the staff member's responsibility to the *Free Press* and to our readers. Examples would include work for an employer who is the subject of *Free Press* news coverage; work for an employer whose employment of a *Free Press* staff member might indicate an endorsement by the *Free Press* or the staff member of his or her product, service or business; a staff member's endorsement of any product or cause (for pay or for free) which might imply an endorsement by the *Free Press;* work for an employer who competes with the *Free Press* for either circulation or advertising revenue. Discuss any such activity in advance with a supervising editor.

The *Free Press* is the exclusive owner of the work for which it pays. Any disposition of that work requires *Free Press* approval. Freelance work is permitted for publications not in direct competition with the *Free Press.*

Appearances on radio or television by staff members are generally permissible, but a supervising editor should be consulted in advance of the appearance. A staff member should not enter into a commitment for regular involvement with a radio or television station without first consulting a managing editor.

Business interests, investments: A staff member may not enter into a business relationship with a news source. A staff member may not make investments which could come into conflict with the staff member's duties. A staff member with investments or stock holdings in corporations should avoid making news decisions that involve those corporations.

Unpublished information gathered by the *Free Press* may not be used by staff members for investment decisions. Staff members should try to ensure the confidentiality of information gathered by the *Free Press* by making every effort to keep such information from reaching anyone who might attempt to use it for personal gain before it is published. Staff members should be careful in dealings with news sources—and particularly those in the investment community—not to disclose before publication the nature of any story that has the potential to affect the price of any stock. And because timing of an investment is often crucial, no one outside the *Free Press* should know in advance the publication date of any such story.

When there is doubt about the appropriateness of a business investment or about any possible conflict of interest, the staff member should discuss the situation with a supervising editor.

Personal relationships: No staff member should write about, report on, photograph or make a news judgment about any individual related to him or her by blood or marriage or with whom the staff member has a close personal relationship. Writing or editing a story about a friend's business, for example, presents a conflict and should be avoided. A staff member who finds himself or herself in a situation where a conflict of interest (or the perceptions of such) becomes likely should consult beforehand with a managing editor about the circumstances.

Travel: We do not accept travel junkets or special media rates from airlines, agencies and governmental travel organizations or free travel with sports teams. In the latter case, we will accept the same discount the team receives. Transportation costs necessary to the performance of *Free Press* duties are paid by the *Free Press*. Inaugural flights, where government regulations prohibit the sale of tickets, will be taken only in cases where there are compelling coverage reasons and then only by the person(s) assigned to such coverage. Unique situations, e.g., military transportation necessary to covering a story, will be handled on a case-by-case basis in consultation with a supervising editor.

Connections: Staff members need to avoid using their *Free Press* positions to obtain personal or financial benefit for themselves, family or friends. We cannot use the company's name to curry favor, imply a threat or pressure, seek personal gain, expedite personal business, or seek special consideration. (For example, it would be improper to use company stationery for a personal complaint letter.)

Political activity: Journalists should avoid work for pay or as a volunteer in a political campaign or organization. If a staff member has a close relative—spouse, parent, child, brother or sister—or a person with whom the staff member has a close and continuing personal relationship, who is involved in a political campaign or organization, the staff member should not cover or make news judgments about the campaign or organization; if the individual circumstances are felt to justify another course of action, a managing editor needs to be consulted. If a staff member feels compelled to seek public office, the executive editor's permission is required.

Grand Forks* (N.D.) *Herald

Because the nature of their profession requires impartiality, journalists must avoid situations where conflicts of interest could occur. It is especially important to remember that the appearance of conflict, even when no conflict exists, can do serious damage to our professional credibility.

Journalists should avoid political involvement beyond voting. In no circumstances may a staff member seek political office or work, for pay or as a volunteer, in a political campaign or organization.

Staff members should not undertake any outside employment that might interfere with their duties at the newspaper or that could lead to a conflict of interest. Staff members may not enter into business relationships with news sources, nor should they make investments that could lead to conflicts of interest. It would be improper for a staff member to use his or her position at the

Grand Forks Herald to obtain any benefit or advantage in commercial transactions or personal business.

No news department employee should serve on any board or committee that common sense dictates could become controversial, and we avoid active involvement in causes of any kind—politics, community affairs, social action, demonstrations—that could compromise, or seem to compromise, our ability to report and edit with fairness. Relatives of staff members cannot fairly be subject to *Grand Forks Herald* rules, but it should be recognized that their involvement in causes can at least appear to compromise our integrity.

Staff members shall not accept appointment to publicity committees of even non-controversial events or organizations.

Staff members may free-lance for publications that are not in direct competition with the *Grand Forks Herald*, but performing work for a competitor is not allowed. Occasional performances on area radio or television programs are permissible, but staff members who make such appearances should be guided by the same rigid standards of fairness and impartiality that apply to the newsroom.

The news and advertising operations within our paper are separate. We do not consider advertisers' requests in any special way when making news judgments, and staff members should seek no commercial advantage beyond those available to members of the public generally.

We pay our own way. Free tickets or passes to sports events, movies, theatrical productions, political banquets and other events for which the public is required to pay an entrance fee shall not be accepted by staff members. Staff members who need to attend events for professional purposes shall pay for tickets and obtain reimbursement from the *Grand Forks Herald*. We do not accept free trips or accommodations or reduced rates for members of the press. If an event or situation is newsworthy, we can afford it. If it isn't newsworthy, we can get along without it.

Staff members should accept no gifts of value from news sources. For example, a bottle of wine or a box of candy should be returned to the donor with an explanation that it is a violation of *Grand Forks Herald* policy to accept gifts. Gifts of insignificant value, such as a calendar or a pencil, may be accepted if it would be awkward to return them. Offers of free food and drinks should be politely refused. It may be necessary to accept such offers to avoid being rude or obnoxious, but they should be rare exceptions.

We must remember that many of the kindnesses offered to the *Herald* and its employees are tendered on the basis of friendship or courtesy and without any self-serving motive. It's important that we avoid appearing rude or narrowly self-righteous in living within the spirit of this policy. We should never assume a stance of outraged innocence. Instead, we should express our appreciation and politely decline, explaining the importance of our policy.

Books, recordings and other items delivered to the *Grand Forks Herald* or to individual staff members for review purposes are the property of the newspaper. They will be distributed, disposed of or returned as senior editors determine which is most compatible with the spirit of this code.

KHON-TV (Hawaii)

All members of the KHON news staff shall govern their personal lives and such non-professional associations as may impinge on their professional activities in a manner that will protect them from conflict of interest, real or apparent.

In order to preclude a real or apparent conflict of interest, news personnel should, under no circumstances, allow their names, voices or likenesses be used in connection with any form of commercial advertising.

As professional journalists, all members of the news staff, reporters, talent, and cameramen are prohibited from accepting gifts, favors, merchandise, travel or accommodations which may be offered regardless of whether any type of consideration may be asked in return. In the case of items or services of minor or insignificant value, the News Director should be consulted if there is any question of propriety.

Violations of this Code of Ethics may result in either dismissal or some other disciplinary action.

National Conference of Editorial Writers

The editorial writer should never use his or her influence to seek personal favors of any kind. Gifts of value, free travel and other favors that can compromise integrity, or appear to do so, should not be accepted.

The writer should be constantly alert to conflicts of interest, real or apparent, including those that may arise from financial holdings, secondary employment, holding public office or involvement in political, civic or other organizations. Timely public disclosure can minimize suspicion.

Editors should seek to hold syndicates to these standards.

The writer, further to enhance editorial page credibility, also should encourage the institution he or she represents to avoid conflicts of interest, real or apparent.

Newspaper Food Editors and Writers Association

The Association believes that the primary responsibility of food editors and writers is to serve the public interest by reporting the news accurately and as objectively as possible.

The Association further believes that essential to this commitment is the absolute separation of food editors' and writers' editorial responsibilities from the influence of their newspapers' advertising departments.

To assure their integrity and preserve their credibility, members therefore accept the following standards:

1) Gifts, favors, free travel or lodging, special treatment or privileges can compromise the integrity and diminish the credibility of food editors and writers as well as their employers. Such offers should be avoided.

2) Similarly, food editors and writers should not use their positions to win

favors for themselves or for others.

3) Secondary employment, political involvement, holding public office or serving in organizations should be avoided if it compromises the integrity of food editors or writers.

4) Because the editorial space allotted to food editors and writers is not an extension of advertising, brand names or names of specific companies or interest groups should be used only in a newsworthy context or for purposes of clarification.

Orange County (Calif.) *Register*

The *Register*'s management and staff shall be committed to the truth uncorrupted by special interest. In this regard, these guidelines are to be used:

Gratuities: Gifts of goods and services may be accepted only if they are of inconsequential value. In areas of question, the staff member should consult with his or her supervisor.

Meals and Drinks: Free meals, drinks, etc., should be accepted only where the meal itself, or the events surrounding it, have news value. Free meals, drinks, etc., are not to be accepted from persons whose primary aim is to directly or indirectly influence the news content of the *Register*. It is recognized that it is sometimes difficult to demand half a check or your fair share after a lunch or dinner. The staff member should use common sense when faced with such a situation.

Tickets: Tickets or passes to any cultural or athletic event may be accepted only for the purpose of coverage of the event.

Junkets: Trips, transportation, lodging, etc., will be taken only where in the judgment of the appropriate editor a clear and obvious news benefit to the *Register* exists. In such cases, the *Register* will pay for all expenses. Exceptions, such as where a monetary value cannot be readily placed on the transportation or lodging, must be approved by the editor. Associates may not use their position with the *Register* for personal gain in any other way.

Outside Activities: Any limitation on outside activities of *Register* news department associates is intended only to protect the *Register*'s reputation, credibility and position as the dominant information source in its primary marketing area. Hence, the following guidelines:

1. Associates may not perform services for the following news media that compete with the *Register* in Orange County: Daily or weekly newspapers home-delivered in the county, radio stations and television stations which serve the county. Appearances on broadcast media must be approved in advance by the associate's supervisor.

2. Associates may not perform services for a primary news source and may not accept any payment for services involved in producing publicity matter which may be submitted for publication in the *Register*.

3. Associates are limited in other free-lancing work only by the above restrictions and by the additional standard that such work will not compromise the integrity of the associate or bring harm to the integrity and reputation

of the *Register.*

4. Associates are limited in civic activity only if it compromises the integrity of the associate or harms the integrity or reputation of the *Register*. Associates should consult with their supervisor when questions of applicability arise. Obviously, civic activity should not be assumed to the point of undue interference with work for the *Register*. Any exception to these guidelines must be approved by the associate's supervisor.

Radio Television News Directors Association
Code of Broadcast News Ethics

The responsibility of radio and television journalists is to gather and report information of importance and interest to the public accurately, honestly and impartially.

The members of the Radio-Television News Directors Association accept these standards and will:

2. Strive to conduct themselves in a manner that protects them from conflicts of interest, real or perceived. They will decline gifts or favors which would influence or appear to influence their judgments.

San Jose* (Calif.) *Mercury News

3. Connections: Employees shall not use their positions with the *Mercury News* to get any benefit or advantage in commercial transactions or personal business for themselves, their families, friends or acquaintances.

For example, they shall not use company connections to:

Get information or a photograph for purposes other than those of the newspaper.

Expedite personal business with, or seek special consideration from, public officials or agencies, such as police.

Seek for personal use information not available to the general public.

Get free, or at a reduced rate not available to the general public, considerations such as tickets, memberships, hotel rooms or transportation.

Employees shall not use the company name, reputation, phone number or stationery to imply a threat of retaliation or pressure, to curry favor, or to seek personal gain.

For example, it is improper for an employee to write a personal letter of complaint to a merchant on company stationery, or to arrange a personal purchase at wholesale or discount rates through the public relations office of a corporation.

4. Meals, Tickets, Travel: As a general rule, we pay our own way.

The *Mercury News* will pay for meals and drinks shared with news sources, for luncheons or dinners which are covered as news events and for restaurant meals reviewed. When the cost of a meal includes a sum tacked on to raise funds (for instance, a $300-a-plate political dinner), we will pay only what we estimate to be the price of the meal if it were to be purchased in a restaurant. (This is not meant to prohibit corporate contributions to charity fund-raisers.)

Whenever complimentary food and beverages are supplied at press events, staff members should calculate about how much their portions cost and then reimburse the coordinator of the event.

Staff members may encounter situations in which it is socially awkward or even impossible to pay for a meal or entertainment. In such circumstances they should exercise good judgment. Such situations should be rare and should not be entered into habitually.

Common sense also should prevail in meals with news sources. It is acceptable to let a source pay for a lunch, so long as one expects to be able to return the favor and pick up the lunch check sometime in the near future.

Free tickets to sports events, movies, plays, fairs, amusement parks and all other entertainment for which admission normally is charged shall not be accepted or solicited.

If the event being covered is a private screening or special press conference for which tickets are not being sold to the public, it is permissible to attend gratis. In other special cases, such as a business seminar or a National League of Cities meeting, a reporter covering the event may attend without paying the registration fee after receiving permission from a supervisor. Special press-box facilities, photo galleries and passes to areas available exclusively to the press are also accepted, provided these are used only by the persons assigned to cover the event. These press passes must never be given or sold to anyone.

Transportation necessary for the performance of professional duties shall be paid for by the *Mercury News* in all possible cases—including travel on a press plane of a political candidate or sports team. The executive editor or editor may give approval for special travel arrangements that would be the sole way to effectively complete an assignment, such as when military transit is involved. In an emergency situation, staff members are encouraged to use common sense and discretion.

For example, if the only transit available to a disaster site is by Army helicopter, a staff member trying to cover that story might accept the transportation and let a supervisor know about it at the earliest opportunity.

For free-lance articles written for the Travel section, the editor shall disclose in print the source of any free trips accepted by the writer.

Society of American Travel Writers

No member shall accept payment or courtesies for an agreement to produce favorable material about a travel destination, service or supplier that is contrary to his or her own professional appraisal.

Members who are or have been employed by or associated with a travel destination, service firm or supplier shall disclose that fact to all potential editors and/or publishers prior to accepting an assignment relating to that destination or involving that service firm or supplier ....

The sole responsibility of the SATW member is to provide his/her readers, listeners or viewers with objective and independent reporting. SATW calls direct attention to the fact that some members represent publications which do not accept complimentary transportation, accommodations or other necessities or amenities of travel. Prospective hosts sponsoring familiarization trips at no charge to invited journalists are requested also to state in the invitation what the full rate or the press or industry rate would be for such trips, giving those members who must pay all or part of the cost of any trip the option to do so ....

SATW and its membership pledges to continue to do everything possible to attain and maintain for travel journalists a position of highest prestige and integrity in the journalistic fraternity. Resolved by The Editors Council in Boston, Mass., April 16, 1989.

In recognition of ethics policies adapted by newspapers and magazines, and by the American Society of Newspaper Editors and the Society of Professional Journalists, members of the SATW Editors council believe no SATW function should involve subsidies from travel industry sources.

Elimination of such subsidies in all SATW functions, including conventions, chapter meetings, board meetings and tours, will result in a stronger and more respected association.

Southern Illinoisan

It is the personal responsibility of all editorial department employees of the *Southern Illinoisan* to avoid any action that will damage the credibility of the newspaper. One way to do this is to avoid any activity that will bring our motives or our news judgments into question.

Some obvious don'ts:

1. Staff members may not seek elective offices. Nor may they engage in campaign activity on behalf of, or in opposition to, any candidate or position.

2. Staff members, unless specifically assigned to do so, should not participate in the events they are assigned to cover. Unless otherwise instructed, every effort should be made to remain an observer of events, not a participant in them, while on assignment.

3. Even in your private life, every effort should be made to avoid involvements in potentially controversial activities in which your connection to the newspaper could give the appearance of a conflict.

4. Staff members may not accept appointment to any public body without first checking with their supervisor.

5. Staff members should not serve in a publicity or public relations capacity for any organization; nor, without authorization from their supervisor, should they write articles bout any organization in which they are a participating member.

6. Staff members may not work on a free-lance or other basis for any other medium competing for news, readership or advertising within the *Southern Illinoisan*'s circulation area. If in doubt about whether a publication is considered a competitor ask the editor.

7. Staff members should check with their supervisors before agreeing to do any writing, photography or editing work for any company or organization within our circulation area. No work of any sort may be done for any political candidate.

Turner Broadcasting System Inc.
Code of Ethics and Business Conduct (January 1992)

In a conflict of interest situation, an employee may have the opportunity to do something that would benefit him or her personally, but would either interfere with the employee's ability to guard the Company's best interest or would appear to interfere with that ability. Therefore, Turner's Code of Ethics requires that both types of activities be avoided: those that create a conflict of interest and those that create the appearance of a conflict of interest.

(Note: The 16-page manual is devoted almost entirely to conflicts of interest; page 17 is an "annual certification" that employee has reviewed, understood, not violated, is currently in compliance and is not aware of any violations of the code.)

Washington* (D.C.) *Post

We have adopted stringent policies on these issues, conscious that they may be more restrictive than is customary in the world of private business. In particular:

We pay our own way.

We accept no gifts from news sources. We accept no free trips. We neither seek nor accept preferential treatment that might be rendered because of the positions we hold. Exceptions to the no-gift rule are few and obvious—invitations to meals, for example, may be accepted when they are occasional and innocent, but not when they are repeated and their purpose is deliberately calculating. Free admissions to any event that is not free to the public are prohibited. The only exception is for seats not sold to the public, as in a press box. Whenever possible, arrangements will be made to pay for such seats.

We work for no one except for the *Washington Post* without permission from superiors. Many outside activities and jobs are incompatible with the proper performance of work on an independent newspaper. Connections with government are among the most objectionable. To avoid real or apparent conflicts of interest in the coverage of business and the financial markets, all members of the Business and Financial staff are required to disclose their financial holdings and investments to the assistant managing editor in charge of the section. The potential for conflict, however, is not limited to members of the Business and Financial staff. All reporters and editors, wherever they may work, are required to disclose to their department head any financial interests that might be in conflict or give the appearance of a conflict in their reporting or editing duties. Department heads will make their own financial disclosures to the managing editor.

We free-lance for no one and accept no speaking engagements without permission from department heads. Permission to free-lance will be granted only if the *Post* has no interest in the story and only if it is to appear in a medium that does not compete with the *Post*. It is important that no free-lance assignments and no honoraria be accepted that might in any way be interpreted as disguised gratuities.

We make every reasonable effort to be free of obligation to news sources and to special interests. We must be wary of entanglement with those whose positions render them likely to be subjects of journalistic interest and examination.

Our private behavior as well as our professional behavior must not bring discredit to our profession or to the *Post*.

We avoid active involvement in any partisan causes—politics, community affairs, social action, demonstrations—that could compromise or seem to compromise our ability to report and edit fairly. Relatives cannot fairly be made subject to *Post* rules, but it should be recognized that their employment or their involvement in causes can at least appear to compromise our integrity. The business and professional ties of traditional family members or other members of your household must be disclosed to department heads.

Wilson* (N.C.) *Daily Times

Reporters may accept free meals or transportation, when offered, in connection with coverage of a news stories. Many civic clubs and other organizations will invite reporters to be their guests in order to accommodate news coverage. If accepting the invitation will make coverage more convenient, it may be acceptable. Invitations should not be accepted simply because a reporter wants a free meal. The *Daily Times* will pay for meals or tickets necessary to the coverage of a story when the sponsoring organization does not offer a free ticket or meal.

Reporters should not make a habit of accepting gifts from news sources. Acceptance of such gifts can leave the impression, correctly or not, in the eyes of the giver or of the public, that something is being "bought" with these gifts.

Small gifts tendered for purely altruistic reasons or because a person genuinely likes a reporter may be accepted. A reporter should avoid offending genuinely benevolent persons by refusing a gracious offer.

If a gift is offered, the reporter should make a judgment: is this a gracious offering born out of caring affection or generosity or is it a bribe cloaked in the guise of a gift? Gifts of substantial value (this policy sets no absolute standard, but gifts worth more than a half-day's pay might be a good criterion) should be refused under any circumstances.

Reporters may hold down part-time jobs, so long as they do not interfere with the primary job. Reporters may not work for advertising agencies, other news organizations or for employers the reporter is likely to encounter as a news source. Reporters may not endorse products.

Chapter Six

Deception

The issue of deception is a significant ethical matter, for it deals with truth, and seeking truth is what journalism is all about. Only recently has the debate over deception reached the stage where media organizations have begun to address the issue head on in their codes of ethics. The discussion has intensified of late because of the invention of digital photography and the ease with which reality can be manipulated, along with the disturbing tendency of so many news operations to turn to surreptitious reporting and hidden cameras as a first rather than a last resort when conducting investigations.

Deception in journalism can take many forms, from outright lying, to misleading, or misrepresenting, or merely being less than forthright. All of these actions are intended to cause someone to believe what is not true.

Our society depends on a level of trust, a belief that people will exchange and share information that is true. Without such trust, interaction among people will be stifled, and the functioning of society will be thwarted.

Given the premium value on truth, when, if ever, is it appropriate for a journalist to deceive someone in gathering information or reporting a story?

Journalists disagree. Some subscribe to a rigid rule, saying that any form of deception to obtain information is unacceptable in a profession whose mission is truthtelling. Others would argue that while deception is to be avoided, it may be acceptable in those rare instances in which the value of the information sought is of overwhelming importance, and the information can be obtained in no other way. Others would suggest there is a distinction among forms of deception, between outright lying and merely not revealing everything, between using hidden cameras in a public place and hiding cameras on the person of someone who is at the same time pretending to be someone else.

The issue of deception places a premium on the ability of individual journalists and news organizations to do solid, ethical decision making. In some cases, deception might allow journalists to come closer to exploring the truth, but those who deceive can cause great harm to the credibility of journalism and may harm individuals who are deceived.

Deception

Checklist

What does it mean to lie? Ethicist Sissela Bok wrote an outstanding book on this subject, called *Lying: Moral Choice in Public and Private Life*. In that book, she says lying is one form of deception. "I shall define as a lie any intentionally deceptive message which is stated." The act of deception, Bok says, can be much broader. "When we undertake to deceive others intentionally, we communicate messages meant to mislead them, meant to make them believe what we ourselves do not believe. We can do so through gesture, through disguise, by means of action or inaction, even through silence."

In an effort to determine when the use of deception at whatever level might be justified by journalists, the participants in an ethical decision making seminar at The Poynter Institute for Media Studies created the following criteria:

When is deception by a journalist justified? What are the criteria for a "Just Lie?" **To justify a lie or deception one must fulfill all of the criteria.**

- When the information sought is of profound importance. It must be of vital public interest, such as revealing great "system failure" at the top levels, or it must prevent profound harm to individuals.
- When all other alternatives to obtaining the same information have been exhausted.
- When the journalists involved are willing to fully and openly disclose the nature of the deception and the reason for it to those involved and to the public.
- When the individuals involved and their news organization apply excellence, through outstanding craftsmanship as well as the commitment of time and funding needed to fully pursue the story.
- When the harm prevented by the information revealed through deception outweighs any harm caused by the act of deception.
- When the journalists involved have conducted a meaningful, collaborative, and deliberative decision making process in which they weigh:
    - the consequences (short- and long-term) of the deception on those being deceived
    - the impact on journalistic credibility
    - the motivations for their actions
    - the deceptive act in relation to their editorial mission
    - the legal implications of the action
    - the consistency of their reasoning and their action.

Case Study #20

ABC and Food Lion

Summary

ABC News journalists have used hidden cameras on a number of occasions over the years, the reports often airing on the network's "PrimeTime Live" program. Some stories revealed dangerous or illegal situations in board and care homes, child care facilities and veterans hospitals. In other cases journalists used hidden cameras to help expose insurance scams and racial discrimination by landlords and real estate agents.

Yet, no "PrimeTime Live" story has generated as much public attention and journalistic soul-searching as the reporting on the Food Lion supermarket chain. To investigate allegations of unsanitary food-handling practices at Food Lion, two ABC producers worked briefly in the spring of 1992 at several of the company's supermarkets in the Carolinas. The producers misrepresented themselves on their job applications, and once employed they concealed cameras in wigs and clothing to record videotape and sound for their story.

The "PrimeTime Live" expose aired in November of 1992. The broadcast reported rat-gnawed cheese and spoiled meat and chicken being washed with bleach and redated for sale past the manufacturer's sell-by date. In interviews, Food Lion employees and former employees attested to being told to take part in such practices, and many former store workers signed affidavits swearing to the same effect.

Food Lion claimed its reputation was severely damaged by the revelations and that it lost $1.7 billion to $2.5 billion in sales and stock value.

Still, Food Lion did not sue for libel where the truth of the report would be the standard. Instead Food Lion sued on fraud and trespass grounds, seeking to show that the ABC employees spent their time on the job at the stores performing their journalistic role instead of performing the work they were hired to do. Food Lion lawyers also said the journalists had made some mistakes in reporting, even helping to create some of the bad conditions they exposed. The plaintiff's lawyers also sought to discredit statements by some people it characterized as union supporters dissatisfied by management at the non-union chain.

So when the case of *Food Lion v. Capital Cities/ABC* went to trial in December 1996, the judge did not allow jurors to view the news report but rather directed them to assume that the facts of the report were true.

The network did not deny that it had used deceptive news-gathering meth-

QUILL
MARCH
1997
published by the Society of Professional Journalists
abc
VERSUS
FOOD LION
When do the
ends justify
the means?

ods, but it did deny committing fraud and trespass. Fraud requires intent to injure, and by performing their supermarket jobs well, the undercover journalists could do no harm as food workers.

The jury found in favor of Food Lion. Although the food chain sought as much as $1.9 billion from ABC, the jury awarded it $5.5 million.

In August 1997, the trial judge judge reduced the punitive damages award to $315,000. Although it publicly maintained that the original jury verdict was justified by the evidence, Food Lion accepted the reduced judgment in October 1997.

Analysis

This case clearly demonstrates how courtroom verdicts are cast in the extremes of black and white while ethical decisions most often emerge from situations painted in multiple shades of gray.

With the law, juries vote on right or wrong after listening to polarizing arguments from two sides of a case. With ethics, there is no defined forum the likes of a witness stand and jury box, and there is no volume of case law. It is the public, and to some degree professional colleagues, who will judge the moral positions of both this major network news organization and this huge supermarket corporation.

In the court of law a federal jury said ABC News and "PrimeTime Live" journalists trespassed and committed fraud when researching accusations that Food Lion supermarkets sold spoiled meat.

The debate over ethics in this case continues in the court of public opinion, focusing on issues of honesty, accuracy and fairness.

There is a pivotal question. Is it ever appropriate for journalists to lie to get to the truth? Put another way, is it ever justifiable for a journalist to violate the principle of honesty in order to honor the principle upon which journalism is founded, a duty to provide the public with meaningful, accurate and comprehensive information about significant issues?

Absolutists will argue that a journalist should never lie, no matter what is at stake. That position avoids the essence of ethical decision making and ignores the unique and essential role journalists play in a democratic society. Ethics involves making difficult choices when faced with competing values, conflicting principles and multiple stakeholders. Ethical decision making often involves choosing a course of action among several options, each of which carries negative consequences.

Journalists can and do face these agonizing dilemmas when reporting on issues of national security, government corruption or public safety. The consequences can be profound, sometimes involving risk to human life, the ruin of a person's reputation or the downfall of an institution or business enterprise. Even on routine stories about health care, crime, education and government, journalists face hard choices about what to report and what to hold back, about when and how to approach vulnerable people and when to step back.

ABC News encountered such ethical dilemmas in the past in deciding to use deception and hidden cameras to get to the truth. "PrimeTime Live" journalists went undercover to produce reports on abhorrent treatment of patients in V.A. hospitals and in board and care homes, spotlighting government regulatory failures that jeopardized the welfare of patients. In another report, "PrimeTime Live" used deception and hidden cameras to document the insidious racial discrimination that threatens the fabric of our society.

To be sure, hidden cameras are overused and misused by both network and local television, and journalists too often use forms of deception and misrepresentation as a shortcut in their reporting.

To be sure, hidden cameras are overused and misused by both network and local television, and journalists too often use forms of deception and misrepresentation as a shortcut in their reporting. These tools have extremely sharp edges, and when improperly used they harm innocent people and erode journalistic integrity. When the tools are overused they become dull, losing their impact.

Hidden cameras and any form of deception should be used judiciously and rarely. They should be reserved for those exceptional stories of great public interest involving significant harm to individuals or system failure at the highest levels. Furthermore, deception and hidden cameras should be used only as a reporting tool of last resort, after all other approaches to obtaining the same vital information have been exhausted or appropriately ruled out. And, news organizations that choose to use deception and hidden cameras have an obligation to assure their work meets the highest professional standards.

There is neither judge nor jury to offer a verdict on whether ABC measured up to such high ethical standards in the Food Lion case. The public and other professionals render that verdict. Perhaps more importantly, ABC must scrutinize its own journalism to see if it met the highest standards.

"PrimeTime Live" must make a convincing argument that the use of deception to get journalists inside Food Lion supermarkets was justifiable. ABC had considerable anecdotal evidence, including dozens of interviews with current and former Food Lion employees, that Food Lion supermarkets were selling tainted meat and fish products and violating other health, safety and employment standards. But ABC News needed firsthand evidence to be sure of the accuracy of those allegations and to document the extent of wrongdoing. While undercover reporting is clearly intrusive and invasive, the journalist's direct observation can heighten fairness to the accused by minimizing reliance on other sources who might bring tainted motives.

ABC must also make a convincing argument that in this case no other reporting methods would provide the same level of verification as undercover reporting. Granted, ABC could have purchased meat and fish products at the counter and tested them, but that approach is not foolproof, nor could it have revealed the behind-the-meat-counter story that would indicate the extent of wrongdoing and the reasons for it.

In the forum on ethics, ABC News must justify the level of expertise it brought to this story. Did the quality of reporting measure up to the highest standards required for a case where it lied to get to the truth? Were the journalists comprehensive and exhaustive in their investigation? Did they offer a contextual as well as factually accurate picture of what was happening at Food Lion?

Finally, there is this critical question: If ABC News used the threat to public health as a reason for the extensive undercover investigation and the use of deception, why did it take so long to ring the warning bell? Why did the network wait six months after going undercover before "PrimeTime Live" aired the report?

ABC had good reasons to appeal the legal ruling in the Food Lion case. It is equally important that ABC hold its own news reporting to the highest standards. Journalists need considerable freedom to do their work on behalf of the public. They have a responsibility to honor that freedom by being ethical and excellent at what they do.

—Versions of this analysis by Bob Steele appeared originally in a Poynter Institute Web Site case study and in an article in *Communication.*

Case Study #21

The Masquerading Mortician

Summary

Free-lance reporter Jonathan Franklin posed as a mortician and entered the mortuary at Dover Air Force Base, the sole Desert Storm casualty processing center, during the Persian Gulf War. He wanted to find out if the military had been underestimating the number of casualties. He found that it had.

On the face of previous reporting he had done on the war dead after the invasion of Panama, Franklin was convinced that the Pentagon was "screwing with the numbers." The Pentagon had forbidden journalists to photograph or witness the unloading of the dead at Dover Air Force Base, and Franklin was stymied in all his above-board efforts to penetrate the cloak of security around the returning dead.

He tried contacting the undertaker who won the government contract to prepare the bodies returning from the gulf for burial, attempted to get the number of dead from airlines shipping the bodies home, and sought unsuccessfully to locate the officers who were informing the families of the dead. After exhausting those avenues of inquiry, Franklin decided to go undercover.

Craig McLaughlin, then managing editor of the *Bay Guardian,* a weekly newspaper in San Francisco, said he chose to run Franklin's freelanced piece, although he usually turns down story ideas involving undercover work. He said he felt it was his responsibility as an editor to show the public what the war really resulted in: not just flashy graphics on the television, but mangled American sons and daughters.

McLaughlin said the deception perpetuated on the military's mortuary "was not a lie directed at an individual. It wasn't an invasion of privacy. It was directed at a government body failing to uphold the Constitution."

McLaughlin gave Franklin's story the green light because it passed his two requirements of undercover work:

1. There are no other means by which the story can be reported.
2. The information in the story is politically vital to the readers, with important public policy ramifications.

Inside the morgue, Franklin was apparently the only journalist to actually see the gulf casualties. He found that many of the combat deaths due to friendly fire were being reported inside the morgue as "training accidents," a practice that also occurred after the Panamanian invasion. And Franklin discovered a source who estimated there were "about 200" combat deaths, compared to the official Pentagon figure at the time: 55.

Franklin's one-page story in the *Bay Guardian* prompted at least one letter to the editor, in which the writer complained only about the gruesome descriptions of the bodies Franklin had seen inside the morgue. The story also won second place in the annual Project Censored awards for the most important stories bypassed by the mass media each year.

Analysis

The use of deception to gain access to information is always an ethical concern. The primary principle of journalism, truthtelling, requires reporters **to be honest themselves in their gathering, reporting and interpreting of information.**

At the same time, there can be rare cases in which the only way to inform the public fully about significant events necessitates misrepresentation or deception. Craig McLaughlin's two criteria outlined in the case above provide the base of a meaningful process for determining when it might be appropriate to be deceptive. There is another important criteria to add: If a journalist uses deception in the news-gathering process, that deception must be disclosed to the public when the story is published. McLaughlin said the *Bay Guardian* demanded that Franklin include that full disclosure in his article. That level of accountability forces journalists to be judicious in their choice of exceptions to the truthtelling principle and requires them to be ultimately accountable to the public.

Journalists must accept that when they are less than honest about who they are in gathering information, whether it be through actively misrepresenting their identity, using hidden cameras or microphones, or passively deceiving someone, they are lying, pure and simple.

In the case of Jonathan Franklin's decision to pose as a mortician at the Dover Air Force Base, that lie must be balanced against the significant public policy interests inherent in this case and the responsibility of the media to hold the government accountable. Furthermore, Franklin's decision to misrepresent himself must truly be the last and only alternative available in gathering and reporting that information.

News organizations and individual reporters who consider using deception should also weigh both the short-term and the long-term consequences of their actions. It is possible that lying may provide access to significant information for a particular story; it also could keep government agencies honest. It is also possible that lying may erode the credibility of journalism and undermine its overall and long-term ability to function effectively as the primary information provider in society.

Case Study #22

Surreptitious Taping and Eavesdropping

Summary

The *Lexington* (Ky.) *Herald-Leader* revealed that boosters had made cash payments to University of Kentucky basketball players, and that those players had also profited illegally by selling their complimentary tickets at inflated prices. Reporters tape-recorded telephone interviews with sources, but did not tell them they were being taped.

David Green, projects editor for the newspaper, said reporters Mike York and Jeff Marx had been assigned to take a hard look at the successful UK basketball program, especially the suspicion that it was built on broken NCAA rules. The reporters got initial confirmation, but all they had were handwritten notes. They feared their sources would deny telling them of the rule violations once the stories were printed. The newspaper, however, had a practice requiring reporters to tell sources when they were being taped. The reporters, in this case, feared the sources would not repeat their allegations if they knew they were being taped. So they asked editors for permission to tape without informing the interviewees.

Green said the editors decided the tapes were needed for the newspaper to avoid facing a flood of lawsuits later. They decided the surreptitious taping would not break faith with their sources because all sources would know they were talking on the record and were expecting to be quoted. The tapes were merely a more complete and accurate form of notes. They also decided that if any sources asked, they would be told their conversations were being taped.

The reporters interviewed 33 former UK players, all but two of whom said they knew of rule violations when they were playing. Every player quoted was on tape and, with a couple of minor exceptions, all went on the record.

The resulting articles, which won a Pulitzer Prize for investigative reporting, produced an explosive, mostly unfavorable reaction from Kentucky basketball fans. When several players denied having made their statements, newspaper editors responded by saying they had cassettes sitting in a bank vault to prove them right. Although they were sued by one person over a small portion of the series, Green said the newspaper editors felt it clear they would have been sued many times over if they didn't have the tapes.

Analysis

This is a tough case. At first blush it certainly looks like the classic example of "the ends justifying the means." After all, the ends included correcting a bad system and winning a Pulitzer Prize. The means, however, were problematic.

The fundamental conflict is between two of the primary principles of journalism: Seek truth and report it as fully as possible, while minimizing harm. This was an important story that needed to be told. The full truth may have caused some harm to the athletic community, but in the long run it produced a better good. A bad system was corrected.

The attitude a news organization takes—its journalistic duty—is to provide that watchdog function, regardless of the consequences. The fact that good consequences emerged is a bonus. However, if the only way that good could have been achieved was to rely on unfair reporting and interviewing, some questions remain unanswered. Most of those questions concern the nature of the reportorial harm.

The newspaper said it kept the tapes to prove the accuracy of the quotes. It even succeeded in convincing the basketball players that it would do no good to complain about being misquoted. But did it not, in the same process, show those sources that they had been deceived, that the press had used whatever means it had at its disposal?

The *Herald-Leader* had a practice of informing sources when they are being taped. It's hardly sufficient to violate a well-designed ethical standard by suggesting that, after the fact, if a specific source asks if he or she is being taped, you'll have to confess to doing so. Who among us wouldn't feel a little sneaky at that point?

Print reporters have grown so accustomed to using tape recorders that they often forget the tool changes the nature of the interviewing process. In a face-to-face interview, permission to tape is usually sought because of the awareness that people behave differently when they know every word and nuance will be captured for posterity. Broadcasters have long known that setting up cameras and lights and turning on the recorder affect the spontaneity of the interview, and they adjust the source-reporter relationship accordingly. Do not the same principles apply during a telephone interview?

News sources have a right to know the ground rules under which interviews are taking place. (See "Source-reporter introduction and checklist.") If the reporters and editors believe they have an ethical justification in changing those rules in the heat of news-gathering, they should carefully work through the pros and cons of the changes, considering the nature of the change, the impact of the change on sources, and the primary responsibilities to report fully and accurately while minimizing harm. All voices should be heard.

Case Study #23

Story or Stunt in Tampa?

Summary

The image had come to be seared into the collective consciousness of America as a portent of terror: a yellow Ryder rental truck parked in front of a bustling federal office building. Only this time, there was no bomb, no explosion, at least not in the literal sense. On this day, March 31, 1997—by no mere coincidence the opening day of the trial of Oklahoma City bomber Timothy McVeigh—the Ryder truck in question was rented to a Tampa Bay-area television news team and parked in front of a building in downtown Tampa.

If the idea and the journalists' news judgment were questionable, at least the action taken by government officials and building security personnel was swift and decisive. As viewers of that evening's WTVT-TV newscast witnessed, a station reporter climbed out of the parked truck and started walking down the street. Security personnel quickly emerged from the federal building, detained the reporter and searched the truck. All of this activity was recorded by a WTVT photographer and aired in that evening's newscast.

No legal steps were taken, but law-enforcement officials were quick to criticize the station for staging the event. WTVT-TV news director Daniel Webster—who was not involved in the planning, production or airing of the story—told the *St. Petersburg Times* the story was a test of the "status of public safety in Tampa." Offering that "if the scenario played out differently ... we might have done a piece that protected people's lives and led to a change in policies." Webster added that "if you had a belief that if you pulled a fire alarm and it didn't work, you might be exposing an issue of public concern."

U.S. Marshal Don Moreland, however, was quoted in the *Times* report on the stunt as saying, "In this case, I think a line was crossed." And officials at another local TV station were skeptical of the way WTVT approached the story, saying their own report on courthouse security was handled without having to stage an actual test of it.

Analysis

While the intent of the journalists in this story may have been noble—to examine the security status at the Tampa Federal Building—the reporting

TV mimics Okla. bombing in security test

The Tampa Tribune

Ryder truck test: news story or stunt?

methods were poorly thought out and outright dangerous. The use of the Ryder truck was insensitive to family members of those who died in Oklahoma City and unfair to the Ryder truck company.

The greatest danger, however, was to public safety, exactly what the journalists were trying to protect. This staged event held all sorts of potentially significant dangers to citizens, the journalists involved, security personnel and public safety officers.

It's not inconceivable that workers in the federal building might panic at the sight of the Ryder truck outside. Passersby on the street might also react in fear, conceivably even attacking the journalists leaving the parked truck. Fortunately, the incident was well handled by security personnel, but it could have led to a shooting. In addition, firefighters or police officers could have been at risk in responding to someone's urgent call for assistance.

This case demonstrates the importance of strong front-end decision making in a newsroom where managers and journalists seriously weigh the consequences of their actions. The risks in the actions of the WTVT journalists far outweighed the benefits. There were alternative reporting methods the television station could have taken to examine the status of security at the Federal building. While less visual, those approaches would have been safer and could have produced meaningful information.

This was a case where those involved ignored journalism ethics and completely forgot about common sense.

Deception

What the Codes Say

Norfolk (Va.) *Virginian-Pilot*

It is our policy for reporters and photographers to fully identify themselves when covering a news event. Some situations will call for judgment: Openly announcing one's presence at the scene of certain news events could impede fair coverage. But reporters, editors or photographers should not lie or be deceptive when asked to identify themselves. Journalists are forbidden from posing as representatives of other professions, including but not limited to law enforcement, the medical fields and military.

San Jose (Calif.) *Mercury News*

Under ordinary circumstances, reporters or photographers ought to identify themselves to news sources. There might be times, however, when circumstances will dictate not identifying ourselves. Only the executive editor or editor may approve such exceptions.

Philadelphia Inquirer

Impersonation undermines the trust that should be implicit in our relationship with the public. Although no guideline can be drawn that would clearly distinguish between enterprise and deception, the use of entrapment or criminal methods to develop a story cannot be condoned. There has been much debate over the appropriateness of such undercover news-gathering activities as the *Chicago Sun-Times'* Mirage Bar and a reporter's masquerading as a prison inmate or mental patient. In rare instances, such methods might be the only way to handle an important story. Staff members may not embark upon such an activity alone. Any such operation would be a project undertaken by The *Inquirer*, after detailed discussion and with the express approval of the executive editor or the managing editor.

Beaumont (Texas) *Enterprise*

Under all but the most extreme circumstances, people have a right to know when they are talking to a reporter. Under no circumstances is an *Enterprise* reporter to obtain information through any other means than by identifying himself or herself as a reporter and interviewing sources on that basis without prior approval from the desk. It may be necessary under extreme, rare circumstances for a reporter to go under cover to get a story vital to the public welfare which is available by no other means, but such a decision rests with the publisher and editor after consultation with company counsel ....

It is acceptable for a reporter to use a tape recorder both during in-person interviews and on the telephone without notifying the party being interviewed so long as the reporter has identified himself or herself as a reporter to the source.

Spokane (Wash.) ***Spokesman-Review***

This goes beyond the ethical question of whether reporters ought to pose as something else. That should not be an ethical question; in fact, we should be honest in describing our role at all times.

This has to do with stressing what to us is basic: identifying ourselves as reporters and naming the newspapers we work for.

We want to avoid the allegation that we somehow cloak the fact we seek information which we intend for public consumption.

Rochester **(N.Y.)** ***Democrat and Chronicle***

We should avoid impersonation. Posing as a prisoner or a mental patient or a salesperson or a public employee in order to report authoritatively rarely produces results that are significant enough to offset the risks that may result. There are two tests for editors to consider in deciding whether to authorize a covert form of reporting. First, would misrepresentation by a reporter violate the rights of individuals that are guaranteed under the Fourth Amendment? Second, is the information being sought of such overwhelming public importance that a reporter can be allowed to undertake impersonation? In any case, a staff member who has a question about the appropriate way to report a story should consult an editor.

Grand Forks **(N.D.)** ***Herald***

Staff members are not to misrepresent themselves to potential sources by disguising their identity or the purpose of their questions. The people we interview should understand they are speaking to a reporter and that their comments may be published. We should be particularly sensitive to the emotional or ignorant source, the person who is not accustomed to dealing with the press or who doesn't appreciate the implications of his or her statements.

Register Citizen **(Torrington, Conn.)**

When initiating an interview for quotes and comment, staff members should clearly identify themselves as working for the *Register Citizen*. Do not assume ordinary citizens are familiar with journalistic ground rules, nor take advantage of unsophisticated sources not familiar with newspaper procedures. When appropriate, clearly explain the difference at the outset between off-the-record, not-for-attribution, background and on-the-record remarks. Make clear the basic rule that if the source wishes information to be off the record he or she should so indicate before the information is provided. If reporters prefer to set special rules for an interview, do so at the beginning of the conversation.

Detroit Free Press

Except in rare and justifiable instances, we do not tape anyone without that person's knowledge. To do otherwise violates a general policy of treating people as we would want to be treated. An exception may be made only if we are convinced the recording is necessary to protect us in a legal action or for some other compelling reason, and if other approaches won't work. Such instances require a managing editor's approval in advance.

Chapter Seven

Diversity

Only recently have news media codes of ethics and books on journalism ethics begun to mention issues related to diversity. It is clear, however, that diversity issues have an important place in any discussion of journalistic ethics.

Diversity is certainly a part of accuracy and fairness, whether it relates to avoiding stereotypes or redefining news to better reflect a multicultural society.

Diversity is about the makeup of news organizations and about who is making decisions. Diversity is about the way story ideas are developed and who does the reporting. Diversity is about inclusiveness in choosing sources and about giving voice to the voiceless.

There is no shortage of horror stories about news media thoughtlessly running roughshod over the sensitivities of various groups in society—ethnic, racial, religious, sexual, physical ability, etc. While lessons can be learned from mistakes, the authors of this book believe we learn best from success. Therefore you will find a relatively positive tone in much of this chapter, including a number of suggestions for news organizations and for individual journalists relating to both staffing and story content. Case studies show how print and electronic journalists can and should practice diversity.

Diversity

Checklist

The following questions, protocols and recommendations for handling issues of diversity come from a variety of sources, including the *Seattle Times*, the Poynter Institute for Media Studies and KRON-TV in San Francisco.

Seattle Times Diversity Checklist

For beat reporters:

- As I examine and explore my coverage area, how do I assess its importance in the lives of people in various groups throughout the area?
- Do I attempt to find out how the actions of the agency or organization I cover affect people in diverse populations in our community?
- Do I communicate with my editor about ways to broaden our focus, so that the newspaper looks at this beat with an eye toward the variety of stories it could produce?
- Do I seek stories that originate with the members of the community affected by this agency or organization, rather than from the players within the organization?
- How do I expand my own lists of contacts and sources?

On general assignment:

- How do I seek story ideas? In what ways can I expand the types of people, places and organizations from which I draw story ideas and angles?
- Where do my assignments come from? How connected are we to various demographic groups in our area? How receptive are we to story suggestions?
- How well do I make use of diverse sources? How do I attempt to expand the paper's ability to tap those sources?
- How do I expand my own lists of contacts and sources?

For editors:

- Am I making diversity a clear priority in the assignment and scheduling of stories?
- Am I giving reporters the time to pursue diverse sources and stories?

- Do I get out of the office in an effort to develop my own sources and contacts in diverse communities?
- Am I challenging my own and others' notions of what constitutes news, in the effort to avoid ethnocentrism?
- Do I seek input from a variety of people within the newsroom evaluating stories and story ideas?

On a story:

- Have I discussed with my editor the possibilities for achieving a sense of diversity in this story?
- Have I sought diverse sources for this story?
- Have I allowed preconceived ideas to limit my efforts to include diversity?
- Am I employing "tokenism," allowing one person to represent a community, or am I seeking true diversity?
- Am I furthering stereotypes—or battling stereotypes—as I seek diversity?
- Am I telling the truth as I see it?
- Am I serving the reader first and foremost?
- What are the likely consequences of publication? Who will be hurt and who will be helped?
- Will I be able to clearly and honestly explain—not rationalize—my decision to anyone who challenges it?
- Do I communicate with my editor about ways to broaden our focus, so that the newspaper looks at this beat with an eye toward its importance in the lives of groups/populations in our area?

Making Connections: A Strategy for Connecting with Diverse Communities (by Aly Colon, The Poynter Institute)

- **Specialists**

  Contact local diversity and/or race relations specialists. Check universities, institutes, diversity consulting firms, companies known for diversity efforts. Meet with diverse people in your own organization.

- **Organizations**

  Contact local organizations that represent diverse groups, i.e. Hispanic Chamber of Commerce, African American Coalition, Asian-American Association, the Deaf Center, etc.

- **Publications and broadcasts**

  Meet with publishers/editors of locally-based publications (newspapers, magazines, newsletters) that focus on race, ethnicity, sexual orientation, gender, disabilities. Subscribe to the publications. Also check with television, radio and cable stations owned by, or oriented toward, diverse groups.

- **Leaders**

  Ask everyone you meet who they respect as knowledgeable people in their communities. Seek out unofficial leaders.

- **List**

  Create a list of people you can turn to in diverse communities who represent different perspectives within their groups.

- **Visits**

  Visit communities different from your own. Eat at ethnic restaurants. Shop at ethnic stores. Meet the owners.

- **Contact**

  Remain in regular contact with people on your diversity list. Meet them for coffee, tea, breakfast or lunch, *in their communities.*

Racial Identification Guidelines (by Keith Woods, The Poynter Institute)

The use of racial identifiers in the media was for decades a means of singling out those who were not white. The practice helped form and fuel stereotypes and continues today to push a wedge between people. We can handle this delicate material better if we flag every racial reference and ask these questions:

- **Is it relevant?**

  Race is relevant when the story is about race. Just because people in conflict are of different races does not mean that is the source of their dispute. A story about interracial dating, however, is a story about race.

- **Have I explained the relevance?**

  Journalists too frequently assume that readers will know the significance of race in stories. The result is often radically different interpretations. That is imprecise journalism, and its harm may be magnified by the lens of race.

- **Is it free of codes?**

  Be careful not to use *welfare, inner city, underprivileged, blue collar, conservative, suburban, exotic, middle class, Uptown, South Side or wealthy* as euphemisms for racial groups. By definition, the White House is in the inner city. Say what you mean.

- **Are racial identifiers used evenly?**

  If the race of a person charging discrimination is important, then so is the race of the person being charged.

- **Should I consult someone of another race/ethnicity?**

  Consider another question: Do I have expertise on other races/cultures? If not, broaden your perspective by asking someone who knows something about your subject. Why should we treat reporting on racial issues any differently from reporting on an area of science or religion that we do not know well?

The **KRON-TV Multi-Cultural Policy** suggests the following guidelines to writing and reporting:

- Ask your subject what he or she wants to be called.
- Avoid references to race in a story unless it is relevant.
- Avoid inflammatory language.
- Avoid stereotypes.
- Avoid double standards.
- Avoid repeating irrelevant information given by a source.
- Use care when using the term "minority."
- Be thoughtful and considerate of people's differences.

Case Study #24

Covering Communities: Taking Risks

Summary

Pat Burson will be among the first to tell you that being a race and community reporter is no small task. She will also tell you that she believes her job is one of the most important in journalism. Burson took on that role at the *St. Paul Pioneer Press* in 1996. She primarily focuses on interracial relations and people and communities of color.

"When you go out to cover communities, it's not easy. You will face obstacles and challenges," Burson says. "It's scary for me to go into different cultures. I'm afraid I'm going to say the wrong thing. But you have to be willing to take a risk."

Pat is African-American, but she points out that "you don't ingratiate yourself with any community overnight, even if you look like them. They need to trust you. They need to know you *really* care. It's a respect issue."

She says a group may have suspicions about you, because too often "we parachute into communities. These people don't even know us and we're saying, 'Tell us what happened!' Then we quickly leave. Sometimes it's like we go on a safari into an unfamiliar community. [We leave and we say] 'I went in. I got out alive. Now I'm back [to the newsroom] to tell the story!'"

Pat Burson says one of the best ways for people to gain confidence in a reporter is for them to get to know you as a person. "I want people to know *me*, not just my newspaper," she says, with strong emphasis on the word *me*.

Her stories for the *Pioneer Press* reflect that trust building approach as she writes about people who are invisible to most of us though important in their own communities. Pat says she gets her best stories by getting out of the office and hanging out for a while in communities, observing people coming and going.

Her lede on a story about a woman who has been running a small convenience store for nearly three decades goes like this:

> To most customers, she is "Mrs. Fletcher." Several call her "Mary." And, occasionally, a few will even call her "Mama."
>
> From her seat behind the cash register of the Selby Avenue Superette in St. Paul, Mary Fletcher has spent nearly 30 years foiling would-be thieves, befriending even the neighborhood's most notorious residents, and bouncing babies on her knees.

Pat Burson says that in reporting on Mary Fletcher and her superette, "I sat there for two days ... to see her open the store ... to smell the store, to see the interaction between owner and customers, to see her open her cash register, to see her hold children."

In many respects, what Pat Burson does is just good, solid, basic reporting. But it involves the challenge of acceptance into different communities where that acceptance doesn't always happen easily or quickly.

"You show respect for individuals by asking questions of them to better understand who they are and how they see themselves," she says. "When she writes about the people on her beat she cares deeply about what she does. "I am the guardian over these stories," she says.

Analysis

Pat Burson is one of a handful of reporters in the country who specialize in covering the race and community beat. She says she is still growing in the job and acknowledges frustrations. Nevertheless, her experiences provide a blueprint for others who accept the important challenge of covering diverse communities, whether full time or on an occasional assignment.

Here are some lessons that Pat Burson says she's learned so far:

• *You have to get over being uncomfortable around people who are different from you.* Covering communities—particularly racial and ethnic communities—means being around people with whom you may have little, if any, regular contact. You just have to get over that. What I try to do is look for the universal, and go from there. Yes, people are different, but remember: We're all the same under the skin. *If you can't get over the differences, you won't gain entry into those communities, and those stories will go untold.*

• *Know the rules before you go into a community.* In most instances, you'd do what we're taught in journalism school: Walk up to an individual, state who you are, the organization you're with and what you want. That doesn't work with all communities. In some, such as the Hmong community, you will need an elder or other respected community leader to escort you into the community. Or you might need to offer something—for instance, in some American Indian communities, it is customary to offer tobacco as a show of respect—before you can gain access to people you would like to interview. I'm not suggesting anything unethical, but *it's important to respect the customs and traditions of the cultures and communities you would like to enter.*

• *Every community deserves to be portrayed in a holistic way.* For example, all black men aren't gang-bangers or drug addicts. All white people aren't racists. And so on. No one person or small group of people in any community defines that entire community. Look for a variety of stories, sources, voices, experiences, etc., for your stories. In the process, you will tell some hard truths, debunk some stereotypes and show readers and viewers the interesting and diverse world we live in.

Case Study #25

Covering Racism: The Fourth "R"

Summary

Among the toughest ethics calls journalists must make are ones dealing with race issues. The *Daily Southtown* faced such dilemmas when it published a series of six stories in May 1992.

"The 4th 'R'" examined the role of race and racism in high schools in Chicago's south suburbs. The *Southtown*, a 57,000-circulation daily, serves that diverse area, including communities whose populations range from virtually all white to virtually all black.

The series evolved from a single story about racism at an all-white high school and a pattern of racist incidents there. In the interest of fairness and context, editors decided to expand the story to other schools to determine whether the situation at the first school was unusual.

"We needed to see what was going on from the kids' perspectives as well as those of administrators and parents," editor Michael J. Kelley said. "Racial integration in the south Chicago suburbs is going to be a major story to us for a long time, and it is important for us to approach it with a scrupulous balance."

Kelley assigned a team of reporters to interview students and faculty members at five high schools with varying racial makeup, to determine their views of race relations and find out what school administrators were doing to help the students adjust to suburban integration.

Editorial page editor Ed Koziarski said the editors and reporters faced a series of ethical questions: "Should we quote teen-age students by name or give them the protection of anonymity? How extensive a forum should we give to blatantly racist views, particularly those expressed by the leader of a white supremacist group? Should we suspend our usual guidelines discouraging use of racial slurs in stories?"

The paper decided to make several exceptions to its usual practices. "Generally we stay away from strong quotes and racial slurs," Koziarski said. However, "language and sensitivity were what this story was about," he said. "We decided early on to quote racial slurs that we would normally avoid, rather than paraphrasing, which would soften the impact of attitudes that were central to the story."

Furthermore, the paper decided to quote the teenagers by name in almost all cases, according to Koziarski, "with the notable exception of a Hispanic

female student who was dating a black student without her parents' knowledge, in order to protect her from her stepfather's potential ire."

The *Daily Southtown* also made other decisions that were exceptions to usual practice. Editor Kelley recognized that he needed to get some additional input on the series because all the editors at the paper were white. He sought the advice of black journalists, including a radio reporter who works out of the paper's office, a former *Southtown* metro editor and a feature reporter at the paper.

That advice included comments about references to Malcolm X in some stories, prompting editors to do more research. Additionally, according to Koziarski, "they noted that in early drafts of the stories, some individuals but not all were identified by race. Because of the subject matter, they recommended identifying every individual by race, and we concurred."

"The 4th 'R'" series was followed by two editorials on the issue of race and racism and follow-up stories on the racial makeup of faculties at the high schools and on teacher training.

Koziarski says the paper received some letters from readers saying the paper "will ruin the community" by running stories on racial issues. There were as many positive letters supporting the series, and Kelley says he received favorable reaction from school administrators.

Kelley said he felt it "was high time we covered integration in the schools," and that his staff handled the stories very responsibly.

"Nothing good ever happens when you keep these things in the dark. The more discussion, the more on the table, the better off we are."

Analysis

The *Daily Southtown* staff members accomplished some important goals in this case. They fulfilled their truthtelling obligation by publishing important stories about a significant issue in their communities. They informed their readers about vital matters, painful though they might be, in the belief that more information is essential to citizens. Furthermore, by publishing this series, they were holding the powerful accountable to recognize problems and to make changes, while at the same time giving voice to individuals and groups who were the victims of injustice and racial hatred.

The paper reflected journalistic excellence and good ethical decision making by committing resources to further probe and develop this story, giving it meaningful context.

Editors chose, for the right reasons, to challenge and make exceptions to some traditions or rules at the paper regarding the use of strong and racist language. Too many news organizations shy away from using such language for fear that it will offend readers, or in the case of broadcast, viewers or listeners. As Koziarski said, "language and sensitivity were what this story was all about."

It was ethically justifiable and courageous for the paper to use the strong language to tell the story of racism in the schools.

It was ethically justifiable and courageous for the paper to use the strong language to tell the story of racism in the schools.

Decisions to identify the individuals by quoting them directly are tough calls. On the one hand, the stories have more impact when there is direct attribution for the comments and viewpoints. At the same time, there is potential harm caused to those individuals when their views are aired publicly.

In such cases, reporters must ensure that the quotes truly express the views of the individuals and that they are being fairly characterized. Given the high stakes for both truthtelling and harm, this reporting necessitates great skill and care at every step in the process.

The *Daily Southtown* demonstrated that it was willing to examine its approach carefully and to choose alternatives to minimize harm, such as withholding the name of one source to protect her from potential harm.

A key aspect of the ethics in this case was the editors' recognition that they needed to increase diversity in the decision making process. By seeking additional views from black journalists, the white editors were able to hear perspectives that prompted several important questions and eventually changes in story content.

That latter experience is a lesson for all news organizations, emphasizing both the importance of having a diverse staff and the need to increase the number of people of color in management. The *Southtown* chose a reasonable alternative in this case, bringing in outside views. Yet it remains clear that newspapers and broadcasters must aggressively broaden minority representation in newsrooms at all levels if journalism is to effectively fulfill its obligations to a diverse public.

Case Study #26

"Nigger": A Word with Power

Summary

The CNN anchor was a study in euphemisms. As *Headline News* went "around the world in 30 minutes," returning inexorably to the O.J. Simpson murder trial one October 1995 day, writers presented anchor David Goodnow with a new way around the word that rocked the trial.

The slurs from retired Los Angeles detective Mark Fuhrman did not flow easily from the mouth of CNN's on-air talent this day. It came out as 'n word" or "racial epithet." At one point, Goodnow said the officer had hurled his insults at a group of "n's."

This wasn't the first time journalists had to figure out how to say "nigger" without offending people. But Fuhrman's titillating, slur-laced tales of corrupt policing in Los Angeles combined with Simpson's international celebrity to force the issue into the face of media decision makers across the country and around the world.

As with most ethical dilemmas, the paths to a conclusion were many. "We changed our policy on it," CNN executive producer David Bernknopf said. "First we started by using it as 'the n word.' Then we decided, 'Who are we hiding this from?' If people know what we are talking about, let's say what people are saying and hope people are mature enough to deal with it."

The euphemisms began sounding absurd, Bernknopf said. "It started sounding like a joke," he said. "We were being a little paternalistic, a little protective. But it's silly to think that we could protect people from a word that's being used every day."

People hear the word and say the word often, said Otis Sanford, deputy managing editor at the Memphis *Commercial Appeal*. Why cover their ears and eyes now? The *Commercial Appeal* didn't. The newspaper decided to use the whole word, just as it did when local members of a fraternity hurled "nigger" at a black man while they beat him and his white friends in 1995.

"The context has to be right," Sanford said. "We should report exactly what was said. No sense in dancing around and trying to be nice. Newspapers can't sanitize this world."

But the word has power. More perhaps, than all of the profanity that gets into the newspaper and onto the airwaves with increasing frequency. "I know its power because I know history and how it would be used," Sanford said. "It was meant to degrade people."

It was just that power, Bernknopf said, that pushed it over the CNN threshold. It was the same power that kept it out of newspapers and off the air elsewhere. That dichotomy identifies the core of the debate.

Saying anything short of "nigger," Bernknopf and others said, would not deliver the full impact—the full truth—of Fuhrman's words. Some have argued that it was the power of the word, all six letters, both syllables, that ultimately fixed the direction of the Simpson trial. To leave it out or disguise it in any way, journalists said, would be to eliminate a critical fact in the case.

Some have argued that it was the power of the word, all six letters, both syllables, that ultimately fixed the direction of the Simpson trial. To leave it out or disguise it in any way, journalists said, would be to eliminate a critical fact in the case.

"The words coming from (Fuhrman's) lips in any context were enough to hang him," said National Public Radio senior editor Greg Smith, whose organization used the tape without beeping out the word. "He used it aggressively, over and over."

But even in a direct quote, coming solely from Fuhrman's lips, "the word itself can still be offensive," Smith said.

Thrust into long discussions and great angst by Fuhrman's words, journalists elsewhere looked for alternatives that included the euphemisms and went beyond them. The *St. Petersburg Times* in Florida and *The State* in Columbia, S.C., took the route of many newspapers when they decided to use "n——" or other euphemisms for every reference to "nigger" that appeared in news stories about Fuhrman. *Times* world editor Chris Lavin said editors recognized that "the word causes pain to people and has a unique history." The paper, he said, had to ask itself, "Is there an overriding reason to cause pain to readers?"

At *The State*, news editor Diane Frea said the paper now groups "nigger" with other obscenities, requiring top management approval before the word can appear in print. "I talked to a colleague who said, 'Every time I see that word in print, it's a slap in my face,'" Frea said. "It's not the paper's place to be slapping our readers."

At KRON-TV in San Francisco, managing editor Lisa White said her station's decision developed through similar collaboration. "The news director said we need to talk with some of the minority members of our newsroom and see how they feel about this," White said. "One of our anchors, Pam Moore, who is African-American, said it would be very difficult for her to read the word, and we relied a lot on her view."

Anchors, the station decided, would not say the word. But managers decided that "we wouldn't make any attempt to censor, soundwise, the words from the trial, to bleep out the word 'nigger' from our tapes," White said. "There wasn't much questioning of that at all."

The station decided to allow graphics to display the whole word. Viewers could see the word "nigger" in a graphic, but what they heard from the anchor was "the n word."

Although there was dissent in the newsroom from those who thought that the station was trying to "sanitize" the news, the decision was firm.

Analysis

How, news organizations wondered, do we allow viewers, listeners and readers to feel the full impact of a racial slur while not perpetuating the injury that such words still can cause?

What is the harm beyond hurt feelings? And isn't the word in such common usage that its harm is minimized? Won't the word ultimately lose its power if the media air it more frequently?

The answer lies in the history of language, said Antonio McDaniel, a professor of sociology at the University of Pennsylvania. "The word has specific meaning," McDaniel said. "It is a solid rallying call for racists of various colors. It is a conceptualization of African people that others have perpetuated for years. There is a degradation of the position of black people in society. Use it as long as you appreciate the gravity of what's being said."

History belies the notion that using the word repeatedly will rob it of its destructive power, McDaniel said. Just as the most profane words in the language, though used frequently, remain offensive in most contexts, so "nigger" retains its most sinister meaning, he said. "We need to place that word in the category with the worst words in the language," he said. "Just because you are desensitized to it doesn't mean that it loses its meaning."

Young people living in a culture saturated with violence from the neighborhood to the newspaper to prime-time programming see nothing wrong with violence, McDaniel said. Likewise, repeated use of "nigger" may make its use more common but no less devastating, he said. "People are saying it in their living rooms, that's true," he said. "But that doesn't mean they want to see it on the front page of the *New York Times*."

For news organizations grappling with this decision, context was everything. KRON's White said the "explosiveness" of the word in the context of an admittedly brutal police officer made its utterance more incendiary. But KRON did decide to say "nigger" when reporting on efforts to remove the novel *The Adventures of Huckleberry Finn* from school reading lists. That issue of context, White said, prevents the station from having a "blanket policy" regarding epithets.

Though journalists disagree on how the word should be handled, most say that it helps to talk—as early and with as many people as possible. It helps to consider the potential harm, to understand the context, to decide whether it's more important to use the specific epithet or whether it will suffice to tell viewers, reader and listeners that someone used an obscene word.

Editors should set a high threshold for using the word, sociologist McDaniel said. "The editor should feel the pressure and weight of this decision as though he's doing something profoundly important, because he is," he said.

The decision should not necessarily produce a precedent, CNN's Bernknopf said, just a better process.

"If it came up tomorrow in relation to another case when the word 'nigger' was used a part of the story we would get into a whole new conversation and start from ground zero again as to whether it was appropriate to use the word," he said. "I don't think there is any precedent other than that we talk about the matter."

—This case was written originally by Keith Woods for The Poynter Institute Web site.

Case Study #27

Covering the St. Petersburg Riot

Summary

Bill McGinty was having a rough night.

As nightside reporter for Tampa Bay's CBS affiliate, WTSP-TV, he was doing his best to cover not just the story of the night but perhaps the story of 1996 in St. Petersburg, Fla. McGinty had spent part of the evening lying atop a station truck, looking through the viewfinder of a camera, watching his car burn. He had never liked the idea of taking the car on reporting assignments, but he never quite envisioned his car being torched.

If McGinty thought he had it bad, he had only to check with his competitors from WTOG-TV down the street. They had one vehicle parked in front of McGinty's and another right behind. Both vehicles went up in flames. The vivid video would lead the network morning programs and appear prominently in many local newscasts around the country. In addition to losing two news vehicles, a WTOG photojournalist was cut on the arm by shattered glass that rained down on him as a crowd hurled bricks and rocks at the station's news truck.

At the same time that night, Tampa Bay's Fox affiliate, WTVT-TV, was broadcasting the fifth game of the World Series; the NBC affiliate, WFLA-TV, was rolling the top-rated program "ER"; and the ABC affiliate, WFTS-TV, was providing live, uninterrupted coverage of the event.

The riots in St. Petersburg, sparked by the shooting of an 18-year-old black motorist by a white police officer, made a lot of people in the Tampa Bay area rethink things they felt they knew about race relations, law enforcement and their community. Most of the images they had to go on came from local television news.

WTSP's McGinty chose not to reveal on the air just what he had been through that night. But viewers could tell—if not from his words, then from his stressed tone and agitated manner. McGinty, who often delivers his reports in an excited manner, was more worked up than usual the night of the rioting.

"We understand this riot is continuing to grow and there is no sign of it being under control," McGinty reported live near the top of the 11 p.m. newscast. A few minutes later another reporter, at the same spot, reported that the riot was under control.

WTSP news director Mike Cavender praised McGinty's work.

"I'm sure there is a point on stories where reporters are too much a part of it

St. Petersburg Times

FRIDAY, OCTOBER 25, 1996

25¢

FULL PAGE OF PHOTOS INSIDE – 8A

Violence, fires erupt after police kill driver

CHAOS: 500 police, firefighters respond; 15 hurt; 10 fires set.

PLEA FOR PEACE: City officials appeal to residents. 1A

INTERSECTION: At the same place 18 years ago, a disturbance. 10A

Police officers, led by Chief Darrel Stephens, right center, and residents clash Thursday at 16th Street and 18th Avenue S after an officer killed a driver during a traffic stop.

■ Suspect shot in stolen car; the disturbance spreads over 200 blocks in St. Petersburg.

School news

A WTOG-Ch. 44 van burns Thursday after the crowd set it on fire. A photographer escaped by using his camera as a shield.

THE TIMES TODAY

Pettitte gets sweep revenge

The Yankees win a classic duel as Andy Pettitte bounces back to beat the Braves' John Smoltz 1-0. New York wins all three games in Atlanta to take 3-2 World Series lead. PAGE 1C

Local

Nation

World

Medigap premiums soaring 20% to 40%

■ A study shows the largest Medigap insurance companies are raising rates too fast for many struggling seniors.

"I need your help between now and Nov. 5," Bob Dole says.

'Wake up, America,' Dole pleads to voters

INDEX

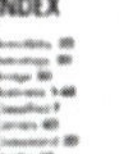

to report on it," Cavender said. "I don't think this was one of those cases ... I don't think that (the fact that McGinty's car was set afire) diminishes his ability to perform. And I didn't think so that evening or I would have made a change."

The injured WTOG photojournalist, Dave DeJohn, was interviewed in the newsroom studio just hours after escaping his flaming news truck. The station's news anchors asked him whether the news media contributed in any way to exacerbating the situation.

"Yeah," DeJohn said. "I was there when this group of African-Americans ... they were giving the police a hard time. I showed up with my camera and once I did, they started acting up a lot more .... They were in the middle of the center of attention, they knew that our cameras were there, yeah, they started going crazy. Then the police came up to us and said, 'Look, take your cameras out of here. The people are acting up. Just get out and they'll settle down.'"

DeJohn said he and other photojournalists packed up their cameras and left.

By 8 or 9 p.m., Tampa Bay journalists knew that residents in St. Petersburg were rioting.

WTVT, the Fox affiliate, had the biggest audience in town that night. By 10 p.m., more than 30 percent of the area's homes with TV sets were tuned in to the World Series on Fox. The station's news director said he had a difficult decision on his hands: Should he interrupt the game to live up to his station's marketing as "Florida's News Leader," or stay with what viewers tuned in to see?

The Fox channel stuck with the game.

"If we were going to do something, it had to be complete," said WTVT news director Daniel Webster. "But we didn't want to do it because, number one, people were watching baseball and that's what they were watching our air for. Number two, this ... was a very volatile situation and restraint was extremely important. You had to be very controlled about the way you presented the information. You were very clearly wanting to be truthtellers but at the same time minimize harm. And the level of potential harm was massive. We felt, in balance, that we should, instead of giving just sort of a little clip, that it needed to be told in its entirety."

ABC affiliate WFTS, the station that decided to broadcast riot coverage "wall to wall" from 10 to 11 p.m., was later criticized by some of its competitors for being repetitive. WFTS viewers who stayed with the station from 10 p.m. on saw the same exploding police car, burning news van, fleeing family and retreating police a number of times. WFTS news director Steve Majors said the station had an obligation to recap the major points of the story.

Analysis

WTVT news director Daniel Webster was just one of many area gatekeepers who relied on two fundamental principles when deciding how to cover the riots in St. Petersburg:

How do you do the best possible job of seeking and reporting the truth, while minimizing harm?

In the case of Bill McGinty and his news director, there was another important question:

How can you report fairly and objectively on an event in which you have an immediate and significant stake? How do you maintain independence in such a situation—or should you?

The choices made by Webster, McGinty and others were not easy ones; in hindsight, some of the choices remain troubling.

Consider the complexity of the dilemma that night. How could assignment editors, reporters, anchors and camera crews be honest, fair and courageous in gathering, reporting and interpreting information that is inherently sensational, while showing the respect and concern for sources and audiences that such a story demands? How could they do so in the pandemonium of breaking and unpredictable events, given the very real possibility that by their mere presence on the scene they were exasperating the turmoil? How could they focus on the causes and consequences of a complex story when their own personal and company vehicles were in flames, and when they felt their own lives were in danger? How could they tell a complete and honest story to the world when knowing the dominant (and repeated) image would be the flaming news vans? And how could they choose between 1) the demands of a massive TV audience who wanted escape and recreation, and 2) the civic but perhaps unappreciated sense that people need to know their community was in chaos?

The unexpected riot in St. Petersburg forced the journalistic decision making processes to kick in, at warp speed.

The unexpected riot in St. Petersburg forced the journalistic decision making processes to kick in, at warp speed. There was no time to call a quiet seminar on how to balance competing principles, no opportunity to bring together a diverse group of stakeholders and seek counsel. There wasn't even time to look up policy statements. If there had been time, journalists would have found that several years earlier, after rioting followed another police shooting of a young African-American man in Tampa, a press-community forum developed a clear set of voluntary guidelines for TV crews. (Given the rapid turnover of television news personnel in the market, it is little wonder that no one remembered that it wasn't necessary to repeat history.) The guidelines:

1—Don't go in with marked vehicles; they often become targets of people who don't want to be on television or resent your being there. Using marked vehicles increases the chances that television will become part of the story. (Of course, most station managers have opted for the promotional value of marked cars over the safety of their employees, and as a result have very few unmarked cars available.)

LOCAL NEWS

Media criticized for disturbance coverage

By KELLY RYAN
Times Staff Writer

ST. PETERSBURG — Residents told members of the media Wednesday night they have lost faith in TV and newspaper reporters who fall short in providing complete and unbiased coverage of race issues.

"They made it seem like it was more than it was," said Jas'Mine Allison, president of student government at the University of South Florida, referring to the much-publicized pictures of a burning news van the night the city erupted in violence.

The three-hour discussion about media coverage of racial issues drew a crowd Wednesday night of more than 100 in the Florida Marine Research Institute auditorium. Talk focused on how media covered the two nights of violence last fall, spurred by the shooting of a black motorist by a white police officer.

Overall, people said the media had failed to provide comprehensive coverage that details the long-standing, racially charged anger among some residents. They criticized the media for not doing a better job of chronicling the positive things being done.

Several people said they resented that their friends and relatives — in Ohio, Germany and New York — were presented with TV images of widespread violence and destruction that did not accurately portray the scope of the violence.

Times photo — BRIAN BAER

Maurice Sebastian, left, of radio station WTMP-AM 1150 speaks to the crowd as Scott Libin from the Poynter Institute listens at a forum on how the media covered two racial disturbances.

They raised questions about the use of loaded words like "riot" and "angry mob." One woman asked how media define "south St. Petersburg," saying it was really central St. Petersburg hit with unrest.

"You should be beating up on us," said Forrest Carr, assistant news director for WFLA-Ch. 8. "Why did we miss this one? Why did we fail to see this coming?"

Eric Deggans, now the *Times* television critic who helped cover the disturbances, urged reporters to judge all sources with equal scrutiny, even institutions. Some pointed out that reporters often refer to the police version of events as fact.

"We were all very scared," Deggans said. "It was a situation where you didn't know what would happen. That can influence your thinking."

Roger Clendening, a member of the National People's Democratic Uhuru Movement and a former *Times* reporter, said the media problems today are the same ones he pointed out to editors years ago.

"The problem is economy, yes," he said. "It's also racism."

2—Don't use lights; bright camera lights may encourage people to throw rocks or other objects for—or at—the camera.

3—Stay back from the action; for the same reasons as given above. Stay out of danger. Stay with police, or, if you prefer, shoot from a distance.

4—Don't go out alone; have someone watch your back. Reporters need to put down their pads if need be to make sure the crew is where it ought to be.

5—Don't put on uncorroborated "eyewitnesses"; just as half a million people probably swear they were in the baseball stadium the night they saw Hank Aaron break Babe Ruth's home run record, many people will talk convincingly saying they saw what happened on the street. This does not mean to accept only the official version of events offered by the police, but extreme caution should be exercised in giving the journalistic stamp of truth to a single person's account in a highly volatile situation.

Mark Barroso, a free-lance videographer and president of the Tampa Bay pro chapter of SPJ, answers with "a loud NO!" to the question, "Should cameras be kept out of civil disturbances?" He said TV crews have brought problems on themselves by not using the sort of common-sense guidelines listed above.

"We need to cover the news, and the pictures are important," he said. "But if you act stupidly and make matters worse, I think even our viewers—who happen to be citizens, too—would support the cops giving us the boot."

Professionals, guided by news and commercial judgments, made some widely divergent calls that October, 1996, night and in the days to follow. Many of the calls were visceral. Days and weeks later, some of those gut level decisions seemed more justifiable than others. Much later, a call for front-end loading the judgment process seems warranted.

When questioning the Tampa Bay news personnel on their decisions, it becomes clear that the events of October 24, 1996 caught "the establishment" off guard. Police and city officials had not recognized that a substantive segment of their metropolitan resort community was near the flash point. Only later, when many voices had been heard and a national task force tried to bridge the gaps in the community were the depths of the problem widely recognized. Journalists, by and large, had overlooked the area of town where many voiceless but frustrated citizens grappled with high unemployment and underemployment, routine and occasionally violent crime and drug problems, etc. Significant efforts in subsequent months to report more fully—and with understanding—on the underlying causes of problems and proposed solutions have been coupled with efforts to cover the routine but previously underreported everyday "news" of ordinary people going about their daily lives.

It is unlikely the news crews in Tampa Bay will be caught off guard if another such incident occurs. If they and community are lucky, and if they learned some lessons from 1996, the experience will not be repeated. But if the unexpected does occur, the response should be based on principle, not on visceral thinking. One benefit of a good ethical *post mortem* is that the front-end loading should be in place, should it be called for.

—This case summary was adapted from an article by Scott Libin of the Poynter Institute, written for *The Weekly Planet*.

Case Study #28

A Columnist's Edge Cuts Skin-deep

Summary

In contemporary sports journalism, the *Miami Herald*'s Dan LeBatard is widely known as a talented, hip, young columnist with an acerbic writing edge that, he proudly proclaims, "sells papers."

So when LeBatard was directed to write a piece during the 1997 NBA playoffs bashing the Knicks and New Yorkers in favor of his hometown Heat—standard sports-page fare for intercity rivalries—what he sent was a postcard from the edge.

Or, from over the edge, his editors would say in apologizing for a column they called "inappropriate ... offensive" and "a failure of the editing process."

Reaction to LeBatard's column, in which he joked that even New York moms are named Vinny and in which he described Knicks center Patrick Ewing as having "a face used by cavemen to scare woolly mammoths," resulted in a protracted public debate in the *Herald* and in the New York press about racial and ethnic stereotyping, with colleagues and competitors alike turning critic on LeBatard.

The column, *Herald* executive editor Doug Clifton wrote in the paper the following week, had raised eyebrows in the sports department before publication, but "the debate didn't go on long enough or proceed high enough up the chain." Sports editor Dave Wilson described the editing process—the column was read by a deputy sports editor and at least two copy editors, including an African-American—as not "thorough enough." There was, Wilson said, "a major meltdown in the editing process."

The most provocative passage proved to be that which poked fun at Ewing's appearance. To some readers, and to the editors at the *Daily News* in New York, where LeBatard's column was run reciprocally as part of the hyped coverage—and to Clifton—the passage about Ewing, who is African-American, was "racially insensitive." The *Daily News* printed LeBatard's column but deleted the Ewing reference, but the next day a *Daily News* writer printed the passage in his own column, in which he denounced LeBatard as a racist and called for his firing.

Fellow *Herald* columnist Richard Steinbach, who is African-American, also castigated LeBatard in print, but another African-American columnist at the *Herald*, Leonard Pitts, while maintaining LeBatard had been too zealous and defending Ewing's looks, denied the remark had any relevance to race and

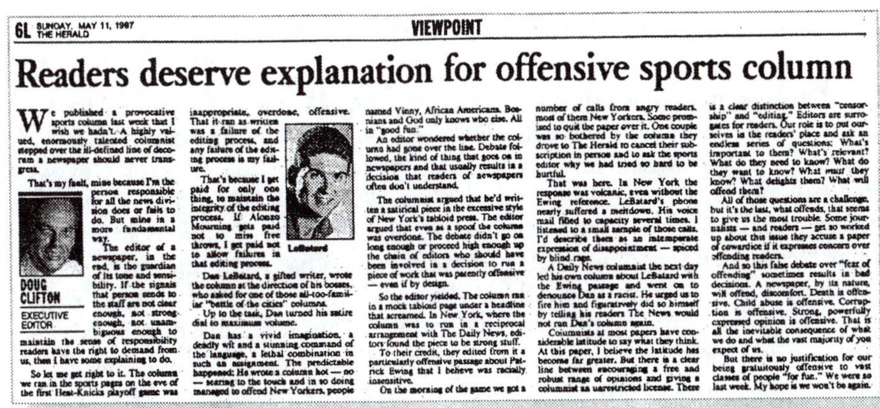

6L SUNDAY, MAY 11, 1997 THE HERALD — VIEWPOINT

Readers deserve explanation for offensive sports column

DOUG CLIFTON
EXECUTIVE EDITOR

We published a provocative sports column last week that I wish we hadn't. A highly valued, enormously talented columnist stepped over the ill-defined line of decorum a newspaper should never transgress.

That's my fault, mine because I'm the person responsible for all the news division does or fails to do. But mine in a more fundamental way.

The editor of a newspaper, in the end, is the guardian of its tone and sensibility. If the signals that person sends to the staff are not clear enough, not strong enough, not unambiguous enough to maintain the sense of responsibility readers have the right to demand from us, then I have some explaining to do.

So let me get right to it. The column we ran in the sports pages on the eve of the first Heat-Knicks playoff game was inappropriate, overdone, offensive. That it ran as written was a failure of the editing process, and any failure of the editing process is my failure.

That's because I get paid for only one thing, to maintain the integrity of the editing process. If Alonzo Mourning gets paid not to miss free throws, I get paid not to allow failures in that editing process.

LeBatard

Dan LeBatard, a gifted writer, wrote the column at the direction of his bosses, who asked for one of those all-too-familiar "battle of the cities" columns.

Up to the task, Dan turned his satire dial to maximum volume.

Dan has a vivid imagination, a deadly wit and a stunning command of the language, a lethal combination in such an assignment. The predictable happened: He wrote a column hot — no — searing to the touch and in so doing managed to offend New Yorkers, people named Vinny, African Americans, Bosnians and God only knows who else. All in "good fun."

An editor wondered whether the column had gone over the line. Debate followed, the kind of thing that goes on in newspapers and that usually results in a decision that readers of newspapers often don't understand.

The columnist argued that he'd written a satirical piece in the excessive style of New York's tabloid press. The editor argued that even as a spoof the column was overdone. The debate didn't go on long enough or proceed high enough up the chain of editors who should have been involved in a decision to run a piece of work that was patently offensive — even if by design.

So the editor yielded. The column ran in a mock tabloid page under a headline that screamed. In New York, where the column was to run in a reciprocal arrangement with The Daily News, editors found the piece to be strong stuff.

To their credit, they edited from it a particularly offensive passage about Patrick Ewing that I believe was racially insensitive.

On the morning of the game we got a number of calls from angry readers, most of them New Yorkers. Some promised to quit the paper over it. One couple was so bothered by the column they drove to The Herald to cancel their subscription in person and to ask the sports editor why we had tried so hard to be hurtful.

That was here. In New York the response was volcanic, even without the Ewing reference. LeBatard's phone nearly suffered a meltdown. His voice mail filled to capacity several times. I listened to a small sample of those calls. I'd describe them as an intemperate expression of disappointment — spiced by blind rage.

A Daily News columnist the next day led his own column about LeBatard with the Ewing passage and went on to denounce Dan as a racist. He urged us to fire him and figuratively did so himself by telling his readers The News would not run Dan's column again.

Columnists at most papers have considerable latitude to say what they think. At this paper, I believe the latitude has become far greater. But there is a clear line between encouraging a free and robust range of opinions and giving a columnist an unrestricted license. There is a clear distinction between "censorship" and "editing." Editors are surrogates for readers. Our role is to put ourselves in the readers' place and ask an endless series of questions: What's important to them? What's relevant? What do they need to know? What do they want to know? What *must* they know? What delights them? What will offend them?

All of those questions are a challenge, but it's the last, what offends, that seems to give us the most trouble. Some journalists — and readers — get so worked up about this issue they accuse a paper of cowardice if it expresses concern over offending readers.

And so this false debate over "fear of offending" sometimes results in bad decisions. A newspaper, by its nature, will offend, discomfort. Death is offensive. Child abuse is offensive. Corruption is offensive. Strong, powerfully expressed opinion is offensive. That is all the inevitable consequence of what we do and what the vast majority of you expect of us.

But there is no justification for our being gratuitously offensive to vast classes of people "for fun." We were so last week. My hope is we won't be again.

Reprinted with permission of The Miami Herald.

suggested the furor boiled down to: "Can you call a black man ugly?"

For LeBatard, and his colleague Pitts, racism in this instance was in the eye of the beholder. LeBatard, a Cuban-American who acknowledges having been the target of ethnic prejudice but claims not to feel its sting as others might, maintained that there was nothing racial in the caveman reference, citing white athletes who have the same facial characteristics. "Why can't it just be about an athlete?" LeBatard wonders aloud. "Why does anyone have to read 'black' into it?"

Executive editor Clifton saw things differently, writing that LeBatard had "gratuitously" offended "vast classes of people," and pre-empting the counter-claim that the newspaper's concern was mere misguided political correctness by labeling that argument "a false debate."

> ***"The real tragedy here would be if there were no lessons learned. In fact, there were hard lessons learned."***
> ***—Dave Wilson***

In retrospect, sports editor Wilson said, the editing process in place wasn't thorough enough. His department has "tightened up the checks and balances—either I or another senior editor gets a look at all columns as early as possible."

"The real tragedy here," Wilson added, "would be if there were no lessons learned. In fact, there were hard lessons learned."

Months after the storm, LeBatard said he remained "confused" by the episode and gun-shy about using all the ammunition in his arsenal of wit. "I can understand being cautious about what I say," the columnist said, "but I don't want to be afraid of what I say. You do that to a columnist, you take away his edge."

Analysis

As the diverging views of Robert Steinbach and Leonard Pitts, two African-American columnists at the *Miami Herald*, show, whether some comments might be racially insensitive is often in the eyes of the beholder. But the overwhelming public and media response to Dan LeBatard's column about New Yorkers and the Knicks, particularly his unflattering remarks about Patrick Ewing, are evidence enough that the remarks could be found offensive.

Despite a reasoned argument that LeBatard's reference to Ewing's resemblance to an ugly "caveman" was never meant to be, nor could have been, construed as racial stereotyping, the fact that so many people drew a racial inference raises the concern that the *Herald* did not give enough thought to how such pejorative comments might be perceived and did not have in place a process for flagging such problems.

From the narrower perspective of one editor, or even a few, it is difficult to foresee how a broader range of readers might react to anything that smacks of the controversial. In such cases, it helps to engage in collaborative decision making. And it helps to collaborate early in the process—during the assigning and planning stages of a story, column or project—as well as later, on deadline, when second thoughts about the appropriateness of language, for instance, might occur to either writer or editor. The collaborative process ought to allow for diversity, and not merely diversity of ethnicity or race; in the LeBatard case, the columnist and one senior editor who approved the piece are members of a minority group, and so is one of the copy editors who read the column. True diversity means a variety of minds and voices. Combined with the truth-telling aspect of voicing what one really thinks, diversity is essential to collaborations.

In the case of the *Herald*'s tabloid-style treatment of the playoffs package, the implications of mimicking a tabloid should have set off alarms among those who conceived of the idea and those who knew it was in gestation. Because the image of the tabloid today often evokes questions of taste and propriety in the minds of most people, editors who choose even to parody one should have been exceptionally careful to scrutinize the content of the package's every component, as well as the impression it gave overall.

Although principals involved in the editing of the LeBatard column—including the writer himself—disagree, in their recollection, of just what was edited out or kept the same, and why and how, all agree that the level of editing and discussion was minimal. In this case, "negligible" might be a more accurate description. Even though three gatekeepers read and, by allowing LeBatard's column to pass through, at least tacitly approved of it, it is clear that in retrospect, *Herald* management regrets that none of the editors pressed whatever concerns they may have had.

Ironically, in the *post mortem* discussions, according to sports editor Dave Wilson, the copy editors have been excluded from accountability and exculpated of blame. Such a top-down, noncollaborative approach can be self-defeat-ing. Every journalist in the process from content generation to publication has some moral and legal, as well as professional, stake in the outcome; each should be viewed positively as a collaborator.

In many, if not most, newsrooms, columnists traditionally have been granted greater leeway in pushing the outside of the envelope. In part, that may be because individual journalists maintain a fierce independence and pride of authorship in their work and do not lightly accept the questioning of it. In part, the freedom given columnists may stem from a lack of misunderstanding of the protectedness of opinion in libel law. LeBatard and his editors agree that the substantive editing of his Knicks column amounted to a simple request to delete and LeBatard's rejection of that request.

In any case, often at the end of the process, rank-and-file copy editors and copy desk chiefs feel they have neither the authority nor the support to question what assigning editors and department heads appear to have approved. Such organizational thinking reduces the work of gatekeepers to mere fact-checking, when instead the work calls for moral wherewithal, as well.

Newsroom managers would be better served, as would writers and editors equally, by having an ongoing editing process that allows for frank and constructive discussion, the goal of which is not to censor, but to publish—and to publish in as responsible a way as possible.

Case Study #29

Portrayal of the Disabled

Summary

It was the type of story that television reporters are often assigned without any advance preparation. Reporter Doug Miller of KHOU-TV in Houston, Texas, was covering a story involving disabled individuals taking part in a water sports event.

Miller and his photographer could have easily shot some video and gathered a few facts and made the story into a 30-second voice-over for the evening newscast. Or they could have done a short report focusing on the difficulties of disabled people in participating in such an event.

But Miller went beyond that. He and his photographer produced a story that concentrated on the feeling of freedom these individuals experienced while in the water. Most were unable to walk and used wheelchairs for mobility. In the story, they expressed the feelings of elation they experienced during their first time free-floating in the water.

What could have been a routine story merely showing the event or a potentially negative story detailing the individuals' difficulty in getting around on land became an informative and visual story about inspiration and success.

Analysis

Telling the truth in a story is much more than just providing facts. This case is an example of a journalist who took the time to recognize the value of a meaningful and fair portrayal of a group of individuals who don't always receive such media coverage.

By focusing on the positive aspects of the human condition, journalists can provide a more enlightened outlook about people who are often regarded as afflicted or handicapped. Reporters and photographers must be willing to try to see situations from the perspective of the subjects of the story. To those who are disabled, an ordinary trip to the beach can be an adventure filled with excitement and wonder.

News organizations can improve their coverage of the disabled by considering various reporting alternatives, such as first-person narratives, photo essays and series reporting. Additionally, it is important to report continuously on how well our society treats those with disabilities, in the job market and in building access. In that reporting, journalists should examine their use of language and images in stories to prevent unfair stereotypical portrayals of the disabled.

Beyond that, news organizations should ensure that their daily reporting includes people with disabilities in routine coverage of all events, whether interviews with stockbrokers, reporting on school programs, or athletic competitions. Newspapers and broadcast stations should also hold themselves accountable in this respect, taking the initiative in hiring and promotion practices to ensure that individuals with disabilities are represented within the news organization and that their voices are regularly heard in the decision making process.

Diversity

What the Codes Say

Detroit *Free Press*

Race, ethnic origin: The race of a person in the news won't be reported unless it is clearly relevant to the story or is part of a detailed physical description. If a strong case cannot be made for mentioning race, it should be omitted.

Racially and ethnically derogatory terms are to be treated as obscenities; such a term should be spelled as an initial followed by hyphens, and be used only in quoted material, when it is essential to a story, and with approval of a managing editor.

Photos or art work which foster racial stereotypes are to be avoided unless there is justifiable news value. In such cases, a supervising editor should be consulted.

Sexism: Women and men should not be treated differently. Physical description and familial connections of a woman are appropriate only if a man would be described comparably in similar circumstances. We generally avoid terms that specify gender, e.g., police officer rather than policeman, although such uses as actor/actress and waiter/waitress are acceptable. Phrases that suggest there is something unusual about the gender of someone holding a job (woman lawyer, male nurse) should be avoided. When referring to members of a group, a construction correctly using THEIR is generally preferable to one requiring HIS or HER.

Photos which foster sexual stereotypes or exploit the subject's physique should have justifiable news value to be used.

Grand Forks* (N.D.) *Herald

A person's race, religion or sex should be reported only when such information is clearly relevant, and staff members are expected to avoid usages that may perpetuate racial, religious or sexual stereotypes. Patronizing references can be as offensive as outright bigotry.

Radio Television News Directors Association

(RTNDA members) will identify people by race, creed, nationality or prior status only when it is relevant.

Independent Newspapers

With a shrinking number of voices setting newspaper standards, the standards are dropping. Marshall McLuhan called television "chewing gum for the mind." Many of today's publishers seem dedicated to turning newspapers into printed versions of television's colorful and glitzy superficiality.

KGNU (Boulder, Colo.)

Seek out more than one, two or three perspectives on an issue. The more interviews, research and diverse resources you use in your program, the closer you will come to "the truth."

Spokane (Wash.) *Spokesman-Review*

Challenge statements, descriptions and assumptions that reflect unfair attitudes about race, sex, age, religion or economic class.

St. Paul* (Minn.) *Pioneer Press

Women/Models—When we use photos of women who pose in scanty attire (bikinis, etc.) do not use their addresses.

Gays—References to homosexuals, lesbians or gays: we will not use language such as "limp wristed," "lavender laddies," "faggots" or "queers." Such language is considered derogatory and in poor taste. However, such terms will be permissible if they are an essential part of a news story or column and are direct quotes of individuals or from theatrical or movie dialogue.

Race—Race should be specified only if it is truly relevant. Do NOT use a person's race in describing criminal suspects or fugitives unless the rest of the description is detailed enough to be meaningful, or unless there are extenuating circumstances that make a suspect's race pertinent. Sketchy descriptions often are meaningless and may apply to a large number of innocent persons.

Rochester* (N.Y.) *Democrat and Chronicle

Staff members keep abreast of current issues, events and developments relating to minority communities. They are alert to the impact on minorities of events in the larger community. They use that knowledge to plan and carry out news coverage. They take the initiative to develop sources in the minority community and to gain perspective in covering minorities and minority points of view. News staffers are aware of the minority perspective or point of view and act to ensure that these elements are included in stories where appropriate. They spot subtleties in stories and headlines that may cast members of minority groups in an unfair light.

Chapter Eight

Photojournalism

Some might say that the photojournalist has the toughest job of all when it comes to journalism ethics.

Photographs and video images tend to generate the most heated of debates within newsrooms. And it's clear that the ire of the public can be easily provoked by a single photo or a short piece of video.

Making ethical decisions about what pictures to take and what to publish or broadcast is no simple matter. The very nature of gathering and reporting the news means that photographers are regularly expected to go into situations involving tragedy, to cover clashes between groups of people and to record the public actions of people who wish to protect their privacy. And photo editors, television producers and others who decide what images the public ultimately will see face equally difficult challenges.

The case studies in this section run the gamut, from recording the horrors of violent accidents to revealing the identities of minors, from documenting deplorable behavior to changing images to protect the sensitive.

What the photojournalists did with their cameras and in their editing is quite interesting. How and why they decided to do what they did is highly instructive.

Additional photojournalism ethics dilemmas can be found in other chapters of this book, nested within the framework of issues on accuracy and fairness, deception, diversity, and privacy.

Photojournalism

Checklist

Questions to ask before taking a photo or recording on videotape:

- Am I invading someone's privacy? If so, is it for an appropriate reason?
- Is this a private moment of pain and suffering that needs to be seen by our readers or viewers?
- Does this photo tell the story I want? Would another photo be more appropriate?
- Am I shooting at a distance that is not obtrusive or potentially revictimizing individuals?
- Am I acting with compassion and sensitivity?

Questions to ask prior to publication/broadcast:

- Do I need more information about facts or context?
- Is there information missing from the content of the photo?
- What is the news value of the photo?
- What is the motivation for publishing the photo or using the video image?
- What are the ethical and legal concerns?
- Who will be offended? Does such offense outweigh the value of presenting the image?
- What are the possible consequences of using the photo?
- How would I react if I were in the photo?
- Are there any alternative ways to present the information to minimize harm while still telling the story in a clear way?
- Will we be able to justify our actions? Would disclosure of our reasoning process that preceded publication help diffuse controversy and misunderstanding?

Case Study #30

On Campus: Tragedy at Ohio University

Summary

In the early hours of April 12, 1996, a vehicle carrying five Ohio University students overturned on a highway on-ramp near the main campus in Athens, Ohio. None of the students was wearing a seat belt. The driver, it was later determined, had a blood-alcohol level of more than twice the legal limit. At least two passengers also were intoxicated. The vehicle, a Jeep Wrangler with a canvas top, rolled several times during the crash. Students were thrown from the vehicle some 100 feet. Three died at the scene, and a fourth died 36 hours later at a Columbus, Ohio, hospital. The fifth student was critically injured.

Two reporters and a photographer from the university's independent newspaper, *The Post*, were on the scene shortly after the accident. The facts and images they gathered were vivid, powerful and disturbing. The photographer recorded the accident site from numerous angles and shot several photos of the dead students. Although authorities had not released names of the accident victims, the reporters learned that they were Ohio University students. After inspecting the vehicle, which sustained little damage in the crash, investigators emphasized to the student reporters that the crash victims had not used seat belts, and that the use of seat belts might have prevented the tragedy.

At 4 a.m., *Post* editor Joe Shaulis and his staff met with reporters and the photographer to determine the substance of the coverage. The most compelling decision concerned which photographs to publish with the story. The photographer presented two choices he felt were most representative of the scene. The first contained a large pool of blood next to the Jeep's canvas top, a spiral notebook and a sandal belonging to one of the crash victims. The second photograph showed the body of one victim surrounded by a coroner and police officers. Much of the body was covered by a sheet, but the victim's pants and sweatshirt were visible. The sheet was blood-stained around the victim's head.

Facing a 6 a.m. press start, Shaulis and his staff had to decide which photographs to use quickly because the front page and at least one inside page had to be redesigned and composed. The editors selected the second image, the one containing the body, because they felt it was the less graphic of the two. They reasoned that the photo conveyed the story's impact without resorting to sensationalism.

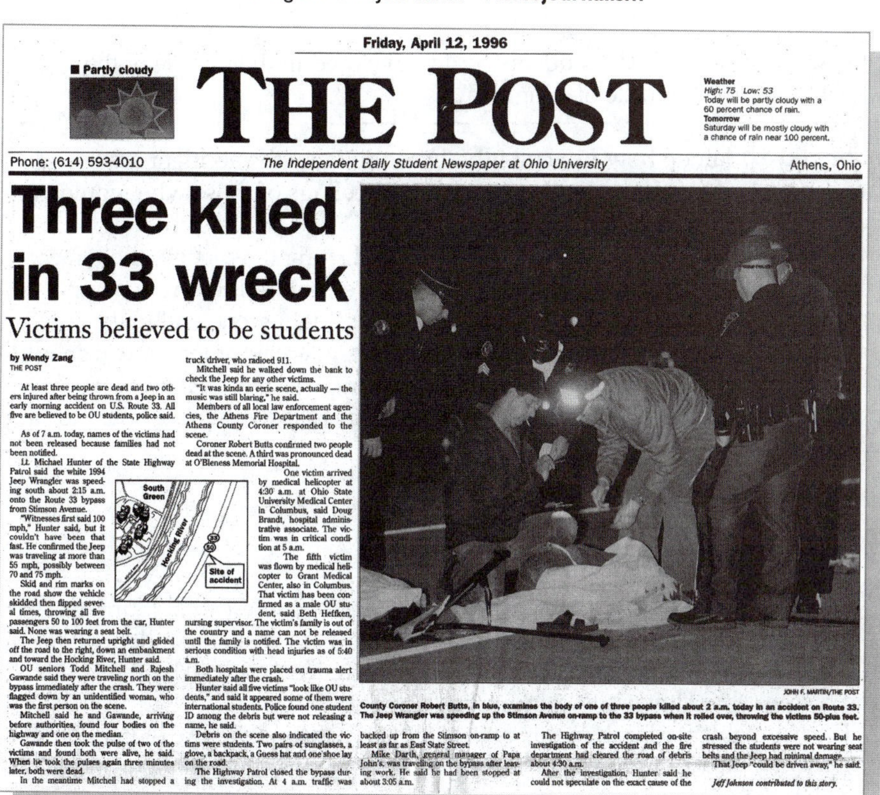

Friday, April 12, 1996

■ Partly cloudy

THE POST

Weather
High: 75 Low: 53
Today will be partly cloudy with a 60 percent chance of rain.
Tomorrow
Saturday will be mostly cloudy with a chance of rain near 100 percent.

Phone: (614) 593-4010 | *The Independent Daily Student Newspaper at Ohio University* | Athens, Ohio

Three killed in 33 wreck

Victims believed to be students

by Wendy Zang
THE POST

At least three people are dead and two others injured after being thrown from a Jeep in an early morning accident on U.S. Route 33. All five are believed to be OU students, police said.

As of 7 a.m. today, names of the victims had not been released because families had not been notified.

Lt. Michael Hunter of the State Highway Patrol said the white 1994 Jeep Wrangler was speeding south about 2:15 a.m. onto the Route 33 bypass from Stimson Avenue.

"Witnesses first said 100 mph," Hunter said, but it couldn't have been that fast. He confirmed the Jeep was traveling at more than 55 mph, possibly between 70 and 75 mph.

Skid and rim marks on the road show the vehicle skidded then flipped several times, throwing all five passengers 50 to 100 feet from the car, Hunter said. None was wearing a seat belt.

The Jeep then returned upright and glided off the road to the right, down an embankment and toward the Hocking River, Hunter said.

OU seniors Todd Mitchell and Rajesh Gawande said they were traveling north on the bypass immediately after the crash. They were flagged down by an unidentified woman, who was the first person on the scene.

Mitchell said he and Gawande, arriving before authorities, found four bodies on the highway and one on the median.

Gawande then took the pulse of two of the victims and found both were alive, he said. When he took the pulses again three minutes later, both were dead.

In the meantime Mitchell had stopped a truck driver, who radioed 911.

Mitchell said he walked down the bank to check the Jeep for any other victims.

"It was kinda an eerie scene, actually — the music was still blaring," he said.

Members of all local law enforcement agencies, the Athens Fire Department and the Athens County Coroner responded to the scene.

Coroner Robert Butts confirmed two people dead at the scene. A third was pronounced dead at O'Bleness Memorial Hospital.

One victim arrived by medical helicopter at 4:30 a.m. at Ohio State University Medical Center in Columbus, said Doug Brandt, hospital administrative associate. The victim was in critical condition at 5 a.m.

The fifth victim was flown by medical helicopter to Grant Medical Center, also in Columbus. That victim has been confirmed as a male OU student, said Beth Heffken, nursing supervisor. The victim's family is out of the country and a name can not be released until the family is notified. The victim was in serious condition with head injuries as of 5:40 a.m.

Both hospitals were placed on trauma alert immediately after the crash.

Hunter said all five victims "look like OU students," and said it appeared some of them were international students. Police found one student ID among the debris but were not releasing a name, he said.

Debris on the scene also indicated the victims were students. Two pairs of sunglasses, a glove, a backpack, a Guess hat and one shoe lay on the road.

The Highway Patrol closed the bypass during the investigation. At 4 a.m. traffic was backed up from the Stimson on-ramp to at least as far as East State Street.

Mike Darth, general manager of Papa John's, was traveling on the bypass after leaving work. He said he had been stopped at about 3:05 a.m.

The Highway Patrol completed on-site investigation of the accident and the fire department had cleared the road of debris about 4:30 a.m.

After the investigation, Hunter said he could not speculate on the exact cause of the crash beyond excessive speed. But he stressed the students were not wearing seat belts and the Jeep had minimal damage.

That Jeep "could be driven away," he said.

Jeff Johnson contributed to this story.

JOHN F. MARTIN/THE POST

County Coroner Robert Butts, in blue, examines the body of one of three people killed about 2 a.m. today in an accident on Route 33. The Jeep Wrangler was speeding up the Stimson Avenue on-ramp to the 33 bypass when it rolled over, throwing the victims 50-plus feet.

The published picture sparked controversy. *The Post* received more than 100 telephone calls and 30 letters to the editor condemning the photograph's publication. Readers aimed much of their criticism at photo editor John Martin, who shot the crash photos. It was the most intense public response to a story the paper had received in at least four years. Most of the letters and phone calls accused the paper of pandering to sensational and voyeuristic tastes. Some readers questioned the propriety of publishing a graphic image in a small, close-knit community such as Athens. The public outcry was so heavy that the accident itself was nearly lost in the controversy over the community's response to the photograph.

In its next edition, however, *The Post* devoted its entire editorial page to the accident and explained the mechanics of its decision to publish the picture. Shaulis and Martin laid out for readers the reasons they believed the photo warranted publication. Shaulis wrote:

> Only an image could convey the seriousness and the impact of an accident .... This picture has lasting value. It will make people think about the accident and why it happened. It will make them think

> about how any O.U. students could have died in the middle of the night, in the middle of a highway.

Martin explained how difficult it had been to view the accident scene and how he and other editors had considered the feelings of those who would be harmed by publication.

After the paper disclosed its reasons for publishing the picture, the tone of the overwhelming majority of the letters to the editors shifted from negative to positive. One reader noted, "If a picture of an accident scene will make one person think twice about doing anything unsafe in an automobile, you should print it." Another reader wondered, "How many lives were saved because people had the image of that picture in their minds as they drove home for the weekend?"

Analysis

This case puts all four principles of the Society of Professional Journalists' Code of Ethics to the test: truthtelling, minimizing harm, being independent, and being accountable. The lessons in ethics were learned well by the *Post* staff and by the Ohio University community.

The inevitable backlash in this case demonstrates how the use of images can increase the intensity of debates about privacy, compassion and reporting of tragedies. Greg Lewis, a former news photographer who teaches at Fresno State, has written that images of tragedy have more impact than words because the photo leaves so little to the imagination. A photograph, he says, "forces an image on the reader, one he or she cannot control. Its presence on the page is almost impossible to ignore, and its reality can be overwhelming." Use of high-impact images often provokes allegations of sensationalism and lack of consideration for the families of victims, and while these are serious considerations, they must be weighed against the role of the journalist in society.

The moral dilemma places the duty of journalists to disseminate functional information that may be of significant instructional value to a mass audience in direct conflict with a duty to refrain from inflicting unnecessary harm to those who have already suffered significant emotional distress. The conflict is sharpened when it is framed by the effect of publication on members of small communities, wherein media play a significant role in defining and reflecting the perspectives of community members.

As information is necessary if individuals are to exercise control over their own lives, the benefits of information distribution are of sufficient value to justify potential harms that distribution may inflict. The need to distribute as much truthful, accurate and compelling information as possible about a local tragedy must be balanced against the need to reduce, or refrain from inflicting, unnecessary harm on family members and friends. In smaller communities, one must also consider harm to the news media's ability to fulfill a role that

THE POST

OPINION

Editorial

Let us mourn with those who mourn

There is a time to feel sorrow, and there is something we all need to learn from it.

Column

Learn from today, hope in the future

My foot in the door

Doonesbury

Garry Trudeau

Letters

More thought

Inappropriate, unnecessary

Keeping Posted

Editor explains use of photo

Photographer saw and felt the scene

THE POST

research shows is significant for community newspapers: to be a mirror of the community's perspectives and values.

Lewis observed that the question of whether some images ought to be published will likely never be answered. Journalists, he said, must set their own standards, "standards that are realistic, carefully thought out, and that you can live with." With that in mind—and motivated by the need to avoid *ad hoc* rationalizing and rely instead upon moral philosophy—the following set of guidelines is proposed to serve as a justification model for journalists faced with a dilemma similar to that which confronted *The Post*:

1. Does this image reflect significant instructional value? How might its publication prevent harm to readers? Is an image necessary to illustrate the instructional value of the story?
2. Is it possible to present the image in such a way that it reflects its instructional value without inflicting undue emotional distress on readers or on the families of victims?
3. Does the image truly qualify as news of instructional value? Or is it the result of a "news event," staged for its shock value?
4. Should disclosure play a role in this case? Would explanation of the reasoning process that preceded publication help to diffuse the controversy?

In working through this case, and others like it, the initial questions in Steps 1 and 3 must be answered in the affirmative if one is to justify publication. Elsewhere, the model permits a good deal of flexibility as one makes judgments based on a sense of compelling but sometimes conflicting moral duties.

Any decision to publish a disturbing image hinges on its instructional value, which is the primary consideration of Step 1. Does the image, by its compelling nature, warn others of imminent harm or danger, or is it exploiting tragedy for the sake of meeting traditional, non-moral news values? If the impact is of great instructional value, the journalist has a moral duty to publish, notwithstanding the harm or criticism that follow. (It is very important to note that harm to others and criticism of the newspaper are very different considerations. Making a decision merely to avoid criticism is far less moral than making one that minimizes harm to others.) In the absence of clear instructional value, there is no debate, and the images that are disturbing or that could inflict unnecessary harm should not be published.

If there is instructional value, and Step 1 has been passed affirmatively, Step 2 suggests that journalists seek ways to present the image so that its instructional value is clear, while at the same time seeking to minimize emotional distress of readers or families of victims. This step, when coupled with the first, meshes nicely with the initial guiding principles of the SPJ Code of Ethics: seek truth and report it, and minimize harm. Research shows that positioning of images below the fold or inside the paper seem to reduce the impact of the disturbing images. Color is also problematic; where images of bodies or blood are concerned, it may be advisable to consider printing in black and white rather than in color. (The rival Athens *Messenger*, the town's commercial paper, had more time than the *Post* to weigh alternatives and selected a black and white photo of a state police officer examining blood stains on the highway.)

Next we turn to the issue of journalistic independence. As they move to Step 3, journalists may wish to consider the motives of people who attempt to manipulate coverage by creating "news events" as a way of making public statements. Instructional value rarely exists in such pseudo-events. The same is true for "news events" staged for their shock value. In the media's self-examination after the Budd Dwyer suicide, for example, the question of manipulation was raised frequently. Did the besieged Pennsylvania state official exploit the media to make a public statement with his suicide? Obviously, that was his intent. While his death and the accompanying circumstances were "news" according to traditional, non-moral criteria of news judgment, the instructional value of the graphic images that depicted the moment of death and its aftermath was nil. On the other hand, it is unlikely that even the most accurate description of the one-vehicle accident in *The Post* case could have served the same instructional purpose without the accompanying photograph. Thus, in the absence of clear and decisive instructional value that goes beyond the realm of manipulation for shock value, we recommend that media seriously consider the ulterior motives behind such events and reject those that fail to meet the instructional-value test.

Finally we take up the issue of media accountability. After the first three steps of the model have been considered and adequate justifications for publication have been identified, it is likely that disclosure of the journalists' intent and reasoning process will help readers understand why they saw disturbing images in their newspaper. Certainly this is true of *The Post* case. The decisive shift in the tone of the public's response demonstrates the value of disclosure in educating readers about the reasoning for publishing in such cases. *The Post* case also leads us to suspect that disclosure will be especially valuable in smaller towns, where the newspaper plays such a vital role in communicating community values and perspectives to readers.

The initial wave of criticism focused on reaction to the photo itself and its effect on friends and family of the victims. Before disclosure, readers were focused on criticizing *The Post* to the point that they seemed to have overlooked the accident and the deaths of four students. Disclosure prompted support for the decision to publish the photo; the intensity of that support was such that it nearly ended the controversy. Letters to the editor supporting the paper's decision indicated that their authors understood the instructional value of the picture. Disclosure fulfilled, at least in part, its aim of educating readers who may have believed that such images have no place in a small-town newspaper.

—This case was written by Paul Husselbee; a longer version was drafted for the *Newspaper Research Journal.*

Case Study #31

Tragedy at the Phoenix Tower

Summary

The image is, as the television news anchors warn, frightful: Buffeted by high winds, an unidentified man stands atop a 375-foot radio tower near a Phoenix shopping center at about noon on a February day in 1997. Below him gathers a crowd, including police alerted to the scene. The man appears to be shouting and gesticulating as he braces himself on a tiny platform with no rails, but his words are lost on the wind.

Then suddenly, after almost two hours, and as police attempt to establish a communications link halfway up the tower, the man reaches for a shirt he has hung on a short pole at one corner of the platform. As he grabs it, he slips backward off the platform and plunges to his death.

Some viewers of local television newscasts in Phoenix that evening saw video footage that juxtaposed scenes of the man on the tower with interviews of witnesses to his fall, punctuated by their horrified reaction. The news reports also depicted the man's fall. KSAZ-TV (Ch. 10), the Fox affiliate in Phoenix, showed the man as he fell off the platform, and only a moment more of his plunge; KTVK-TV (Ch. 3), on the other hand, aired about five seconds of the man's plunge, cutting away just before he would have hit the ground.

The city's largest newspaper, the *Arizona Republic*, printed two photographs from the scene: a closeup of the man on the platform and longer view of the man in free-fall, about a third of the way from the top. The picture combination visually and geographically dominated the front page of the newspaper. Although no story accompanied the photos, the headline, which appeared above the fold, read "Tragic drama atop tower." The caption said police "were unsure whether the man intended to commit suicide or had climbed the tower for a thrill."

Don Henninger, the newspaper's managing editor, said the decision to publish the photos was reached as a result of an afternoon of discussions about their appropriateness. Discussions involved the photo editor, an assistant managing editor and the photographer. "One thing we talked about was whether this was a suicide," Henninger said. "At the time police didn't know—or weren't saying—whether it was a fall or a jump. If it was a suicide, we wouldn't have run them.

"Since we didn't know, and there were all these other things to consider, with the people crowded around out there—it captured a lot of interest; peo-

WEATHER

SPORTS

Coyotes beat Blackhawks, 3-2

BUSINESS

Valentine candy hearts for the '90s

'The Beautician and the Beast' WEEKEND

FINAL EDITION

THE ARIZONA REPUBLIC

50¢

Friday, February 7, 1997 — Phoenix, Arizona

Plan would boost funds for Indians

Spending intended to offset Congress' cuts

President Clinton unveils his budget for fiscal year 1998, which outlines his spending plans over five years.

Clinton takes wraps off budget proposal

GOP is skeptical books would balance

U.S. leads in child homicides

26 nations rated on youth violence

Tragic drama atop tower

An unidentified man's trip to the top of a Phoenix radio tower ended in death Thursday. With his coat hung on a lightning rod, the man leaned against the light at the top of the tower at Tower Plaza, gesturing and yelling to people in the parking lot below, but his words were carried away on the wind. After about two hours, as police attempted to set up two-way communication equipment halfway up the tower, the man appeared to slip as he moved around on the platform, witnesses say. He grabbed the lightning rod, but it bent, and the man plunged 375 feet to his death. Phoenix police, who are investigating the incident, said they were unsure whether the man had intended to commit suicide or had climbed the tower for a thrill.

ASU studies 'gift' premium for best tickets

Move may doom booster clubs

Math whiz, 17, finds SAT error, board red-faced

INSIDE

2 bills would curb photo-radar use by Arizona cities

Set up in Scottsdale, this photo-radar unit targets speeding drivers, but the Legislature may target it.

Triple Crown or Grand Slam? 2 airlines waging prize fight

AT A GLANCE

ple knew about it and were hearing about it—we decided to go with it."

The *Republic,* Henninger said, has a policy against running news of suicides, although "there are always cases where you'll break what might be stated policy," he added. The tower pictures represented "dramatic news, no question about it," he said. "Getting that kind of photograph doesn't happen very often."

Doug Bannard, news director at KSAZ-TV, said that although his station does not routinely air news reports and video footage of suicides, it deemed this incident newsworthy because "it caused a commotion, with hundreds of people lined up on the ground watching it, causing traffic problems." Still, Bannard said, there was "quite a good debate in the newsroom" over whether to air the story. For the station, Bannard said, the decision to run with it came after its review of the footage determined the man appeared to slip rather than step off the platform. The key decision, Bannard said, was not "whether" to report the story, but "how." It was Bannard's decision, he said, to edit the footage to show the man slipping off, but not to show him plunging or to show his jacket fluttering to the ground. As a follow-up to the report, Bannard's station investigated how easy it was to gain access to that and several other such towers in the Phoenix area. As a result of the incident, he said, security was tightened at the towers.

The key decision, Bannard said, was not "whether" to report the story, but "how."

Not all Phoenix media reported the incident. KPHO-TV, KPNX-TV and KNXU-TV chose not to. At KNXU, an ABC affiliate, news director Jeff Klotzman said that although the footage made for "compelling video," he and his colleagues considered the incident a suicide that did not meet their criteria for newsworthiness. "The only thing we would have reported out of this story was the traffic problem that resulted, and we had no footage of that," Klotzman said.

Nor does Klotzman's station have a written policy to cover the decision making that goes with such stories. "Everything is reviewed on a case-by-case basis," he said. In this case, Klotzman, an executive producer, and the managing editor—with input from the reporter and photographer at the scene—decided not to air footage. Still, he said, he "didn't want to throw any stones at Channel 3 or Channel 10" for their decisions to go with the story. "In fact," he said, "I would stand at the head of the line to defend their decision."

Analysis

The coverage of this story highlights the tension between the principles of truthtelling and minimizing harm. This incident had a fair amount of news value, not the least of which was the matter of how this man gained access to the tower and what kind of security exists at similar towers in the Phoenix area.

At the same time, a decision to report the story carried the potential for harm to any number of stakeholders. Family members or friends of the man on the tower could suffer from seeing his death plunge. Viewers or readers might be upset by seeing the tape or still image of the fall. It's even possible that someone seeing this bizarre incident might try to climb one of those towers on a dare or to commit suicide. There is also the question of exploitation of the people watching the drama unfold, unfairly using these bystanders as characters in a morality play.

That potential harm can be addressed in several ways. As Doug Bannard of KSAZ emphasized, the key here is how the journalists go about their work. That applies to the news gathering in the field as well as the decisions on airing or publishing the story and the pictures.

In several instances, Phoenix television reporters interviewed bystanders during this drama asking people why they were watching the man on the tower and then recording their horror after the man fell to his death. Granted, the bystanders were there of their own volition, but the intrusion on their grief seemed unwarranted.

It is also appropriate to question the plan of the story in the *Arizona Republic*. If editors thought the incident at the tower warranted front page treatment, why didn't they offer more information beyond the photos and cutline? The images are certainly compelling, but there is little context to help readers understand this event and what it meant.

This incident offers us a case where the use of alternatives is important. The newspapers and the television stations could determine coverage by degrees and by tone, ranging from ignoring the story to blowing it out of proportion.

That degree and tone are determined by how much time or space is given to the story; by the size of headlines or the choice of video in teases; by the style of the writing or the delivery; by the size of the picture or the amount of tape used; by the placement of the picture on the page or the video in the newscast. And, most importantly, that degree and tone are determined by the focus of the story. If the emphasis is on the security issues or on the heroic efforts of rescuers, you have one kind of story. If the focus is on the rubbernecks who watched the drama or on the fall itself, you have a very different kind of story.

Tone and degree have much to do with the distinction between coverage that is legitimate and measured and coverage that is sensationalistic and gratuitous.

Case Study #32

Dear Reader: "An Indelible Photo"

Summary

Seconds after a Northern California jury convicted Richard Allen Davis of murdering 12-year-old Polly Klaas, a press-pool photographer took a picture of Davis, who held up both of his middle fingers. The *San Jose Mercury News* decided to publish the picture on its front page accompanied by a "Dear Reader" box soliciting reader response and explaining its reasoning for running the controversial photograph.

Mercury News executive editor Jerry Ceppos told readers that the picture showed Davis' "contempt for the system that convicted him."

"Ever since Davis' arrest, I've wanted to know about the character of a man who could kill Polly Klaas," Ceppos wrote in a front-page column. "Ever since it became clear the jury would convict him, I've wanted to know how he would react, what he's thinking.

"Even though it's unclear who the target of the gesture is, I believe the photograph tells us something about Allen's contempt for the system that convicted him. While the picture is vulgar, it does give us some insight. In fact, I suspect that it will become one of those indelible photographic images that will come to represent a terrible episode in American life."

Ceppos concluded the column, writing, "I'd be interested in your views, too."

More than 1,200 readers responded by fax, phone and mail — 815 in favor of running the picture and 431 against.

In a subsequent column, Ceppos wrote that he was grateful for the relationship he had fostered with his readers, saying it was clearly "their newspaper." He added that asking for readers' opinion made them "feel part of the newspaper."

Managing editor David Yarnold had suggested the note to readers during a *Mercury News* editors' meeting, which included Ceppos, the photo editor and news editor. Ceppos decided to add the invitation for readers to comment on the picture.

"In this case the picture was so jarring and so different from what the *Mercury News* usually does that we felt we owed readers an explanation—on the front page, right under the picture," Ceppos said.

"The key issues were taste and whether this guy should be given such a prominent platform. In the end, we decided that this photograph told us even

THE POLLY KLAAS CASE: DAVIS FOUND GUILTY

Now, life or death?

Convicted on all counts, defiant killer awaits sentencing

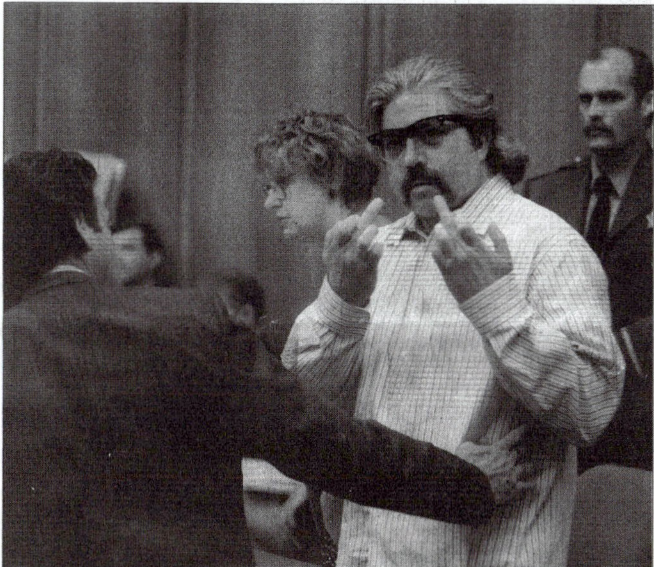

JOHN BURGESS — POOL PHOTOGRAPH

After standing impassively as the guilty verdicts were read at length, Richard Allen Davis turns suddenly and gestures to the television camera. Then he winked in the direction of the Klaas family and kissed the air.

■ **Next:** Special circumstances make him eligible for capital punishment.

BY SANDRA GONZALES
Mercury News Staff Writer

Seconds after hearing the guilty verdicts, Richard Allen Davis told the world what he thought.

He didn't say a word.

With both middle fingers extended, Davis suddenly turned in the direction of the TV camera and Polly Klaas' family and winked his right eye and kissed the air.

Polly Klaas Kidnapped during a 1993 slumber party.

"He was showing us what he is: just a contemptible little punk who's been flipping off society from Day 1," said Marc Klaas, father of the girl Davis had just been convicted of killing. "This is the beginning of the end for Richard Allen Davis."

For the 15 minutes before he made his vulgar salute, Davis had remained mostly impassive while the court clerk read the 21-page verdict forms proclaiming him guilty of the kidnapping and murder of Polly and eligible for the death penalty.

Klaas, who sat in the front row of the San Jose courtroom with his parents, clasped a district attorney's investigator with one hand and held onto his mother with his other.

Much of the time, Klaas kept

See DAVIS, Back Page

Dear reader,

The decision to publish the front-page photograph of Richard Allen Davis' obscene gesture wasn't an easy one.

Let me tell you why we decided to do it.

Ever since Davis' arrest, I've wanted to know more about the character of a man who could kill Polly Klaas.

Ever since it became clear that the jury would convict him, I've wanted to know how he would react, what he's thinking.

Even though it's unclear precisely who the target of the gesture is, I believe the photograph tells us something about Allen's contempt for the system that convicted him.

While the gesture is vulgar, it does give us some insight. In fact, I suspect that it will become one of those indelible photographic images that will come to represent a terrible episode in American life.

For those reasons, I thought the photograph was worth publishing. I'd be interested in your views, too.

Jerry Ceppos
Executive Editor
(408) 920-5456 Fax: (408) 288-8060
E-mail: JCeppos@AOL.com

JOHN BURGESS — POOL PHOTOGRAPH

Marc Klaas clutches the hand of former Petaluma police Sgt. Mike Meese as verdicts are read.

Arrogance, stupidity, contempt: Killer has it all

JIM TROTTER

A WORD to Richard Allen Davis, killer of Polly Klaas.

You're toast, sleaze bag.

Of all the stupid stunts that anyone could expect to see from a man whose life is in the hands of a Superior Court jury, Davis topped them all Tuesday afternoon when he turned in the specific direction of the TV camera and in the general direction of the family of the murdered child and flipped them off with both hands.

Gave them a little wink and a gesture of contempt with his mouth, too.

A kiss and two birds from a sociopath who is trying to avoid the death penalty. The jury found Davis guilty Tuesday of all 10 counts with which

See TROTTER, Back Page

more than we already knew about the mindset of Richard Allen Davis."

Five other Bay Area newspapers published the photo of the obscene gesture on their front page. The *Marin Independent Journal* ran the photo on its editorial page with an accompanying editorial. The *San Francisco Chronicle* published the photo on its front page but without an editor's note. The newspaper reported more than 130 negative phone calls, and several readers canceled their subscriptions. Only one Northern California newspaper using the press-pool photographer, the *Sacramento Bee,* decided not to publish the photo, allowing the text to convey Davis' message. The *Bee's* drop-head read: "Killer flips off camera after verdicts read." Reporter Patrick Hoge referred to the act in his third paragraph, writing, "Silently, menacingly, Davis winked, kissed the air and flashed an obscene gesture with both hands."

Bee Executive Editor Gregory Favre said that editors who said they published the photo to show "what type of person Davis really is" were looking for an excuse to run it.

"You run that picture for shock value only," Favre told *Editor & Publisher.* "There was no other redeeming value in it. We didn't run it to show that Davis is a despicable, disgusting, contemptible human being. What he did spells that out thousands of times more than any picture could ever do."

Analysis

Sometimes reasonable individuals pursuing the same goal radically disagree on a course of action. Editors Ceppos and Favre both wanted to tell the story of what happened in the courtroom at a crucial moment in that celebrated trial. They landed on opposite ends of the decision making spectrum, though both would argue they reported the truth of that story and properly served their readers. Ceppos, and editors at other papers, used the picture to carry the impact. Favre believed words alone would accomplish the task.

They landed on opposite ends of the decision making spectrum, though both would argue they reported the truth of that story and properly served their readers.

While Ceppos could talk himself blue in the face trying to defend Favre's challenge that he was just looking for an excuse to run the picture, the *Mercury News* editor took the best course of action to justify his decision. He held himself and his paper accountable by taking a public stance on why they ran the photo.

The principle of accountability says "Journalists should clarify and explain news coverage and invite dialogue with the public over journalistic conduct."

Ceppos tied his *Dear Reader* column to the photo to explain the paper's decision to run what many would term an offensive picture. This real-time explanation, used judiciously, is an excellent tool of accountability and a key element of the ethical decision making process. Additionally, when editors have to write down and publish the how and why of a decision, they are required to be reflective. They know their judgment and logic will be scrutinized in a very public forum. And, knowing that they will likely face dissent from some readers, they must anchor their decisions in a principle that at least will be respected, even if disagreed with.

Ceppos took the additional step of urging readers to give the paper feedback on the decision to publish the photo. The pro and con vote on the use of the photo is interesting, but not nearly as important as the fact that more than 1,200 readers made the effort to respond to Ceppos' invitation.

That invitation and the response to it speak loudly of the importance of news organizations creating an ongoing dialogue with those they serve. Such conversations, whether about dramatic photos or the coverage of complex and controversial issues, help news organizations better understand the communities they serve. Just as importantly, the conversations should help the public better understand the essential role journalism plays in a democratic society. To be sure, disagreements on course of action will continue, but they can exist out of mutual respect.

Case Study #33

Covering Victims: Storytelling with Power and Respect

Summary

It was a powerful photograph by any definition. It was also one that was very disturbing to everyone who viewed it. The image was made by newspaper photographer Kenneth Lyons on the evening of July 29, 1993. You see the body of 15-year-old Jeff "Shorty" Davis, as he lies dead on the pavement of the parking lot outside a convenience store in Hampton, Virginia.

Davis had just been shot to death by a 16-year-old who tried to rob him as Jeff left the convenience store. The police investigation was continuing and the body remained uncovered and lit by the lights from the police cameras.

This stark image was one of many pictures presented by Lyons to the editors of the *Daily Press* in Newport News-Hampton, Virginia, as they made the decision on how to cover the story.

The paper's managing editor (now editor), Will Corbin, had a strong, visceral reaction to the image of Davis' lifeless body, saying, "No way will we use that photo." He felt the image violated the rule of "no dead bodies in the paper," a standard shared by many newspapers. Running the photo seemed too great a risk. Readers would be offended and perhaps very angry with the paper, and the photo would be invasive and harmful to the family members of Jeff Davis.

Despite his strong initial reservations, Corbin kept the conversation alive. He brought more voices into the discussion to hear different points of view. Some argued that this photo was important to the story, challenging the no dead bodies rule. That challenge led the discussion to what reasons exist for publishing the photo. Why was it newsworthy? Why was it an essential part of the story of this murder?

As the discussion in the newsroom continued, a consensus emerged that the readers would better comprehend the larger context of this murder by first observing the stark image of the dead body of Jeff Davis.

Will Corbin explained the decision to use the photo in a column he wrote to readers of his paper.

> This photograph would make our readers angry in a way that was worth upsetting them. It would leave a lasting and indelible

Another tragedy of youth

The body of Jeff Davis Jr., 15, lies near a Pembroke Avenue convenience store in Hampton Thursday night. He was gunned down during an attempted robbery. A 16-year-old suspect has been charged with capital murder. Photos by **Kenneth D. Lyons**/Daily Press

DAVIS. Would have been a sophomore in high school.

Father: 'My kid lost his life for nothing'

By Matt Murray
Daily Press

HAMPTON

This morning, Jeff Davis Jr. — "Shorty," they called him, or "Little Jeff" — was supposed to climb into a car with his father and his younger brother and drive down to Tarboro, N.C.

There, he was supposed to sit down with 250 relatives at a family reunion, to talk about rap music and the Dallas Cowboys and how someday Shorty Davis — who is 6 feet tall and 170 pounds — would play football for the Tar Heels of North Carolina.

Tonight, he was supposed to eat too much — as he always did — at a big dinner, with chicken, string beans, potatoes, cabbage, yams, collard greens and sweet potato pie.

Instead, he is dead, a few weeks before his 16th birthday, and his family is coming to Hampton to mourn.

"I am hurt," his father, Jeff Davis Sr. said Friday evening. "My kid lost his life for nothing.

"You can cut a limb on that tree and it will grow back," he said, "but people don't come back."

Jeff Davis Jr. was killed Thursday night just after leaving a convenience store at 2131 W. Pembroke Ave., not too far from his father's house. He was there with a friend, about 9:30 p.m., to buy some Famous Amos chocolate chip cookies, his favorite.

Shortly before, he had talked on the phone to his mother, Leona "Kay" Williams, who lives in Newport News. He told her he was looking for a job.

In the parking lot of the store he ran into a close family friend, "Uncle Ben" Williams, 33, who was just walking into the store to buy a Pepsi. He is not related to Jeff's mother.

"The first thing I heard was, 'Hey Uncle

Please see **Father/A4**

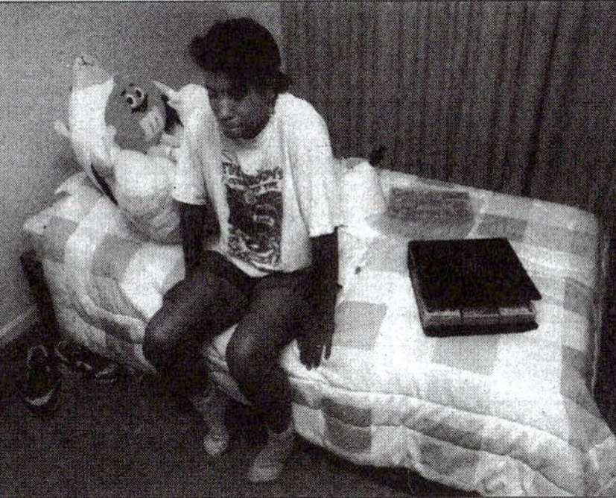

Leona Williams sits inside her son's room Friday night. Some of his friends would get into trouble, but Jeff Davis would avoid getting involved, she said.

IT'S AN EPIDEMIC

■ Violence claims the lives of six teenagers daily in this country. The homicide rate among those 18 and younger has doubled since 1985 — and tripled in many inner-city neighborhoods. Criminologists and public health officials are trying to understand and treat what they consider a major epidemic. **Story, A4.**

Hampton teen fatally shot outside store

By David Chernicky
Daily Press

HAMPTON

Jeff "Shorty" Davis Jr. would have been a high school sophomore this fall. But he was gunned down during an attempted robbery on the streets of Hampton Thursday night.

His suspected killer, a 16-year-old, has been charged with capital murder.

Jeff had a promising future. He idolized Michael Jordan and Charles Barkley and wanted to be a professional athlete, his relatives said.

His accused killer, Shawn Hicks of the 700 block of Birch Street, dropped out of school and had been in a program for juvenile delinquents, according to Hicks' mother.

Jeff, 15, and a teen-age friend had walked to a convenience store about a half-mile from Davis' father's home on Pennsylvania Avenue.

The store manager said Jeff bought three small bags of Famous Amos chocolate chip cookies and his friend bought

Please see **Teen/A4**

impression as a troubling icon of our times. It would frighten them and sicken them and make them think and talk and maybe even act. And that would be a good thing, because too many kids are dying, and not enough people are asking why. This wasn't somewhere else, wasn't the make-believe violence of television. The picture would do what words could not: make the tragedy of Little Jeff Davis inescapable for our readers. Then, maybe, he wouldn't have lost his life for nothing.

Once the editors decided it was legitimate to use the photo they still recognized the concern for re-victimizing the family. The editor of the paper went to the family to talk with them about how they would feel if the photo were to run. The editor found support from the family members who said, "If this will do some good, run it." The family did ask the paper to use an additional picture of Jeff when he was alive. The editor agreed.

Analysis

This case is a classic example of how the ethical decision making process often plays out in newsrooms. The initial "no way will we run this photo" position mirrors what happens when strong gut reactions drive the initial discussion and when emotion and polarized thinking restrict good decision making. That initial reaction also suggests how newsrooms can be trapped by what we call "rule obedience," that is, an over-reliance on either written or unwritten dicta that prevent good ethical decision making. In this case the "no dead bodies" rule stopped—at least for a period of time—the exploration of alternative treatments of the story, including using the photo for very good reasons.

Once the editors decided it was legitimate to use the photo they still recognized the concern for re-victimizing the family.

To the paper's credit, the process did not end with that gut reaction and rule obedience. The consideration of journalistic purpose and the understanding of the ethical concerns produced a reasonable solution that included measures to minimize the harm to the family members.

It was appropriate for the paper to go to the family to seek their input on the use of the photo. To be sure, if the family had opposed the photo's use, the editors would have faced a new dilemma. But at least they would have known more and been able to make a better ethical decision.

Once they knew how the family felt, the editors could turn to how they would play the story and the photos. With further research, they designed a presentation that was respectful and yet powerful:

- They published the murder scene photo in black and white because of concern that some readers might be offended by blood in the color photo.

They paired the photo of Jeff's lifeless body with a family photo of Jeff.

• They took the story beyond an isolated murder and put it in the context of an epidemic as described by experts. They included information and statistics about murder as a profound social issue beyond the cold hard facts of one killing.

• They told readers something about who Jeff Davis was beyond the fact that he was a murder victim. They expanded the story to include the pain felt by the family members of Jeff Davis.

Despite their good decision making process, the editors still received negative reaction from some readers. Most critics focused on the picture, which they felt was insensitive to Jeff's family.

Such criticism led Corbin to write the column a week later explaining how and why the paper did what it did. Corbin says this example of reader reaction "underscores the value of explaining at the beginning what happened."

That point is worth emphasizing, as it connects to the SPJ Code of Ethics section focusing on accountability. While writing to readers to explain past decisions is a legitimate approach, editors should consider being more proactive in revealing their decision making process. When possible, they can explain their reasoning in a column or sidebar at the time the story and/or photo runs so that readers will have the context of the decision in relation to the product itself. With that approach, the explanation is viewed less as a rationalization and a response to criticism and more as a justification explaining the principles behind the decision.

The editors at the *Daily Press* demonstrated a good ethical decision making process in the way they handled the coverage of Jeff Davis' murder. To be sure, not everyone will agree with their decision to publish the photo or with how they treated the story.

Nevertheless, the process the *Daily Press* used reflects an attention to journalistic principles, a genuine concern for ethical issues, a recognition of the consequences of the decision on various stakeholders, and a willingness to explore alternative approaches to maximize truthtelling and to minimize harm to vulnerable individuals.

News organizations that value ethical decision making hone their skills at this process in the same way that they develop their skills in reporting, writing, and editing. A newsroom that is practiced in this skill of ethical decision making is much more able to resolve dilemmas quickly and effectively—even on deadline.

(In preparing this case study on the shooting death of Jeff Davis, we talked with his mother. Leona Williams told us that looking back on the newspaper's coverage of her son's death in 1993, she still feels the reporting and the use of the picture were appropriate. She also said she believed it appropriate for us to use the picture of Jeff's body for this case study.)

Case Study #34

Abortion Protests in Milwaukee

Summary

The *Milwaukee Journal* faced ethical challenges in its coverage of large groups of abortion protesters who gathered in Milwaukee during the summer of 1992. The anti-abortion protesters used a variety of approaches to make their case to the public, including blocking access to abortion clinics and allowing their children to be arrested.

Many of the ethical questions faced by the newspaper related to photojournalism, as described by *Journal* graphics editor Geoff Blaesing.

"Do we want to show pictures of fetuses in jars? Do we want to picture all of the signs, some quite graphic? Do we want to publish pictures of women going into abortion clinics? And, causing the most discussion, do we want to publish pictures of minors who are protesting and getting arrested on their parents' behalf?"

Blaesing said "photographing the events was generally easy. I told the staff to shoot what looked good and not worry about any of the aforementioned questions. Senior editors debated what to publish. Show fetuses in jars? No. Show some of the graphic signs? Yes, but carefully chosen. Pictures of women going into the clinics? No. Minors getting arrested? At first no, but it became a focal point of the story here as the city attorney announced he would charge parents and guardians with contributing to the delinquency of minors when minors were arrested."

Analysis

What criteria should editors apply in deciding which photos to publish? This issue balances the truthtelling principle against the minimizing harm principle. There are also important questions to be asked about the paper's honoring of the independence principle. By asking some of the "Doing Ethics" questions, we can get clarity:

- What did the *Journal* know and need to know? What was its journalistic purpose? What were its ethical concerns?
- How much weight should it place on the significance of this issue? How valuable was the information the readers would receive? Were these protests truly important and of legitimate consequence, or were they merely staged

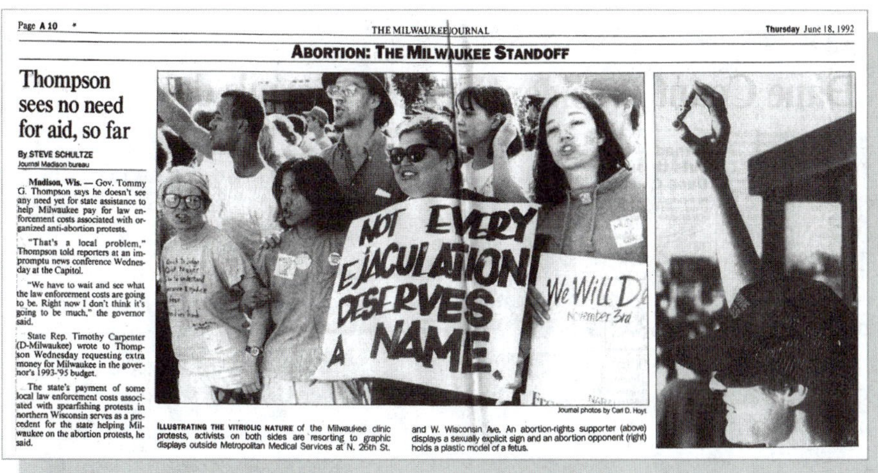

Page A 10 • THE MILWAUKEE JOURNAL Thursday June 18, 1992

ABORTION: THE MILWAUKEE STANDOFF

Thompson sees no need for aid, so far

By STEVE SCHULTZE
Journal Madison bureau

Madison, Wis. — Gov. Tommy G. Thompson says he doesn't see any need yet for state assistance to help Milwaukee pay for law enforcement costs associated with organized anti-abortion protests.

"That's a local problem," Thompson told reporters at an impromptu news conference Wednesday at the Capitol.

"We have to wait and see what the law enforcement costs are going to be. Right now I don't think it's going to be much," the governor said.

State Rep. Timothy Carpenter (D-Milwaukee) wrote to Thompson Wednesday requesting extra money for Milwaukee in the governor's 1993-'95 budget.

The state's payment of some local law enforcement costs associated with spearfishing protests in northern Wisconsin serves as a precedent for the state helping Milwaukee on the abortion protests, he said.

Journal photos by Carl D. Hoyt

ILLUSTRATING THE VITRIOLIC NATURE of the Milwaukee clinic protests, activists on both sides are resorting to graphic displays outside Metropolitan Medical Services at N. 26th St. and W. Wisconsin Ave. An abortion-rights supporter (above) displays a sexually explicit sign and an abortion opponent (right) holds a plastic model of a fetus.

public relations events designed to manipulate media coverage and public opinion? Even if the protests were staged events, did the ensuing arrests elevate the news value to the community? Did the tactics of the protesters, such as having their children arrested, give the story more significance?

• What organizational policies and professional guidelines did the paper need to consider?

• What was the paper's policy on identifying juveniles? Was this case an exception to that policy, given the role of the parents? What harm would be caused to the children?

• What was the precedent at the paper for showing images that were very graphic and likely to offend readers? Was it justifiable to run the risk to be accurate in covering the story? How would the editors respond to anti-abortion advocates who argue that the image of the fetus in the jar is what the abortion issue is all about, and not to publish that picture means the paper is both inaccurate and unfair in its coverage?

• Is it appropriate for editors to tell photographers not to worry about ethical questions in the field, to leave such questions to editors? Is it possible that merely taking the pictures of women going into the abortion clinic could cause significant harm to the women, even if those pictures were never published? Is it likely that the presence of photographers at the protests changed the basic nature of the protests?

• Did the editors include people of different perspectives and backgrounds in the decision making process? Was there diversity in terms of gender? Ethnicity? Age? Were there individuals who could argue different sides of the abortion issue?

• Were the editors open-minded in their decision making process to envision how they would have felt if in the shoes of the subjects of the story? What if they were the women using the clinics? The protesters? The children being arrested? The readers?

• Did the journalists give consideration to the impact of their coverage, for both short- and long-term consequences? What was the value of the information to the public? Were the journalists compromised by protesters who were manipulating the media? How much harm was caused to the various subjects of the story?

The editors originally said "no" to publishing photos of children being arrested. That decision may have been a gut reaction prompted by the ethical journalistic tradition of not identifying, in most cases, juveniles who have been arrested. At a higher level of reflection and reasoning, the editors recognized that parents were being charged with contributing to the delinquency of minors. Beyond that justification, editors might have decided to publish photos of children being arrested because that was a central and essential part of the unfolding story.

• Did the significance of the abortion issue, the calculated tactics of the protesters and the wide-scale arrests of children outweigh whatever harm might be caused to the children by identifying them in the paper? Did the value of the information being disseminated outweigh whatever harm might be caused to readers who were offended by what they saw in the paper?

• Was the paper willing to publicly explain how it made its decisions and why it published some information and pictures and did not publish other information and images?

Case Study #35

A Photo-digital Cover-up

Summary

A copy editor at the Louisville *Courier-Journal* reviewing a full-size proof of the Sept. 14, 1996, first edition of page A-1 noticed something amiss. The lead photograph, of a stripper high-kicking toward the ceiling, made it appear as if the woman were wearing nothing beneath her sweater.

The copy editor took that concern to the night news editor, who consulted with an assistant managing editor and the night picture editor and determined—mistakenly—that no alternative images existed. With another edition's deadline approaching, they decided to digitally manipulate the photo they had in place.

Using Adobe PhotoShop, they were able to extend the hem of the sweater below the stripper's waist and hide the problematic dark leotard underwear. The change was made in time for the final edition of the paper, which goes to most readers.

According to then-presentation editor Robert King, who wrote about the incident in a posting on the Poynter Institute for Media Studies website, none of the editors involved in the decision felt comfortable about it. But they felt they had to make a choice between possibly offending thousands of readers and performing what they knew to be an ethically wrong manipulation of a photograph. They chose the latter.

No readers called to complain about the images—only about the content of the accompanying story, King said, although a local television station noticed the switch between editions and reported it as a news story.

According to King, the executive editor agreed that digital manipulation "was something we would never want to do. In fact, we should never do it." Nevertheless, he agreed that the correct decision had been made.

The incident, however, led the paper to prohibit digital manipulation of news photos under any circumstances; to clearly label, in credit lines, an image as either "illustration" or "photo"; to abide by limits when using dodge, burn and color-correction settings; and to communicate more clearly among editors about problematic images.

What if kids don't leave the nest? — Features, D1

The Courier-Journal

INDIANA EDITION

Students' casual attitudes fuel rise in drug use

IU official blames cuts in programs for prevention

Lead-paint hazards must be disclosed

John Kennedy Jr., girlfriend wed

Florida, next UK foe, tops football polls

Cell-phone towers concern Hoosiers

Scientists combing solar system for life

Adult entertainment thrives

Perot focuses his ire on GOP for debate snub

Turning little dolls into big dollars

Court case stalls Louisville's fight against nude dancing

COMING TOMORROW

History hidden in opera house

FORECAST

Partly sunny

INDEX

What if kids don't leave the nest? — Features, D1

The Courier-Journal

METRO EDITION

Who knows secrets of world trade? Barbie knows

'Made in China' is misleading label for doll

Lead-paint hazards must be disclosed

John Kennedy Jr., girlfriend wed

Florida, next UK foe, tops football polls

Teens get a taste of life's rougher side

Water pipe floods downtown building

Adult entertainment thrives

Perot focuses his ire on GOP for debate snub

NRA cuts 30 workers, television program

Group's money woes stem from costly membership drive

Turning little dolls into big dollars

Court case stalls Louisville's fight against nude dancing

FEWER ADULT BUSINESSES

COMING TOMORROW

History hidden in opera house

FORECAST

Partly sunny

INDEX

Wedding band missing for 52 years

Ring's return seals memory of airman's love

Analysis

It is important to recognize the solid decision making process that the editors at the *Courier-Journal*—and at other newspapers and news magazines—have developed for dealing with these manipulation issues. The *C-J* now has a systematic procedure for making such decisions, including who is involved in the process, what criteria should be considered and what level of disclosure the paper must make to the readers.

As the technology becomes more available and more sophisticated, photo manipulation cuts across the wide spectrum of journalism publications. Magazines such as *National Geographic, Time, Newsweek, TV Guide* and the *Atlantic Monthly* have altered photos. Newspapers such as the *Orange County* (Calif.) *Register,* the *St. Louis Post Dispatch,* the *New York Times,* and the *Columbus* (Ohio) *Dispatch* have doctored pictures to some degree.

In the case of the *Register*, the paper altered a photo for its 1984 Olympics special edition by clearing smog out of a photo of the Los Angeles skyline and making the sky a brighter blue. That paper also used digital imaging to clone in a zipper on the photo of a young boy whose fly was down when his picture was taken. Top editors later said they would not have allowed such digital manipulation had they been involved in the decision making.

Most photojournalists are very conservative about making any changes electronically in photographs. And most, if not all, news organizations do not condone photo manipulation.

National Geographic electronically moved one of the Great Pyramids of Egypt to make a photo fit the design on the magazine's cover. *TV Guide* superimposed Oprah Winfrey's head onto Ann Margaret's body for a composite cover photo. The *Post Dispatch* electronically removed what editors felt was an obtrusive Diet Coke can from a photo of an awards ceremony in its own newsroom.

Most photojournalists are very conservative about making any changes electronically in photographs. And most, if not all, news organizations do not condone photo manipulation. Yet the temptation to use what technology has given us appears at times too good to pass up. It's important that newspapers develop procedures for dealing with this issue.

Photojournalists and editors can ask themselves several important questions in the process of ethical decision making:

• If I have to alter this photo to make it acceptable to my readers, does it need to run?

• Can I get another photo that will illustrate the story just as well?

• If I alter the photo, am I willing to tell my readers how and why I made the changes?

A key step in the decision making process is for the journalists to ask themselves about their motivations for manipulating a photo. The act is potentially deceptive, and there should be an overriding reason for the image to be altered. When such alteration takes place, it is essential for the paper to hold itself accountable, to tell readers what changes were made and why.

Coordination between photographers and editors is important in this process. Problem photos submitted on deadline offer editors little choice beyond either not running the photo or altering it. With more time to make decisions, more alternatives become available.

In the case of the *Courier-Journal*, the validation for using the altered photos may have been legitimate: protecting the readers of a family newspaper from exposure to what appeared to be a breach of community standards.

But manipulation for the sake of expediency or for design purposes or for self-serving motives is not an acceptable practice for a profession whose integrity relies on truthtelling.

The National Press Photographers Association approved a statement of principle in 1990 to add emphasis to their concern over this issue:

> As journalists we believe the guiding principle of our profession is accuracy. Therefore, we believe it is wrong to alter the content of a photograph in any way that deceives the public .... altering the editorial content of a photograph, in any degree, is a breach of the ethical standards recognized by the NPPA.

And the Associated Press has a specific standard on altering photographs:

> Simply put, the Associated Press does not alter photographs. Our pictures must always tell the truth .... The contents of a photograph will never be changed or manipulated in any way .... The integrity of AP's photo report is our highest priority. Nothing takes precedence over credibility.

The *St. Louis Post-Dispatch* developed the following policy in the wake of misgivings about photo manipulation after the paper ran the altered photo of the Diet Coke can.

> One of the functions of the Scitex system is to enhance the technical quality of photographs to be published in the *Post-Dispatch.* To assure the integrity of our visual reportage, the system may not be used to distort or change the image in a way that misleads the reader, be it for news or feature display.

While it is highly unlikely that there will be a unanimous position on the issue of digital manipulation, news organizations can develop strategies to lead them toward good ethical decisions. A group of photojournalists and photo editors gathered at The Poynter Institute for Media Studies in 1991 to discuss such decision making. The group developed and endorsed the following "protocol" for making decisions on digital manipulation. This protocol has been used by numerous newspapers in developing their own policies.

> Abuse of the technological changes by members of the publishing community have negatively affected the public's perceptions of photojournalism's credibility .... It is our policy that content alterations of documentary photographs is unacceptable using past or present techniques of technology. If significant reasons exist to challenge this policy, it will be addressed in the following manner:
>
> **No discussion needed**—dodging/burning areas that do not change content; correction of technical defects in a photo.
>
> **Discussion required**—photo with potential breach of community standards.
>
> **Discussion needed**—photos that may offend community standards.
>
> All photo illustrations should be labeled as such. Whenever possible, the cutline should contain an explanation of any special effects used in the creation of an illustration when the photo technique may cloud the reader's understanding of the photo.

Photojournalism

What the Codes Say

Rochester (N.Y.) *Democrat and Chronicle*

All photographs are accurate representations of the situations they portray. Nothing recreated, staged or posed is represented as a candid situation. Previously shot photographs are not represented as fresh and new. Photographers are alert to situations in which straightforward photography might create an impression contrary to the facts. They avoid cropping a photograph in a way that would misrepresent the situation. They point out questionable photographs or situations and discuss proper treatment of them with editors.

San Jose (Calif.) *Mercury News*

In the interest of integrity and fairness, photographers and editors should exercise caution in the use of "set-up" photographs. In the same way that reporters do not make up quotes, photographers do not reconstruct scenes or events with the purpose of making them appear as if they were "found" moments.

However, photographers are often called upon to make environmental portraits or do illustrative photography. In no way should such photographs be approached or treated as anything but what they are. They are either portraits or are demonstrative of a situation. Both should be clearly labeled.

That means that care should be taken in writing captions so they do not suggest the picture is something it is not. For example, is Clark Kent working in his study or is he simply in his study (for purposes of a portrait)? Is Lois Lane actually practicing her technique of boomerang tossing or is she demonstrating her technique of boomerang tossing (for purposes of a photograph)? Such distinctions make a difference ....

Ordinarily, consent is implied if a photographer approaches a subject, indicates that he/she is a newspaper photographer and asks for names and other facts. In some circumstances, written releases may be required (at mental health institutions or orphanages, for example).

Racine (Wis.) *Journal Times*

The following protocol must be followed if there is any question about the accuracy of the color of a photo, or whether there are details that should be altered in consideration of acceptable community standards such as accidental inclusion of genitals or obscene gestures or language:

A newsroom consultation group shall discuss the question. The group shall include: the page editor; the photographer, when possible; the director of photography, when possible; the top newsroom editor available; the editor of the section where the photo will appear.

The editor of the newspaper shall have the final say. The group will reach a consensus decision if the editor is not available. Any members of this group who are not present for the discussion should be left a message about the question that arose, and how it was resolved.

Detroit Free Press

News photos are not to be changed in any way that might mislead readers. Do not move, eliminate (except by cropping), alter or add to the content in a news photo. Feature photos may be manipulated, but such pictures must be clearly labeled, such as: composite photo, photographic recreation, photo dramatization; a fuller explanation in print with the art may be appropriate.

Independent Newspapers

The natural tendency at many community newspapers is simply to imitate the photo coverage in metropolitan newspapers. This is usually a mistake. Community newspapers have an entirely different mission. At Independent Newspapers, the first part of our mission statements says we publish purposeful newspapers that encourage and support meaningful community involvement. That mission should be the guiding force behind our photo coverage. Our photos should show local people in the act of participating in their community.

St. Paul* (Minn.) *Pioneer Press

Dead Bodies—Avoid use of photos of dead bodies (especially local) unless covered. Of course, there will be exceptions that must be cleared with the managing editor.

General Policy—Do NOT run photos of the governor, mayor, etc. signing proclamations, receiving plaques, looking at a check or piece of paper, etc. Avoid posed news photos of politicians immediately prior to elections.

Added on July 27, 1989:

Under no circumstances shall documentary photographs be manipulated, changed, or altered to any degree, by any method or medium, including electronic manipulation.

Documentary photographs shall not be set up, i.e., manufactured by the photographer.

Any manipulation of feature photos can be done only under the supervision of the director of photography in conjunction with the managing editor and the associate editor of features.

Code for Coverage of Victims

The National Victim Center strongly endorses the following media code of ethics for journalists whose work brings them in contact with crime victims. We firmly believe that the components of this code—when adopted by media professionals—will result in more sensitive and understanding coverage of violent crime victims.

I shall:

- ... avoid photographing or filming crime scene details or follow-up activities such as remains of bodies or brutality, instruments of torture, disposal of bodies, etc.; and
- Notify and ask permission from victims and their families before using pictures or photographs for documentaries or other news features.

I shall not:

- Photograph, film or print for publication photographs of victims, graphic crime scenes or victims in the courtroom without permission;
- Print, broadcast, photograph or film lurid or graphic details of the crime ....

Texarkana* (Texas) *Gazette

Dead Body Policy (editorial memo, Oct. 9, 1989)

Effective today, we will initiate a kinder, gentler photo policy that precludes dead bodies in photos. There may be some exceptions to this, if there is compelling news value. But as the norm, we will cease to show bodies under sheets, or in bags, or on stretchers, or in any other state of demise. I can't rationalize to myself how body photographs add anything to the value of our newspaper. Instead, I think many of our readers would find them offensive.

I would also extend this policy to people who are severely injured and likely to die. This of course is a judgment call, but in such cases we need to take both with-victim and without-victim photographs.

The guiding philosophy behind the policy is one of compassion for th victim's friends and family and an empathy for the sensibilities of our readers. Instead of being an exploitative, shocking newspaper, I want the *Texarkana Gazette* to be known as a sensitive paper.

I realize this doesn't make for gripping, high-profile photos, but I think it does make for a newspaper more in step with this community.

Sioux Falls (S.D.) *Argus Leader*

News photos in advertisements: Photographs taken specifically for news columns shall not be used in advertisements unless approved by the executive editor or managing editor.

Sarasota* (Fla.) *Herald-Tribune

The introduction of electronic photo editing technology to the *Herald-Tribune* brings with it concerns about the use of the image manipulation capabilities of the tools in our daily production.

The technology gives us the ability to easily alter the content or create new photograph that could deceive the reader and ultimately damage the credibility of the *Herald-Tribune*.

IT HAS ALWAYS BEEN THE POLICY OF THE *HERALD-TRIBUNE* THAT CONTENT ALTERATION OF PHOTOGRAPHS IS UNACCEPTABLE USING PAST OR PRESENT TECHNOLOGY.

If significant reason exists to challenge this policy it will be addressed in the following manner:

No discussion needed:

• Dodging or burning of areas in the photograph that do not change the content, for instance, lightening or darkening areas of the photograph to make them reproducible in the newspaper.

• Correction of technical defects in a photo, for instance, repairing line hits in a photo or erasing line noise.

Discussion required:

• Photographs with the potential to breach community standards, including accidental inclusion of genitals, obscene gestures, offensive cultural elements.

• Photographs that may offend community standards, including gruesome or emotionally distressing photographs.

• Discussion is also required to use the electronic image manipulation capabilities to create an illustration using photographic elements. It should be noted that this protocol does not preclude the use of the technology to create illustrations using the particular advantages of the tools, but does require that the resulting illustration not closely resemble a real life scene and requires that the resulting illustration be labeled as to its creative elements.

The discussion group should include:

• Photographer, top newsroom executive, photo editor, section editor, and anyone who might lend an enlightened argument for or against the usage.

Some of the questions that should come up in the discussion should include:

• What are the alternatives: Can another photo convey the same message and eliminate the concerns?

• Is possession of the technical capability to alter a photograph justifying the proposed manipulation?

• Is all of the necessary information available for discussion: Story and photo readily available?

• Is there any missing information from the photograph?

• What is the news value of the particular photograph?

• Are there legal or ethical concerns about running the photo?

• Who might be offended and why?

• What are the possible consequences of publishing the photo?

• Will we be able to justify our decision?

Photo credits and labeling:

• Any time the content of a photograph has been altered, the extent of the alteration and the technique should be clearly explained in the cutline or credit, adhering to the style of the *Herald-Tribune*.

• The emphasis should be on adding as much detailed information as possible.

Chapter Nine

Privacy

There are few greater conflicts than the need for free information flow versus the rights of individuals to personal privacy. The public has a need for much information that others, for a variety of motives, would like to keep private.

There is value in citizens' knowing about certain activities of public officials, even though the officials may wish to restrict flow of that information. There is also value in the public's knowing about meaningful details of accidents, tragedies and crimes, even though the gathering and distribution of such details might invade someone's sense of privacy. Such stories highlight the journalist's dilemma in balancing the competing ethical principles of truthtelling and minimizing harm.

Public discussions that ultimately may bring some benefit often cannot begin without some invasive and harmful disclosure. A story about the spread of AIDS and the failure of society to respond may present this disease as just another abstract threat unless specific names are attached to the story.

Stories that make allegations of criminal activity or unethical behavior, ranging from government corruption to child abuse, are less accurate and potentially unfair if individuals involved go unidentified. To identify individuals is certain to cause some harm, however.

Reports on crime are necessary to inform citizens of both their own safety and to provide them with information on the performance of those responsible agencies of government. On the other hand, coverage of crime is bound to cause some invasion of privacy.

Harm from privacy invasion is almost certain, but it is more difficult for a journalist to fully identify benefits from an intrusion. Thus, it is important to recognize that the primary ethical obligation of journalism is to inform the public by seeking truth and reporting it as fully as possible. That obligation must then be balanced against the obligation to respect individuals and their privacy.

The challenge for journalists is to be courageous in seeking and reporting information, while being compassionate to those who are being covered.

Privacy

Checklist

- How important is the information I am seeking? Does the public have a right to know? A need to know? Merely a desire to know?
- What level of protection do individuals involved in the story deserve? How much harm might they receive? Are they involved in the news event by choice or by happenstance?
- How would I feel if I were being subjected to the same scrutiny?
- How can I best weigh the concerns of highly vulnerable individuals whose privacy may be invaded? Should I talk directly with them to better understand the impact my actions could have on them? Will that additional step provide alternatives to allow meaningful reporting while minimizing harm?
- Do I know the facts of the story well enough? What else do I need to know?
- What can I do to minimize the privacy invasion and the harm? Can I broaden the focus of the story by including more "victims," thereby minimizing harm to a select few? Can I postpone the story without significantly jeopardizing information to the public?
- Do I need to include in the decision making other individuals to gain more perspective?
- Should I be focusing more on the system failure or the big-issue picture as opposed to focusing intensely on individuals?
- Can I clearly and fully justify my thinking and decision? To those directly affected? To the public?

Case Study #36

"Outing" Arthur Ashe?

Summary

In April 1992, a *USA Today* reporter called former professional tennis star Arthur Ashe and asked if Ashe had AIDS. Ashe would neither confirm nor deny the story, although he had previously confided in family and some friends, including at least two journalists, that he did indeed have AIDS. He had contracted the HIV virus from a heart surgery blood transfusion in the mid-1980s, and he had known for more than three years that he had AIDS.

Editors at *USA Today* told Ashe that the paper would not report his AIDS without on-the-record sources. They also said they were pursuing the matter despite his objection. Their position was that a prominent, although retired, sports figure with AIDS was important news.

The next day, Ashe called a press conference to announce he had the disease. His announcement alluded to rumors and half-truths about his condition and expressed anger at what he felt was intrusion by the media into his privacy. Of particular concern was the effect of disclosure on his young daughter in light of public attitudes toward AIDS. Ashe became the first celebrity to disclose he had contracted the disease from something other than sex or drug abuse.

"I am angry that I was put in the position of having to lie if I wanted to protect my privacy," he said.

The 48-year-old Ashe, who won the U.S. Open tennis championship in 1968 and Wimbledon in 1975, was the most prominent black male tennis player in history. He retired from professional tennis in 1980, but continued to maintain public visibility through his television commentaries on tennis, his involvement with apartheid issues in South Africa, and his public comments on the exploitation of college and high school athletes.

Analysis

While public disclosure that a person has any of hundreds of diseases may not raise questions of privacy invasion, such volatile topics as AIDS and rape generate emotionally protective public responses. Some argue that the disclosure of information about those who have AIDS or those who have been raped has a unique stigma attached. Others question whether the stigma will dissi-

VIA SATELLITE — THE NATION'S NEWSPAPER — 50 CENTS

USA TODAY

No. 1 IN THE USA . . . 6.6 MILLION READERS A DAY

YOU MUST REMEMBER THIS

50 YEARS LATER – PLAY IT AGAIN: 'CASABLANCA' SALUTE, 5D

THURSDAY

BOGART, BERGMAN

THURSDAY, APRIL 9, 1992

NEWSLINE

WALL STREET:

CAPITOL HILL PERKS:

BRITISH VOTE:

MAJOR

CATERPILLAR:

CHURCH SEXISM:

ENVIRONMENTAL DAMAGE:

BRUISING CAMPAIGN:

IMAGE REPAIR:

IRAQI MOVE:

TODAY'S DEBATE:

MONEY:

SPORTS:

LIFE:

WEATHER:

USA SNAPSHOTS®

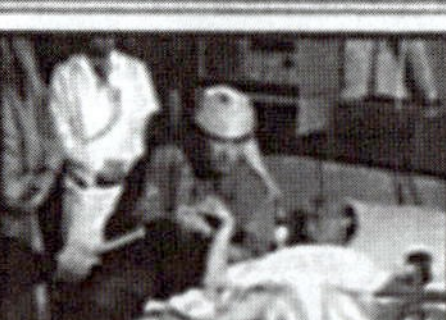

'God saved Arafat for us'

By Lee Michael Katz
USA TODAY

REACTION, CAREER ON COURT, 1-3C

'Everything with grace'

Ashe: AIDS 'just another' crisis to overcome

EMOTIONAL DAY:

U.S. stocks rattled by Japan drop

Cold drugs useless, sniffs panel

Hung jury feared in Noriega trial

COVER STORY

Star wanted this news to stay 'private'

GLORY DAYS:

Light shed on black hole

For USA TODAY subscription and customer service . . . call 1-800-USA-0001

pate without more public, specific discussion on the topic, including the use of names of prominent victims.

Arthur Ashe's anguish and the pain to his family cause reporters and editors to question again why they are willing to inflict such trauma. However, decisions should come from a balance of arguments for both sides.

It is not adequate to argue "newsworthiness" about a public figure without some supporting list of social benefits. For example, Ashe's case may confirm to some people for the first time that the disease is not solely a sex-and-drugs product, creating a very different example of a celebrity victim for audiences to observe. Such a disclosure adds a dimension that may affect attitudes people bring to contacts and relationships with AIDS victims. Perhaps disclosure of Ashe's affliction may not change attitudes toward the disease, but the principle of an open society suggests that more will change from publishing important stories than from keeping such stories under wraps.

It is not adequate to argue "newsworthiness" about a public figure without some supporting list of social benefits.

The Arthur Ashe case exemplifies the precarious balance between the principles of maximizing truthtelling and minimizing harm. This case speaks to the continuing challenge journalists face in weighing the harm of reporting certain information against the benefits of revealing that information.

Those who would argue that journalists should not have pushed Arthur Ashe into a corner, essentially forcing him to go public, place the most weight on the minimize-harm principle. They believe that the harm caused to Ashe and his family is tremendous, recognizing that such revelations could have a serious impact on him, his reputation, his family or his career.

They would argue that having AIDS is a private matter, and one should retain the choice over when and how it would be revealed. They would argue that compassion necessitates honoring Ashe's privacy. They would argue that revealing Ashe's medical situation is merely using him as a means to a journalistic end.

On the other hand, those who argue in favor of pursuing such information and reporting it place the most weight on the maximize-truthtelling principle. They believe significant information would benefit the public.

They would argue that AIDS is the top health, social and public policy issue of the decade. They would argue that revealing how Arthur Ashe contracted AIDS, through a blood transfusion years ago, is important, as is the subsequent information about how blood supplies are now much safer. They would argue that Ashe's continued high public profile makes what happens to him meaningful to a great number of people, including those who might find inspiration from him or those who might financially invest in him in some way.

They would argue that Ashe's position as a member of the board of directors of a major insurance company makes him part of the public debate over

AIDS, given the controversy about how insurance companies treat people with AIDS. Finally, they would argue that while Ashe clearly suffered from the pressure of the revelation, the harm to him or his family was not nearly that great given the way in which he contracted AIDS, through a blood transfusion. While some would still shun him, most people would be more likely to feel sympathy and empathy rather than revulsion or disdain.

Whether the benefits outweigh the anguish is still the decision of the individual reporter or editor. At least two journalist friends who knew of Ashe's illness chose not to tell. Such a choice, while an acceptable exercise of independence, inevitably raises questions of consistency. How far would the journalists go in refusing to disclose information about friends, when they would routinely publish that same information about others?

To those journalists who would reveal that Ashe has AIDS, there is an additional responsibility. They should publicly justify their action, explaining how and why they decided as they did.

Case Study #37

Unmasking the Grand Forks Angel

Summary

For three weeks, reporter Liz Fedor, her colleagues at the *Grand Forks* (N.D.) *Herald* and a herd of television, radio and newspaper journalists from as far away as Miami had included in their reporting news of some $15 million donated to 1997 Red River Flood victims by an anonymous "angel." The Angel stories centered mostly on the details of when, where, and how much money was being disbursed, and to whom.

Owing to the vague rumor that the Angel was a millionaire from California who had never been to North Dakota, some early reports speculated that she was either entertainer Oprah Winfrey, singer Madonna or McDonald's heiress Joan Kroc.

"What she had done was more important than who she was," says Fedor, the hometown paper's lead reporter on flood coverage overall. "I thought it silly for news organizations, especially our paper, to spend resources on finding out her I.D. There were plenty of other stories on the flood to be done."

And, defying the ravages of the flood, the *Grand Forks Herald* continued to publish throughout, providing essential information to water- and fire-weary residents. The paper, editor Mike Jacobs said, "achieved an almost mythic role of heroism in the community."

Then, on a weekend in late May, an official who had been the local governments' liaison to the Angel and who had steadfastly kept her identity a secret, inadvertently led Fedor's paper to uncovering that secret—something the newspaper had not been pursuing all that aggressively. East Grand Forks, Minn., Mayor Lynn Stauss, who along with Grand Forks, N.D., Mayor Pat Owens was being interviewed by Fedor, let on that the Angel had toured the flooded region the night before. Stauss, knowing that other media in Grand Forks and nearby Minneapolis-St. Paul knew the Angel's identity but had honored her request for anonymity, began worrying that Fedor and her editors would not respect the Angel's wish for privacy. Stauss asked Fedor not to go to Grand Forks International Airport and "go checking on tail numbers of airplanes."

Fedor did not do that, but, she said, bound by her duty as a reporter to her editors, called to let them know and to allow them to decide what to do with the information. Two other reporters followed up the tip and, checking airport records for the tail numbers as well as credit-card purchases for fuel, deter-

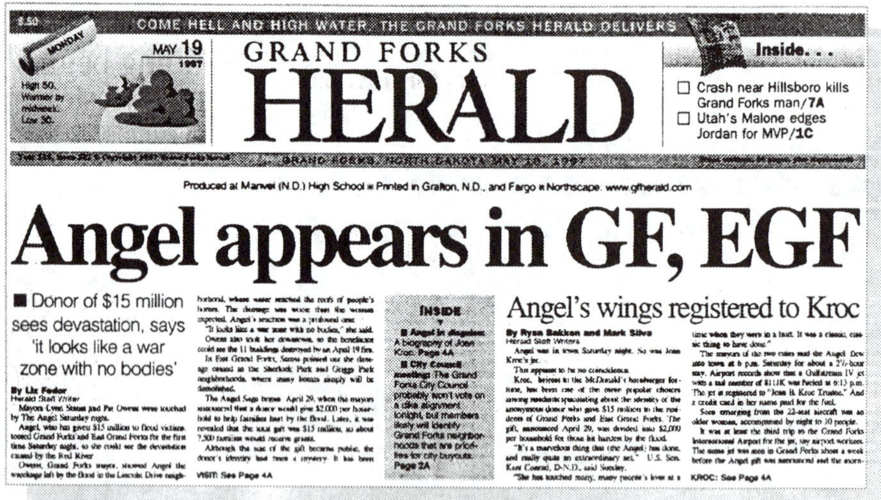

$.50 COME HELL AND HIGH WATER, THE GRAND FORKS HERALD DELIVERS

MONDAY MAY 19 1997

High 50. Warmer by midweek. Low 30.

GRAND FORKS

HERALD

Inside. . .

- Crash near Hillsboro kills Grand Forks man/**7A**
- Utah's Malone edges Jordan for MVP/**1C**

GRAND FORKS, NORTH DAKOTA MAY 19, 1997

Produced at Manvel (N.D.) High School * Printed in Grafton, N.D., and Fargo * Northscape: www.gfherald.com

Angel appears in GF, EGF

■ Donor of $15 million sees devastation, says 'it looks like a war zone with no bodies'

By Liz Fedor
Herald Staff Writer

Mayors Lynn Stauss and Pat Owens were touched by The Angel Saturday night.

Angel, who has given $15 million to flood victims, toured Grand Forks and East Grand Forks for the first time Saturday night, so she could see the devastation caused by the Red River.

Owens, Grand Forks mayor, showed Angel the wreckage left by the flood in the Lincoln Drive neighborhood, where water reached the roofs of people's homes. The damage was worse than the woman expected. Angel's reaction was a profound one.

"It looks like a war zone with no bodies," she said.

Owens also took her downtown, so the benefactor could see the 11 buildings destroyed by an April 19 fire.

In East Grand Forks, Stauss pointed out the damage caused in the Sherlock Park and Griggs Park neighborhoods, where many homes simply will be demolished.

The Angel Saga began April 29, when the mayors announced that a donor would give $2,000 per household to help families hurt by the flood. Later, it was revealed that the total gift was $15 million, so about 7,500 families would receive grants.

Although the size of the gift became public, the donor's identity had been a mystery. It has been

VISIT: See Page 4A

INSIDE

■ **Angel [illegible]:** A biography of Joan Kroc. **Page 4A**

■ **City Council meetings:** The Grand Forks City Council probably won't vote on a dike alignment tonight, but members likely will identify Grand Forks neighborhoods that are priorities for city buyouts. **Page 2A**

Angel's wings registered to Kroc

By Ryan Bakken and Mark Silva
Herald Staff Writers

Angel was in town Saturday night. So was Joan Kroc's jet.

This appears to be no coincidence.

Kroc, heiress to the McDonald's hamburger fortune, has been one of the more popular choices among residents speculating about the identity of the anonymous donor who gave $15 million to the residents of Grand Forks and East Grand Forks. The gift, announced April 29, was divided into $2,000 per household for those hit hardest by the flood.

"It's a marvelous thing that (the Angel) has done, and really quite an extraordinary act," U.S. Sen. Kent Conrad, D-N.D., said Sunday.

"She has touched many, many people's lives at a time when they were in a [illegible]. It was a classic, classic thing to have done."

The mayors of the two cities said the Angel flew into town at 6 p.m. Saturday for about a 2½-hour stay. Airport records show that a Gulfstream IV jet with a tail number of 811JK was fueled at 6:13 p.m. The jet is registered to "Joan B. Kroc Trustee." And a credit card in her name paid for the fuel.

Seen emerging from the 22-seat aircraft was an older woman, accompanied by eight to 10 people.

It was at least the third trip to the Grand Forks International Airport for the jet, say airport workers. The same jet was seen in Grand Forks about a week before the Angel gift was announced and the morn-

KROC: See Page 4A

mined whose private jet had arrived in Grand Forks for the weekend. Publisher Mike Maidenberg and Jim Durkin, the senior editor in the newsroom, after some discussion with other editors—including editor Jacobs, who called in from out of town—decided to go ahead with an article for the Monday paper that disclosed what it believed to be the identity of the Angel: Joan Kroc.

The publisher and the editors weighed what Jacobs characterized as "truthful information of interest—what I presume to be the heart of the profession we're in" versus "community approbrium." Given the newspaper's stature in the community and the perception that, as Fedor said, "everyone was in this thing together," the decision might have been easy but not necessarily pleasant. "We had achieved the one thing few papers ever do," Jacobs said, "and it feels good to be loved. We knew the consequence would be a sharp reversal of that, or at least a return to a more normal role—investigatory rather than affirmational."

Indeed, public reaction to the disclosure was swift and largely unfavorable, especially among readers (the newspaper's own poll revealed that 85 percent of respondents in the community thought the name should not have been published; 7 percent agreed with the decision to publish) from Stauss, who felt betrayed, and city attorney Howard Swanson, who had urged the *Herald* not to divulge Kroc's name. "Don't, don't, don't," the paper quoted him as saying. "You do that and you destroy an awful lot of things. This is irresponsible. There is no reason to identify anybody."

A day later, publisher Maidenberg and editor Jacobs jointly signed a front-page column defending their decision under the headline "The Herald's first commandment: Never hold the news." In the column, they asserted that once reporters had uncovered Kroc's identity, the newspaper could not withhold what it believed was compelling information.

Says Fedor, who believes her distance and detachment from the decision to disclose kept her from appearing to have been compromised with her sources: "They had a very short time frame in which to make the decision. They had just a couple of hours to decide to run the story. I don't believe there was ever a question to publish if we had it."

She acknowledged that on the face of it, others might characterize the Angel disclosure as a decision "made for competitive media reasons." She added: "The decision that editors needed to make was: Should the *Grand Forks Herald*—the hometown newspaper—make the decision to print what it knew to be the Angel's identity or allow someone from outside to break the story?"

Analysis

The journalists at the *Grand Forks Herald* knew they had a tough call and they knew the criticism would come their way no matter what their decision. This case clearly demonstrates the clash between competing principles.

The newspaper recognized its journalistic responsibility to seek truth and report it as fully as possible. The reporter and the editors believed the public deserved to know the identity of this anonymous "angel" whose multi-million dollar contribution was a major development in one of the most important stories in the history of Grand Forks. The primary challenge they faced was determining if the revelation of Joan Kroc's name, once they verified it, was truly significant news. The newspaper believed it was.

The journalists at the Grand Forks Herald knew they had a tough call and they knew the criticism would come their way no matter what their decision. This case clearly demonstrates the clash between competing principles.

It can also be argued that among the reasons to report the truth is to combat rumor and to clarify confusion. There was a missing piece to this major flood story, and the absence of that piece left open possibilities ranging from suspicion to frustration. Furthermore, a contribution of $15 million may have repercussions related to public policy. The public deserved to know about any connections between the anonymous donor and city officials and any strings attached to the use of the money.

Editors then had to weigh that truthtelling responsibility against the potential harm caused by revealing Mrs. Kroc's name. Would publishing that information damage reputations? Would it undermine the flood relief effort? Would it deter others from making anonymous contributions? Would it greatly damage the paper's relations with public officials? Would it erode the paper's

COME HELL AND HIGH WATER, THE GRAND FORKS HERALD DELIVERS

GRAND FORKS
HERALD

Inside. . .

- GF landfill now holds tons of mementos of city's past/**1B**
- Varmints players finding housing hard to find/**1C**

GRAND FORKS, NORTH DAKOTA MAY 20, 1997

Produced at Manvel Public School • Printed in Grafton, N.D., and Fargo • Northscape: www.gfherald.com

The Angel Flap

Flood of complaints follows newspaper's disclosure of donor

By Mark Silve and Liz Fedor

■ Area residents blast the Herald for identifying Grand Forks' Angel

— Page 6A

Kroc

The Angel flew to Grand Forks on Saturday evening to inspect damage. The Grand Forks Herald reported Monday that it was McDonald's heiress Joan Kroc who flew in. Until then, the Angel's identity had been a secret. Controversy swirled Monday over the newspaper's report.

On the radio waves

▲ Radio talk show host Scott Hennen took plenty of calls Monday morning after a Grand Forks Herald story identified McDonald's heiress Joan Kroc as a weekend visitor to the flooded city. Hennen said he tried to prevent the Herald from identifying Kroc as the philanthropist known as "the Angel" who gave residents $15 million.

Ed Schafer,
N.D. governor

Dave Norman,
president KCNN radio

Pat Owens,
GF mayor

Howard Swanson,
GF city attorney

Lynn Stauss,
EGF mayor

The Herald's first commandment: Never hold the news

The Flood of 1997 is over — sort of

■ River below 28 feet

McVEIGH TRIAL

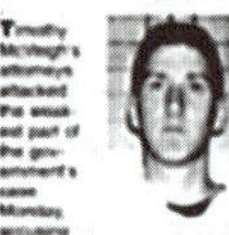

— Page 3A

School repairs may top $40 million

■ It could be curtains for South, Lincoln and Belmont

By Steve Schmidt

credibility with readers?

And, the *Herald*'s editors had to grapple with the issue of journalistic independence. Sure, some public officials were strongly opposed to the paper revealing the "angel's" name. That was their right and it might have been quite appropriate for them to take that stance.

But the duty of the newspaper in a community is not the same as the duty of public officials. A newspaper best serves citizens by providing them with meaningful, accurate information about significant issues and events. The *Herald* grappled with that conflict as it addressed the fourth principle of the SPJ Code of Ethics: accountability. It shared its decision making process with the public, not merely to make excuses for its behavior, but to widen the dialogue about journalism ethics.

A news organization should be extremely cautious when considering withholding information. Yes, there might be very rare instances when that is appropriate, when the harm that can occur is so profound that it outweighs the value of the truth to be told. However, those cases where important truth is spiked should be as rare as a 100-year flood.

Case Study #38

Public and Private Jewell

Summary

For a few months after the bombing at Centennial Park during the Olympic Games in Atlanta, few figures were as public as Richard Jewell.

A 33-year-old security guard on duty in the park in the early morning hours of July 27, 1996, Jewell had discovered an abandoned knapsack containing a bomb and quickly moved people away minutes before it exploded. Two people died as a result of the bombing, and Jewell, a young man seeking a career in law enforcement, was hailed as a hero who had saved perhaps many more lives.

Three days later, in its Olympics special edition, the afternoon *Atlanta Journal* reported that Jewell was under surveillance and was the focus of the federal investigation into the bombing. Suddenly, the would-be hero, lauded for his ambitions, was painted in a dramatically different light. "Jewell ... fits the profile of the lone bomber," the *Journal* wrote. The story, which did not attribute the information to any source, was news to Jewell.

That afternoon, a CNN anchor read the *Journal* story on air. Soon, CNN confirmed through its own unnamed sources that Jewell was a suspect. Wire services, network news operations and most newspapers picked up the story as the big news of the day. "Hero or villain?" questioned a *Boston Herald* headline. "Hero now bomb suspect," declared *USA Today*.

Dallas Morning News national editor Pam Maples told *American Journalism Review* that readers who had seen Jewell's story "all over TV" expected to read more about it in the morning paper. *Seattle Times* national editor Greg Rassa told *AJR*: "Won't we appear foolish for being the only medium in the country not to name Jewell?"

Other news outlets, such as the *New York Times*, played down the information, noting that Jewell had not been named on the record as a suspect.

For the next two months Richard Jewell was in the news almost daily. Law-enforcement officials, pressured to resolve the case, held frequent news conferences but were unable to pin anything substantive on Jewell. Journalists, perceiving a frenzied public interest, continued on their own to dig up facts about Jewell. He lived with his mother, they reported. His apartment was tiny, they reported. He wore a baseball cap and was overweight, they reported.

On Oct. 26, the FBI exonerated Jewell, stating that, barring any new evidence, Jewell was no longer a target of the Olympic bombing investigation.

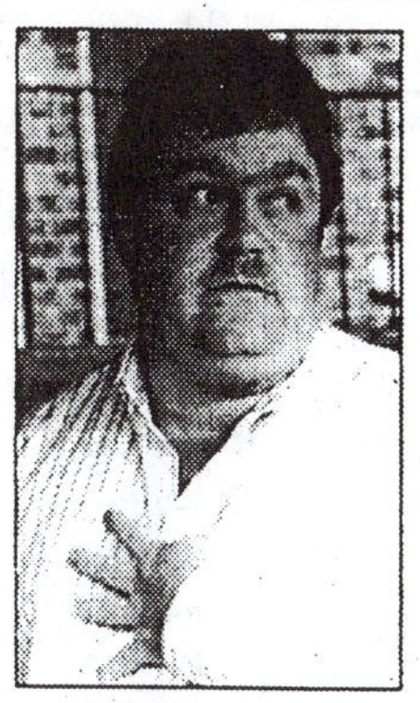

"There will always be people out there who believe Richard is the bomber. There will always be people who stare. There will always be whispers of recognition."

– A lawyer of former Olympic bombing suspect Richard Jewell, left.

A life ruined?

The media certainly share the blame

Nauman: Media ethics code little help to Richard Jewell

The Accused

How Richard Jewell And His Lawyers Seek Revenge on the Media

Cleared in Olympics Blast, He Gets Cash From NBC, Tips From Sympathizers

Stick to facts

Richard Jewell case not news media shining moment

On Oct. 28, Jewell spoke at a news conference. He said he had endured "88 days in hell," and said the news media "cared nothing for my feelings as a human being."

Under threat of a libel suit, NBC and CNN moved quickly to settle with Jewell before a claim was ever filed. The Atlanta *Journal-Constitution* stood by its coverage, maintaining it had done nothing wrong by merely reporting on various law-enforcement investigations and by reporting details about someone who was thrust into the spotlight by those investigations. On Nov. 8, the newspaper said, "It was not illegal, immoral or unethical to publish the story about the FBI's investigation of Richard Jewell."

Testifying before the Senate Committee on the Judiciary Subcommittee on Terrorism, Technology and Government Information in December 1996, Steve Geimann, then president of the Society of Professional Journalists, said: "We, the media, blew it in July. Our coverage of the bombing and the search for a suspect was, in hindsight, excessive, overblown and unnecessarily intruded into the life of Mr. Jewell."

Analysis

Hindsight does offer us a different lens to view our actions, and it's not surprising that many journalists offered *mea culpas* when the Justice Department cleared Jewell. This case, however, offers us lessons far beyond what played out in Atlanta that summer of the Olympic Games. The lessons speak to how we honor the principles of truthtelling, independence, and minimizing harm, and how news organizations can be more accountable in their professional duty.

The lessons speak to how we honor the principles of truthtelling, independence, and minimizing harm, and how news organizations can be more accountable in their professional duty.

Joann Byrd, editorial page editor of the *Seattle Post-Intelligencer* and former ombudsman at the *Washington Post*, suggests that the main lesson journalists can draw from the Jewell case "is that law enforcement people may be wrong. This is only one of the recent cases where journalists went even farther than law enforcement in our presumption that police suspicions were right."

Byrd says the media coverage would have been very different if "journalists had presumed from the start that the FBI's focus on Jewell was wrong: We would have pressed the FBI about other suspects every day. We would have gone to sources—including previous employers—who had good experiences with Jewell. We would have done our best to reconstruct his alibi, and to give attention to his lawyers and his mother and anyone else who would provide a different picture of him."

Byrd argues that journalists should not presume that law enforcement is wrong in such investigations, but recognize that the "law enforcement work is preliminary—more preliminary than all of our disclaimers made it sound this time."

The quest for truth in a high-profile, developing story requires journalists to be at their very best. In this case, too many journalists were over-zealous in pursuing Jewell and exhuming his background. Too few journalists were aggressive in examining the law enforcement officials and investigating the strength of the case against Jewell.

It was probably inevitable that news reports would at some point tie Richard Jewell's name to the FBI investigation. He was already at the center of the case, given his role as a security guard at the scene of the bombing. It would have been difficult if not impossible to merely report that the investigation was focusing on a security guard. Some people would assume it was Jewell, given his central role in the incident. Some might point fingers at other Olympic Park security guards, causing harm to their reputations.

Keith Woods, associate in ethics at The Poynter Institute, says it was not improper to name Jewell as the man law enforcement was investigating. Woods says the ethical failures really occurred in the choices journalists made *after* identifying Jewell as a suspect. Woods refers to "the placement of a story, the tone of the storyteller, the framing of the story. Declaring that Jewell 'fit the profile' of a bomber went beyond the media mandate. Describing him as all but a maladjusted mama's boy, as one print story did, is not what the First Amendment demands of journalists."

Indeed, the intense coverage of Jewell often painted him as a trapped man. Over and over we saw slow-motion video of Jewell walking away from his truck in the parking lot of his home. Over and over we saw him at the center of a swarm of photographers and reporters. Over and over we heard about when he crashed his police car into another squad car during a previous job. The tone of the video and the words in many of the stories often portrayed him as a loser at best, a killer at worst.

In writing about the case after Jewell was cleared by the Justice Department, Woods said "this new pseudo-psychology journalism that we have seen emerge in the past decade is anathema to informed reasoned public discourse. It is sophisticated rumor-mongering. It encourages quick judgment and mob mentality. Worst of all, it happens every day in smaller, less dramatic ways, when the lives of 'suspects' are investigated and explicated by journalists single-mindedly seeking facts to validate the accusations.

"We gnash our teeth and wring our hands over Richard Jewell, but I worry about those many less-public people who are bitten each day by rabid watchdogs."

Case Study #39

A "Cool" Decision Not to Photograph

Summary

The day 19-year-old Clifford Harris arrived at a Florida courthouse to testify in a multimillion dollar lawsuit against the Ford Motor Co., a newspaper and television photographer were waiting outside.

Four years earlier, Harris had been severely burned and lost three limbs in a car crash that claimed the lives of two of his teenage friends. Harris, who was embarrassed to emerge from his room or look in the mirror after the accident, dreaded having to testify and show his face in public. Even more, he feared having his picture circulated in the newspaper and broadcast to thousands of people watching local television news.

But when Harris, in his wheelchair, passed the media photographers outside the courthouse, both kept their cameras at their side. After talking with Harris' attorney, they had decided not to photograph the disfigured 19-year-old.

"We hear so much about the media, that they're so cold, that they're vultures," said Harris' mother, Karen D'Amario. "Well, they held back with Cliff. I was very, very impressed."

St. Petersburg Times photographer Robin Donina Serne, who was assigned to cover the trial, spoke with her editor before Harris was scheduled to testify.

"She told me she trusted me as a photojournalist," Serne said. "She said I would know best what to do being in the courtroom."

Serne spoke with Harris' attorney about taking the teenager's photograph from behind so as not to reveal his disfigured face. But the attorney "vehemently objected," arguing that the very act of taking the picture would "traumatize" Harris. A psychologist had offered the same opinion earlier in the trial.

Serne, a newspaper photographer of 13 years, returned to the newsroom without snapping a picture of Harris.

"It felt funny," she recalled. "But I knew in my mind I had done the right thing. I was taking responsibility as a person gathering information. So often we shoot blindly without fully understanding why we are taking photos and thinking responsibly."

The next day, the *Times* published a picture of Harris and his mother hugging one another, a family snapshot taken before the crash.

The *Tampa Tribune,* which also was covering the trial, had decided beforehand not to send a photographer the day Harris testified. The *Tribune* printed a family photograph, also taken before the accident, of Harris hugging his dog.

Tribune reporter Robin Shaw had seen photographs of Harris after the crash and agreed with Harris' attorney that taking the teenager's picture would have a devastating effect.

"It wouldn't have seemed to do any public good to photograph him," said Shaw. "We wanted to do what was best for the boy."

Outside the courtroom, Harris' attorney also asked a cameraman from WTSP-Ch. 10, who was shooting images of the trial for all the area's media, not to photograph Harris. WTSP talked with a representative of a competing Tampa Bay television station, and they decided not to videotape Harris.

"There was no compelling need for him to be in our coverage," Mike Cavender, then-WTSP vice-president for news, told the *St. Petersburg Times*. "We did tape the audio part of his testimony, so we had what I thought was important."

A jury eventually ruled that Ford Motor Co. had no liability in Harris' 1992 crash. In May 1997, however, a judge ordered a new trial after learning that two jurors had failed to disclose their involvement in two unrelated lawsuits.

Harris and his mother remain angry at Ford, but they continue to praise the media's coverage of the trial.

According to D'Amario, when she told her son of the media's decision not to photograph him the day he testified, he responded, "Really? Cool. Tell them I said, 'Thank you.'"

Analysis

Pictures are sometimes worth a thousand words, and it's possible that the image of the horribly disfigured Clifford Harris would be compelling in a storytelling sense. And the picture would be true. And it would be relevant to the central issue of the story.

That said, we must always remember that we, as journalists, are human beings, not robots. We are more than electronic button pushers.

It is accepted that journalistic duty often requires us to intrude on people who want no part of us and to give the public information that they sometimes would rather not hear about. Journalists are not unlike physicians in that respect. Journalists have a duty to inform; physicians, the duty to heal. Sometimes the procedure and the diagnosis are unpleasant to those on the receiving end.

> ***(J)ournalistic duty often requires us to intrude on people who want no part of us and to give the public information that they sometimes would rather not hear about.***

Yet neither the physician nor the journalist must treat the patient or the story subject as a means to an end. We have an ethical responsibility to treat human beings with respect and as ends in and of themselves.

Clifford Harris and his family had endured pain beyond comprehension. Even though he was the central figure in this high-profile case, this young man deserved a considerable measure of compassion.

As photojournalist Robin Donina Serne said, "I knew in my mind I had done the right thing ...." She and the others photojournalists and news managers took responsibility for their actions.

This case exemplifies several important decision making steps.

The journalists involved seriously weighed the competing principles of truthtelling and minimizing harm. They chose alternatives that allowed them to honor both principles, giving greater weight to the extreme vulnerability of the young man.

The decisions were enhanced by good "front-end" decision making by those involved. They spotted the ethical land mines early, deliberated with colleagues, weighed consequences, considered alternative actions, and made thoughtful decisions.

The public was still served. Clifford Harris was respected.

Case Study #40

Megan's Law: "Naming" a Dilemma

Summary

In July 1994, 7-year-old Megan Kanka of Hamilton Township, N.J., was kidnapped, raped and murdered, allegedly by a neighbor who, unbeknown to the community, was a twice-convicted sex offender.

Less than two weeks after her body was found, New Jersey lawmakers pushed through an emergency measure requiring police to notify communities when certain sex offenders move into a neighborhood. It was called Megan's Law, and it sparked a national drive, fueled by presidential politics, to pass a federal law bearing the same name and intent.

The case also renewed debate among news organizations trying to identify the line that separates their responsibility to the public and their responsibility to vulnerable individuals.

That debate came to focus on the case of E.B., an Englewood, N.J., man who successfully petitioned a federal appeals court in 1996 to prevent authorities from carrying out Megan's Law, which requires police to notify neighbors, day-care centers and schools whenever convicted sex offenders move into a community.

E.B. confessed to the 1969 rapes and gruesome murders of two Virginia boys, one of whom he buried alive. He admitted those crimes in 1976 while in prison and undergoing therapy after molesting three boys in New Jersey. He served his sentence and was released in 1989. He and his wife bought a house and lived in Englewood for more than six years without notice.

Then came Megan's Law and the lawsuit. And then came the Guardian Angels and their leader, Curtis Sliwa.

Unhappy and impatient with the legal processes preventing the wholesale dissemination of names and information, Sliwa's group printed fliers bearing the man's identity and declaring, "E.B., we know who you are." They handed out the fliers in the neighborhood where he lived. A political activist broadcast the man's name on Sliwa's radio show.

At the *North Jersey Herald & News*, a copy editor noted that a story about those events bore E.B.'s full name. "The copy editor said, 'We've got a story here with a name in it. Do we want to run this?'" *Herald & News* editor Ian Shearn said, "That story was barreling right toward the press. We pulled it."

Thus, one news organization in the area confronted the ethical dilemma of choosing between public information and individual privacy. The involvement of community activists such as the Guardian Angels challenged the media to make independent decisions about identifying E.B. as public support of Megan's Law grew.

From the moment the lawsuit was filed, E.B.'s true identity was available and legally could have been printed and broadcast. It took little research to figure out he was the man who confessed to choking and raping a 14-year-old Petersburg, Va., boy and burying him alive, then stabbing a 13-year-old boy 21 times after raping him. The boys lived a block apart.

"We run the names of shoplifters in (nearby) Bayonne. We're not going to run the name of a man who killed two kids—tortured and raped them? I don't see the point of that."
—John Oswald

The state Associated Press tracked down the name quickly, then had to decide what to do with it. The decision: Withhold the name until the courts rule.

"We had the full range of discussion with good arguments on both sides," said Mark Mittelstadt, AP New Jersey bureau chief. "We tried to act responsibly without contributing to the problem. This was a tough one."

John Oswald, managing editor for the *Jersey Journal*, had no trouble figuring out his newspaper would become the first in the state to run E.B.'s real name. With a local peg for the story (the politician who named E.B. on the radio lives in the *Journal*'s coverage area), the newspaper's leadership came to a deadline decision.

"It seems like a really basic point of information," Oswald said. "We run the names of shoplifters in (nearby) Bayonne. We're not going to run the name of a man who killed two kids—tortured and raped them? I don't see the point of that."

E.B.'s decision to challenge Megan's Law in court made him a public person, Oswald said. The fact that E.B. was trying to derail a law of such national prominence and statewide popularity gave the story all the news value it needed to propel his real identity into the newspaper, Oswald said.

"There weren't great hours of debate going on about it" at the *Journal*, he said, inasmuch as the issue first surfaced on deadline after a television station broadcast E.B.'s name. A small group of editors at the *Journal* debated the question for "about an hour," Oswald said.

By contrast, the Bergen County *Record* convened more than 20 people—editors, reporters, even a former prosecutor now writing about legal affairs—in a meeting editor Glenn Ritt said "eventually turned into a seminar." The discussion lasted about three hours, Ritt said, and yielded a decision to wait until the courts had ruled before deciding whether to release E.B.'s name.

"We didn't want to make an ad hoc policy that we would have to revisit the next time this kind of case came up," Ritt said.

The *Record* did have an opinion, though. In its editorial, "Why we're not naming E.B.," the newspaper said his crimes "were monstrous, and we believe the community has a right to know who he is. But we also believe that in a nation of law, the court should be given time to rule on the case."

For the news organizations involved, the case prompted great soul-searching and few clear answers. "I don't know if there's a right or wrong answer, only the one we came to," AP's Middlestadt said.

Analysis

Even the most difficult of ethical dilemmas *do* have right or wrong answers to them. That's what ethics is about. But few cases have two clear choices.

To publish E.B.'s name strictly for competitive reasons would be ethically unsupportable, since it does not rely on a moral principle. To publish E.B.'s name by caving in to pressure from authorities also would be ethically questionable, since it violates the principle of independence. To make an immediate decision about publishing without considering one's professional duty or the significant consequences of the action is ethically indefensible.

At the same time, there are several possible *right* answers to this dilemma, though they may be grounded in different ethical principles.

Most of the newsroom decision makers worried about the potential consequences of publishing E.B.'s name in such a charged environment, where the threat of violent vigilantism was thought to be high. They also worried about the swamp they might walk into by journalistically embracing the legislative and legal movement to get more and more information about crime and criminals out to the public.

Those papers who held back on naming E.B. gave strongest weight to the principles of minimizing harm and independence.

To make an immediate decision about publishing without considering one's professional duty or the significant consequences of the action is ethically indefensible.

Using a different principle, the *Jersey Journal's* John Oswald saw his paper's responsibility as clear; to tell the truth and name E.B. Oswald found no reason to hold back, believing the public benefit of disclosure outweighed any potential of harm.

No matter how the courts rule in this and similar cases, news organizations will continue to face similar tough calls when the public's right to know clashes with an individual's right to privacy.

"Where do you stop?" asked Shearn of the *Herald & News*. "Do you print the name and address? Do you print the model of the car? The license plate number? His picture? Do you tell people where he works? Where he drinks? And is the newspaper the venue to do that?"

The difficulty in answering such questions must not deter the effort to make good ethical decisions. News organizations can use the guiding principles of truthtelling, independence and minimizing harm as a moral compass in that decision making process. And, once a decision has been reached, it is also morally appropriate to go public with your thought process, letting the readers know that the tough calls were not made capriciously. These principles help you recognize and resolve conflicting loyalties to different stakeholders.

Good decisions require some reflection and reasoning. We must not be trapped by our gut reactions when an ethical issue clearly strikes a strong emotional chord. A high-stakes issue deserves attention. To borrow from a time-honored warning: *stop* your reaction; *look* at what you know and what you don't know; and *listen* to what others have to say.

Good ethical decisions are a product of collaborative decision making, even on deadline. Different voices will raise legitimate concerns and potential alternative actions.

A decision must be made. Make it a justifiable one.

—This case study was originally written by Keith Woods for The Poynter Institute web site.

Privacy

What the Codes Say

Norfolk (Va.) ***Virginian-Pilot***

There are inevitable conflicts between an individual's desire for privacy and the public good or the right to know about the conduct of public affairs.

Reporters and photographers should make judgments in the light of common sense, decency and humanity, keeping in mind that we do not encourage them to badger a person who has made it clear he does not want to be interviewed or photographed.

(Note exceptions: People involved in a criminal activity being dragged to court, etc.)

Our newspapers are edited under the guidelines that copy and photographs should not pander to morbid curiosity about details of vice, crime or personal tragedy.

Australian Journalists' Association

At times of grief or trauma, always act with sensitivity and discretion. Never harass. Never exploit a person's vulnerability or ignorance of media practice. Interview only with informed consent.

Grand Forks **(N.D.)** ***Herald***

We must remember that many people place a high value on their privacy, and we should honor that basic interest unless there are compelling reasons to the contrary. When people thrust themselves into the public spotlight, either momentarily or over time, they forfeit to some degree their right to privacy. In many other circumstances, the public's legitimate right and need to know must take precedence. Because it is vital that we reserve to ourselves the authority to make such decisions, it is equally vital that we make them carefully and responsibly.

Philadelphia Inquirer

Most of the people mentioned in the news columns are public officials, whose official activities are legally the subject of scrutiny, or public figures, who often seek out publicity. However, private citizens who have not sought public notice are frequently surprised, and sometimes upset, when they are approached by reporters or find themselves written about. This is especially true in tragic situations. Staff members should approach stories with both a desire to inform the public and compassion for the individuals involved.

A private citizen who is thrust unwittingly and unwillingly into a public situation is likely to be unfamiliar with news-gathering practices. Staff members should clearly identify themselves when approaching such inexperienced people and treat them with courtesy.

Relatives of public officials and public figures are sometimes newsworthy solely because of their family position. Such stories can, however, be overdone. They should be handled thoughtfully and not be simply voyeuristic.

When it is decided that a person in a news story should not be named, such as a rape victim or a witness in possible danger, care should be taken not to identify the person through other specific references, such as home address, place of work or school attended.

A person's mental or physical infirmities, sexual preference or the like generally should not be referred to unless it is relevant to the story.

Victims, witnesses to crimes, accused persons and jurors can be subjected to harassment. Therefore, we do not generally give exact addresses, but use more general references, such as "Broad Street near Callowhill Street," "the 200 block of Pine Street," or, especially for a short street, "Emery Lane, Phoenixville." Exceptions should be approved by the executive editor or managing editor or, in their absence, by the editor in charge.

San Jose* (Calif.) *Mercury News

The *Mercury News* is sensitive to the privacy of victims of rape and child molestation, or of subjects who clearly would be in physical danger by publication of their names and addresses. Exceptions to this rule may be made in some circumstance, but they must be approved by the executive editor or editor.

Ordinarily, consent is implied if a photographer approaches a subject, indicates that he/she is a newspaper photographer and asks for names and other facts. In some circumstances, written releases may be required (at mental health institutions or orphanages, for example).

Spokane (Wash.) *Spokesman-Review*

Journalists should recognize the individual rights of privacy of people involved in the news. There are inevitable conflicts between the privacy of individuals and the public good or the public right to know about the conduct of persons in regard to public affairs. Newsworthiness, common sense, humanity, and the law are factors which should be considered in each case.

Legality Only One Measure:

The legal standard, however, is not the only standard by which to measure a story or a picture. What is legal, in other words, is not necessarily what is ethical or what is in good taste.

It is perfectly legal to identify rape victims, for instance. But these newspapers do not identify rape victims, even when they testify in open court. It is legal, too, to publish pictures of victims of fatal accidents or pictures of persons displaying any number of private emotions as long as they are in public situations. But good taste may dictate against the use of such shots.

There can be few hard-and-fast rules governing the use of stories and pictures that have the potential to be offensive to great numbers of readers. There are exceptions to every rule. Even the rape rule has exceptions: We do identify rape victims in some instances, such as when a woman sues her convicted rapist for civil damages, or when a wife charges her husband with rape.

In the absence of specific rules, the important point is to consider the implications of using material that might prove objectionable to many of our readers.

National Victim Center (Texas)
Victim's Rights and the Media

Never feel that because you have unwillingly been involved in an incident of public interest that you must personally share the details and/or your feelings with the general public. If you decide that you want the public to be aware of how traumatic and unfair your victimization was, you do not automatically give up your right to privacy. By knowing and requesting respect for your rights, you can be heard and yet not violated ....

You have the right to grieve in privacy.

Grief is a highly personal experience. If you do not wish to share it publicly, you have the right to ask reporters to remove themselves during times of grief.

Chapter Ten

Source/Reporter Relationships

Sources are the foundation of a journalist's success, developed and nurtured and often protected for the future. The reputation a reporter or newspaper or television station has for protecting sources who provide sensitive information is a part of the continuing dynamic of successful journalism.

At the same time, audiences and conventional wisdom expect sources to be fully identified as a way of assessing and assigning media credibility. Audiences generally have a right to detailed information held by reporters and editors. Only an argument of seeking a greater good, or trying to avoid grievous harm, can justify not identifying the sources of information.

Remember, a large part of the argument over the Brock Adams story, discussed earlier, dealt with the decision by the *Seattle Times* to publish politically damaging accusations based on anonymous sources. Therefore, use of anonymous sources or abuse of cited regular sources is a decision to be carefully considered.

When an editor decides to keep sources confidential, the editor should recognize that the reputation of the newspaper or station is being placed on the line, asking audiences to accept the information on faith.

Confidentiality is not the only ethical concern journalists face when dealing with sources. Indeed, the fundamental relationship between journalists and their sources has been subjected to moral scrutiny because it is, by nature, a "use and be used" relationship. Writer Janet Malcolm, in a two-part *New Yorker* series and a subsequent book titled *The Journalist and the Murderer*, leveled the charge that:

> Every journalist who is not too stupid or too full of himself to notice what is going on knows that what he does is morally indefensible. He is a kind of confidence man, preying on people's vanity, ignorance, or loneliness, gaining their trust and betraying them without remorse .... On reading

> the article or book in question, (the source) has to face the fact that the journalist—who seemed so friendly and sympathetic, so keen to understand him fully, so remarkably attuned to his vision of things—never had the slightest intention of collaborating with him on his story but always intended to write a story of his own. The disparity between what seems to be the intention of an interview as it is taking place and what it actually turns out to have been in aid of always comes as a shock to the subject.*

Journalists by and large disagreed with Malcolm's strident point of view. However, her charges did cause some healthy soul searching within the industry. If nothing else, Malcolm caused journalists to recognize the tenuous nature of the reporter-source relationship. The bottom line is a warning to keep a professional distance or to behave so honorably during the interviewing and the writing that sources are not deceived.

* Source: Janet Malcolm, *The Journalist and the Murderer.* New York: Vintage Books, 1990, pp. 3-4.

Source/Reporter Relationships

Checklist

- All else being equal, provide full identity of your news sources. The story is more credible, and future sources will recognize your basic ground rules. Generally, confidentiality should be granted only to protect someone who is relatively powerless or who is in a position to lose the capacity to continue as a solid source of information. In addition, the story should be of overriding public importance.
- Make sure sources understand the basic ground rules concerning on-the-record, off-the-record, not-for-attribution, etc.
- Do not abuse naive news sources, and don't be abused by sophisticated ones. Don't put words in their mouths, but at the same time don't let them dictate to you only the story they want to tell. You're a journalist, not a flack.
- Before promising confidentiality, try to obtain the same information from sources willing to be quoted.
- Do not permit "after the fact" requests for confidentiality.
- Don't let anonymous sources use the cloak of anonymity to attack other individuals or organizations.
- Make sure you understand your newsroom's policy on confidentiality before promising it to sources. You may need the consent of your editors, and/or you may have to share the source's identity with your supervisor. Professional burdens of trust must expand to include the reporter, editor, and sources, always with an eye to the needs of the public.
- Once you promise confidentiality, keep your promise. Ask yourself how far you and your news organization are willing to go to keep that promise. Are you willing to tell your source that he/she and you are likely to be subpoenaed in case of a libel or invasion-of-privacy suit? Are you willing to go to jail?
- Always bear in mind the power of the press when dealing with sources. You are in a position to cause harm or benefit. Use that power with great discretion. Do your sources know you are a reporter? Do you and they assume that everything they reveal is fair game for publication?
- Are you willing to spell out in your news stories the methods you used to gain information from sources and why you may be protecting confidentiality?

Case Study #41

Crack Reporting in Detroit

Summary

The *Detroit Free Press*, after an exhaustive look at the effect of crack cocaine on Detroit and its suburbs in late 1989, produced "24 Hours: The Drug Menace," a special section.

Journalists working the project were repeatedly warned "to stay as much as possible at arm's length" from involvement in the story, Heath J. Meriwether, the paper's executive editor, recalled in an interview with *Editor & Publisher*.

However, photographer Manny Crisostomo bought sausage from Tim, a crack addict, and paid Tim $20 for a Sony Walkman. Each purchase allowed the drug user to buy crack. After buying the radio, the photographer and reporter Pat Chargot did not mention the incident to their bosses. Crisostomo later said buying the radio was for the journalists' safety.

The explanation of the incident by the photographer, who earlier in the year had won a Pulitzer Prize, was that the competitive *Free Press* newsroom and the requirements of producing the "24 Hours" feature led to what happened. The photographer and reporter were suspended without pay for three and two days, respectively.

The spending of money by the photographer, which in turn allowed the addict to spend money for cocaine, raised a number of questions on the *Free Press* project.

After buying the sausage from Tim, the reporter-photographer team was allowed to observe the addict's life for 24 hours. Crisostomo and Chargot drove Tim and friends to find crack.

Meriwether said the newspaper felt Tim and his friends were going to the crack houses anyway.

"Our staffers were really just along for the ride, and driving enabled us to retain control of the situation should personal safety become an issue," he said.

The purchase of the radio became known to *Free Press* editors when Chargot, writing a follow-up story about Tim, "realized that the story ... was going to compound the problem. Her conscience couldn't abide continuing the lie," Meriwether said.

While working on the project, the reporter and photographer were asked by editors if they had provided any money to the addicts. They said they had

SUNDAY, OCT. 15, 1989 • DETROIT FREE PRESS

COMMENT

SPECIAL SECTION

24 HOURS

THE DRUG MENACE

Life, death, crack: Night and day with the high, the horror

6 P.M. Friday: Tim's on the launching pad.

A 24-year-old crack addict who grew up in Roseville, Tim is at his sister's apartment in Hamtramck, cranking up for another night of "hustling" — doing whatever it takes to get crack cocaine.

He's downed a fifth of Night Train wine and two beers because he wants his "attitude to be right. I don't want to think about anything . . . just about what I want to do when I'm out there — get high. It's like going to the bathroom. You're only in there for one reason. You really have to go."

6:07 P.M.: Across from the 12th Street Missionary Baptist Church in west Detroit, kids play basketball on a court laid by the church to attract young people from the troubled streets.

"Other than this, I would be at a friend's house or in the streets," says David Johnson, 15. "There's a lot of chances for me to be in trouble. Crack is all over. There's too much crack. You get tired of it."

The Rev. Robert Moorman, 47, director of the Pilgrim Village Basketball Association Substance Abuse Program, supervises the game. A former crack addict who went to prison twice on drug-related charges, Mr. Moorman wears a pin signifying he's been drug free for a year.

6:23 P.M.: At Orchard and Paddock, two blocks from Wood Park in Pontiac, five young men stand around two cars parked in front of telephone booths. Nearby residents say the corner is a drug communications center.

"Yo! Whatcha want? Whatcha need?" one of them yells, walking toward a passing car.

6:30 P.M.: On this 60-degree, full-color fall evening, Tom Cremonte zips along a winding, two-lane blacktop headed to Milford from Brighton.

As a huge, nearly full moon rises over the rolling countryside, small lakes and impressive homes of northwest Oakland County, Cremonte observes that this is "the kind of night where everyone is going to be out looking for their hop. Everyone knows it's going to be a real good party night."

Dressed in gray jeans, a Michigan State University T-shirt and a cap that reads "MIA/POW Never Forgotten,"

See 24 HOURS, Page 5E

10:30 P.M.: They've shined shoes in a bar and sold a radio on the street to buy $20 worth of crack. Now, parked in a Detroit alley near Richardson and Mt. Elliott, Dave takes a hit from a crack pipe while Tim waits his turn. They think they've been shorted. "This ain't two dimes," says Tim.

PAULINE LUBENS/Detroit Free Press

7:35 P.M.: Marie Henderson, 46, sings a gospel song at a tent revival in the parking lot of Harbor Light Center, a rehabilitation facility run by the Salvation Army off Cass on Park Avenue in Detroit. After 25 years of addictions, most recently to crack, she says, she left Harbor Light in March clean. "I'm blessed . . . I'm free," she says. "I intend to stay free one day at a time." Later in the evening, in Harbor Light's third-floor ward for recent arrivals, Aaron Moore, 20, of Detroit will explain that watching his best friend die of a crack overdose prompted him to seek treatment. "I'm saying to myself, 'That could have been me.' "

6:20 P.M.: A Detroit narcotics officer questions four men who kneel on the concrete walkway outside an apartment building on East Ferry, near Beaubien, after a raid. Not all the men handcuffed and cabled together are arrested; police lead those who are into a van. "They ain't got nothin,' " one suspect says in the van. "They can't get nothin.' "

not. But Chargot claimed the withholding of direct information from editors was more deception than lie; that editors did not ask direct questions that might have elicited the truth.

Crisostomo said the situation with the three persons in his back seat was getting out of hand with Tim and his addict friends getting loud and nearly fighting for a few "microscopic" bits of crack. That's when he bought the radio, he said. Chargot said she resisted the radio transaction because she felt the journalists were not in danger.

Meriwether said the reporter and photographer deceived their editors about the incident, and a bond of trust was broken that was critical to how journalists do their jobs.

Crisostomo said: "Think about this: How does somebody who has been working (on the *Free Press*) for eight years … how come there was no one here I would trust to tell this to?"

He said there was pressure from both management and himself to produce. The paper encouraged him to buy booze and meals to get close to a crack addict, he said. If there had been more time to get the project completed, he said he might not have bought the radio. One other point: This was his first major effort since the Pulitzer and he "wanted to hit a home run."

Analysis

Several questions are raised by this case:

- Do the pressures of producing a major story under deadline pressure lead editors or reporters or photographers to take ethical shortcuts?
- Under what conditions can a reporter or photographer deceive an editor?
- How does a journalist deal with a guilty conscience?

Editors have an obligation to anticipate the kind of problems that reporters and photographers will run into and should have guidelines for handling them. Given the guidelines, reporters and photographers deserve a work climate in which they can talk with an editor.

> ***The pressure journalists feel to produce is part of the normal tension and creativity in a newsroom.***

Obviously in this case, it was necessary to build a relationship with an addict so that his life could be observed and photographed. However, buying the radio and the sausage from Tim raises significant ethical questions. These purchases by the photographer gave the addict money to buy crack cocaine, which amounted to letting the source break the law. The problem is compounded in this instance because the reporter and photographer agreed not to tell their editors and, in fact, deceived both editors and the public by not disclosing, under questioning, that they had provided money with which the addicts fed their habit.

The pressure journalists feel to produce is part of the normal tension and creativity in a newsroom. In this instance, a Pulitzer Prize winner felt additional pressure by having just won a prestigious award. One thing that newsroom management can do is be sensitive to this kind of situation and help the journalist deal with the pressure to produce excellent stories. Management must always share the responsibility for both the ethical guidelines that are created and the ethical culture in which journalists work.

Case Study #42

Crossing the Border

Summary

A Copley News Service reporter, S. Lynne Walker, and photographer, Jeffrey Brown, accompanied a 21-year-old Mexican immigrant from central Mexico to Chicago, a 3,500-mile, 13-day journey that included illegally crossing into the United States. Walker and Brown also witnessed Luis Muñoz purchase a fake green card in Los Angeles before hopping on a flight with him to Chicago.

The story ran as a 14-part series in Copley's flagship, the *San Diego Union-Tribune,* and was picked up on the wire by several other newspapers throughout the country. Copley-owned newspapers in Illinois, which initiated the series because of an influx of illegal immigrants in the Chicago area, published the account of Muñoz's journey in a special section called "A Journey to the Promised Land."

Readers raised questions about the ethics of reporting such a story. Some called for Walker and Brown to be prosecuted for aiding and abetting an illegal act. Others charged that Walker and Brown had glorified Muñoz and illegal immigration. Readers accused the newspaper of providing a blueprint for immigrants on how to cross the border illegally.

Walker and Brown said they merely played the role of reporter-observer. They said they paid none of Muñoz's expenses during the trip and never aided and abetted him in a crime. Instead, they wanted to put a face on illegal immigration, to help people understand why anyone would undertake such a treacherous and dangerous journey.

"We knew there would be criticism," Walker said. "We wanted to give people an inside look at why people cross the border (illegally) every day, and why it's impossible to stop it."

The journey started in Muñoz's hometown north of Mexico City. Walker and Brown, a photographer with the Copley-owned Waukegan *News-Sun* in Illinois, rode a bus with Muñoz to Tijuana, then struck a deal with smugglers to sneak them across the border.

Walker and Brown said they told the smugglers they were journalists. The smugglers were skeptical, suspecting that Walker and Brown were American authorities, but eventually agreed to shepherd them across the border with Muñoz. The smugglers planned to charge Muñoz $450, while charging Walker and Brown half that amount because they were Americans.

"We never misled anybody," Walker said. "Our problem was convincing

IMMIGRATION: A COPLEY NEWSPAPERS SPECIAL REPORT

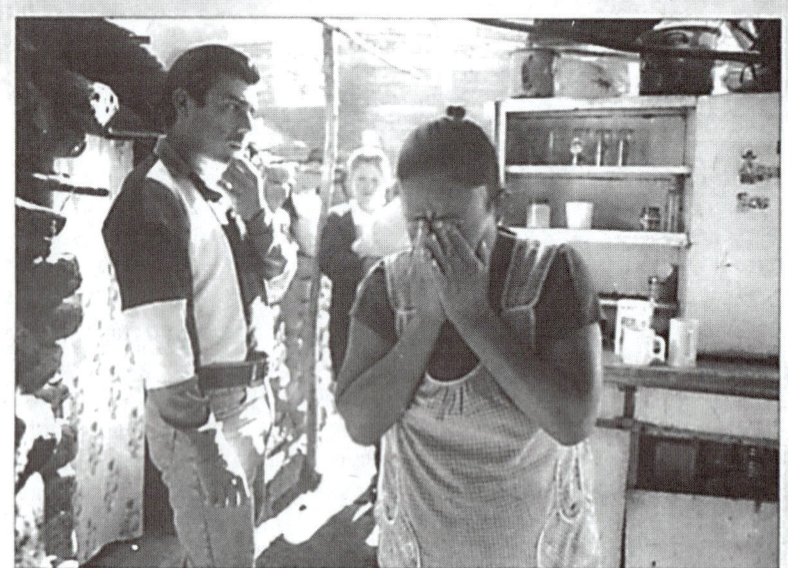

UNDOCUMENTED

A JOURNEY TO THE PROMISED LAND

By S. Lynne Walker
Copley News Service

Turn to Page 2

2 Luis' journey begins as he travels to the U.S./Mexico border. Coyotes must decide when and where he will cross.

3 A frightening ride through San Diego County brings Luis to a safehouse and the beginning of his new life.

4 Luis joins two brothers in northern Illinois. In a matter of hours, he's washing dishes in a restaurant kitchen.

everyone that we were journalists."

Walker and Brown had previously discussed with Copley editors their plan to cross into the United States without passing through a legal port of entry—a misdemeanor offense. Walker and Brown said the story was compelling enough to warrant breaking the law.

"There was no other way to do the story," Walker said.

In a mountainous area east of Tijuana, Mexican authorities apprehended the smugglers, along with Muñoz, Walker and Brown, and drove them to jail.

Walker and Brown identified themselves as journalists. The Mexican authorities asked them to testify against the smugglers, but Walker and Brown refused, after calling the U.S. consulate in Tijuana. The Mexican police eventually released Walker, Brown and Muñoz, and they returned to Tijuana.

They found another smuggler who was successful in shuttling them across the border into San Diego, then on to north San Diego County where they were put in a "safe house." Another smuggler drove them to Los Angeles.

After Muñoz purchased the fake documents, the three flew on a jet to Chicago. There, Muñoz secured a job as a dishwasher, where he earned almost 10 times his salary in Mexico.

Brown was selected as a finalist for the 1997 Pulitzer Prize in feature photography for his work chronicling the journey.

Analysis

Can you report accurately on someone with whom you have broken laws, whom you have watched violate a number of laws, with whom you have been arrested (and against whom you have refused to testify), and with whom you have shared a 3,500-mile journey?

This reporter and photographer said they could; the two parties remained largely independent of each other. They wrote a series to chronicle the odyssey and shed some light on the problems of illegal immigration in the United States.

Neither critics nor Pulitzer jurors seemed to think the shared experience would affect the reporting. Critics concentrated on the lawbreaking and the message the stories sent to the world.

Neither critics nor Pulitzer jurors seemed to think the shared experience would affect the reporting.

Clearly, the journalists tried to be unintrusive flies on the wall to the Mexican immigrant's journey, but were necessarily involved to the extent they were arrested with him in Mexico, committed the misdemeanor of illegal entry themselves, and watched him violate numerous U.S. immigration laws. The journalists must be trusted on this, but it is difficult to see how the emotional bond of shared experiences would have affected the ultimate story. They did the immigrant no favors and will probably never see him again. The power of the immigrant, in short, is negligible.

Balancing those concrete actions are the abstract benefits of readers informed in detail about the experiences (and presumably the mindset) of one alien determined to find a better life for himself in a country whose laws do not welcome him.

The role of information is often underrated by critics of the media. However, at least some of the critics recognized the power of the information to upset the status quo of immigration laws and practices (glorifying immigration and providing a blueprint for illegal immigrants).

It is difficult to see how Muñoz himself would affect the ultimate story of the journey, but the reporter's and photographer's presence through those 3,500 miles could not have helped but color the story, probably to its benefit. Presumably, experiencing the trip would shape the journalists' attitudes toward the system, toward immigrants, and toward other elements they would have encountered.

However, virtually any experience journalists have will affect their outlook and influence their writing and photography. The question would be whether the experience created a bias that would result in an unrealistic image projected by the ultimate story.

These journalists, and their project, suggested they were looking to experience what illegal immigrants experienced and to project that experience as accurately as they could for readers.

The Pulitzer nomination suggested they were able to do that.

One who has a commitment to the distribution of information must conclude that the information gathered and distributed more than offset in social value the damage done by law violations and observations of violations. Information is a critical commodity, and the test is whether the image created by the journalists in the aftermath of their journey was an accurate recounting of the experiences of an immigrant.

Critics of the Copley News Service project would do well to consider the nature of the source-reporter relationship in this project and the potential benefits and costs of the project to the source, to U.S. immigration policies and to the readers. In addition, they should ask what makes any story compelling enough to break a law, and, if journalists do decide to break laws, what degree of accountability do they and their employees owe "the system"?

Case Study #43

Fertility Fraud

Summary

At first, the story seemed implausible: Doctors at a highly-acclaimed Southern California fertility clinic were stealing eggs from women patients, fertilizing them and implanting the embryos in other women who eventually gave birth. Women whose eggs were stolen were becoming mothers and didn't know it.

The story started as a news tip from a source who called the *Orange County Register*. Reporters tracked down one case, obtaining medical records and interviewing the woman whose eggs were harvested without consent. Soon, reporters learned that doctors had stolen eggs from dozens of women. Reporters from all *Register* editorial departments became involved in the stories.

The unprecedented nature of the crimes opened unprecedented journalistic problems. The reporters had evidence that stolen eggs resulted in live births. They also knew that the women didn't know their eggs had been stolen and that the women who gave birth didn't know they had been implanted with stolen eggs. All of the patients had spent tens of thousands of dollars in desperate attempts to conceive.

In the *Register* newsroom, editors and reporters held discussions about how to report the stories. They set up a conference call with an ethicist, Michael Josephson of the Josephson Institute of Ethics in Marina Del Rey, Calif., who helped reporters develop a strategy for contacting and questioning women whose eggs were stolen.

> ***Putting the rights of sources above publishing the story gave reporters a sense of relief, Nicolosi said. They were not pressured to get sources to speak on the record at all costs.***

"We talked things through to find out the questions we should be asking of ourselves," said *Register* executive editor Ken Brusic.

From the start, *Register* reporters and editors decided that the rights of the patients would "reign supreme," said Michelle Nicolosi, a reporter who interviewed many of the victims. "We wanted to put a human face on this story, but we didn't want to hurt people to do it."

Putting the rights of sources above publishing the story gave reporters a sense of relief, Nicolosi said. They were not pressured to get sources to speak on the record at all costs. In fact, editors at the *Register,* which has a strict policy forbidding the use of unnamed sources, agreed to allow reporters to break the rule for the fertility stories because of their sensitive nature.

Reporters first contacted fertility patients by phone, explaining the story they were working on and telling the women that they had their medical records. Reporters brought the records to patients' homes.

Said Nicolosi: "We told them, 'Here, these records are yours. Would you like to share them with us? Would you like to talk about them?'"

Most of the women granted interviews. Many spoke on the record. Others asked that their names not be published. The *Register* honored their request.

To learn more about fertility concerns and issues, Nicolosi joined an on-line fertility chat room. She sent a message to chat room participants, identifying herself as a reporter, and asked to join as a "fly on the wall to listen to your problems, what your life is like." Reading the conversations helped Nicolosi to better understand women with fertility problems, allowing her to interview the women with greater sensitivity, she said.

The *Register* published more than 240 stories about the fertility scandal in one year. The three doctors involved in the scandal were indicted. Two fled the country. The *Register's* reporting not only furthered the investigation and prompted regulatory reforms, but it put the revelations into context, explaining the science, ethics and law of the fertility industry. In 1996, the *Register* received a Pulitzer Prize in investigative reporting for its series of stories.

Nicolosi believes the *Register's* approach and treatment of sources on the fertility stories could be applied to everyday reporting.

"We put an extra step in the (reporting) process," Nicolosi said. "We took a look at our needs *and* our sources' needs. Normally, we don't talk about the consequences of our actions. Does the story merit the intrusion? But if we did it for the (fertility) stories, why couldn't we do it more on other stories?"

Analysis

This is a complex and fascinating case study in source-reporter relationships. It puts to the test several "standards of practice" outlined in the SPJ Code of Ethics:

- Journalists should identify sources whenever feasible. The public is entitled to as much information as possible on sources' reliability.
- Always question sources' motives before promising anonymity. Clarify conditions attached to any promise made in exchange for information. Keep promises.
- Show compassion for those who may be affected adversely by news coverage. Use special sensitivity when dealing with children and inexperienced sources or subjects.
- Recognize that private people have a greater right to control information

about themselves than do public officials and others who seek power, influence or attention. Only an overriding public need can justify intrusion into anyone's privacy.

• Be vigilant and courageous about holding those with power accountable.

In short, this case study demands a careful balancing of the fundamental principles of truthtelling and minimizing harm.

The *Register* took great, and laudable, care to protect vulnerable sources who involuntarily became a part of a news story because they had unknowingly relinquished eggs, or because they were victims of fraudulent fertility.

That the public was made aware of the overall scheme is of tremendous credit to the *Register*. However, some thought should be given to the damage done by the withholding of names to see whether some justifiable balance was achieved.

This is a case in which the *Register* decided early on to withhold information from its paying audience. It certainly may have been for good reason, but any institutional decision to withhold a body of relevant information raises questions about the contract that is established between the news media and their subscribers. When subscribers plunk down their sixpence for the daily news, do they expect to know what the newspaper knows, or do they rationally agree to receive only part of what is a relevant report of the day? Generally, a democratic society would limit the amount of information a news organization would withhold.

Numerous questions may be asked in the matter of whether more facts, rather than fewer, should have been distributed as part of the truthtelling obligation. (For instance, as a result of the reporting of this story some families had to confront the embarrassing truth about biological parenthood, while others, equally armed with information, could avoid the truth merely by virtue of asking the paper for anonymity.) Whether the emotional satisfaction of not publicly embarrassing principals in the case overcomes a troubling question of unintended consequences that may accrue from the deletions is a question editors must deal with. Discussing the potential problems of maintaining the confidentiality of those involved is one way of assuring a rational rather than an emotional decision.

Case Study #44

Connie Chung and Newt's Mom

Summary

The veteran CBS news personality and host of *Eye-to-Eye with Connie Chung* was interviewing the parents of Newt Gingrich, perhaps the second most powerful politician in the world and soon to become speaker of the U.S. House of Representatives. In the course of the interview, which was conducted in December 1994 and aired the next month, Kathleen Gingrich let on that her son held no high regard for the wife of perhaps the most powerful politician in the world.

With cameras recording in the comfortable surroundings of the Gingrich home, and urging Kathleen Gingrich to disclose her son's private comments about Hillary Rodham Clinton, Chung said:

"Why don't you just whisper it to me, just between you and me?"

Gingrich replied: "She's a bitch. About the only thing he ever said about her."

Hardly said in a whisper, the response spoke volumes—if not about the Gingrich-Clinton relationship, then about relationships between journalists and their sources.

Promoting the interview, CBS released the quote two days before the Jan. 4, 1995, broadcast. Kathleen—and, by extension, Newt—Gingrich's words became front-page news in many papers and a top story on the evening network telecasts.

Newt Gingrich reacted swiftly and vociferously, implying that his mother—a starstruck innocent—had been victimized by an unethical reporter. He described Chung's question and the very act of asking it as "despicable."

"I think Connie Chung owes Mrs. Clinton an apology and she owes my mother an apology," he said, adding that the question and the broadcast of the answer were ploys designed to drive up ratings.

Chung denied she had taken advantage of Kathleen Gingrich. She said Gingrich was in a "playful mood" and "knew exactly what she was doing as three cameras were videotaping her."

In the flurry of media criticism that followed, there were few heroes to be found among the players in this case.

Chung was roundly criticized. "Connie Chung lied," wrote syndicated columnist Colman McCarthy. "'Between you and me' ought to mean exactly that." Wrote Gina Lubrano, reader representative at the *San Diego Union-*

Tribune, "In her duplicity, Chung displayed an appalling lack of ethics that should be of concern to all journalists."

CBS, too, was taken to task for exploiting—"marketing"—the quote, which was never explained in fuller context.

Others defended Chung and CBS for merely doing their job—reporting what was said—and for recognizing that, despite the way Chung set the ground rules for the question, Kathleen Gingrich's quote was newsworthy enough to transcend that agreement and to weather whatever storm of outrage resulted.

For his part, Newt Gingrich was able to make political hay out of the whole affair, attacking the media while defending his mother, while a vulgar comment involving his biggest domestic political nemesis echoed around the country for weeks.

And even Kathleen Gingrich was held up to criticism for not maintaining her son's confidence. "I can't tell you what he said," she had playfully told Chung. And then, Kathleen Gingrich did just that.

Analysis

Connie Chung's primary responsibility was to generate information for her audience. In this case, in a comfortable, homey, benign setting, she was teasing out from a source a bit of information about two of the most politically powerful people in the United States, the speaker of the U.S. House and the activist wife of the nation's president.

At the same time, deception is a corrosive, socially destructive device that victimizes the target by causing that person to believe something the deceiver herself does not believe. Such actions tear at a society's social fabric.

Deception in the search for information may be more justifiable in the reporter-source war when the source is a seasoned veteran determined to hang onto the information being sought.

Deception in the search for information may be more justifiable in the reporter-source war when the source is a seasoned veteran determined to hang onto the information being sought. In such a case the contest between reporter and source may be a fairly equitable battle of wits with able opponents playing a well-established game. In-game deception is an honorable part of American gamesmanship—witness feints and fakes in football, basketball and baseball to throw opponents off balance.

Now, was Mrs. Gingrich the innocent Newt says she was (in which case one wonders why he let her into the cage with Chung in the first place), or was she a seasoned warrior engaging in the normal battle of wits between reporter and source? Different people will answer that question differently, and therein lies an emotional discussion with few objective answers.

Nevertheless, give CBS credit for allowing itself to be held accountable by leaving Chung's whispered assurance in the final presentation. Keep in mind the "just between you and me" phrase could have been edited out, and subsequent Gingrich outrage would merely have been speculative.

It is difficult to see the harm of the quote, except for an inevitable, unmeasurable reduction in media credibility and a rise in suspicion among innocent sources, confirmed in their notion that reporters are mad bombers lying in wait to lay waste to hard-earned reputations. Seasoned sources, on the other hand, are aware that deceptions—whether for good or ill—are always a stick of dynamite in the vigorous reporter's tool box as the reporter mines for elusive information.

Case Study #45

Keeping a Promise to a Source

Summary

Political campaigns can be full of pitfalls for journalists caught between candidates under stress. In a case in Minnesota, editors of the Minneapolis *Star Tribune* and the *St. Paul Pioneer Press Dispatch*, acting under traditional prerogatives, overrode a reporter's promise to a source and disclosed the source's name.

On condition he not be identified, the source, an employee of an ad agency working for the Republican lieutenant governor candidate in Minnesota, had given reporters embarrassing information about the other lieutenant governor candidate in the closing days of the campaign. The information showed the candidate had been arrested nearly 20 years earlier on a shoplifting charge.

Feeling the campaign tactic of disclosing information of questionable relevance in such a way was a bigger story than the shoplifting information, editors at both the *Star Tribune* and the *Pioneer Press Dispatch* independently disclosed the source of the information.

The reporters' source was fired from the agency, took legal action against the newspapers and won a U.S. Supreme Court ruling in 1991 that promises of confidentiality may be legally enforceable under state law.

Despite the court decision, a question still exists about whether the newspaper might not morally justify disclosure of the source's name, despite the promise of its agent (the reporter), and despite legal rulings to the contrary. Editors have generally assumed that even though reporters' assurances to their sources are important, circumstances can justify an overriding of the reporters' judgment. The question of overriding legal consideration when making an ethical call is also important.

Analysis

A number of significant questions are raised in this case:

- Is it reasonable for a reporter to be able to assure a source of confidentiality and expect the news organization to support the promise?
- Should a reporter be required to consult with editors before offering source confidentiality?
- How important should a story be to warrant discrediting the reporter and

damaging the news organization's credibility?

• What kind of discussion should take place in the newsroom before a reporter's promise is violated? What weight should the reporter's input have in the discussion?

• Would other stakeholders, particularly the news audiences and the sources, feel the breaking of a promise was justifiable?

The ethical conflict in this case is between two virtues: 1) the right of the source to expect a promise to be kept and 2) the feeling of the editors that the audience needed the information about the source. Audiences' need for that information should be so great that damage done by the breaking of a reporter's (and hence, the newspaper's) promise is acceptable.

The key ethical question may lie in editors' motives. If their intent was to inform readers about a campaign tactic they considered questionable, justification comes fairly easily. If, however, editors were even subconsciously trying to embarrass a candidate by trying to expose the candidate's agent, ethical justification becomes prohibitively difficult. Generally, any good that may come from embarrassing the candidate will be more than offset by damage to the newspaper's reputation among sources, and probably among readers. Violations of promises have a heavy burden to produce some greater good. In this case, that "good" would be a fully informed readership presumably better able to make a voting decision.

As in other ethics issues, editors are obliged to search their own minds for motives. In their social role, editors can most easily defend an action that places audience interest first, and can be justified to the audience. Editors should acknowledge to their readers or listeners that publication of the source's name was not a matter taken lightly, recognizing that future coverage may be at risk because other sources will be reluctant to confide in reporters.

Source/Reporter Relationships

What the Codes Say

Sioux Falls (S.D.) ***Argus Leader***

Our allegiance to the First Amendment should be as strong as our commitment to the public's welfare. This includes protection of sources, notes and photographs from those who would seek to abridge those rights.

Rochester **(N.Y.)** ***Democrat and Chronicle***

The use of unidentified sources raises questions about the credibility and fairness of stories and about our ability to support our stories factually.

Anonymous sources are to be avoided except as a last resort. Legitimate efforts must be made to get sources on the record; only when those effort have been exhausted will the use of anonymous sources be considered.

San Jose **(Calif.)** ***Mercury News***

The *Mercury News* should strive to avoid the use of unidentified sources. Reporters shall make every effort to get sources to speak on the record. When that is impossible, reporters shall make every effort to get the information elsewhere.

We will attribute information to anonymous sources only when news value warrants and it cannot be obtained for attribution.

If an unidentified source must be used, the reason shall be given in the story. The story shall also make a strong effort to indicate the source's credibility by describing the source as fully as possible without identifying him or her.

Wilson **(N.C.)** ***Daily Times***

The use of "off the record" assurances should be avoided. Such promises are seldom worth the dilemmas they can create. If a reporter gives a promise that information will be "off the record," however, he must not violate that trust. This does not preclude using that knowledge to obtain the same information from another source, if that is possible.

Cable News Network

Generally, you should not assume that the source understands the meaning of such phrases as "off the record" or "on background" or that the source's understanding is the same as yours; when in doubt as to the meaning or mutual understanding of these terms or any agreement made with a source, be specific.

Norfolk (Va.) *Virginian-Pilot*

Editors, reporters, artists and photographers are forbidden from working for the CIA, FBI or any other governmental intelligence or law enforcement agency. It is common practice for reporters and photographers to trade basic information with law enforcement personnel during the coverage of a news event, but active, covert cooperation will not be allowed.

KTVQ-2 (Billings, Mont.)

Subject: Off the Record Comments and Confidential Sources

The easy answer is to avoid both at all costs!

Off the record comments can get you in trouble. Here are a couple of rules that may help:

- Tell your source that you don't accept off the record remarks! Usually, they want to tell you badly enough they will tell you on the record anyway.
- Don't fall for any of that "Blah, Blah, Blah ... and of course this is all off the record." It's off the record ONLY if you agree to it before you're told about it, not after the fact.
- "Deep Background" information is useful if you are able to get information that somewhere down the road will help you understand how things work, and will lead you to places where you can get useful material confirmed. Otherwise, avoid it.

Confidential sources. The networks use them all the time and attribute by saying, "A White House source says ...." Fine for them, not for us. You are NOT AUTHORIZED to offer confidentiality to a news source. You need to have the senior news staff member on duty to OK using a source in confidence. Even at that, you need to make triple sure the information you receive from them is SOLID.

In All Cases ... ask yourself WHY this individual doesn't want to be connected to the information they want to provide. Are they lying to you? Are the documents incomplete ... or fakes? Do they have an ax to grind?

American Society of Newspaper Editors

Pledges of confidentiality to news sources must be honored at all costs, and therefore should not be given lightly. Unless there is clear and pressing need to maintain confidences, sources of information should be identified.

Columbus* (Ga.) *Ledger-Inquirer

We disclose news sources unless there is a clear and compelling reason not to do so. The same principle applies to use of names of writers of letters to the editor. When it is necessary to protect the confidentiality of a source, we clearly explain why. And we honor that confidentiality until and unless we are released from it by the source.

Detroit Free Press

We avoid promising sources or subjects of news stories an opportunity to review articles, photos or artwork before publication. In the rare instance when a pre-publication review might be justified, the decision will be made by a supervising editor with the knowledge of the staff members involved. In cases when a partial review may be desirable—to check technical data, for example—a supervising editor should be consulted.

We avoid promising sources that they will be treated in a particular way in a story in exchange for information ....

Attribution, unnamed sources: Our readers usually are best served when we can identify news sources by name. We should work hard to identify the source(s) although there will be instances when the pursuit of truth will best be served by not naming a source. Sources will be named unless the reason not to do so is an overriding consideration. Except in a justifiable instance, we will not allow an unnamed source to use us to attack an individual or an organization. We will work hard to corroborate information from any unnamed sources. A decision to use unnamed sources will be made with the advice and consent of a supervising editor.

Confidentiality: Since the U.S. Supreme Court has ruled that the First Amendment does not extend to journalists the absolute right to protect the confidentiality of news sources, reporters on their own cannot guarantee sources confidentiality in a published story. If a demand is made after publication for the source's identification, a court may compel us to reveal the source. In circumstances where the demand for absolute confidentiality is made as a condition for obtaining the story, that situation needs to be discussed with a supervising editor before a commitment is made. Trust works both ways—the editor must be able to trust the reporter fully, and vice versa.

Philadelphia Inquirer

The ability to assure the confidentiality of sources is so fundamental to the press' vigorous coverage of matters of public importance that the identity of such sources must be scrupulously protected.

Sources—The source and quality of the information that a newspaper presents to its readers cannot always be self-evident. Ideally, we like to give our readers the maximum possible indication of where information comes from so that they can assess its authority. Practically speaking, some people—indeed, some institutions—prefer to provide valuable information without taking credit or responsibility for being the source of it. We constantly weigh the value of information against an obligation to respect a confidence, and we often weigh it under the pressure of deadline.

The use of unnamed sources is a primary cause of public mistrust of the press and the information it provides. Therefore, unnamed sources should be used sparingly and in consultation with an editor. Quoting unnamed sources should not just be an easy alternative to documenting the information from the public record or seeking out someone willing to be named.

Anonymity should not be conferred on a source merely out of a staff member's presumption that the information provided by the individual is sensitive or that the individual would like to be anonymous. To the contrary, the assumption always should be made that information is fully on the record unless some other ground rule is clearly asserted and the information is accepted on that basis. If a source does request anonymity, the staff member and the source should agree on the following: what information may be attributed; what information is not to be attributed; what information is confidential; how the source is to be identified; that a supervising editor may know the identity of the source; and under what circumstances, if any, the identity of the source may be made public.

No set of guidelines can define situations in which less-than-complete sourcing is appropriate. However, the following approaches can help to illustrate the difficulties we face in striving to fully inform the reader:

- Information that is not generally available should, if possible, clearly be from a reporter's own observations or should be attributed. A story should make it evident, for example, that a narrative of an event was reconstructed from later interviews or derived from documents ....
- Unfortunately, it is a common practice in Washington for high-level policy makers to talk to the press under a variety of rules concerning attribution. Sometimes, the information is obviously important; other times, it is an apparent trial balloon; in still others, it might simply be self-serving politically. Because we can scarcely deny our readers this information, we often must accept such arrangements regretfully and give our readers as much definition of the source as the ground rules will allow. It may be useful to cite reasons why the unidentified source might have wanted the information to become public, such as to affect a policy debate or as a consequence of political conflict.
- In stories in which a person or organization is the focus of in-depth reporting, the use of unnamed sources frequently plays an important role. In such cases, the importance of the information or the sensitive position of the source may warrant the use of material when it is not possible to identify the source by name and qualifications. In such circumstances, we must enter carefully into arrangements to protect such sources and also give the reader as much information as possible as to the nature of each source.

Because such terms as "background" and "off the record" often are used differently, reporters should make sure that they and their sources agree on the ground rules. Usually, the meaning of these terms is: not for attribution—the statements may be quoted directly but the source must not be named; background—the general thrust of the statements may be used but they may not be quoted directly, and the source must not be named; deep background—only the general thrust of the statements may be used and no indication of a source is permitted; off the record—the information may be used only for the reporter's understanding or perspective and may not be used in a story.

Reporters must be free to use their judgment in granting confidentiality to a source of information. However, it is important to keep in mind that the agreement of confidence is between the source and the newspaper. An editor has the right to know with whom the confidence is made and will share the commitment to keep the confidence.

In using information provided by a source, the reader should be given the maximum amount of guidance possible. For example, it is preferable to attribute to "an official in the mayor's office" or to "a senior law enforcement official" rather than to "a source."

If an unnamed source is quoted making a derogatory statement about a person or an organization, the comment should be one that enhances the public's understanding of a crucial issue. Here, reporters and editors should apply additional safeguards: The statement should be corroborated by public record or by named sources, or the source should have a record of reliability as well as knowledge of the facts. Of course, as with all critical comments, the object of the criticism should be sought out to be given an opportunity to respond if possible.

Phoenix (Ariz.) Newspapers Inc.

The newspapers recognize the rare instance in which an entire story is based upon a confidential source and acknowledge the need to protect such sources. No such sources may be used except when the public has an overriding interest in the material and there is no other way to get it. A senior editor must know the source's identity. The reason such a source is being used must be explained in the story. In the case of wire stories based solely on confidential sources, the news editor on duty must approve their use. The use of confidential sources merely to enhance or add perspective or information to an otherwise attributed story is acceptable, but the reader should be given as much information as possible about the source; for example, "a leading GOP legislator" instead of "a source."

Spokane (Wash.) *Spokesman-Review*

Attribution of information with identifiable sources is vitally important in writing news stories. Use of unnamed sources is discouraged. In most cases, sources should be told that editors might not publish the information provided unless: 1) sources are attributed in the stories, 2) other sources or documents can be obtained to confirm the information, or 3) if circumstances warrant, the source's identity is divulged to at least one editor to allow an adequate basis on which to judge the credibility of the information.

If a news source is granted anonymity, the decision to maintain that confidentiality rests solely with the reporter(s) and/or editor(s) involved in granting that guarantee

Before using information from anonymous sources, attempts should be made to obtain that information from sources who can be quoted.

Traverse City **(Mich.)** *Record-Eagle*

Off the Record: Fairness is a major factor in establishing a newspaper's credibility. Responding to fairness concerns is always difficult and much more so when a newspaper reports information attributed to off-the-record or anonymous sources.

Such information will be allowed in stories in rare instances and only when the reporter is granted prior approval from the city editor or editor.

The editor must be informed in any cases an off-the-record or anonymous sources are used in a story.

Anonymous sources: Anonymous sources cannot be quoted in stories without the approval of the city editor or editor.

Use of pseudonyms or the phrase "who asked not to be identified," also must be cleared by the city editor or editor.

Use of pseudonyms or the above phrase should be used rarely.

Whenever pseudonyms are approved, the reporter must know the name of the source. If asked, the reporter must also give the name to the city editor and editor. The anonymous person should be informed of the policy before an interview. All these details should be worked out before the initial interview.

Radio Television News Directors Association

Recognize the need to protect confidential sources. (Broadcast journalists) will promise confidentiality only with the intention of keeping that promise.

Beaumont **(Texas)** *Enterprise*

The readers have a right to evaluate what is being reported in a newspaper by who is saying it. In that regard, the *Enterprise* will strive at all times to attribute all reportage to news sources by name.

In our pursuit of news and background for editorial comment, we should:

1. Always seek the best, most qualified source. Seek the highest-ranking person or the authorized spokesman rather than talking to a receptionist or secretary and quoting that person as a source for the business or institution. In any story which reflects on the character of reputation of an individual, seek out the individual referred to, himself or herself, for a comment—not a publicist or aide. In any sensitive story where the person evades comment, we should detail for the reader the good faith effort the newspaper made to get the source's side of the story before we publish without it.

2. In any sensitive story likely to stir controversy or the possibility of libel suit, any sensitive information should be attributable to at least three sources.

3. Only in the most extreme situations should it ever be in the best interests of the readers to use an anonymous source. Should that extreme situation arise, anonymity will be granted to sources only under the following conditions:

a. The source must understand that if the newspaper learns he or she has lied by design or by omission, the agreement is off.

b. The newspaper would reserve the right, if it were sued and the anonymous source were the only way to prove the truth of the statements, to subpoena the source as a witness.

c. In all cases, the reporter must share the identity of the source with the editor.

d. Wherever possible, the reporter should get any source accorded anonymity to give his or her information in a sworn affidavit.

e. Obviously, cases will arise in which a reporter may not have the time to clear granting anonymity with an editor and thus may have to make a field judgment on whether to commit to anonymity. But the reporter should understand and make it clear to the source that if the editor overrules him in granting anonymity, the source's identity will be protected in any case, and any information the source may have given is not usable as attributed to that source. However, the reporter also should make it clear that while protecting the source's identity, the reporter can use the information for background and leverage to get another source to provide the sane information. If another source does give the same information, it is fair game for the newspaper to issue it as attributed to the alternate source.

4. Sources should understand that once a reporter identifies himself as a representative of the newspaper, everything the source says from that point on is on the record unless the source and reporter reach a mutual agreement to go off the record. Once reporter and source agree to go off the record, the commitment is in force until both agree to go back on the record.

Washington* (D.C.) *Post

The *Washington Post* is pledged to disclose the source of all information when at all possible. When we agree to protect a source's identity, that identity will not be made known to anyone outside the *Post*.

Before any information is accepted without full attribution, reporters must make every reasonable effort to get it on the record. If that is not possible, reporters should consider seeking the information elsewhere. If that in turn is not possible, reporters should request an on-the-record reason for concealing the source's identity and should include the reason in the story.

In any case, some kind of identification is almost always possible—by department or by position, for example—and should be reported.

No pseudonyms are to be used.

Annotated Bibliography on Journalism Ethics

Media Ethics Online

Links change frequently, so we've decided not to include a list with this bibliography. Instead, please check **http://spj.org/ethics**, the ethics area on the Society of Professional Journalists' web site, for links to media ethics sites.

Journalism Ethics Books and Journals

Altschull, J. H. (1990). *From Milton to McLuhan: The ideas behind American journalism*. New York: Longman. 447 pages. With this book, Altschull explores the intellectual concepts that form the basis of Western civilization and shows how the practice of journalism has been indelibly influenced by the evolution of the American intellectual tradition.

Arnett, R.C. & Makau, J.M. (Eds.). (1997). *Communication ethics in an age of diversity*. Urbana, IL: University of Illinois Press. 270 pages. Fourteen leading communication scholars integrate cutting-edge research with real-world dilemmas as they address ethical problems associated with demographic shifts, as well as technological and cultural changes in the context of communication.

Black, J. & Barney, R. D. (Eds.). (1985-current). *Journal of Mass Media Ethics*. Mahwah, NJ: Lawrence Erlbaum Associates. The *Journal of Mass Media Ethics* is published quarterly (semiannually 1985-1989) and provides up-to-date articles on a variety of ethical issues and philosophies concerning the media. *JMME* runs "Cases and Commentaries" and book reviews on media ethics.

Black, J. (Ed.). (1997). *Mixed News: The Public/Civic/Communitarian Journalism Debate*. Mahwah, NJ.: Lawrence Erlbaum Associates. 280 pages. This volume explores some of the most central issues in journalism today, from theoretical and practical approaches. More than a dozen scholars and journalists contribute to the lively debate about public journalism.

Bok, S. (1978). *Lying: Moral choice in public and private life*. New York: Random House. Bok examines the nature and consequences of lying and offers a systematic justification model of deciding whether or not such acts are ethically defensible.

Bugeja, M.J. (1996). *Living ethics: Developing values in mass communication*. Needham Heights, MA: Allyn & Bacon. 344 pages. The book aims to help journalists and students build, test and improve their professional values.

Christians, C. G., Rotzoll, K. B., & Fackler, M. (1995). *Media ethics: Cases and moral reasoning*. (4th Ed.) White Plains, NY: Longman. 350 pages.

The authors have designed a textbook that uses case studies and the Potter Box to study various ethical situations.

Christians, C., Ferre J.P. & Fackler, P.M. (1993). *Good news: Social ethics & the press.* New York: Oxford University Press. 265 pages. In this book, the three authors formulate a new model for ethical behavior in journalism rooted in the community instead of individuals. They argue for a fundamental change in the press's world view that has practical implications for such areas as truth telling, privacy and social justice.

Cohen, E. D. (Ed.). (1992). *Philosophical issues in journalism.* New York: Oxford University Press. 273 pages. This book is a collection of articles on philosophical issues that confront journalists. Some of those issues include newsworthiness, morality, free speech, privacy, objectivity, and news distortion.

Cooper, T.W., Christians, C.G., Plude, F.F., & White, R.A. (Eds.). (1989). *Communication ethics and global change.* New York: Longman. 385 pages. This book is a collection of essays that represents a major attempt to present and analyze the many different perspectives that inform communication ethics around the world. The 23 editors and contributors represent six continents and include many of the best-known scholars on media ethics.

Day, L. A. (1997). *Ethics in media communications: Cases and controversies.* Belmont, CA: Wadsworth. (2nd ed.). This book contains chapters on moral development, moral reasoning, truthfulness, privacy, confidentiality, economic pressures, antisocial behavior, morally offensive content, social justice, stereotypes, the juvenile audience, and taste/morality.

Elliott, D. (Ed.). (1986). *Responsible journalism.* Beverly Hills: Sage. 192 pages. This book is a collection of nine essays on press responsibility. Contributors include John Merrill, Ralph Barney, Theodore Glasser, Everette Dennis, Clifford Christians, Louis Hodges, and Martin Linsky.

Fedler, F. (1989). *Media hoaxes.* Ames: Iowa State University Press. Fedler compiles a history of media hoaxes. He examines journalism's most successful hoaxes, divides them into common themes, and comments on modern journalism and how it deals with hoaxes.

Fink, C. (1988). *Media ethics in the newsroom and beyond.* New York: McGraw-Hill. 323 pages. Fink places political, economic, and spiritual events of the 1980s and the press' role in reporting these stories in a perspective that is highly readable and useful to the social scientist and the training journalist. The book blends philosophical and practical approaches to create a leading new book on ethics.

Fuller, J. (1996). *News values: Ideas for an information age.* Chicago: University of Chicago Press. 251 pages. Fuller, former publisher of the *Chicago Tribune,* explores the fundamental issues—ethical and practical—confronting newspapers today. He argues that intellectually honest "news values" do exist and can continue to guide journalists even in today's competitive marketplace.

Goldstein, T. (Ed.). (1989). *Killing the messenger: 100 years of media criticism.* New York: Columbia University Press. 272 pages. *Killing the Messenger* is an anthology of some of the most provocative writing that has been done in this century about the press. It is a collection of pieces that offer different perspectives on many of the issues that plague the press.

Goldstein, T. (1985). *The news at any cost: How journalists compromise their ethics to shape the news.* New York: Simon & Schuster. 301 pages. The book talks about ethical issues which journalists confront by using the author's experience as a reporter to present and discuss the issues. The book contains anecdotes and quotations or observations from other journalists about the issues.

Goodwin, G. & Smith, R.F. (1994). *Groping for ethics in journalism.* Ames, IA: Iowa State University Press. (3rd Ed.) 369 pages. Goodwin has written a book that tries to assess the current status of ethics in the field and present it in a manner that might help journalists think through their ethical problems. The authors interviewed 150 working journalists and media watchers.

Gordon, A.D., Kittross, J.M. & Reuss, C. (1996). *Controversies in media ethics.* White Plains, NY: Longman. 316 pages. The book provides students and media practitioners with a carefully constructed set of arguments focusing on 13 controversies facing journalists today.

Hausman, C. (1990). *The decision-making process in journalism.* Chicago: Nelson-Hall Publishers. 140 pages. This book examines how experienced journalists made decisions regarding newsworthiness, accuracy, fairness, logic, freedom from distortion, liability for libel or invasion of privacy, ethical professional practice, and the possible consequences of the story.

Hausman, C. (1992). *Crisis of conscience: Perspectives on journalism ethics.* New York: HarperCollins Publishers. 214 pages. Hausman offers a four part book on historical and modern perspectives of journalism ethics.

Hulteng, J.L. (1985). *The messenger's motives: Ethical problems of the news media (2nd ed.).* Englewood Cliffs, NJ: Prentice-Hall. 239 pages. Using cases and examples, Hulteng's book is a text to help members of the public, people who manage and work in the news business, and students who hope to make careers in the field become more knowledgeable about the nature of ethical problems of the media.

Isaacs, N. E. (1986). *Untended gates: The mismanaged press.* New York: Columbia University Press. 258 pages. Isaacs presents an interesting and insightful examination of the standard sins of journalism from an insider's perspective.

Jaksa, J. A. & Pritchard, M. S. (1988). *Communication ethics: Methods of analysis.* Belmont, CA: Wadsworth Publishing Company. 172 pages. This book is an ethics textbook that focuses on the issues of lying and deception and provides an examination of methods of analysis of these issues.

Jensen, J.V. (1997). *Ethical issues in the communication process.* Mahwah, NJ: Lawrence Erlbaum Associates. 236 pages. The book discusses ethical concerns as they occur in the communication process, examining the communicator, the message, the medium, the audience and the situation in which the communication takes place.

Johannesen, R. (1990). *Ethics in human communication (3rd ed.).* Prospect Heights, IL: Waveland Press. 343 pages. The best description of this book is a "sampler." Johannesen ranges over a variety of ethical questions and perspectives, all examined through the lens of rhetoric.

Kaplar, R.T. & Maines P.D. (1995). *The government factor. Undermining journalistic ethics in the information age.* Washington, DC: Cato Institute. 100 pages. The authors pose a challenge to journalists and policy makers to think seriously about journalistic freedom and responsibility. The book documents how journalists let government rules and regulations decide what is ethical.

Kittross, J. M. (Ed.) *Media Ethics.* Boston, MA: Emerson College. This semi-annual journal, published in magazine format, carries provocative articles by working journalists (and other media professionals) and academics, plus numerous news items and reviews.

Klaidman, S. & Beauchamp, T. L. (1987). *The virtuous journalist.* New York: Oxford University Press. 246 pages. This book provides a moral framework for evaluating many issues that face journalists on a daily basis. The framework includes an examination of what the authors call central moral concepts and the authors employ that framework to evaluate journalists' conduct in several areas.

Knowlton, S.R. & Parsons, P.R. (Eds.). (1995). *The journalist's moral compass.* Westport, CT: Praeger Publishers. 246 pages. An anthology of 24 readings that discuss the guiding principles of journalism and the major issues that challenge them.

Knowlton, S.R. (1997). *Moral reasoning for journalists: Cases and commentaries.* Westport, CT: Praeger Publishers. 220 pages. An up-to-date collection of more than two dozen real-life cases that illustrate the moral issues facing contemporary journalists. The cases are presented in substantial detail to provide students with a realistic sense of the complexity of issues facing journalists today.

Lambeth, E. B. (1992). *Committed journalism: An ethic for the profession.* Bloomington: Indiana University Press. (2nd Ed.) 224 pages. Lambeth proposes a system to energize the process of moral reasoning by journalists. The system is based on the weighing of five principles he has derived from ideals, codes and practices in the field.

Lee, M. & Solomon, N. (1990). *Unreliable sources: A guide to detecting bias in news media.* New York: Carol Publishing Group. 419 pages. This book presents the argument that the economic and social structure of U.S. mass media necessarily leads to a news product that serves elite vested interests rather than the public interest and supports the argument with plenty of facts, figures and morality tales.

Lester, P. M. (Ed.). (1996). *Images that injure: Pictorial stereotypes in the media.* Westport, CT: Praeger Publishers. 282 pages. The book begins with essays discussing media responsibility and factors that lead to stereotyping. It is followed by 29 essays on how media stereotype many groups, such as African-Americans, women, men, elderly, handicapped, etc.

Merrill, J.C. (1997). *Journalism ethics: Philosophical foundations for news media.* New York: St. Martin's Press. 248 pages. Merrill focuses on the philosophical and theoretical underpinnings that support the daily routine of journalism. He explores such concepts as individualism, communitarianism, propaganda and responsibility, providing journalists and aspiring journalists with a systematic way of considering various ethical actions and helps them make responsible, well-informed decisions.

Merrill, J. C. (1989). *The dialectic in journalism.* Baton Rouge; Louisiana State University Press. 259 pages. Merrill synthesizes the three ethical strains of previous works to produce a theory of moral philosophy that is more coherent and powerful than his previous attempts. Using his dialectic approach, he analyzes a wide range of thinking about journalism and philosophy.

Merrill, J. C. & Barney, R. D. (Eds.). (1975). *Ethics and the press: Readings in mass media morality.* New York: Hastings. This 338-page anthology was one of the first books in the current (post-World War Two) wave of books about journalism ethics. It provides a balance between practical and philosophical essays.

Merrill, J. C. & Odell, S. J. (1983). *Philosophy and journalism.* New York: Longman. 190 pages. This book establishes both philosophical and journalistic frameworks from which the journalist can think about the issues. It provides logical systems that journalists can apply in the process of developing a coherent foundation for their journalistic beliefs and values.

Meyer, P. (1987). *Ethical journalism: A guide for students, practitioners, and consumers.* New York: Longman. 262 pages. This book seeks out the best of journalism scholarship on ethics, combines it with contemporary examples of difficulties faced in the news industry, presents discussions of efforts made in the industry to cope with such problems, then sets out a paradigm of ethical accounting that can reasonably be undertaken by those carrying out the day-to-day tasks of journalism.

Olen, J. (1988). *Ethics in journalism.* Englewood Cliffs, NJ: Prentice Hall. 127 pages. Olen focuses on the moral dilemmas that confront journalists and examines the ethical problems of journalists from a philosopher's point of view.

Patterson, P. & Wilkins, L. (1998). *Media ethics: Issues and cases.* New York: McGraw Hill Publishers. (3rd ed.). 300 pages. This book uses a case study technique for teaching ethics, providing a practical approach to ethical theory.

Pippert, W. G. (1989). *An ethics of news: A reporter's search for truth.* Washington, DC: Georgetown University Press. 156 pages. Pippert's central thesis is that journalists should pursue truth, and in so doing, grapple with the dimensions of justice and peace in any assignment. In the first part of the book, he lays out his ethical theory, and in the second he demonstrates how the theory is to be applied.

Rivers, W. L., & Mathews, C. (1988). *Ethics for the media.* Englewood Cliffs, NJ: Prentice Hall. 307 pages. Rivers and Mathews analyze the strengths and weaknesses of the media and their adjuncts as they play their roles in society. Issues and topics addressed include sexism, investigative reporting, news-gathering, freedom of the press, privacy and photojournalism, and media codes.

Schmuhl, R. (Ed.). (1984). *The responsibilities of journalism.* Notre Dame, IN: University of Notre Dame Press. 138 pages. Schmuhl has compiled a number of essays from print and broadcast journalists, businessmen, ethicists, philosophers and government representatives on various ethical questions that plague journalism.

General Issues in Journalism Ethics

Beechner, S. (1996). Not on my life! Disillusionment with broadcast journalism. *Media Ethics,* 7:2, pp. 16, 25. A summer intern finds that her individual morality conflicts with the television news business.

Blankenburg, W. B. (1995). Measuring morality in newspaper management. *Journal of Mass Media Ethics,* 10:3, pp. 147-153. This paper examines the ethics of resource allocation by newspaper management. The notion of quality is used to link ethics and economics in publishing. A quantitative standard of moral behavior in budgetary policy is offered.

Blevens, F. (1995). Newspaper monopolies: profits and morality in a captive market. *Journal of Mass Media Ethics,* 10:3, pp. 133-146. The closing of a newspaper violated the spirit, if not the intent of the Hutchins Commission report, as applied through a corporate ethics formula. The author concludes that the foundation of ethics should move from the newsroom to the boardroom.

Byerly, C.M. & Warren, C.A. (1996). At the margins of center: Organized protest in the newsroom. *Critical Studies in Mass Communication,* 13:1 pp. 1-23. The author's study finds that reporters often take an active part in changing attitudes and news styles in some newsrooms.

Callahan, C. (1994). When a journalist is kidnapped. *American Journalism Review,* September, pp. 37-39. Several news organizations hold the story of an AP reporter kidnapped in Somalia until after the reporter is released. The incident raises the question of whether journalists treat their own differently than others.

Case, T. (1994, Oct. 29). The APME ethics code. *Editor & Publisher,* p. 13. The Associated Press Managing Editors decide to revise a perfunctory 1975 code of ethics, after rejecting a proposed 10-page code that sparked controversy among members.

Courtright, J.L. (1996). Postmortem of an ethics code: The national religious broadcasters' EFICOM. *Journal of Mass Media Ethics,* 11:4, pp. 223-235. Courtright examines the ethics code of an association of religious broadcasters.

Cunningham, R. (1994). Good stories: Competition can get in the way. *Quill,* June, pp. 14-15. Sound ethical decision making often loses out during the heat of deadline pressure, especially when two competing papers—the *Boston Globe* and *Boston Herald,* in this case—are critical of each other.

Dalton, T.A. (1994). Another one bites the dust. *Quill,* Nov./Dec., pp. 39-41. The article discusses the declining number of ombudsmen at newspapers.

Demers, D. (1993). Effect of corporate structure on autonomy of top editors at U.S. dailies. *Journalism Quarterly,* 70:3, pp. 499-508. The article addresses a common belief among journalists and scholars that the growth of corporate newspapers is robbing journalists of their professional autonomy.

Ehrlich, M. (1995). The ethical dilemma of television news sweeps. *Journal of Mass Media Ethics,*

10:1, pp. 37-47. Do television stations produce "sleazy" or sensationalistic stories to boost their rating during sweeps week?

Fallows, J. (1996). Why Americans hate the media. *The Atlantic Monthly,* February, pp. 45-56, 62-64. Fallows contends that journalists don't share the same interests as the public they supposedly represent, particularly with regard to politics. An excerpt from Fallows' book, *Breaking the News.*

Harper, C. (1995). Did the Unabomber set a precedent? *American Journalism Review,* November, pp. 13-14. Harper believes the decision by the *New York Times* and *Washington Post* to print the Unabomber's 35,000-word manifesto has opened a Pandora's box. He predicts future criminals will demand a stage to speak from.

Kamen, J. (1993). A matter of "live" and death. *American Journalism Review,* pp. 27-31. Kamen explores the effects of live media coverage on two events: the siege of the Branch Davidian complex in Waco, Texas, and a prison uprising in Lucasville, Ohio.

Kaplar, R.T. & Maines, P.D. (1995). The role of government in undermining journalistic ethics. *Journal of Mass Media Ethics,* 10:4, pp. 234-247. The authors contend that the government erects barriers to the development of technologies such as cable TV that can offer journalists a more ethically hospitable environment.

Kirtley, J. (1995). Were the media negligent in Waco? Did the Unabomber set a precedent? *American Journalism Review,* November, pp. 46-47. Kirtley contends that a journalist's sole responsibility should be to report news to its audience. "Conforming to the government's definition of responsible journalism is a recipe for disaster," she says.

Kovach, B. (1994). Focusing our values. *Nieman Reports,* Winter, pp. 2, 11-13. Kovach explains how the media mix values, namely through the adoption of entertainment values in the newsroom, and how economics has contributed to the trend.

Lieberman, T. (1995). Plagiarize, plagiarize, plagiarize ... only be sure to always call it research. *Columbia Journalism Review,* July / Aug., pp. 21-26. Editors and other news professionals often look the other way when it comes to plagiarized material.

Lind, R. A. (1996). Care and justice in audience evaluations of ethical issues in TV news. *Journal of Mass Media Ethics,* 11:2, pp. 82-94. Lind investigates viewer evaluations of television news stories.

Lind, R.A. (1996). Race and viewer evaluations of ethically controversial TV news stories. *Journal of Mass Media Ethics,* 11:1, pp. 40-52. Lind studies how whites and blacks perceive news coverage of three events. The perceptions of the two groups are markedly different.

Lule, J. (1993). Radical rules: I.F. Stone's ethical perspective. *Journal of Mass Media Ethics,* pp. 88-102. Lule examines the complex, sometimes paradoxical ethical standards of I.F. Stone, one of America's great journalists.

Luna, A. (1995). An economic philosophy for mass media ethics. *Journal of Mass Media Ethics,* 10:3, pp. 154-166. This article, with a foundation in economic models and principles, contends that a news organization may use ethics as a means to prevent potential loss and therefore sustain or increase gains. The theory is based on pragmatic assumptions that ethics may be quantified as a cost or a benefit.

Mathews, C. (1994). Ethical codes and beyond. *Nieman Reports,* Spring, pp. 73-76. Mathews comments on efforts of the Associated Press Managing Editors Association to convert its existing statement of general principles into a more specific set of ethical guidelines.

McKinzie, B.W. (1994). How papers with and without ombudsmen resolve disputes. *Newspaper Research Journal,* Spring, pp. 14-24. A survey finds that most editors and publishers don't like giving control of their newspaper's image to an ombudsman.

McManus, J. (1992). Serving the public and serving the market: A conflict of interest? *Journal of*

Mass Media Ethics, 7:4, pp. 196-208. The article deals with the conflict between journalism's interest in serving the public and its corporate interest in selling newspapers.

McMasters, P. (1996). Ethics and free expression. *Media Ethics,* 7:2, pp. 17-18, 23. McMasters argues against journalism codes of ethics, saying they are unrealistic in the media business.

Meyer, P. (1994). Moral confusion: The what, why, and how of journalism is changing. *Quill,* Nov./Dec., pp. 31-33. A shift in the economic structure of media organizations will make it impossible for them to separate the business side from the editorial side, Meyer says.

Miller, M.C. (1996). Free the media. *The Nation,* June 8, pp. 9-15. Miller constructs a map showing the vast economic and political interests of the companies that own the four major news networks.

O'Neill, M.J. (1994). Who cares about the truth? *Nieman Reports,* 48:1, pp. 11-14. O'Neill says the merging of news and entertainment has hurt the credibility of journalism and the quality of information the public receives.

Pritchard, D. (1993). The impact of newspaper ombudsmen on journalists' attitudes. *Journalism Quarterly,* 70:1, pp. 77-86. Though ombudsmen often influence the behavior of newspaper staff (journalists work more carefully under an ombudsman's scrutiny), they seldom change attitudes.

Ratzan, S. (1994). Ethical health communication. *Media Ethics,* May, p. 7, 21. Ratzan believes that the media have an obligation to help educate the public about AIDS.

Rich, F. (1996, May 18). Media amok. *The New York Times,* p. 15. Rich supports his hard-hitting criticism of recent media mergers with specific examples of how they already have compromised media integrity.

Roberts, E. (1996). Corporate journalism and community service. *Media Studies Journal,* 10:2-3, pp. 103-107. *New York Times* managing editor Gene Roberts says corporate concern with the bottom line is driving local and state government news coverage into oblivion.

Seigenthaler, J. (1994). News junkie interviews himself on ethics. *Nieman Reports,* Summer, pp. 64-70. Seigenthaler believes that journalists have a high sense of ethics, and a strongly worded code of ethical conduct is not needed.

Shepard, A. (1994). Legislating ethics. *American Journalism Review,* Jan./Feb., pp. 37-41. Shepard looks at the pros and cons of detailed codes of ethics for newspapers.

Slattery, K. (1994). Sensationalism versus news of the moral life: Making the distinction. *Journal of Mass Media Ethics,* 9:1, pp. 5-15. Slattery provides journalists with a method of determining whether coverage of a "sensational" story is morally justifiable.

Smith, K.Z. (1996). Klein lied and that's wrong. *Quill,* September, p. 11. Smith criticizes Newsweek columnist Joe Klein for denying that he was the author of the bestselling novel Primary Colors.

Starobin, P. (1995). A generation of vipers. *Columbia Journalism Review,* March/April, pp. 25-32. Starobin criticizes cynicism among journalists.

Stein, M.L. (1994, Sept. 3). Good citizens make good reporters. *Editor & Publisher,* pp. 28-29. *Washington Post* columnist William Raspberry argues that reporters have a responsibility to be "good citizens" in the communities they cover.

Stein, M.L. (1995, June 10). Twice burned. *Editor & Publisher,* pp. 13, 35. Bob Wisehart, television critic for the *Sacramento Bee,* is forced to resign after plagiarizing on two occasions. The article offers some answers on why he did it.

Traska, M.R. (1996). Identity trivial, idea isn't. *Quill,* September, p. 10. In discussing *Newsweek* columnist Joe Klein's authorship of *Primary Colors,* Traska says that journalists should have the right to publish books anonymously. He argues that journalism ethics do not apply to literature.

White, H.A. (1996). The salience and pertinence of ethics: When journalists do and don't think for themselves. *Journalism and Mass Communications Quarterly*, 3:1, pp. 17-27. Journalists who rely more on internal motivations than ethical guidelines make more consistent ethical decisions, according to White.

Wilkinson, J. S., & Fletcher, J. E. (1995). Bloody news and vulnerable populations: an ethical question. *Journal of Mass Media Ethics*, 10:3, pp. 167-177. The results of a controlled experiment involving television news stories about auto accidents suggests that blood shown on screen makes a difference in the perceived emotional impact of the story. The quest for hard-hitting news and high ratings, the authors say, ought to be tempered with the knowledge that some viewers are adversely affected by graphic scenes of human suffering.

Woo, W. F. (1993). Redrawing the line between what readers and advertisers need. *ASNE Bulletin*, April, pp. 11-14. Woo writes that a good number of journalists compromise themselves in order to placate advertisers.

Accuracy and Fairness Issues

Akhavan-Majid, R. (1995). How community involvement affects editors' role. *Newspaper Research Journal*, 16:4, pp. 29-41. The author shows evidence that editors who are active in community organizations are less likely to criticize local government and businesses.

Artwick, C.G. (1996). Media held hostage: TV faces harrowing times when broadcasts go live. *Quill*, July / Aug., pp. 20-23. Broadcasters face tough ethical decisions when providing live television coverage of hostage situations.

Aufderheide, P. (1995). Vernacular video. *Columbia Journalism Review*, Jan. / Feb., pp. 46-48. The article discusses the increase in "camcorder journalism," the use of small-format video taken by private individuals and broadcast on television news.

Baldwin, D. (1994). A matter of life and death. *American Journalism Review*, June, pp. 40-45. Journalists often feel like they are playing God when asked to report on transplant patients who need organs. How do they decide which patients get coverage and which do not?

Berger, J. (1994). Hit-and-run journalism. *Nieman Reports*, Summer, pp. 67-70. Facing increased pressure to beat the competition, more and more journalists are neglecting to confirm facts. This has led to an increase in false allegations about public figures.

Budiansky, S. (1995, Jan. 9). The media's message. *U.S. News & World Report*, pp. 45-48. Journalists often interject "attitude" or "edge" into their stories, a practice that has contributed to the public's hatred of the media.

Cochran, W. & Steele, B. (1995). Computer-assisted reporting challenges traditional news-gathering safeguards. *ASNE Bulletin*, January, pp. 12-16. Editors and journalists face new ethical challenges due to the increased use of new technology, such as electronic message boards, the Internet and government computer files.

Connell, J. (1994). Virtual reality check: Cyberethics, consumerism, and the American soul. *Media Studies Journal*, 8:1, pp. 153-159. The article examines ethical considerations along the information superhighway.

Cramer, C. (1994). Ethical problems of mass murder coverage in the mass media. *Journal of Mass Media Ethics*, 9:1, pp. 26-42. The article analyzes *Time* and *Newsweek*'s coverage of mass murders, which shows evidence of disproportionate, perhaps politically motivated coverage.

Ehrlich, M. C. (1995). The ethical dilemma of television news sweeps. *Journal of Mass Media Ethics*, 10:1, pp. 37-48. The study, a comparison of two local TV newsrooms during sweeps ratings periods, examines whether news workers and news organizations can balance the pressure of producing sensationalistic or sleazy news that attracts viewers with the opportunity to produce more substantive news by giving reporters more time—off and on the air—to explore issues.

Germer, F. (1995). Are quotes sacred? *American Journalism Review,* September, pp. 34-37. Germer questions to what extent journalists should alter quotes.

Gilles, P. (1996). Hard-luck stories: How to avoid getting burned. *The Editor,* May/June, pp. 12-14. When covering people "down on their luck," reporters should be skeptical, ask questions, trust their intuition, check sources, assume nothing, and stay objective, says Gilles.

Giobbe, D. (1996, June 1). Better late than never. *Editor & Publisher,* pp. 14-15. In 1992, the *Northwest Arkansas Times* printed unsubstantiated rumors about a mayoral candidate attacking his character. Four years later, under a new executive editor, the newspaper apologizes.

Holley, J. (1996). Should coverage fit the crime? A Texas TV station tries to resist the allure of mayhem. *Columbia Journalism Review,* May/June, pp. 27-33. An Austin (TX) television station decides that a crime story must meet certain ethical guidelines before it will air.

Killenberg, G. M. & Anderson, R. (1993). What is a quote? Practical, rhetorical and ethical concerns for journalists. *Journal of Mass Media Ethics,* 8:1, pp. 37-54. Killenberg and Anderson suggest that journalists have the freedom to alter quotes, and therefore, the duty to alter them in an ethical way—in context and true to nonverbal communication as well as spoken words.

Kurtz, H. (1993). Why the press is always right. *Columbia Journalism Review,* May/June, pp. 33-35. Kurtz argues that while the press spends its time dishing out criticism, it doesn't do a responsible job of correcting its own errors.

Lowery, D. T. & Shidler, J.A. (1995). The sound bites, the biters, and the bitten: An analysis of network TV news bias in campaign '92. *Journalism and Mass Communication Quarterly,* 72:1, pp. 33-43. Network TV news used a substantially higher percentage of negative sound bites to skewer the Bush-Quayle ticket than it did in coverage of Clinton-Gore and Perot-Stockdale.

Mauro, T. (1995). Reporters must learn to use the Internet wisely. *ASNE Bulletin,* February, p. 14. Mauro says reporters should check the accuracy of information gleaned from online resources just as they would information gained through any other source.

Rieder, R. (1996). The admiral and the "V" clips: *Newsweek* was pursuing a legitimate story when it sought to interview Admiral Boorda. *American Journalism Review,* July/Aug., p. 6. Rieder defends *Newsweek* for pursuing allegations that Boorda had worn military commendations that he did not earn. The admiral committed suicide rather than submit to reporters' questioning.

Schroll, C. J., & Kenney, R. J. (1997). Public virtue: A focus for editorializing about political character. *Journal of Mass Media Ethics,* 12:1, pp. 36-50. This article argues that a firm and consistent editorial focus on a politician's public virtue would serve well as the essence of journalistic communication about political character. The authors also discuss expectations that readers, opinion columnists and newspaper editors should keep in mind as the "character issue" is brought forth in the press.

Schwar, J. L. (1995). In the spirit of the law: An ethical alternative to the Fairness Doctrine. *Journal of Mass Media Ethics,* 10:2, pp. 83-94. This article, which argues that the doctrine was unconstitutional, presents an alternative model for regulation of broadcast media that preserves the First Amendment.

Speckman, K.R. (1994). Using databases to serve justice and maintain the public's trust. *Journal of Mass Media Ethics,* 9:4, pp. 235-243. Speckman looks at the ethical concerns raised when the media use government databases for their stories.

Starr, D. (1996). The danger of adversary reporting. *Media Ethics,* Spring, pp. 7, 2, 8. Starr says that no reporter can be both adversative and objective when covering government. He warns that if the adversary approach to news reporting becomes the norm, newspapers and television stations will lose their credibility.

Stoker, K. (1995). Existential objectivity: Freeing journalists to be ethical. *Journal of Mass Media Ethics*, 10:1, pp. 5-22. This article critically examines the concept of objectivity and proposes that journalists improve ethical behavior by developing an existential ethic emphasizing individual responsibility.

Taylor, S. (1993). The standup syndrome. *American Journalism Review*, July / Aug., pp. 35-38. Taylor writes that when television reporters go on camera, they often leave attribution and objectivity behind.

Vergobbi, D. (1993). Journalist as source: The moral dilemma of news rescue. *Journal of Mass Media Ethics*, 7:4, pp. 233-245. Vergobbi looks at the moral issues surrounding "news rescue," when a reporter furnishes another news agency with the facts of a story because the reporter's own paper withholds the information.

Ziesenis, E. B. (1991). Suicide coverage in newspapers: An ethical consideration. *Journal of Mass Media Ethics*. 6: 4, pp. 234-244. This article reviews literature on imitative suicide and discusses implications of suicide stories on people in crisis. In addition, it explores the options for suicide coverage and gives suggestions for more ethical coverage that could save people's lives, rather than reinforcing suicide as an option.

Conflicts of Interest Issues

Avis, E. (1991). Have subsidy will travel. *Quill*, March, pp. 20-25. This article examines the ethical dilemma of subsidized travel that is freely used by many publications. Nowadays, however, more editors are heeding ethical alarms and shunning such subsidization.

Bagdikian, B. H. (1989). Economics and the morality of journalism. In M. C. Emery & T. C. Smythe (Eds.), *Readings in mass communication: Concepts and issues in the mass media* (382-392). Dubuque, IA: William C. Brown Publishers. Ethical standards that apply to journalists don't seem to apply to the corporations who employ and control these individuals. This essay traces the rising corporate conflicts of interest and acknowledges the rising professional standards of the journalists hired.

Cranberg, G. (1995). Paying for news is polluting all the press. *ASNE Bulletin*, February, pp. 20-21. Cranberg says the media should tell the public when they pay their sources.

Cunningham, R. (1996). CIA out of bounds when it uses us (journalists) as spies or "cover." *Quill*, April, pp. 14-15. The article addresses the controversial issue of American intelligence officials posing as journalists as a cover for covert operations.

Eddings, K. (1994). Should gays cover gay issues? *Columbia Journalism Review*, March/April, pp. 47-49. Most editors would assign gay reporters to cover gay issues due to their insight and ability to bring in different points of view.

Fiske, F. (1996). Interlocking interests: The masthead symposium. *The Masthead*, 48:2, pp. 5-11. The wife of syndicated columnist George Will was communication director for Bob Dole's campaign. The symposium presents differing opinions from editorial writers on whether Will had a conflict of interest in writing about the 1996 presidential campaign.

Fitzgerald, M. (1993, Jan. 22). Cottage industry for sportswriters. *Editor & Publisher*, p. 9. More and more sportswriters are moonlighting as commentators on talk-radio and television. The article looks at the conflicts that can arise.

Gunther, M. (1995). All in the family. *American Journalism Review*, October, pp. 36-41. Gunther reports on the growing problem of conflicts of interest that arise when news organizations become part of big corporations with diverse interests. He says that journalists will be forced to engage in "journalistic incest" when covering corporate "parents and siblings."

Hoyt, M. (1996). Chuck gate: When can journalists act like citizens? *Columbia Journalism Review*, May/June, pp. 57-60. The article looks at political contributions made by a New York television anchor to Republican candidates for president.

Lederman, D. (1992). The home-town team: It can bring people together, but media risk integrity by giving in to boosterism. *Nieman Reports*, 46:1, pp. 29-34. Media coverage of sports and athletes must be thoughtful and balanced. Sports journalists are often criticized for uncovering crime or corruption in sports, but an over-protective media is not providing the truth to readers, who need to hear the entire story.

Lesly, E. (1991). Realtors and builders demand happy news ... and often get it. *Washington Journalism Review*, 13:9, pp. 21-23. Some revenue-hungry newspapers are siding with advertisers against their readers, so that newspapers are sacrificing integrity in news for dollars.

Mills, K. (1993). Taking it to the streets: What are the limits of activism for journalists? *American Journalism Review*, July/Aug., pp. 22-26. The article explores to what extent journalists can become involved in the communities they cover without creating a conflict of interest.

Pekow, C. (1994). Two-career dilemma: How couples avoid professional conflict. *Quill*, Nov./Dec., pp. 26-30. The article looks at how journalists who are married to newsmakers avoid conflicts.

Shepard, A. (1994). Talk is expensive. *American Journalism Review*, May, pp. 21-42. Shepard looks at "celebrity" journalists and their practice of taking speaking engagements that pay exorbitant sums of money.

Shepard, A. (1996). Schmoozing with the stars. *American Journalism Review*, July/Aug., pp. 20-25. Shepard raises questions about "celebrity dinners" in which Washington reporters schmooze with government officials and Hollywood stars.

Singer, J. (1996). Virtual anonymity: Online accountability in political bulletin boards and the makings of the virtuous virtual journalist. *Journal of Mass Media Ethics*, 11:2, pp. 95-106. Communication online via political bulletin boards raises ethical concerns about anonymity and accountability.

Tate, C. (1991). Outside activities: When does a journalist's personal opinion become a public issue? *Columbia Journalism Review*, March/April, pp. 12-15. The title says it all. The ethical issue discussed here is a reporter's involvement with the issues he/she covers. Can reporters or should reporters be able to express political opinions or be activists for such causes as nuclear energy and abortion?

Ward, B. (1995). Crossing the line? *American Journalism Review*, Jan./Feb., pp. 12-13. The speaking fees that "20/20" consumer reporter John Stossel receives from special-interest groups raise questions of integrity and conflict of interest.

Warren, J. (1996). Speaking-for-pay issue churns ethical questions. *The American Editor*, pp. 12-13. Ward says it's wrong for journalists to accept big money for public speaking engagements.

Winternitz, F. (1996). Muckraking or buckraking. *Quill*, July/Aug., pp. 60-61. The article looks at celebrity journalists who charge large fees to speak before corporations and groups.

Wolfson, L.W. (1992). The beltway allure. *Quill*, March, pp. 24-29. The article looks at journalists who "cross the line" and take jobs in the federal government.

Deception Issues

Baker, R. (1993). Truth, lies, and videotape. *Columbia Journalism Review*, July/Aug., pp. 25-29. The article focuses on the questionable use of hidden cameras for investigative reporting.

Banda, S. (1995). Working undercover: Fine lines of deceptions and lies. *IRE Journal*, No. 18, p. 14.

An interview with a *Wall Street Journal* reporter who secured a job at a poultry processing plant and later wrote a story about the poor working conditions there.

Borden, S. (1993). Empathic listening: The interviewer's betrayal. *Journal of Mass Media Ethics*, 8:4, pp. 219-226. Borden argues that reporters should not deceive interview subjects by pretending to agree with what they are saying by nodding or using other encouraging responses.

Bovee, W. G. (1991). The end can justify the means—but rarely. *Journal of Mass Media Ethics*, 6:3, pp. 135-145. Journalists sometimes say that the end does not justify the means, but they can act otherwise. Even if there are only rare instances in which the end can justify the means, some guidelines are needed to determine when those situations exist. The author proposes six questions for application to this thorny issue and for avoiding extremes of moral laxity and false scrupulosity.

Braun, P. (1992). Deception in journalism. *Journal of Mass Media Ethics*, 3:1, pp. 77-83. In uncovering extreme cases of corruption, journalists may be justified in using deception, so long as they remain within the law, according to Braun.

Denniston, L. (1994). Going too far with hidden camera? *American Journalism Review*, April, p. 54. In a story on sanitation conditions at slaughterhouses, CBS news persuades a worker to wear a hidden camera in a meat-packing plant.

Elliott, D. & Culver, C. (1992). Defining and analyzing journalistic deception. *Journal of Mass Media Ethics*. 7:2, pp. 69-84. Elliott and Culver clarify those acts that should count as deception and bracket borderline cases—cases about which reasonable people might disagree as to whether they ought to count as deceptive acts.

Hodges, L. W. (1988). Undercover, masquerading, surreptitious taping. *Journal of Mass Media Ethics*, 3:2, pp. 26-36. Hodges explores the moral dimensions of undercover investigations by reporters for their deception characteristics. Three test questions are posed for the justifying of deceptive tactics in gathering information. The morality of surreptitious taping is also discussed.

Linn, T. (1991). Staging in TV news. *Journal of Mass Ethics*, 6:1, pp. 47-54. Three justifications used by television news crews for staging of events are examined in this article: the convenience of editing, the convenience of time, and the convenience of story.

Lissit, R. (1995). Gotcha! *American Journalism Review*, March, pp. 11-21. The article examines the legal and ethical issues surrounding the use of hidden cameras by the news media.

Diversity Issues

Asian Pacific Americans: A handbook on how to cover and portray our nation's fastest growing minority group. (1989). National Conference of Christians and Jews, Asian American Journalists Association, and Association of Asian Pacific American Artists, 96 pp.

Brislin, T. & Williams, N. (1996). Beyond diversity: Expanding the canon in journalism ethics. *Journal of Mass Media Ethics*, 11:1, pp. 16-27. The authors call for journalism educators and professionals to expand their knowledge of ethics as practiced by minority groups.

Case, T. (1995, Sept. 9). After the revolution. *Editor & Publisher*, pp. 9-10. Are liberal African-American voices being silenced as conservatives dominate Congress and storm op-ed pages? Some say yes, while others disagree.

Entman, R. (1994). Representation and reality in the portrayal of blacks on network television news. *Journalism Quarterly*, pp. 509-520. Entman's study finds that network television news often stereotypes African Americans.

Freeman, G. (1991). What's in a name? *Quill*, May, p. 39. What terms should news media use when identifying members of minority groups? Opinions—and stylebooks—differ.

Gersh-Hernandez, D. (1993, July 31). Portrayals of Latinos in and by the media. *Editor & Publisher,* pp. 12-13. Latinos are underrepresented as employees in the mainstream media, and issues of interest to the Latino community are largely ignored by the press, according to the National Association of Hispanic Journalists.

Haiman, R. (1992). We're all journalists—so why don't you hear what I mean? *ASNE Bulletin,* July/August, pp. 4-11. Report of an ASNE convention program titled "Face to Face: Race and Gender"

Heider, D. (1996). Completeness and exclusion in journalism ethics: An ethnographic case study. *Journal of Mass Media Ethics,* 11:1, pp. 4-15. Heider brings to light the ongoing problem of underrepresentation of people of color in the media.

Hill, M. & Thrasher, B. (1994). A model of respect: Beyond political correctness in the campus newsroom. *Journal of Mass Media Ethics,* 9:1, pp. 43-55. The authors propose ways to help student journalists make responsible decisions about news content that may be outside their cultural experience.

Jensen, R. (1994). Banning "Redskins" from the sports page: The ethics and politics of Native American nicknames. *Journal of Mass Media Ethics,* 9:1, pp. 16-25. Jensen argues that media outlets have an ethical and political responsibility to stop using sports team names that a majority of American Indians find offensive.

Leberman, S. (1995, Aug. 26). Controversial policy. *Editor & Publisher,* pp. 14-15. The article discusses a Connecticut Jewish news weekly's decision not to publish interfaith wedding and engagement announcements.

Lind, R. A. (1995). Race and viewer evaluations of ethically controversial TV news stories. *Journal of Mass Media Ethics,* 11:1, pp. 40-52. A study of more than 100 African-American and European-American journalists found no simple relationship between race and judgments of whether selected stories should be aired. When story relevance was considered, the relationship became clearer, suggesting a complex relationship between viewers' lived experience, story content and story evaluation.

Pease, T. (1990). Ducking the diversity issue: Newspaper's real failure is performance. *Newspaper Research Journal,* Summer, pp. 24-37. The author suggests that we've paid too much attention to issues of hiring minorities and diversifying newsrooms, while avoiding the tougher questions of content, coverage, and newspapers' role in a pluralistic society.

Schroth, R.A. (1995). "But it's really burning": Tragedy and the journalistic conscience. *Columbia Journalism Review,* Sept./Oct., pp. 43-45. Schroth believes journalists have an obligation to provoke new perspectives on a tragedy through their writing, which may help the healing process.

Shaw, D. (1990). Coloring the news: A special report. *Quill,* May, pp. 14-23. This special report, written by *Los Angeles Times* Pulitzer prize-winning media critic David Shaw, concludes that news media coverage of minorities still focuses on negative news such as crime and poverty, and that one reason for press insensitivity to racial matters is that newsrooms themselves do not reflect society's diversity. The *Quill* articles (taken from a four-part series which ran in the *Times*) contains useful resources and data about minorities.

Simurda, A. (1992). Living with diversity: Talking it through in three newsrooms. *Columbia Journalism Review,* January/February, pp. 19-24. Simurda interviewed dozen of staffers at the Portland *Oregonian, Cincinnati Enquirer,* and the *Hartford Courant* , three newspapers that are attempting to increase multicultural diversity in the newsroom and in news coverage.

Tucker, C. (1994). Can militant minority reporters be objective? *Nieman Reports,* Spring, pp. 82-83. As news organizations seek staffs that are ethnically diverse, news managers are confronted with the question of whether reporters from groups that have suffered discrimination can resist becoming advocates.

Photojournalism Issues

Bryant, G. (1987). Ten-fifty P.I.: Emotion and the photographer's role. *Journal of Mass Media Ethics*, 2:2, pp. 32-39. Professional newspaper photographer Garry Bryant offers a personal testimonial on the effects his job has had on him, as well as the public. He proposes a four-step model to use when deciding whether or not to shoot questionable photos.

Gross, L. , Katz, J. S., & Ruby, J. (Eds.). (1988). *Image ethics: The moral rights of subjects in pho - tographs, film, and television.* New York: Oxford University Press. 382 pages. This book is a collection of essays by various media artists about ethical issues that confront them. This collection presents two central tensions: The first arises from the intense but diffused ambivalence many of the cited film makers bring to the acknowledgement of ethical issues; the second is derived from the polarization of the roles of the media artist/worker in society.

Harris, C. R, (1991). Digitization and manipulation of news photographs. *Journal of Mass Media Ethics*, 6:3, pp. 164-174. Harris argues that the advent of computer-assisted digital manipulation has raised new ethical concerns in news photography. He calls for some systematic decision making and accountability by establishing protocols rather than a code of ethics.

Lester, P. (Ed.). (1990). *NPPA Special Report: The Ethics of Photojournalism.* Durham, N.C.: National Press Photographers Association. 101 pages. This anthology is a thorough treatment of ethical issues arising in photojournalism and videography. War stories and philosophy are neatly combined in a provocative.

Lester, P. (1991). *Photojournalism: An ethical approach.* Hillsdale, NJ: Lawrence Erlbaum Associates. Lester includes chapters on finding a philosophical perspective, victims of violence, rights to privacy, picture manipulations, and juggling journalism and humanism.

Cunningham, R. (1995). Photographs continue to confound newspapers' readers and editors. *Quill*, March, pp. 16-17. Photographs such as those of the Oklahoma City bombing upset readers. Editors who publish such photos wrestle with the public criticism.

Fitzgerald, M. (1993, Oct. 23). Controversial photo. *Editor & Publisher*, pp. 14-15. Photo of a dead U.S. soldier being dragged through a mob of jeering Somalis enrages some readers, divides editors.

Gillies, P. (1995). Ethics specialists have suggestions to guide decision. *The Editor*, February, pp. 14-16. The article looks at the handling of disturbing photos that include "heart-wrenching" images.

Gillies, P. (1995). Would you run these photos? Ethics specialists have suggestions to guide decision. *The Editor*, pp. 14-16. Two viewpoints on how to decide whether to run a disturbing photo.

Grigsby, B. (1996). Grips and grins, other neat jobs—rise of the pseudo-event: The emperor wears no clothes. *News Photographer*, September, pp. 20-21. Grigsby addresses the question of how to report and photograph staged events. He urges journalists and photographer not to go along with the "intended charade" of the event's sponsor.

Grigsby, B. (1996). People photos require trust, responsibility. *News Photographer*, July, pp. 10-11. Rigsby, photo editor for the *Philadelphia Inquirer*, discusses the responsibilities photographers have to their human subjects.

Mahon, B. (1996, March 2). All the news that's fit to manipulate. *Editor & Publisher*, pp. 234-248. Mahon looks at the dangers of altering and enhancing photographs for print.

Meltzer, B. (1995). Digital photography: A question of ethics. *Learning and Leading with Technology*, 23:4, pp. 18-21. With the increase in popularity of computers and photo-manipulation software, Meltzer urges students to think more critically about what they are doing when they enhance an image or change a photograph.

O'Brien, S. (1993). Eye on Soweto: A study of factors in news photo use. *Journal of Mass Media*

Ethics, 8:2, pp. 69-87. O'Brien analyzes how newspapers deal with graphically violent photos.

Overholser, G. (1996, Sept. 22). Up in arms over a falling down. *Washington Post,* C6. Angry readers criticize the *Washington Post* for publishing a photograph of Bob Dole falling from a stage while on the campaign trail.

Shipman, M. (1995). Ethical guidelines for televising or photographing executions. *Journal of Mass Media Ethics,* 10:2, pp. 95-108. Shipman believes there is no compelling reason to allow televising or photographing executions.

Upshaw, J. & Russial, J. (1994). Chronicle. *Columbia Journalism Review,* Jan./Feb., pp. 9-11. Examines how a daily newspaper, a weekly, and a local television station handle pictures of the same tragedy.

Privacy Issues

Benedict, H. (1996). Reporting the crime can risk further victimizing the victim. *Newspaper coverage of Rape: Dilemmas on Deadline,*pp. 7-13. Benedict urges reporters not to use colorful adjectives and cliches when reporting on rape victims.

Bianchi, L. (1995). Rape and student journalists. *Quill,* Nov./Dec., pp. 40-41. The article examines difficulties in publishing stories of campus rape in college newspapers, including policies for publishing victims' names.

Black, J. (1996). Rethinking the naming of sex crime victims. *Newspaper coverage of Rape: Dilemmas on Deadline,*pp. 14-24. The author offers a systematic and ethically justifiable model for working through the dilemma of handling sex crimes.

Bowman, P. (1996). A personal account: Media treatment evolved into an assault itself. *Newspaper Coverage of Rape: Dilemmas on Deadline,* pp. 28-31. Patricia Bowman describes the consequences of the media's "intrusive" reporting before, during and after the William Kennedy Smith trial in 1991.

Cochran, W. (1996). Computers, privacy, and journalists: a suggested code of information practices. *Journal of Mass Media Ethics,* 11:4, pp. 210-222. The author calls for the creation of a code that recognizes journalists need to be more receptive to privacy concerns and to reassure the public they will be sensitive in dealing with private information in electronic databases.

Garrison, B. & Splichal, S. (1994). Reporting on private affairs of candidates: A study of newspaper practices. *Journal of Mass Media Ethics,* 9:3, pp. 169-183. To what extent should the character of political candidates be examined by the media? This study examines attitudes of newspaper editors, finding that their attitudes appear to approximate those of the public.

Germer, F. (1995) How do you feel? *American Journalism Review,* June, pp. 37-42. Reporters offer differing views on how they feel when interviewing victims of tragedy.

Giobbe, D. (1996, Aug. 3). Over the line? *Editor & Publisher,* p. 18. A *New York Post* reporter is arrested after posing as a family member of a passenger on ill-fated TWA Flight 800. The reporter illegally attended a private prayer service for the families of victims.

Goldstein, T. (1996, Oct. 5). Rush to judgment? Do journalists use enough restraint in competitive situations? *TV Guide,* pp. 34-37. Goldstein criticizes the "herd mentality" of the news media in their handling of Richard Jewell as a suspect in the Olympic bombing in Atlanta.

Hausman, C. (1994). Information age ethics: Privacy ground rules for navigating in cyberspace. *Journal of Mass Media Ethics,* 9:3, pp. 135-144. Hausman examines the public's presumed right to know versus the individual's right to know in the context of recent advances in communication and information technology.

Haws, D. (1996). Rape victims: Papers shouldn't name us. *American Journalism Review,*

September, pp. 12-13. Haws surveys 18 rape victims named in the *Winston-Salem* Journal. All of them say they did not want their names in the newspaper.

Hodges, L., Giles, R.H., Steele, B., Woods, K., Byrd, J., Bailey, B. L., & Shriver, D. W. Jr. (1996). Journalists, the FBI, and the Olympic bomb. *Journal of Mass Media Ethics,* 11:4, pp. 246-256. The Richard Jewell case is discussed in the Case and Commentaries section.

Husselbee, L. P. (1994). Respecting privacy in an information society: A journalist's dilemma. *Journal of Mass Media Ethics,* 9:3, pp. 145-156. As more personal information about private citizens becomes available in computerized databases, journalists have a moral obligation to respect the privacy of individuals, Husselbee says.

Lipsyte, R. (1992, April 10). None of us needs other people's fears. *The New York Times,* Section B; Page 13, Column 1. Robert Lipsyte column on questions of ethics in media pressure that compelled Arthur Ashe to make public announcement that he suffers from AIDS.

Meyers, C. (1993). Justifying journalistic harms: Right to know vs. interest in knowing. *Journal of Mass Media Ethics,* 8:3, pp. 133-146. Journalists often confuse having the right to know with having a curiosity in knowing, which results in unethical behavior that infringes on the privacy of individuals.

Paul, N. (1994). Some paradoxes of privacy. *Journal of Mass Media Ethics,* 9:4, pp. 228-230. Paul, who directs the Poynter Institute's library and Web site, outlines conflicts created by the clash of the right to know and the right to privacy, and the issues they raise for journalists.

Quindlen, A. (1992, March 4). The right call. *The New York Times,* Section A; Page 23, Column 1. Anna Quindlen Op-Ed column praises *Seattle Times* for articles on sexual misconduct and harassment charges against Sen. Brock Adams; says women who have given accounts in sworn statements are not named but are described in enough detail to give credibility to allegations.

Record, P. (1994). Hard call: Using brutal terms to define a brutal crime. *Newspaper Coverage of Rape. Dilemmas on Deadline,* p. 25. Record, ombudsman at the *Fort Worth Star-Telegram,* argues that it's often necessary to include graphic details in the reporting of heinous crimes.

Ricchiardi, S. (1996). Children of War. *Quill,* September, pp. 17-21. Discusses the ethical implications of documenting war through the eyes of children.

Seymore, A. (1995). News media must fulfill social responsibility without adding to the pain of rape victims. *Newspaper Coverage of Rape: Dilemmas on Deadline,* pp. 26-27. Seymore says coverage of rape should be handled in a way that educates the public about the horrors of rape and protects the victim from revictimization.

Shepard, A. (1996). Going to extremes. *American Journalism Review,* October, pp. 38-43. A bomb explosion ignites a media feeding frenzy against security guard Richard Jewell. Though Jewell was never charged in the explosion, his privacy was violated and reputation destroyed.

Shribman, D. (1991, May 17). Public backs inquiries of official acts by politicians, not their private lives. *The Wall Street Journal,* Section A; Page 16, Column 1. Americans give news media high marks for examining official and financial activities of public officials but take dim view of inquiries into their private lives, *Wall Street Journal*/NBC News poll shows.

Stein, M.L. (1994, Jan. 8). Identifying parents who rape their children. *Editor & Publisher,* p. 14. The *Spokane* (WA) *Spokesman-Review* polls readers to decide whether to publish name of rapist.

Van Gelder, L. (1990). Straight or gay, stick to the facts. *Columbia Journalism Review,* Nov./Dec., pp. 52-53. Van Gelder focuses on how to deal with the issue of sexuality in news stories. Do we "out" public figures? Do we hide homosexuals in the closet so their lifestyle doesn't look too appealing? This article looks at both sides of the issue of sexuality as news worthy.

Why Arthur Ashe kept it secret. (1992, April 10). *The New York Times,* Section A; Page 36, Column 1. Editorial on Arthur Ashe's disclosure that he contracted AIDS from blood transfusion after surgery says his anger at media is misplaced and should be aimed at cruel public attitudes that have compelled him to keep condition secret; suggests tennis great turn his formidable talent for advocacy to AIDS issue.

Williams, R. B. (1995). Ethical reasoning in the process of gathering news for television: privacy and AIDS testing. *Journal of Mass Media Ethics,* 10:2, pp. 109-120. In a computer simulation experiment, consequentialist forms of reasoning were found dominant among the journalist-subjects. Non-consequentialist thinking also was demonstrated, and the nature of ethical reasoning was highly individualized.

Winch, S. P. (1996). Moral justifications for privacy and intimacy. *Journal of Mass Media Ethics,* 11:4, pp. 197-209. This article analyzes arguments for the right to privacy, showing how some are more convincing than others. Winch also offers a practical argument for recognizing a universal right to privacy over intimate relationships and information.

Source/Reporter Relationships Issues

Borden, S. (1995). Gotcha! Deciding when sources are fair game. *Journal of Mass Media Ethics,* 10:4, pp. 223-235. The article examines information that was questionably obtained by journalists in violation of the expectations of the source.

Cunningham, R. (1995). Saving life becomes ethical dilemma for veteran reporter. *Quill,* May, pp. 14-15. A *Washington Post* reporter, covering a story about prostitution, helps a prostitute escape from her pimp.

Hechler, D. (1992). The source you shouldn't talk to. *Columbia Journalism Review,* March/April, p. 48. This article makes a case for not interviewing child victims even when we don't identify them. By forcing the victim to relive the incident in an interview we re-victimize her/him.

Hoyt, M. (1991). Malcolm, Masson and you. *Columbia Journalism Review,* March/ April, pp. 38-44. Hoyt examines the issues surrounding the Masson-Malcolm libel suit, and discusses the legal and ethical ramifications for journalists.

Malley, J. (1993). The Waco watch. *Columbia Journalism Review,* May/June, pp. 50-55. The media are criticized for playing the role of conduit between Branch Davidian cult leaders and government negotiators, a role thrust on the media by both sides of the confrontation.

Miller, M. (1996, March 11). Devroy's choice. *The New Republic,* 214:11, pp. 15-18. Miller criticizes the Washington press corps for not revealing the hidden motives behind anonymous sources.

Mott, P. (1991). Small-town leaks. *Quill,* March, p. 35. Small papers face greater ethical problems in using anonymous sources for stories that involve subjects who are familiar to the readers. Is it necessary to pursue a story, discovered through an anonymous tip or leak, that could do serious damage to the reputation and career of a minor public official as doggedly as a leaked story about, say, the Iran-Contra affair?

Sachs, A. (1993). No time for ethics: When a cop wants your press card. *Columbia Journalism Review,* May/June, p. 14. A New Jersey newspaper columnist surrendered his press credentials to police to help them end a hostage crisis. A police officer posed as a reporter and arrested a gunman holding two people.

Salisbury, B. (1991). Burning the source. *Washington Journalism Review,* September, pp. 18-22. The *St. Paul Pioneer Press* reporter tells how he promised Dan Cohen confidentiality, then exposed him on orders of an editor. The case wound up in the Supreme Court.

Selcraig, B. (1994). Buying news. *Columbia Journalism Review,* July/Aug., pp. 45-46. Journalists are finding more sources unwilling to speak unless they get paid.

Shepard, A. (1994). Anonymous sources. *American Journalism Review,* December, pp. 19-25. The O.J. Simpson story raises increased concern over the use of anonymous sources.

Shepard, A. (1996). Show and print. *American Journalism Review,* March, pp. 40-44. The practice of showing or reading a story to a source before publication is debated.

Weinberg, S. (1990). So what's wrong with pre-publication review? *Quill,* March, pp. 26-28. Weinberg talks about his method of practicing pre-publication review and how it has led to more accuracy and fairness in his writing. He advocates the use of pre-publication review and challenges traditional objections.

Index

O

P

Q

R

S

T

W

Y